Student Guide
and
Workbook

Student Guide
and
Workbook

for use with
macroeconomics
Canadian edition
FOURTH EDITION
N. GREGORY MANKIW
AND
WILLIAM SCARTH

Roger T. Kaufman
Smith College

William Scarth
McMaster University

WORTH PUBLISHERS

Student Guide and Workbook by Roger T. Kaufman and William Scarth
for use with Mankiw/Scarth **Macroeconomics**, Fourth Canadian Edition

© 2011, 2007, 2001, 2000, 1997, 1994, 1992 by Worth Publishers

Printed in the United States of America

ISBN 13: 978-1-4292-5695-7
ISBN 10: 1-4292-5695-8

Second printing, 2011

Worth Publishers
41 Madison Ave.
New York, NY 10010
www.worthpublishers.com

Contents

Preface

To the Student

Macroeconomics Canadian Edition by Gregory Mankiw and William Scarth is an exciting textbook in which you will learn how to apply a variety of economic models to some fascinating macroeconomic questions. Although these models are not complicated, it is easy, initially, to become confused about the relationships they represent, and consequently not to fully appreciate their power and usefulness. We have found that students understand the underlying concepts much better if they actively take part in constructing economic models and applying them. This Student Guide provides a variety of ways to engage you in this type of active learning. Each chapter of the Student Guide is divided into five or six sections:

The **Fill-in Questions** give you the opportunity to review and check your knowledge of the key terms and concepts presented in the chapter. Note that some of the terms are used more than once.

The **Multiple-Choice Questions** allow you to test yourself on the chapter material. There are 12 to 25 multiple-choice questions for each chapter, ranging from easy to difficult.

The bulk of the Student Guide consists of a series of **Exercises** for each chapter. These exercises contain step-by-step presentations and applications of the models discussed in the textbook. You will be asked to complete tables of data, plot graphs, and illustrate shifts in curves. The exercises can be answered entirely in the Student Guide. When you are given a choice of two or more underlined alternatives, circle the correct one. After completing each exercise, we strongly encourage you to spend two minutes reviewing it to reinforce the concepts. We also suggest that you try to work through some of the exercises *before* the lecture material is discussed. The only mathematics required in this section is simple algebra and an understanding of the slopes of lines. A mathematical review of these concepts is contained in the Exercises for Chapter 1.

The **Problems** ask you to apply the models on your own. We have made a concerted effort to include problems on policy-oriented questions from both Canada and abroad. These problems are similar to the questions you might expect to be asked on an examination. You should complete them on a separate sheet of paper. Several of these problems require the use of calculus, and these are marked **C** (see the Key to Symbols table on page xvi). Some problems that are more challenging are marked with a **CH**. The symbol **A** is used to designate a question, exercise, or problem discussed in the appendix to the textbook chapter. Although the answers to most of the problems appear at the back of the Student Guide, the problems marked **O** have been suggested to your instructor as prime candidates for homework assignments and exams; their answers are not given here.

Most chapters include one or two **Data Questions,** in which you are required to find actual economic data to answer the question. Because different students will be using this Guide in different years, and since data get revised, we have not provided answers to the data questions. Because we are aware of your busy schedules, the data for all of these questions are available from three sources:

- the Statistics Canada Website, and

- the *Canadian Economic Observer*

for Canadian data, and

- the *Economic Report of the President* Web site,

for data pertaining to other countries. The *Canadian Economic Observer* is published monthly by Statistics Canada, and there is a very useful annual historical supplement available through university libraries, via the Web. This source, and the *Bank of Canada Review* (published quarterly contain almost everything that will be needed. As noted, both of these publications are available on the Internet. Suggestions about how to use the Web are offered in the *Economic Data on the Internet* section of this *Student Guide*—immediately following the Preface.

Questions to Think About often go beyond the material presented in the textbook and ask you to think critically about the model itself or some application of the model. This material will probably not be covered in class and it will almost never appear on an examination, but your professor would be thrilled if you told him or her that you were interested in discussing it (and he or she believed you!). We should warn you, however, that good economists disagree about the correct answers to some of these questions. Consequently, no answers are provided. However, developing your ability to think critically will enhance your education in macroeconomics, so we encourage you to tackle some of these questions.

The answers to all but the specially marked Problems and the Questions to Think About are printed at the back of the Student Guide.

Although you may want to complete all the questions for each chapter, you may be limited by time constraints. The Exercises have been especially helpful for most of our students, but you should decide which of the sections of questions and problems are most helpful for you. We can assure you, however, that your understanding of macroeconomics will be substantially deeper and longer-lasting if you complete most of the Student Guide. If you have any specific comments, please send them to William Scarth (scarth@mcmaster.ca).

To the Instructor

This Student Guide is designed to involve students in active learning. We have found that students who have reconstructed the economic models themselves and applied them independently have a much deeper and longer-lasting understanding of the material.

The difficulty many students have with the models taught in intermediate macroeconomics precludes their appreciation of the usefulness of these models in answering important macroeconomic questions. This situation leads some instructors to spend more time than they would like on the formal models and less time on important applications. Others respond by glossing over the models. It is our hope that Greg Mankiw and Bill Scarth's textbook and this Student Guide will allow you to teach a course in which students understand both the relevant macroeconomic models and their applications.

The Student Guide is printed on perforated pages. With the exception of the **Problems,** the answers to all of the questions can be written directly into the Student Guide. Consequently, instructors may wish to make parts of the Student Guide required assignments.

(You should be aware, however, that the answers to all but the specially marked Problems, the Data Questions, and the Questions to Think About are printed at the back of this Student Guide.)

Each chapter of the Student Guide includes five or six sections:

The **Fill-in Questions** review the Key Concepts listed at the end of each chapter of the textbook. We have made these questions a bit more challenging by using some of the concepts more than once.

The 12 to 25 **Multiple-Choice Questions** for each chapter range in difficulty from easy to difficult. Several of these questions are suitable for examinations.

The bulk of the Student Guide consists of a series of **Exercises** for each chapter. In this section, students are guided step-by-step through the models presented in the chapter. We have found that students benefit greatly from solving simple algebraic models, plotting data on grids, and illustrating the comparative static results themselves. Because the Exercises for some chapters are quite long, you may wish to give your students guidance about which exercises you consider most important. We have experimented successfully with assigning exercises *before* the material is covered in class. This forces the student to read the assignment and engage the material, albeit at an elementary level. Each exercise begins with a brief description. The only mathematics required in this section is simple algebra and an understanding of the slopes of lines. A mathematical review of these concepts is contained in the Exercises for Chapter 1.

The questions in the **Problems** section are similar to those in the Problems and Applications section of the textbook. In these problems, students are asked to apply the models on their own. Many of the problems concern policy applications involving Canada or specific foreign countries. Several of these problems require the use of calculus, and these are marked **C** (see the Key to Symbols table on page xv). Others are more challenging and noted by a **CH**. The symbol **A** is used to designate a question, exercise, or problem discussed in the appendix to the textbook chapter. Although the answers to most of the problems appear at the back of the Student Guide, the answers to those problems marked with a **◘** are printed only in the *Solutions Manual*. Consequently, they can be used for homework assignments and exams.

Most chapters include one or two **Data Questions**, in which students are required to obtain actual economic data to answer the question. We believe students should be able to make reasonable estimates of the current inflation rate, unemployment rate, and gross domestic product, and that they should have experience accessing data from the Web and analyzing it within a spreadsheet. Guidance on how to access the data is given on page xi.

In the last section, several **Questions to Think About** go beyond the material presented in the textbook. By including this section, we hope to motivate the talented and industrious students to think more deeply about the models themselves and their applications. Although we rarely have enough time to cover this material in class, we have a number of special lunches each term and invite any students who wish to discuss these questions. You may want to cover some of them if time permits.

We hope you and your students find the Student Guide to be useful in developing their knowledge and skills. If you have any specific comments, please send them to William Scarth (scarth@mcmaster.ca).

Roger T. Kaufman
William Scarth

Economics Data on the Internet

As noted in the Preface, the most convenient source of economic data is the Internet. Here is a bit of advice on how to use this resource. The most recent observations on many major series are available on Statistics Canada's website:

> http://www.statcan.ca

You have two options: (i) click on *Find Statistics*, then *Subjects* and then the category you want (such as labour, prices, national accounts); (ii) click on *Find Statistics*, then on *Summary Tables*, and then enter the keyword you want (such as unemployment rate). While convenient, this free-access site provides only the most recent observations.

Entire historical times series can be had as follows. On your own university website, you can go to the library page and click on *e-resources*. Then, retrieve—under *journal title*—the *Canadian Economic Observer*—a summary publication produced by Statistics Canada. Once at this page, click on *Canadian Economic Observer Historical Supplement* (choosing the HTML view option). You can then choose from the various tables that are available. The series reference numbers in these tables are the ones that are given in the source entries for each table in the text.

A good source of international data is the Appendix of an American publication—the latest issue of the *Economic Report of the President*. This document is available on the Internet:

> http://www.gpoaccess.gov/eop/index.html

Other useful websites include those of the Federal Department of Finance, the Bank of Canada, the Canadian Association of Business Economists, the Canadian policy "think tanks," the *Economist* magazine, and several international organizations. The websites are listed here for your convenience:

http://www.fin.gc.ca
The Federal Department of Finance site has a *Frequently Asked*

Questions section, as well as the annual *Budget* documents (each Spring) and the annual *Fiscal Update* (each Fall).

http://www.bankofcanada.ca/
The Bank of Canada site has useful *Frequently Asked Questions* as well (under the *Monetary Policy* heading). Further, the last four years of data on most macroeconomic series of general interest are included in the tables at the end of each of the quarterly issues of the Bank of Canada *Review*. This publication is available by clicking on *Publications and Research*, and then on *Periodicals*.

http://www.cabe.ca
The Canadian Association of Business Economists site gives links to many interesting sources of information, including the macroeconomic analyses provided by the economics departments of Canada's major chartered banks, and Bill Goffe's general gateway site for economic issues.

http://www.cdhowe.org
The CD Howe Institute publishes many commentaries on the Web.

http://www.irpp.org
The Institute for Research on Public Policy publishes a journal (available on the Web) entitled *Policy Options*.

http://www.csls.ca
The Centre for the Study of Living Standards focuses on productivity growth issues.

http://www.fraserinstitute.ca
The Fraser Institute in Vancouver emphasizes the advantages of a more "hands off" approach to policy.

http://www.policyalternatives.ca
The Canadian Centre for Policy Alternatives emphasizes a more "hands on" approach; early each year the Centre's "alternative budget" is published on the Web.

http://www.caledoninst.org
The Caledon Institute of Ottawa focuses on social policy. Nevertheless, students in macroeconomics will be interested in their studies on unemployment.

http://qed.econ.queensu.ca/pub/jdi/deutsch/
The John Deutsch Institute at Queen's has a conference each spring which evaluates the federal government budget.

http://www.economist.com
The *Economist* magazine's website.

http://www.oecd.org
The Organization of Economic Cooperation and Development has studies and commentaries on all macroeconomic issues on the Web.

http://imf.org
The International Monetary Fund has some very readable articles in the "Economic Issues" section of the "Publications" part of their website.

http://www.brook.edu
The Brookings Institution in Washington has numerous reports of interest to students of macroeconomics.

http://rfe.org
This "resources for economists" site is probably the most comprehensive source for economics data and information in general that is available on the Internet. It is maintained and updated regularly, sponsored by the American Economics Association, and is easy to use.

Key to Symbols

C   This problem requires the use of calculus.

CH   This problem is especially challenging.

A   This question, exercise, or problem includes a topic discussed in the appendix to the textbook chapter.

□   This problem does not have its answer printed in the Student Guide.

Student Guide
and
Workbook

chapter 1

The Science of Macroeconomics

Fill-in Questions

Use the key terms below to fill in the blanks in the following statements. Each term may be used more than once.

deflation
depression
endogenous
exogenous
inflation
macroeconomics
market-clearing

microeconomics
models
price flexibility
price stickiness
real GDP
recession
unemployment

1. _____*Macro*_____ is the study of the economy as a whole. It focuses on issues such as economic growth, inflation, and unemployment. _____*Micro*_____ is the study of the economy in the small. It focuses on the individual firm, industry, or consumer.

2. _____*Real GDP*_____ measures the total income of everyone in the economy. A period in which this measure is falling is called a(n) _____*Recess*_____ if the decline is small, and a _____*Depres*_____ if the decline is severe.

3. During depressions many people lose their jobs, so _____*unemp*_____ rises substantially.

4. An increase in the general level of prices is called _____*inflation*_____.

5. Economists construct _____*models*_____ to assist them in understanding the real world.

6. One of the purposes of an economic model is to show how the _____*exogenous*_____ variables affect the _____*endogenous*_____ variables, where the former come from outside the model and the latter are determined within the model.

7. With regard to prices, most macroeconomists believe that _____*price flexibility*_____ is a reasonable assumption for studying long-run issues but that _____*price sticky*_____ is a better assumption for studying short-run issues.

8. Models that exhibit price flexibility are examples of __Market Clearing__ models.

Multiple-Choice Questions

1. Macroeconomists study all of the following issues EXCEPT the:
   a. determinants of inflation.
   b. relative market shares of General Motors and Ford.
   c. growth of total production in Canada.
   d. amount of imports and exports between Canada and Japan.

2. An example of a controlled experiment is:
   a. astronomers formulating the "big bang" theory of the origin of the universe by making observations through the Hubble telescope.
   b. economists analyzing the effects of an increase in the money supply by examining output, interest rates, and inflation following a large increase in the money supply.
   c. biologists modifying Darwin's original theory of evolution after examining newly found fossils.
   d. physicians testing the effects of aspirin on the incidence of heart disease by following two groups of men who differ only in their intake of aspirin.

3. If real GDP is growing rapidly, which of the following is most likely to occur?
   a. a recession
   b. a depression
   c. higher unemployment
   d. inflation

4. The variable that is likely to be exogenous in a model that explains production in a small firm within a large industry is the:
   a. amount of output produced by the firm.
   b. price of the firm's inputs.
   c. number of workers hired by the firm.
   d. amount of machinery employed by the firm.

5. All of the following are reasons why wages and/or prices may be sticky in the short run EXCEPT:
   a. long-term labour contracts often set wages for up to three years in advance.
   b. many firms leave their product prices unchanged for long periods of time in order to prevent current customers from "shopping around."
   c. it is costly for firms to print new price lists and advertise frequently changing prices.
   d. firms are already charging the highest prices people will pay, so there is no reason to change them.

6. The market in which the assumption of continuous market clearing seems to be LEAST applicable is the:

   a. stock market.

   b. market for wheat.

   c. labour market.

   d. market for federal government bonds.

Exercises: Review of Basic Math

In this first set of exercises, we review some basic mathematical concepts that are an essential part of this course. If you have any difficulty with these concepts, you should discuss your math background with your instructor as soon as possible.

1. **Percentage Change** *In this exercise, we review the calculation of percentage change.*

   The percentage change in a variable Q that changes in value from Q_0 to Q_1 may be calculated by using the equation:

   $$\text{Percentage Change in } Q = 100 \times \frac{Q_1 - Q_0}{Q_0} \qquad \text{(1-1)}$$

   Use the equation to calculate the percentage changes in the following examples.

   a. $Q_0 = 100; Q_1 = 120$

   $$\frac{Q_1 - Q_0}{Q_0} \quad = \quad \frac{120 - 100}{100} \quad = 20\%$$

   b. $Q_0 = 20; Q_1 = 85$

   $$= 38\%$$

   c. $Q_0 = 50; Q_1 = 40$

   $$= -20\%$$

2. **Graphs, Slopes, and Simultaneous Equations** In this exercise, we review how to plot pairs of points on a graph, calculate slopes and intercepts of lines, and solve two linear equations simultaneously.

a. Consider the equation

$$Y = \tfrac{1}{2}X + 3. \tag{1-2}$$

In Table 1-1, list the values of Y according to Equation 1-2 for each of the stated values of X.

Table 1-1

(1) X	(2) Y
0	$Y = (1/2)(0) + 3 = 3$
1	$Y =$ _____
2	$Y =$ _____
3	$Y =$ _____

b. Plot these four pairs of points on Graph 1-1 and connect them.

Graph 1-1

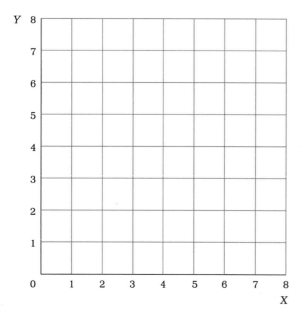

c. Recall that the *slope* of a curve indicates the amount by which the variable measured on the vertical axis increases when the variable measured on the horizontal axis increases by one unit. The slope may be measured by "rise over run" or $\Delta Y/\Delta X$, that is, the change in Y divided by the change in X. What is the numerical value of the slope of this curve? Explain how you derived this result.

d. The *Y intercept* of a curve is equal to the value of the variable measured on the vertical axis when the curve intersects that axis. Alternatively, it is the value of Y when $X = 0$. What is the numerical value of the Y intercept of this curve? How did you derive this answer?

e. Now consider the equation

$$Y = -2X + 8 \qquad \text{(1-3)}$$

In Table 1-2, list the values of Y according to Equation 1-3 for each of the stated values of X.

Table 1-2

(1) X	(2) Y
0	$Y = (-2)(0) + 8 = 8$
1	$Y = \underline{\hspace{2cm}}$
2	$Y = \underline{\hspace{2cm}}$
3	$Y = \underline{\hspace{2cm}}$

f. Plot the preceding four pairs of points on Graph 1-1 and connect them.

g. Calculate the slope and Y intercept of the equation in Part e.

h. Determine algebraically the values of X and Y that satisfy both equations by setting Equations 1-2 and 1-3 equal to each other. Check your answer by determining visually where the two curves intersect.

i. Explain why setting these two equations equal to each other yields the coordinates at the intersection.

3. **Exponents** *In this exercise, we review the use of positive and negative exponents, which are used occasionally in the text.*

a. When n is a whole number that is greater than or equal to 1, the expression y^n is equal to the product of n y's multiplied by each other. Thus, $y^1 = y$, and $y^3 = y \times y \times y$. By convention, $y^0 = 1$.

Calculate each of the following:

$2^3 = $ _____.

$3^2 = $ _____.

$5^1 = $ _____.

b. The expression y^{-n} is equal to $1/y^n$. Therefore, $y^{-2} = 1/y^2$ and $y^{-3} = 1/y^3$.

Calculate each of the following:

$2^{-3} = $ _____.

$3^{-1} = $ _____.

$10^{-3} = $ _____.

c. Finally, recall that the expression $y^n \times y^p = y^{n+p}$, that is, we add exponents when we multiply. Thus, $2^2 \times 2^3 = 2^5$. This can easily be confirmed by noting that $2^2 \times 2^3 = 4 \times 8 = 32 = 2^5$. (Remember, however, that $y^n \times z^p$ *does not equal* $(yz)^{n+p}$.)

Compute each of the following using the multiplication rule for exponents and confirm your answers by calculating the product directly:

$5^2 \times 5^3 =$ _____.

$6^3 \times 6^{-1} =$ _____.

$4^{1/2} \times 4^{1/2} =$ _____.

(Recall that $y^{1/2}$ is equal to the square root of y.)

Problems

Answer the following problems on a separate sheet of paper.

1. According to the textbook, natural scientists often conduct research via controlled experiments, whereas macroeconomists typically rely on natural experiments.

   a. What is a controlled experiment, and how does it differ from a natural experiment?

   b. Why are controlled experiments usually considered to be preferable for scientific research?

   c. Why can't macroeconomists typically perform controlled experiments?

2. Consider the market for coal.

   a. Draw hypothetical market supply and demand curves for coal, label them S_1 and D_1, and illustrate the initial equilibrium price and quantity.

   b. Suppose that the price of oil, which is an alternative fuel, triples. Draw the new supply and demand curves for coal on your preceding graph and label them S_2 and D_2. (*Hint:* one of the curves does not shift from its original position.) What happens to the equilibrium price and quantity of coal?

   c. Now return to the initial equilibrium price and quantity for coal. Suppose that the government imposes restrictions on strip mining that significantly increase the cost of producing coal. Draw the resulting supply and demand curves for coal on your graph and label them S_3 and D_3. What happens to the equilibrium price and quantity of coal?

Question to Think About

1. The textbook discusses how economists build models—simplified representations of reality—to explain how the world works. How important do you think each of the following criteria should be in evaluating whether a model is good? (There is no single correct answer to this question.)

    a. Accuracy in prediction.

    b. Reasonableness of the assumptions.

    c. Simplicity of the model.

    d. Consistency with other models.

chapter 2

The Data of Macroeconomics

Fill-in Questions

Use the key terms below to fill in the blanks in the following statements. Each term may be used more than once.

consumer price index
consumption
core inflation
depreciation
personal disposable income
flow
GDP deflator
government purchases
imputed value
investment
labour force
labour-force participation rate

Laspeyres
national income accounting identity
net exports
nominal gross domestic product
nominal gross national product
Okun's law
Paasche
real gross domestic product
recession
stock
unemployment rate
value added

1. _____N, GDP_____ measures the current dollar value of the final goods and services produced in a given time period within a country's borders. _____R, GDP_____ measures the value of final goods and services measured at constant prices.

2. The _____Uemployment Rat_____ is the percentage of the _____Labour force_____ that does not have a job.

3. A firm's _____Value added_____ is equal to the value of its output minus the value of the intermediate goods it purchases.

4. _____Okun's law_____ depicts a negative relationship between the percentage change in GDP and the change in the unemployment rate.

5. The _____CPI_____ traces the price of a fixed market basket of goods over time. Because the basket remains fixed as we move forward in time, this measurement is an example of a(n) _____Laspeyres_____ index.

$$R \, GDP = \frac{N \, GDP}{GDP \, def} \qquad \therefore \qquad GDP \, def = \frac{N \, GDP}{R \, GDP}$$

6. The ___GDP deflator___ compares the price of the current mix of output in GDP with what the current mix of output would have cost in a particular base year. It is calculated as ___N GDP___ divided by ___R. GDP___. Because the mix of output changes as we move forward in time, this measure is an example of a(n) ___Paashe___ index.

7. One of the more important distinctions in macroeconomics is the one between stocks and flows. Your personal wealth is an example of a(n) ___stock___ whereas your income is an example of a(n) ___flow___.

8. ___depreciation___ measures the reduction in value of the economy's stock of plants, equipment, and residential structures as these wear out.

9. The ___LF Participation Rate___ measures the percentage of the economy's adult, noninstitutional population that is in the labour force.

10. The amount of income consumers have available to spend or save after paying taxes and receiving government transfer payments is called ___Personal disposable income___.

11. Since homeowners do not pay rent, when the national income accounts estimate consumption they use a(n) ___imputed value___ of what the rent on their house would be.

12. In a(n) ___recession___, the ___unemployment___ rises and real gross domestic product falls.

13. There are two measures of income for an open economy. ___N. GNP___ is the nominal income earned by domestic citizens both here and abroad. ___N. GDP___ is the nominal income earned domestically by both domestic citizens and foreigners.

14. According to the ___National Income Accounting identity___, GDP is equal to the sum of ___Consump Investment___, ___Gov purchases___, and ___NX___.

15. ___Core inflation___ measures the increase in price of a consumer market basket that excludes food and energy prices. It is viewed as a better measure of ongoing inflation trends than the CPI.

Multiple-Choice Questions

1. All of the following are flow variables EXCEPT:
    a. disposable personal income.
    c. personal wealth.
    b. consumption expenditures.
    d. gross domestic product.

2. During periods of inflation:

   a. nominal GDP rises at the same rate as real GDP.

   b. nominal GDP rises at a faster rate than real GDP.

   c. nominal GDP rises at a slower rate than real GDP.

   d. one cannot infer anything about the relative rates of growth of nominal and real GDP.

3. Suppose that in 2008 General Motors experienced a large increase in its inventories of unsold cars. Then in 2008:

   a. total income exceeded the total expenditure on goods and services.

   b. total income was less than the total expenditure on goods and services.

   c. total income was still equal to the total expenditure on goods and services, because increases in inventories were counted both as part of expenditure and as part of income.

   d. General Motors' investment was negative.

4. Suppose Stelco sells steel to Chrysler for $5,000, and then this steel is used in a Voyager van that is sold to a new car dealer for $20,000. The car dealer then sells the car to a family for $25,000. In this scenario GDP has risen by:

   a. $50,000.   **c.** $25,000.

   b. $30,000.   **d.** $10,000.

5. The value-added of a particular company is equal to:

   a. its sales.

   b. its profits.

   c. its sales minus its cost of intermediate goods.

   d. zero in the long run.

6. Suppose you purchase a new home for $250,000 and move in. In the national accounts, consumption expenditures:

   a. rise by $250,000.

   b. rise by $250,000 divided by the number of years you expect to live in the house.

   c. rise by the imputed rent on the house, which is equal to what the market rent would be if it were rented.

   d. are unchanged.

7. The GDP deflator is defined as:

   a. nominal GDP/real GDP.   **c.** nominal GDP – real GDP.

   b. nominal GDP × real GDP.   **d.** nominal GDP + real GDP.

8. On occasion the GDP deflator can rise while real GDP falls. When this phenomenon occurs, nominal GDP:

   a. must also rise.

   b. must also fall.

   c. remains constant.

   d. can rise, fall, or remain constant.   *why, magnitude*

9. In the national accounts, investment is divided into three subcategories that include all of the following EXCEPT the:

    a. purchase of new plants and equipment by firms.

    b. purchase of stocks on the Toronto Exchange. *Tonster*

    c. purchase of new housing by households and landlords.

    d. increase in firms' inventories of goods.

10. All of the following would be counted as a government purchase of a good or a service EXCEPT:

    a. the purchase of a new military helicopter.

    b. your grandmother's receipt of her monthly Old Age Security benefit.

    c. the construction of a new dam by Quebec Hydro.

    d. the hiring of a new police officer by the city of Vancouver.

11. The largest component of GDP in Canada is typically:

    a. consumption.   **c.** government purchases.

    b. investment.   **d.** net exports.

12. If OPEC were to collapse and the price of imported oil were to fall dramatically, then:

    a. the GDP deflator and the consumer price index (CPI) would fall at the same rate.

    b. the GDP deflator would probably fall at a faster rate than the CPI.

    c. the CPI would probably fall at a faster rate than the GDP deflator.

    d. nothing would happen to either the CPI or the GDP deflator.

13. All of the following could reduce the unemployment rate EXCEPT a(n):

    a. reduction in the number of people who are unemployed.

    b. increase in the number of people who are employed.

    c. decrease in the labour force unaccompanied by any change in the number of people who are unemployed.

    d. increase in the number of people who have given up looking for work.

14. Okun's law depicts a relationship between the:

    a. percentage change in real GDP and the change in the unemployment rate.

    b. percentage change in nominal GDP and the change in the labour force.

    c. absolute change in real GDP and the percentage change in the unemployment rate.

    d. absolute change in real GDP and the percentage change in the GDP deflator.

15. Suppose the unemployment rate at the beginning of the year is equal to 5 percent. According to Okun's law, the following statement is FALSE:

    a. if the unemployment rate is unchanged during the year, real GDP must have risen by about 4 percent.

    b. if the average unemployment rate for the year rises to 7 percent, real GDP must have fallen by about 2 percent in that year.

    c. if the average unemployment rate for the year falls to 3 percent, real GDP must have risen by about 7 percent in that year.

    d. if the average unemployment rate for the year stays at 5 percent, real GDP must have remained constant.

16. If a Canadian citizen is employed by a Canadian company in Brazil, the income that she earns is:

    a. part of Canadian GDP and Brazil's GNP.
    b. part of Canadian GDP and Brazil's GDP.
    c. part of Canadian GNP and Brazil's GNP.
    d. part of Canadian GNP and Brazil's GDP.

17. If the GDP deflator grows by 4 percent from one year to the next and real GDP grows by 3 percent, then nominal GDP will:

    a. rise by approximately 1 percent.
    b. fall by approximately 1 percent.
    c. rise by approximately 7 percent.
    d. rise, but by somewhere between 1 percent and 7 percent, depending on the initial level of GDP.

    $$R = \frac{N}{d}$$

18. If labour productivity Y/L falls from one year to the next, then:

    a. output Y must have fallen.
    b. labour input L must have risen.
    c. the percentage change in L must have been less than the percentage change in Y.
    d. the percentage change in L must have been greater than the percentage change in Y.

19. The federal government increases the Canada Pension Plan benefits to the elderly each year by an amount that allows the elderly to maintain the same standard of living. This is done by making the percentage change in benefits:

    a. equal to the percentage change in the CPI.
    b. somewhat smaller than the percentage change in the CPI.
    c. somewhat greater than the percentage change in the CPI.
    d. equal to the percentage change in the GDP deflator.

20. Percentage changes in the CPI tend to overstate inflation because:

    a. people substitute away from goods whose relative price has risen.
    b. the continual introduction of new goods makes consumers better off even if prices do not fall.
    c. improvements in product quality tend to be underestimated by government agencies.
    d. all of the above.

21. Male and female labour force participation rates have converged for all of the following reasons EXCEPT:

    a. women now earn as much as men.
    b. new technologies have reduced the time it takes to do household tasks.
    c. improved birth control methods have led to a reduction in the number of children per family.
    d. political and social attitudes about working women have become more favourable.

Exercises

1. **Intermediate and Final Goods, Value-Added, and GDP** *In this exercise, we review the distinction between intermediate and final goods and illustrate how GDP can be calculated by totaling the production of final goods and services or by totaling firms' value-added.*

   a. Suppose that an economy consists of only four firms: Intel, Samsung, IBM, and Sleeman's. Suppose that this year Intel manufactures 1 million computer chips, which it then sells to IBM for $200 each for IBM to use in the manufacture of its computer systems. Similarly, Samsung produces 1 million computer monitors, which it sells for $300 each to IBM, again to use in its computer systems. IBM uses these components and its own to manufacture and sell 1 million computer systems at a price of $1,200 each. Sleeman's, on the other hand, produces 200 million six-packs of beer, which it sells on a special sale for $9.00 per six-pack. Assume, furthermore, that Sleeman's does not buy any new computer systems during the year. The GDP for this simple economy is the dollar value of the final goods produced during the year. Identify each of the following as a final or an intermediate good. (Circle the correct answer.)

      - Intel computer chip: final/intermediate good.
      - Samsung computer monitor: final/intermediate good.
      - IBM computer system: final/intermediate good.
      - Sleeman's beer: final/intermediate good.

   b. GDP is calculated by multiplying the unit price of each final good by the number of units produced. Calculate the GDP for this simple economy.

   c. Recall that the value-added for each firm is equal to its sales minus the cost of its intermediate products. Calculate the value-added for each of the four firms in Table 2-1 and confirm that the total is equal to GDP. (Use the space provided after the table for your work.)

Handwritten in margin:
$1,000,000 \cdot 1,200$
$+$
$200,000,000 \cdot 9$
$= 3,000 \text{ mil}$

Table 2-1

	(1) Value-Added per Unit	(2) Number of Units	(3) Company Value-Added
Intel	200	1 mil	200
Samsung	300	1 mil	300
IBM	700	1 mil	700
Sleeman's	9	200 mil	1800
Total			3000

2. **Nominal and Real GDP** *In this exercise, we calculate nominal and real GDP for a simple economy. We then calculate real GDP growth using two base years and discuss the differences.*

   a. Suppose that an economy consists of only two types of products: computers and automobiles. Sales and price data for these two products for two different years are as follows:

Table 2-2

(1)	(2)	(3)	(4)	(5)
	No. of		No. of	
	Computers	Price per	Automobiles	Price per
Year	Sold	Computer	Sold	Automobile
2000	500,000	$6,000	1,000,000	$12,000
2010	5,000,000	$2,000	1,500,000	$20,000

Nominal GDP in any year is calculated by multiplying the quantity of each final product sold by its price and summing over all final goods and services. Algebraically, this can be written as $\Sigma_i P_i Q_i$, where P_i and Q_i represent the price and quantity sold of the ith final good or service. Assuming that all computers and automobiles are final goods, calculate nominal GDP in 2000 and in 2010.

$N\ GDP_{2000}$ $(500\ 000)(6000) + (1000\ 000)(12\ 000) = 15\ 000\ 000\ 000$

$N\ GDP_{2010}$ $(5\ 000\ 000)(2000) + (1500\ 000)(20\ 000) = 40\ 000\ 000\ 000$

   b. Real GDP in any year is calculated by multiplying that year's quantities of goods and services by their prices in some base year. Therefore, using 2000 as the base year, real GDP in 2000 is equal to nominal GDP in 2000. From Part a, this equals ___15 bill___.

   c. Calculate real GDP in 2010 using 2000 as the base year.

   48 bill

d. Calculate the percentage change in real GDP between 2000 and 2010 using 2000 as the base year.

$$\frac{48-15}{15} = 220\%$$

e. Calculate real GDP in 2000 and 2010 using 2010 as the base year.

$$RGDP_{2000} = Q_{2000} \times P_{2010} = 21.6il$$

$$RGDP\ 2010 = 40$$

f. Calculate the percentage change in real GDP between 2000 and 2010 using 2010 as the base year.

$$\frac{40-21}{21} =$$

?

g. Explain why your answers to Parts d and f are different.

3. **The GDP Deflator and the Consumer Price Index** *In this exercise, we calculate the consumer price index and GDP deflator using the data in Table 2-2 from Exercise 2. We then illustrate how and why the percentage changes in these two price indices can differ.*

a. The CPI in a given year is equal to the cost of a fixed market basket of consumer purchases in that year divided by the cost of that same market basket in a base year. Although the cost of the basket changes, its composition remains the same as in the base year. For ease in reporting, the official CPI is equal to this ratio multiplied by 100. Note that the ratio of these costs in the base year necessarily equals 1. Thus, if 2000 is the base year, the reported CPI for 2000 would equal 1 × 100 = 100. If the fixed market basket is the total amounts of computers and automobiles purchased in 2000, use the data in Table 2-2 to calculate the CPI in 2010, using 2000 as the base year (which is often denoted as "2000 = 100").

Basket 2000 = 15 000   CPI 100

Basket 2010 = 21 000   CPI

$$\frac{21 - 15}{15} = .4 = 1 + .4 = 1.4 \Rightarrow 140$$

or, better way   21/15 = 1.4 ⇒ 140

b. The GDP deflator for any year is equal to nominal GDP in that year divided by real GDP. Again, it is common practice to multiply this ratio by 100. Calculate the GDP deflator in 2010, using 2000 as the base year (2000 = 100).

$$\frac{N\,GDP_{2010}}{R\,GDP_{2010}} = \frac{40\,000}{48\,000} = .8\bar{3} = 83.\bar{3}$$

c. The GDP deflator is often used to "deflate" nominal GDP in order to calculate real GDP. This is obvious from your calculations in Part b. If we did not know real GDP but did know both nominal GDP and the GDP deflator, we could calculate it by dividing nominal GDP by the GDP deflator (divided by 100). Using the numbers from Part b, this gives us __40 000__ / __83.3 ×100__.   No!
Economists often use price indices, like the GDP deflator or the CPI, to calculate real (inflation-adjusted) values.

40 000 / (0.83) = 48 000

d. Calculate the percentage changes in CPI and the GDP deflator between 2000 and 2010.

$$CPI \qquad 100 =7 \quad 140 = 40\%$$

$$deflator = 1 =7 \; .83 \; = -17\%$$

e. Explain why your answers in Part d are so different from each other, and relate your explanation to the difference between Laspeyres and Paasche indices.

Laspeyres CPI

Paasche def

4. **Working with Percentage Changes** *In this exercise, we illustrate how to approximate the percentage changes in products and quotients.*

   a. Economists often find it useful to examine percentage changes in variables. The percentage change in real GDP from one year to the next, for example, represents economic growth during the year. The percentage change in the CPI or GDP deflator represents the rate of inflation during the year. The percentage change of the product of two variables is approximately equal to the sum of the percentage changes in each variable. (This approximation is valid only for relatively small percentage changes.)

   b. Recall that nominal GDP = $P \times Y$, where P is equal to the GDP deflator and Y equals real GDP. Consequently, the percentage change in nominal GDP is approximately equal to the percentage change in P *plus* the percentage change in Y. Consider the data in Table 2-3:

Table 2-3

(1) Period	(2) Nominal GDP (PY)	(3) % Change in PY	(4) P	(5) % Change in P	(6) Y	(7) % Change in Y
1	100		1.00		100	
		_1.0506_		_2 %_		_3 %_
2			1.02		103	

Calculate the percentage changes in Y and P between Periods 1 and 2 in Table 2-3 and complete Columns 5 and 7.

c. Recall that % Change in PY (nominal GDP) is approximately equal to % Change in P + % Change in Y. Using your answers in Columns 5 and 7,

% Change in PY = ___2___ % + ___3___ % = ___5___ %.

Place this number in Column 3 in Table 2-3.

d. Now compute Nominal GDP in Period 2 exactly by calculating PY in Period 2 =

___1.02___ × ___103___ = ___105.06___ . Consequently, the actual % Change in nominal GDP is equal to 100 × (___105.06___ − 100)/100 = ___5.06___ %.

Note the accuracy of our approximation.

e. If % Change in PY = % Change in P + % Change in Y, one can subtract % Change in Y from both sides to obtain:

% Change in PY − % Change in Y = % Change in P.

This is another application of percentage changes. Recall that the GDP deflator = (Nominal GDP)/(Real GDP), or $P = PY/Y$. The percentage change in a quotient is approximately equal to the % Change in the numerator *minus* the % Change in the denominator. Suppose you did not know the level of P in Table 2-3, but you knew the percentage changes in PY and Y in Columns 3 and 7. You could then calculate

% Change in P = % Change in PY − % Change in Y = ___2___ %.

f. As another example, consider labour productivity Y/L, which represents output per worker. Its percentage change from one year to the next is approximately equal to % Change in Y plus/~~minus~~ % Change in L. Consequently, if Y grew by 5 percent in a year and L grew by 2 percent, then labour productivity would grow by approximately ___3___ percent.

$$\%\Delta \, Y/L \approx \%\Delta Y - \%\Delta L$$

$$\%\Delta \, PY \approx \%\Delta P + \%\Delta Y$$

$$\therefore$$

$$\%\Delta PY - \%\Delta Y \approx \%\Delta P$$

5. **The Differences between GDP and GNP** *In this exercise, we discuss the differences between GDP and GNP by examining a series of transactions.*

   a. In an open economy, there are two different measures of total income: gross domestic product (GDP) and gross national product (GNP). GDP defines output according to geographical boundaries. It includes the output produced (and the income received) by everyone within the borders of the country. GNP, on the other hand, includes the output produced (and the income received) by every citizen of that country, regardless of whether he or she is currently living in the country. With these differences in mind, complete Table 2-4.

   ### Table 2-4

(1) Event	(2) Included in Canadian GNP	(3) Included in Canadian GDP
1. Blue Rodeo perform a concert in Vancouver	Yes	Yes
2. Blue Rodeo perform a concert in London (UK)	Y	N
3. The Rolling Stones perform a concert in Vancouver	N	Y
4. The Rolling Stones perform a concert in London (UK)	N	N
5. Toyota earns profits from its car factory in Ontario	N	Y
6. Ford earns profits from its car factory in England	N ?	N

6. **Semilogarithmic Graphs** *In this exercise, we graph the growth of real GDP on a semilogarithmic graph and illustrate how straight lines on a semilog graph represent constant percentage (rather than absolute) changes over time.*

   a. Economists often use semilogarithmic graphs to make some interesting comparisons. In this exercise we shall see how these graphs work. Consider the following hypothetical economy:

Table 2-5

(1) Year	(2) Real GDP ($ in billions)
1970	100
1980	150
1990	200
2000	280
2010	420

Plot and graph these five points on Graph 2-1.

Graph 2-1

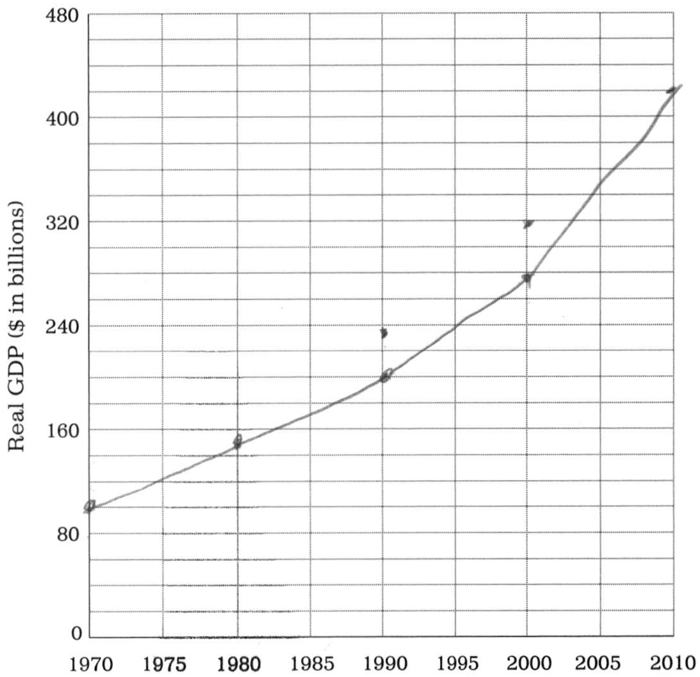

Note that the slope of the line connecting the points is greatest between 2000 and 2010, the decade in which real GDP rose by $140 billion. Similarly, the slope is smallest between 1970 and 1990, when real GDP rose by only $50 billion in each decade. The point to be remembered is that on a conventional graph, segments having equal slopes reflect equal *absolute* changes in the variable that appears on the vertical axis.

b. In economics we frequently want to compare *percentage changes* rather than absolute changes. For this purpose, semilogarithmic graphs can be very helpful. In conventional graphs the numbers on the vertical axis are spaced proportionately. Consequently, 150 lies above 100 by the same distance that 200 lies above 150. In semilogarithmic graphs, however, the numbers on the vertical axis are spaced proportionately according to their *logarithms*. You don't need a calculator to calculate logarithms. As you can see from Graph 2-2 below, the numbers are already marked on the vertical axis. Plot and connect the data from Table 2-5 on this graph.

Graph 2-2

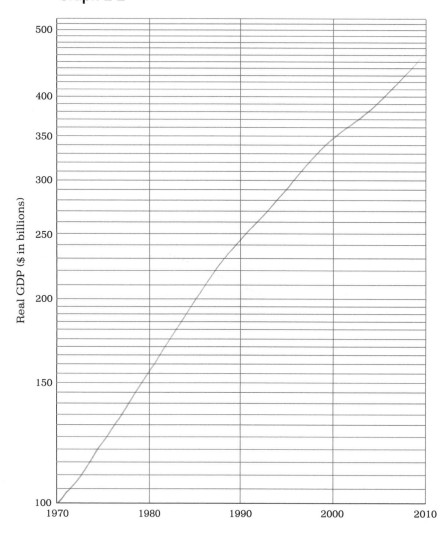

Note that the slope of the line now reaches a maximum on two segments: 1970–1980 and 2000–2010. This is true because the slope of a line segment in a semilogarithmic graph is directly related to percentage changes. The percentage change in real GDP is 50 percent in each of these two decades; hence, the slopes of the segments are equal. The percentage changes in real GDP in the other decades were smaller (33 percent in the 1980s and 40 percent in the 1990s). Consequently, the slopes of their line segments on a semilogarithmic graph are smaller, even though the absolute change of $80 billion during the 1990s was the second highest.

One obvious question you may have is, which graph is better? This depends upon the particular question you are addressing. If you are interested in comparing absolute changes, use a conventional graph. If you are interested in comparing percentage changes, use a semilogarithmic graph.

Problems

Answer the following problems on a separate piece of paper.

1. Consider the following data for 2008:

	($ in billions)
Personal consumption expenditure	$891.2
Government expenditure	367.0
Investment expenditure	317.9
Imports	536.8
GDP	1,600.1

   Calculate exports.

   [handwritten:] NX = EX − IM
   24 = EX − 536.8
   EX = 560.8
   1 600.1 − 8 962 − 367.0 − 317.9 = 24 = NX

2. When computing gross domestic product, economists multiply the price of individual goods by the quantity in order to compare apples and oranges. Why do you think they use prices rather than another common measure, such as the weight of each unit of the good?

3. In the national income accounts, expenditures on one's education (for example, university tuition) are treated as consumption. Some economists believe these should be treated as investment. Why?

4. In 2008, both GDP and GNP per capita in the United States were about $47,000 (U.S.) per person. In the same year, GNP per person was $540 in Bangladesh, $304 in Ethiopia, and $104 in Burundi. Does this mean that the standard of living in the United States was 87 times as great as that in Bangladesh, 155 times that in Ethiopia, and 452 times that in Burundi? Why or why not?

5. For *each* of the following transactions, indicate whether it represents an increase in the Canadian gross domestic product, and, if so, state whether it represents Canadian consumption, investment, government purchases of goods or services, or net exports.

   a. You buy a new Ford Taurus automobile.

   b. You buy a used computer from a friend.

   c. You buy 100 shares of General Motors stock.

   d. Toyota builds a new factory in Ontario.

   e. General Motors' inventories of steel rise by 50,000 tonnes.

   f. The government sends your grandmother her monthly Canada Pension Plan cheque.

   g. The government buys a new submarine for $1 billion.

6. Suppose a family purchases a new home for $300,000 and borrows the entire amount from the bank. The family pays $15,000 in interest on their new mortgage during the first year. The house would rent for $1,000 per month, or $12,000 per year. How are these transactions included in the national accounts?

7. Some Canadians are concerned about Japanese investment in Canada, especially when Japanese firms buy existing Canadian firms. Suppose that a Japanese firm buys an existing Canadian firm and sends some of its Japanese managers to run the firm with Canadian workers. If the firm's output is unchanged and the former Canadian managers remain unemployed, what happens to:

   a. Canadian GNP?

   b. Canadian GDP?

8. Suppose the entire economy consists of only two types of products: computers and automobiles. Sales and price data for these two products for two different years are shown below.

Year	Quantity of Computers Sold	Price per Computer	Quantity of Automobiles Sold	Price per Automobile
2000	2	$10,000	10	$5,000
2010	15	$ 4,000	20	$8,000

   a. Assuming that all computers and automobiles are final goods, calculate nominal GDP in 2010.

   b. Calculate *real* GDP in 2010 in 2000 dollars.

   c. Use the relationship between nominal and real GDP to calculate the GDP deflator in 2010 using 2000 prices (i.e., using 2000 as the base year).

Data Questions

The questions in these data sections require you to obtain actual macroeconomic data. For advice on how to access the data, see the Preface and the Economic Data on the Internet section on p. xi.

As described in Chapter 2 of the textbook, the labour force is either employed or unemployed. While it is most common to summarize this information by reporting the unemployment rate, interpretation is then complicated by considerations such as the discouraged worker effect. Some analysts feel that some of these interpretation difficulties are avoided by focusing on the employment rate.

1. Plot a graph showing the employment rate (annual average data for Canadians over fifteen years of age) 1976 to the present (Statistics Canada series v2461266).

   a. When was the employment rate highest?

   b. How does the recovery after the recession of the early 1990s compare to the recovery after the recession of the early 1980s? Can you think of reasons for this difference?

   c. Why does the discouraged worker effect influence the unemployment rate more than the employment rate?

2. Plot a graph showing the participation rate (annual average data for Canadians over 15 years of age) 1976 to the present (Statistics Canada series v2461455).

   a. Explain how your graph illustrates the change in the labour force attachment of women.

   b. Explain how your graph illustrates the discouraged worker effect.

Questions to Think About

1. According to Okun's Law, the unemployment rate falls by only about one percentage point when GDP rises by about two percentage points. Why do you think that the unemployment rate responds less than one-for-one with the increase in the nation's output?

2. If you had to choose only one measure to represent the level of economic well-being in a country, which of the following would you choose? Why?

   real gross domestic product per capita
   real gross domestic product per working hour
   the literacy rate
   the infant mortality rate
   life expectancy
   the degree of income inequality
   the unemployment rate
   the average level of education

Q 8

$$R = \frac{N}{d}$$

$$d = \frac{N}{R}$$

a $15 \cdot 4000 + 20 \cdot 8000 = 220\ 000$

b $15 \cdot 10\ 000 + 20 \times 5000 = 250\ 000$

c $d = \frac{N}{R} = \frac{220}{250} = .88 = 88$

chapter 3

National Income: Where It Comes From and Where It Goes

Fill-in Questions

Use the key terms below to fill in the blanks in the following statements. Each term may be used more than once.

accounting profit
Cobb-Douglas production function
competition
constant returns to scale
consumption function
crowding out
diminishing marginal productivity
disposable income
economic profit
Euler's theorem
factors of production
factor prices
financial intermediaries

loanable funds
marginal product of capital
marginal product of labour
marginal propensity to consume
national saving
nominal interest rate
private saving
production function
public saving
real interest rate
real rental price of capital
real wage

1. _Factors of Production_ are the inputs used to produce goods and services.

2. _Factor Prices_ are the amounts paid (per unit) to the factors of production.

3. If a firm hires an additional unit of labour while keeping other inputs constant, its production increases by the _MPL_; if it hires an additional unit of capital while keeping other inputs constant, its production increases by the _MPK_.

4. The _Production function_ expresses mathematically how the factors of production determine the amount of output produced.

5. If we double the amounts of labour and capital, and output also doubles, the production function is said to have _constant returns to scale_

6. Under perfect _competition_, profit-maximizing firms hire labour until the _MPL_ equals the real wage. They hire capital until the marginal product of capital equals the _real rent of capital_.

3

7. The ___real wage___ is what a worker is paid (per hour) measured in units of output rather than in dollars.

8. ___Accounting profit___ includes both economic profit and the return to capital.

9. According to ___Euler's Theorem___, if a production function has constant returns to scale and each factor of production is paid its marginal product, then the sum of these factor payments equals total output. Consequently, ___Economic Profit___ equals zero.

10. One special production function that exhibits a constant ratio of labour income to capital income is $Y = F(K, L) = AK^{\alpha}L^{1-\alpha}$. This is called the ___Cobb - Douglas Production function___.

11. Most production functions exhibit ___diminishing marginal productivity___ whereby each additional unit of input increases total output by smaller and smaller increments, all other things being equal.

12. The ___consumption function___ depicts the relationship between consumption and disposable income. Its slope, called the ___MPC___, represents the fraction of each additional dollar of ___disposable income___ that people spend on consumption.

13. The ___i, nominal interest rate___ is the rate investors pay to borrow money. It is equal to the ___r, real interest rates___ plus the rate of inflation.

14. According to the national accounts identity, ___national savings___ equals $S = I$ investment.

15. Disposable income minus consumption equals ___private saving___.

16. An increase in government purchases decreases ___public savings___. If private saving remains unchanged, the interest rate increases and investment decreases. Consequently, an increase in government purchases results in the ___crowding out___ of investment.

17. The interest rate may be viewed as the equilibrium price in the market for ___loanable funds___. Saving represents the supply of ___loanable funds___, and investment represents the demand for ___loanable funds___.

18. Banks, insurance companies, and pension funds are all examples of ___financial intermediaries___ insofar as they take money from savers and make loans to those who have investments to make

Multiple-Choice Questions

1. The production function is a mathematical law that:

   a. relates factor prices to the amounts of inputs demanded.

   b. relates marginal products of factors of production to factor prices.

   c. relates factors of production to the amount of output produced.

   d. always has constant returns to scale.

2. The variable that is held constant for a given production function is the:

   a. amount of labour input.   **c.** amount of capital input.

   b. amount of output.   **d.** production technology.

3. An economy's aggregate income equals:

   a. the total number of dollars earned by workers.

   b. aggregate output.

   c. the number of dollars received by producers as profits.

   d. the total rent collected by the owners of capital.

4. A competitive firm takes:

   a. the prices of its outputs as given, but not the prices of its inputs.

   b. the prices of its inputs as given, but not the prices of its outputs.

   c. the prices of both its inputs and its outputs as given.

   d. neither the prices of its inputs nor the prices of its outputs as given.

5. Profit is:

   a. total revenue minus total cost.

   b. the price of output minus the price of input.

   c. the amount of money paid by a company to its stockholders as dividends each year.

   d. the amount of money earned by firm managers.

6. Constant returns to scale occur when:

   a. output doubles when the amounts of all factor inputs double.

   b. output remains constant over time.

   c. the marginal productivity of labour equals the marginal productivity of capital.

   d. the marginal products of capital and labour do not change.

7. The production function that illustrates diminishing marginal product of labour is:

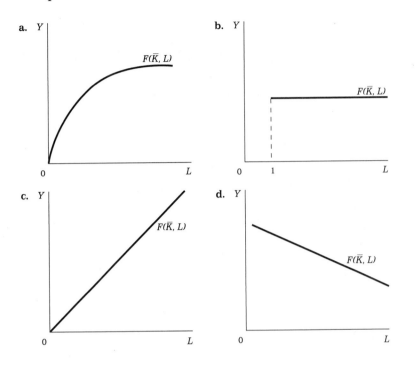

8. A profit-maximizing firm will hire labour up to the point where:
   a. the marginal product of labour equals the marginal product of capital.
   b. the marginal product of labour equals the real wage.
   c. marginal revenue equals zero.
   d. the real wage equals the real rental price of capital.

9. The FALSE statement below is:
   a. the extra revenue a firm gets from an extra unit of capital equals the marginal product of capital times the price of output.
   b. the extra revenue a firm gets from an extra unit of labour equals the marginal product of labour times the wage.
   c. a perfectly competitive firm's labour demand curve is the *MPL* schedule.
   d. constant returns to scale and profit maximization together imply that economic profit is zero.

10. According to Euler's theorem, the sum of all factor payments will equal total output if each factor of production is paid its marginal product and if:
    a. the production function has constant returns to scale.
    b. the production function displays diminishing marginal productivity.
    c. the amounts of capital and labour employed are equal.
    d. firms maximize profits.

11. Which of the following transactions is viewed as investment in the national income accounts?

    a. You buy 100 shares of stock in Apple Computer Corporation.
    b. You buy an Apple Macintosh computer to help your children do their home-work.
    c. Apple Computer Corporation builds a new factory to manufacture computers.
    d. You eat an apple.

12. Which of the following transactions is viewed as investment in the national income accounts?

    a. You buy $1,000 of federal government bonds.
    b. Richard, a carpenter, builds himself a log cabin.
    c. The Art Gallery of Ontario buys a painting by Picasso for $20 million.
    d. Your family buys a newly constructed home.

13. The interest rate on a loan depends on:

    a. the term of the loan.
    b. the riskiness of the loan.
    c. the currency denomination of the loan.
    d. all of the above.

14. The FALSE statement about national saving is:

    a. national saving is the total amount of savings deposits in banks.
    b. national saving is the sum of private saving plus public saving.
    c. national saving reflects the output that remains after the demand of consumers and the government has been satisfied.
    d. national saving equals investment at the equilibrium interest rate.

15. With total output fixed and national saving unrelated to the interest rate, an increase in government purchases increases:

    a. national saving.
    b. public saving.
    c. the equilibrium interest rate.
    d. private saving.

16. With total output fixed and national saving unrelated to the interest rate, an increase in taxes will:

    a. shift the vertical saving schedule to the left.
    b. decrease investment.
    c. increase consumption.
    d. decrease the equilibrium interest rate and increase investment.

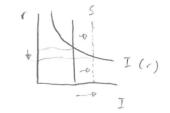

17. If national saving is positively related to the interest rate, a technological advance that increases investment demand will:

    a. have no effect on the amount of national saving.
    b. shift the investment demand curve to the left.
    c. increase both investment and the equilibrium interest rate.
    d. have no effect on consumption.

18. Public saving is equal to:

    a. taxes plus government transfers minus government purchases.
    b. taxes minus government transfers minus government purchases.
    c. taxes plus government transfers plus government purchases.
    d. the government budget deficit.

19. If the nominal interest rate is 8 percent and prices are rising at 5 percent per year, the real interest rate is:

    a. 8 percent.
    b. 3 percent.
    c. 13 percent.
    d. –3 percent.

20. If consumption $C = 100 + 0.8(Y - T)$, disposable income equals 1,000, and $Y = 2,000$, then the marginal propensity to consume is:

    a. 0.5.
    b. 900.
    c. 0.8.
    d. 0.9.

21. All the following are characteristic of the Cobb-Douglas production function EXCEPT:

    a. constant returns to scale.
    b. diminishing marginal productivity of labour.
    c. constant marginal productivity of capital.
    d. a constant ratio of labour income to capital income.

Exercises

1. **Labour Demand and the Nominal Wage** *In this exercise, we derive the demand curve for labour in terms of the nominal wage by equating the nominal wage to the marginal product of labour multiplied by the price of output.*

   Continuing the example introduced in the textbook, consider the data in Columns 1 and 2 for a fictitious bakery—we'll call it the Bread and Butter Bakery.

Table 3-1

(1) No. of Workers (L)	(2) No. of Loaves Baked per Hour	(3) Marginal Product of Labour (MPL)	(4) Price per Loaf	(5) Price per Loaf × MPL	(6) Nominal Wage Rate (W)	(7) Real Wage Rate (W/P)
0	0				$8	8
		20	$1	$20	$8	8
1	20					
		16	$1	16	$8	8
2	36					
		12	$1	12	$8	8
3	48					
		8	$1	6	$8	8
4	56					
		4	$1	4	$8	8
5	60					
		2	$1	2	$8	8
6	62					

This company has a fixed amount of capital equipment. As it hires additional workers, total bread production increases, but by smaller and smaller increments.

a. Using the data from the first two columns of Table 3-1, graph the production function for the Bread and Butter Bakery on Graph 3-1.

Graph 3-1

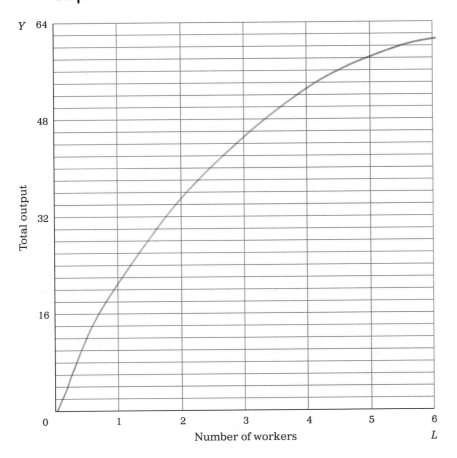

This curve has a positive slope. What does this tell us about the production function of this firm?

The slope decreases as the firm hires additional workers. What does this tell us?

The phenomenon just described is called the property of *diminishing marginal productivity*. As more inputs (here, labour) are added to a fixed amount of other inputs (here, capital), output will rise by smaller and smaller increments. (At some point the bakery could become so crowded that total output might even fall.)

b. Recall from the text that the *marginal product of labour (MPL)* is defined as the extra amount of output the firm gets from hiring an additional unit of labour. When the Bread and Butter Bakery hires its first worker, bread production rises from 0 to 20 loaves per hour. Consequently, the marginal product of labour of the first worker is 20. These data are shown in Column 3 of Table 3-1. Using the definition of *MPL*, complete the remainder of Column 3.

c. Now use the data from Columns 1 and 3 of Table 3-1 to complete Graph 3-2. The point for $L = 1$ is already shown on this graph. Note that this curve has a negative slope, illustrating that the marginal product of labour declines as more workers are hired. This is another example of the law of diminishing marginal productivity.

Graph 3-2

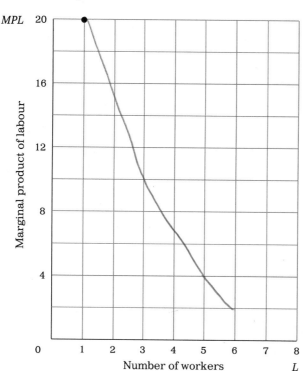

d. The number of workers that the Bread and Butter Bakery will hire depends on the production function and on two additional items: the wage rate the bakery must pay and the price it receives for each loaf of bread. As in the textbook, we assume that the firm operates in perfectly competitive input and output markets. Consequently, the baker will not drive up the wage of bakers if it hires additional employees or drive down the price of bread if it sells more bread. Assume initially that the market price for a loaf of bread is $1. Thus, as the firm hires additional workers, its revenues from sales will rise by $1 multiplied by *MPL*. For the first worker this will equal $1 × 20 = $20. Use this information to complete Columns 4 and 5 of Table 3-1.

e. Now assume that the market wage for each baker is $8 per hour. Complete Column 6 of Table 3-1 appropriately.

The Bread and Butter Bakery will hire an additional baker only when the extra sales revenue she generates exceeds or equals her wage of $8 per hour. (Although the bakery's profits will also be the same if it hires one fewer baker, we shall assume throughout this exercise and the next that more labourers will be hired as long as profits either increase or do not decrease.) Consequently, how many bakers will the bakery hire?

f. Note that when the fourth baker was hired, bread production rose by eight loaves, which were sold for an additional $8. This increase exactly offsets the baker's wage of $8, so she was hired. Algebraically, at this equilibrium

$$W = P \times MPL. \tag{3-1}$$

A fifth baker was not hired because his wage of $8 would have exceeded the $4 in extra revenue he would have generated. Indeed, he would be hired only if the nominal wage rate fell to $4. Similarly, a sixth baker would be hired only if the nominal wage rate fell to $2. Using all of this information, we can now draw the Bread and Butter Bakery's demand curve for labour on Graph 3-3. For each of the wage rates depicted on the vertical axis, plot the number of bakers who will be hired by using the rule $W = P \times MPL$ and connect the points.

Graph 3-3

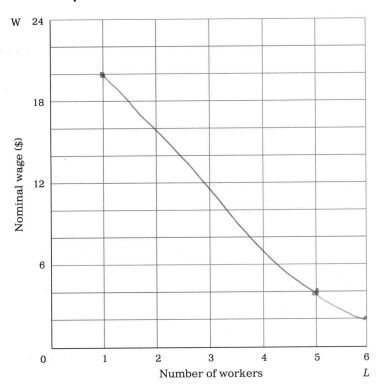

2. **Labour Demand and the Real Wage** *In this exercise, we derive the labour demand curve in terms of the real wage.*

a. As the textbook describes, one can divide $W = P \times MPL$ by P to rewrite the profit-maximizing rule as

$$\frac{W}{P} = MPL, \tag{3-2}$$

where W/P is defined as the real wage. Whereas the nominal wage represents a worker's remuneration in dollars, the real wage represents her remuneration in terms of the amount of goods and services (in this case, loaves of bread) she can purchase. To illustrate this, complete Column 7 of Table 3-1 in Exercise 1. Since $P = \$1$, $W/P = W/\$1$; therefore, the numbers in Column 7 of the table are the same as those in Column 6, although the units are now loaves of bread. Similarly, since $P = \$1$, we could also write W/P instead of W on the vertical axis on Graph 3-3.

b. Now suppose that the price of bread rises to $2 per loaf and the nominal wage rate doubles to $16 per hour. Assuming that the amount of bread produced by each worker remains the same, complete Table 3-2.

Table 3-2

(1) No. of Workers (L)	(2) No. of Loaves Baked per Hour	(3) Marginal Product of Labour (MPL)	(4) Price per Loaf	(5) Price per Loaf × MPL	(6) Nominal Wage Rate (W)	(7) Real Wage Rate (W/P)
0	0				$16	8
		20	$2	$40		
1	20				____	____
		____	____	____		
2	36				____	____
		____	____	____		
3	48				____	____
		____	____	____		
4	56				____	____
		____	____	____		
5	60				____	____
		____	____	____		
6	62				____	____

c. How many workers would the Bread and Butter Bakery now hire?

d. We can illustrate this new labour demand curve graphically in two ways. One way is to find the number of bakers the firm would hire at each nominal wage (just as we did in Exercise 1a). For example, the bakery would hire the first baker only if the wage rate fell to $40, because this is the amount by which revenues rise when the first baker is hired. Similarly, the second baker would be hired only if the nominal wage fell to $_____. Use this type of analysis to draw the Bread and Butter Bakery's demand curve for labour on Graph 3-4. Assume that the price of bread equals $2 per loaf and remember that bakers will be hired according to the rule $W = P \times MPL$. Note that this curve lies to the <u>right/left</u> of the demand curve in Exercise 1f.

Graph 3-4

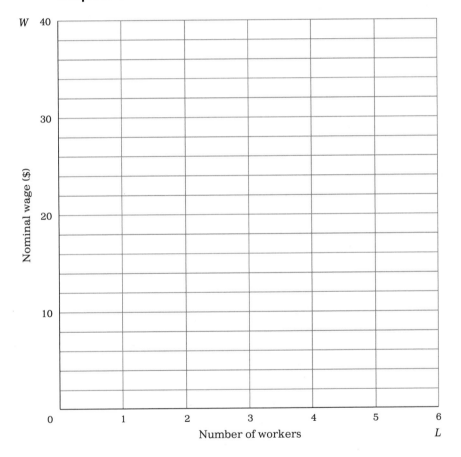

e. A second way to illustrate the labour demand curve graphically is to use the real wage W/P as the variable on the vertical axis and to draw the labour demand curve as a function of the real wage. Use the data from Column 3 of Table 3-2 to complete Table 3-3 and find the number of bakers hired at varying real wages.

Table 3-3

(1) Nominal Wage (W)	(2) Price of Bread (P)	(3) Real Wage (W/P)	(4) Number of Bakers Hired
$20	$1	_____	_____
40	2	_____	_____
16	1	_____	_____
32	2	_____	_____
12	1	_____	_____
24	2	_____	_____
8	1	8	4
16	2	8	4
4	1	_____	_____
8	2	_____	_____

From the data in this table, draw the labour demand curve in terms of the real wage on Graph 3-5. Note that this curve will not shift when inflation increases W and P by the same proportion.

Graph 3-5

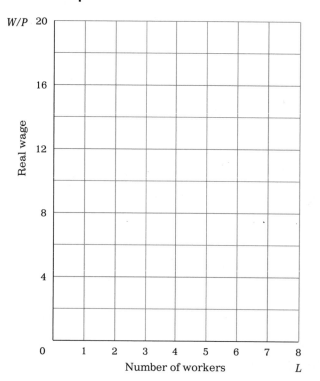

f. In Exercises 1 and 2, we derived the labour demand curve in terms of its nominal and real factor prices, that is, the nominal and real wages. Other factor inputs can be treated in an analogous fashion. For example, we could just as easily draw a table depicting the increase in bread production when the bakery adds more ovens (capital) while holding the number of bakers (labour) constant. This table would allow us to compute the marginal product of capital (*MPK*). We would then equate the *MPK* to the real factor price of capital, *R/P*—called the *real rental price of capital*—in order to determine how many ovens the Bread and Butter Bakery would need to maximize its profits. The curve representing the demand for capital would then be a downward-sloping function of the real rental price of capital.

3. **The Cobb-Douglas Production Function**   *This exercise utilizes a simple Cobb-Douglas production function to illustrate some of the concepts discussed in the textbook—constant returns to scale, diminishing returns, and Euler's theorem. Students who know calculus may choose to do Problem 3 instead of, or in addition to, this exercise.*

    a. Consider the following Cobb-Douglas production function:

    $$Y = K^{1/2}L^{1/2} = \sqrt{KL}.$$ (3-3)

    Compute the value of *Y* for *K* = 100 and *L* = 25.

    b. Define the term *constant returns to scale*.

    Now show that the production function depicted by Equation 3-3 has constant returns to scale by completing Table 3-4. (You will need a calculator.)

Table 3-4

(1)	(2)	(3)
K	*L*	$Y = K^{1/2}L^{1/2}$
100	25	_____
200	50	_____
2,500	625	_____

When you doubled the amounts of capital and labour to 200 and 50, respectively, total output <u>doubled/remained constant/fell by half</u>. When you increased the amounts of capital and labour 25-fold to 2,500 and 625 (from 100 and 25), respectively, total output <u>increased 25-fold/doubled/remained constant/fell</u>. This phenomenon, called *constant returns to scale,* is characteristic of all Cobb-Douglas production functions. Mathematically, this occurs because the exponents on the inputs in the Cobb-Douglas production function sum to 1.0. You may wish to prove this.

c. Using the original values, where $K = 100$ and $L = 25$, compute the marginal product of labour at $L = 25$ by calculating how much output would rise if an additional worker were employed. This can be done by substituting $L = 26$ and $K = 100$ in the production function and noting the increase in Y. Note that in this exercise, as in the textbook, the *MPL* is calculated as the change in output when 1 unit of labour is *added*. This is different from Exercises 1 and 2 where the *MPL* is calculated as the change in output when 1 unit of labour is *subtracted*. (You will need a calculator to solve for $26^{1/2}$. Round off your answer to the nearest hundredth.)

Recall that, in equilibrium, firms will hire workers until the *MPL* equals the real wage W/P. Given your answer to the first part of Part c, if firms in the economy had decided to employ 25 workers, what would the equilibrium real wage have to be?

d. Start again at the original values of $K = 100$ and $L = 25$, and compute the marginal product of capital at $K = 100$ by calculating how much output would rise if an additional unit of capital were employed. This can be done by substituting $K = 101$ and $L = 25$ in the production function and noting the increase in Y. (You will again need a calculator. Round off your answer to the nearest hundredth.)

Recall that, in equilibrium, firms will hire capital until the MPK equals the real rental price of capital R/P. Given your answer to the first part of Part d, if firms in the economy had decided to employ 100 units of capital, what would the equilibrium real rental price of capital have to be?

e. Now we will compute the constant factor shares in this Cobb-Douglas production function.

Step 1   From Part a you found that when $K = 100$ and $L = 25$, $Y =$ _____.

Step 2   From Part c you discovered that the marginal product of labour and the equilibrium real wage at $L = 25$ were both equal to _____. Consequently, total real labour payments, $(W/P) \times L$, are equal to _____.

Step 3   Labour's share of total output is equal to total labour payments divided by total output, or $[(W/P) \times L]/Y =$ _____.

Step 4   From Part d you found that the marginal product of capital and the equilibrium real rental cost of capital at $K = 100$ were both equal to _____. Consequently, total real payments to capital, $(R/P) \times K$, are equal to _____.

Step 5   Capital's share of total output is equal to total payments to capital divided by total output, or $[(R/P) \times K]/Y =$ _____.

Step 6   Note that in a Cobb-Douglas production function, labour's share is always equal to the exponent on the labour input variable in the production function, and capital's share is equal to the exponent on the capital input variable.

Step 7   To see how Cobb-Douglas production functions yield constant factor
CH   shares even as inputs vary, verify that the relative shares would remain constant if K remains equal to 100 but L equals 625. To see this, it is necessary to recompute Y, MPL, W/P, MPK, R/P, and total factor payments for both capital and labour when $L = 625$. If you know calculus, it is easier to see this by answering Problem 3g.

f. Finally, add up the total factor payments from Part e, Steps 2 and 4, and compare the sum with your answer to Part a to illustrate Euler's theorem. This theorem states that if a production function has constant returns to scale and each factor of production is paid its marginal product, then the sum of these factor payments equals total output.

4. **The Consumption Function** *In this exercise, we introduce the marginal propensity to consume and the simple consumption function.*

   a. As described in the textbook, consumption expenditures may be specified as a function of disposable income, where the latter is equal to GDP minus taxes, $Y - T$. Even if disposable income equals zero, people still need to eat, so they will consume out of their wealth, and consumption will still be positive. For each $1 increase in disposable income, consumption rises by $MPC, where MPC represents the *marginal propensity to consume,* defined as the fraction of each additional dollar of disposable income that is spent on consumption. Consider the following *consumption function:*

$$C = 125 + 0.75(Y - T). \qquad \text{(3-4)}$$

   Use Equation 3-4 to complete Table 3-5.

Table 3-5

(1) Disposable Income $(Y - T)$	(2) Consumption
$ 0	_____
100	_____
200	_____
500	_____
800	_____
1,000	_____

   b. Plot the points from Table 3-5 on Graph 3-6 and connect them.

Graph 3-6

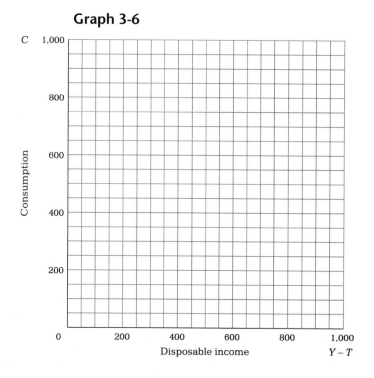

c. What is the value of the *y* intercept of this curve?

d. The slope of this curve is _____. Explain why the numerical value of the slope is also equal to the marginal propensity to consume.

5. **Taxes, Transfers, Budget Surpluses, and Budget Deficits** *In this exercise, we illustrate how the government budget surplus (or deficit) is related to government purchases, taxes, and transfers.*

a. As the textbook suggests, in most economic models *T* is equal to total taxes minus government transfer payments. Some economists call these *net taxes,* which are equal to what households pay to the government in total taxes minus what they receive from the government in the form of transfer payments.

According to this definition:

If total taxes = 100 and government transfers = 0, net taxes *T* = _____.

If total taxes = 100 and government transfers = 50, net taxes *T* = _____.

If total taxes = 100 and government transfers = 150, net taxes *T* = _____.

b. The *government budget surplus* is equal to total government tax revenues minus total government outlays, where the latter consist of both transfer payments and government purchases of goods and services. Since net taxes *T* already equals total taxes minus transfers, then, ignoring interest payments on the public debt, the

$$\text{Budget Surplus} = T - G. \qquad \text{(3-5)}$$

The *budget deficit* is equal to the negative of the budget surplus:

$$\text{Budget Deficit} = -(T - G) = G - T \qquad \text{(3-6)}$$

Use Equations 3-5 and 3-6 to complete Table 3-6.

Table 3-6

(1) Net Taxes (*T*)	(2) Government Purchases	(3) Budget Surplus	(4) Budget Deficit
200	100	_____	_____
200	200	_____	_____
100	200	_____	_____
−100	100	_____	_____

6. **The Saving-Investment Identity** *In this exercise, we assume, as in the textbook, that the total output of the economy is fixed and that the factors of production are fully utilized. We then show that national saving is equal to investment.*

Assume that there are two factors of production, K and L, and that they are both fully employed at $K = \bar{K}$ and $L = \bar{L}$. Furthermore, assume that the economy is described by the following set of equations:

$$Y = \bar{Y} = F(\bar{K}, \bar{L}) = 1{,}200, \qquad \text{(3-7)}$$
$$Y = C + I + G, \qquad \text{(3-8)}$$
$$C = 125 + 0.75(Y - T), \qquad \text{(3-9)}$$
$$I = I(r) = 200 - 10r, \qquad \text{(3-10)}$$
$$G = \bar{G} = 150 \text{ and} \qquad \text{(3-11)}$$
$$T = \bar{T} = 100. \qquad \text{(3-12)}$$

These equations show the following:

Equation 3-7 represents the production function and the fact that the economy is operating at full employment when $Y = 1{,}200$.

Equation 3-8 is the national accounts identity.

Equation 3-9 is the consumption function, whereby consumption is a function of disposable income, $(Y - T)$.

Equation 3-10 is an investment equation in which investment falls by 10 whenever the interest rate rises by 1 percentage point.

Equations 3-11 and 3-12 imply that government purchases and taxes are set exogenously at 150 and 100, respectively.

a. Substituting these values for Y and T in the consumption function, solve for the level of consumption.

$$C = 125 + 0.75 \ (Y - T) = \underline{\hspace{6cm}}.$$

b. Rearranging Equations 3-7 and 3-8, we obtain

$$\bar{Y} - C - G = I. \qquad \text{(3-13)}$$

As the textbook describes, the left-hand side of Equation 3-13 is equal to national saving S:

$$S = \bar{Y} - C - G. \qquad \text{(3-14)}$$

This is the amount of saving that remains after the demands of consumers and the government have been satisfied. As Equations 3-13 and 3-14 illustrate, national saving must equal investment I:

$$S = I. \qquad \text{(3-15)}$$

Substitute the values for Y, C, and G in Equation 3-14 and solve for the initial equilibrium values of both S and I.

$$S = I = \bar{Y} - C - G = \underline{\hspace{6cm}}.$$

Finally, substitute this value of I in the investment equation and solve for the real interest rate.

$$I = 200 - 10r = \underline{\hspace{4cm}}. \quad r = \underline{\hspace{4cm}}.$$

c. In the model we developed in Parts a and b, national saving is assumed to be a fixed amount that is unrelated to the interest rate. Consequently, it is depicted as a vertical line on Graph 3-7. Complete the graph by drawing the curve representing the investment equation. (This is most easily done by solving the investment equation for r—that is, by isolating r on the left-hand side of the equation.) Indicate the slope of the investment curve, the initial equilibrium interest rate, and the initial levels of saving and investment.

Graph 3-7

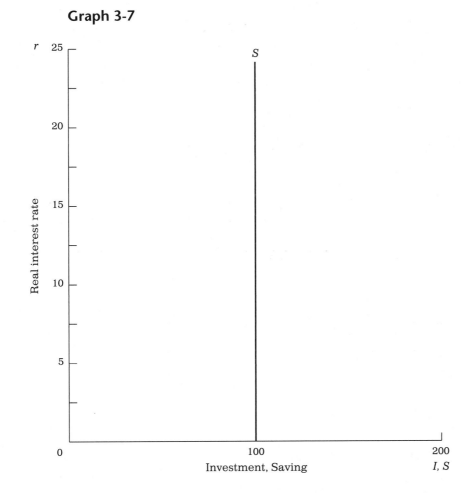

d. Economists often divide national saving into two parts in order to separate the saving of households from that of government. This is done by subtracting from and adding taxes T to the right-hand side of Equation 3-14. Therefore,

$$S = I = (Y - T - C) + (T - G). \tag{3-16}$$

The term in the first set of parentheses is equal to disposable income minus consumption. This is called *private* (or household) *saving*. Recall that the term in the second set of parentheses is the government budget surplus, which is equal to *public saving*. Given your answers in Part b, calculate the initial levels of public and private saving and verify that they sum to the level of national saving.

7. **Shifts in the Saving and Investment Curves** *In this exercise, we use the saving-investment identity to analyze the effects of changes in government purchases, taxes, and technology on the level of investment and the equilibrium interest rate.*

Assume the same model as in Exercise 6.

$$Y = \bar{Y} = F(\bar{K}, \bar{L}) = 1{,}200$$
$$Y = C + I + G$$
$$C = 125 + 0.75(Y - T)$$
$$I = I(r) = 200 - 10r$$
$$G = \bar{G} = 150$$
$$T = \bar{T} = 100.$$

Using the same initial equilibrium values, let us now see what happens when there is a change in fiscal policy or in the investment equation.

a. Graph 3-8 depicts the same initial equilibrium as in Exercise 6. Suppose that government purchases increase by 50 to 200. If $\bar{Y}$ and T remain fixed at 1,200 and 100, respectively, consumption would remain constant at $C = 950$. Consequently, saving S would have to <u>rise/fall</u> by _____ to have

$$S = Y - C - G = \underline{\hspace{4cm}}.$$

Graph 3-8

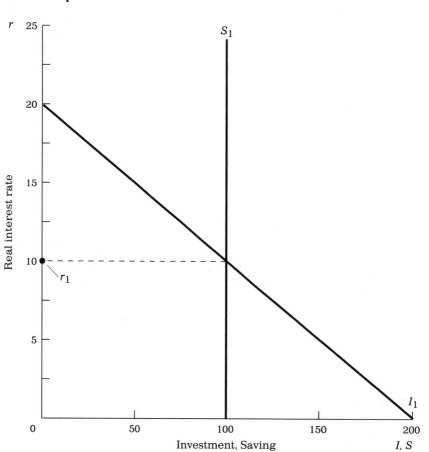

This would shift the vertical saving line to the left/right by _____.
Illustrate this shift on Graph 3-8 and label the new line S_2.

b. For the supply of output to remain equal to the demand for output,
investment would also have to rise/fall by _____ to
_____. This would be accomplished by a shift in/move-
ment along the investment curve. Consequently, the interest rate would rise/fall.
Solve for the new level of the interest rate by substituting this new value for
investment into the investment equation; illustrate the new equilibrium interest
rate on Graph 3-8 and label this point r_2.

c. In Parts a and b, you found that if GDP is fixed at full employment Y, an increase
in government purchases would increase/decrease national saving. This would
increase/decrease the real interest rate and thereby increase/decrease investment. Thus, an increase in government purchases is said to crowd out investment.

d. Now suppose that we start again at $G = 150$ and taxes are reduced by 20 to 80.
Given a value of $\overline{Y} = 1,200$, this would increase/decrease the level of consumption
to

$$C = 125 + 0.75(1,200 - 80) = \text{_____}.$$

Consequently, national saving would increase/decrease to

$$S = Y - C - G = \text{_____}.$$

This would shift the vertical saving line to the left/right by _____.
For output to remain in equilibrium, investment would also have to
rise/fall by _____ to _____. This would be accomplished
by a shift in/movement along the investment curve. Consequently, the interest
rate would rise/fall. Thus, a decrease in taxes also crowds out investment.

e. Finally, suppose that a technological breakthrough increases investment
   demand such that investment rises by 100 at each interest rate. Consequently,
   on Graph 3-9, the investment curve shifts to the right/left by 100. Draw the new
   curve and label it I_2.

Graph 3-9

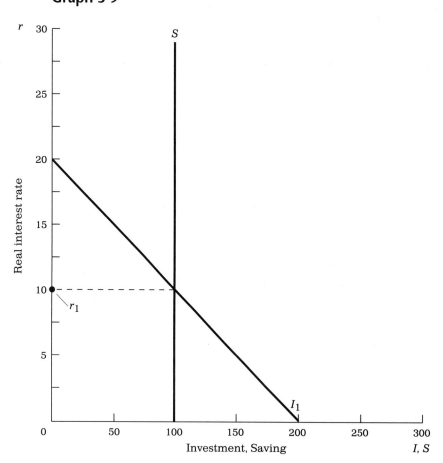

If $\overline{Y}$ initially remains unchanged, national saving will increase/remain con-
stant/decrease and the vertical saving line will shift right/not shift/shift left. As
a result, the interest rate would rise/fall, and we would move along the new
investment demand curve until investment equaled _____.

f. The result in Part e would be different if saving were positively related to the interest rate. A higher interest rate might reduce consumption and increase saving. If this were true, the saving schedule would have a positive/negative slope, as on Graph 3-10.

Graph 3-10

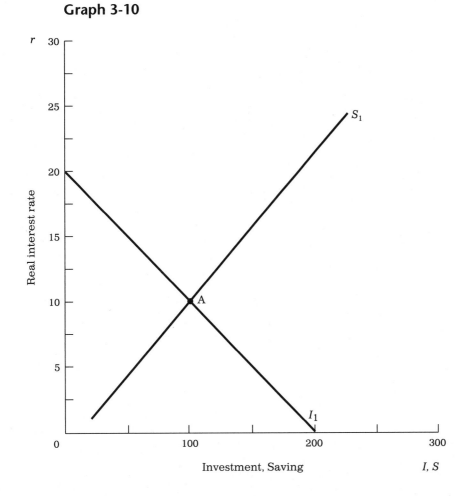

Now suppose that a technological breakthrough increases investment demand at each interest rate by shifting the investment demand curve to the right/left by 100, as in Part e. Draw the new investment curve on Graph 3-10, label it I_2, and label the new equilibrium Point B. The technological breakthrough would now tend to increase/decrease both the interest rate and the level of investment.

8. **The Identification Problem** *In this exercise, we illustrate the identification problem.*

Consider the situation depicted below, in which the saving schedule is positively sloped, as in Exercise 7f, rather than vertical.

Graph 3-11

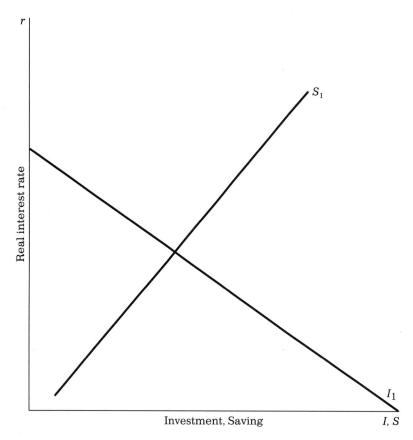

a. In Exercises 7b and 7d, we saw that an increase in government purchases or a reduction in taxes would increase/have no effect on/decrease national saving. Starting from the initial position S_1 on Graph 3-11, these policy changes would shift the saving schedule to the right/left. Draw the new saving schedule and label it S_2. The investment demand curve would not shift, but we would move along it to the new equilibrium. Consequently, the interest rate would rise/remain constant/fall, investment would rise/remain constant/fall, and we would observe a positive/negative relationship between the interest rate and investment.

b. Similarly, a reduction in government purchases or an increase in taxes would increase/decrease national saving. Starting again from S_1 on Graph 3-11, this set of policy changes would shift the saving schedule to the right/left. Draw the new saving schedule on Graph 3-11 and label it S_3. The investment demand curve would not shift, but we would move along it to the new equilibrium. Consequently, the interest rate would rise/fall, investment would rise/fall, and we would again observe a positive/negative relationship between the interest rate and investment.

c. Reviewing Exercise 7f, however, we see that a technological breakthrough that increases investment demand would shift the investment curve to the right/left and increase/decrease both the interest rate and investment. Similarly, a reduction in investment demand would shift the investment curve to the right/left and increase/decrease both the interest rate and investment. This would result in a positive/negative relationship between the interest rate and investment.

d. After putting the results from Parts a through c together, we see that one cannot predict whether the relationship between the interest rate and investment will be positive or negative. If the economy experiences shifts primarily in its saving schedule, the relationship will be positive/negative, but if it experiences shifts primarily in its investment demand curve, the relationship will be positive/negative.

Problems

Answer the following problems on a separate sheet of paper. Complete tables in the spaces provided.

1. How would Graphs 3-1 and 3-2 in Exercise 1 look if each additional worker added the same amount to total output, that is, if there were constant rather than diminishing returns?

2. Apples grown in British Columbia and Nova Scotia are sold at the same price. Farm workers in both provinces work in a perfectly competitive labour market and receive identical wages. Suppose, however, that economists have discovered that the *average* product of labour in British Coumbia apple orchards is 50 percent greater than in Nova Scotia. The average product of labour is defined as total output divided by the number of workers (or worker-hours).

   a. Explain why the following statement could easily be false: Since the average product of labour is different in these two provinces, British Columbia and Nova Scotia apple orchards obviously follow different economic rules in hiring workers; the firms in Nova Scotia must not be maximizing profits.

   b. Suppose that all orchards in the two provinces are currently maximizing profits and evaluate the following statement: Because the average product of labour is higher in British Columbia, Canadian apple production would increase if farm workers moved from Nova Scotia to British Columbia apple orchards.

3. This problem uses calculus to derive the same results as Exercise 3 concerning the **C** Cobb-Douglas production function.

   Consider the following Cobb-Douglas production function:

   $$Y = 60K^{1/3}L^{2/3}.$$

a. Complete Table 3-7. (You will need a calculator.)

Table 3-7

(1)	(2)	(3)
K	L	$Y = 60K^{1/3}L^{2/3}$
64	8	_____
128	16	_____
192	24	_____

Explain how these results illustrate the property of constant returns to scale.

b. Derive the algebraic expression for the marginal product of labour by differentiating the right-hand side of the production function with respect to L.

c. Evaluate the expression you just derived—that is, find the numerical value of MPL—when $K = 64$ and $L = 8$.

Recall that, in equilibrium, firms will hire workers until their MPL equals the real wage W/P. Given your answer to the first part of Part c, if firms in the economy had decided to employ eight workers, what would the equilibrium real wage have to be?

d. Derive the algebraic expression for the marginal product of capital by differentiating the right-hand side of the production function with respect to K.

e. Evaluate the expression you just derived—that is, find the numerical value of MPK—when $K = 64$ and $L = 8$.

Recall that, in equilibrium, firms will hire capital until the MPK equals the real rental price of capital R/P. Given your answer to the first part of Part e, if firms in the economy had decided to employ 64 units of capital, what would the equilibrium real rental price of capital have to be?

f. Illustrate how Cobb-Douglas production functions result in constant factor shares that are equal to the exponents on the respective factors of production. To show this, calculate total real labour payments, total real payments to capital, and labour and capital's shares of total output when $K = 64$ and $L = 8$.

g. Use the algebraic expressions you derived for the marginal products of capital and labour (your answers to Parts b and d) to prove your result from Part f algebraically.

h. Finally, show that this production function satisfies Euler's theorem.

4. Soon after being elected in the 1990s, the Federal Liberals proposed to reduce government spending and increase taxes as proportions of GDP.

   a. What effect would this have on the government budget deficit?

   b. State and explain what the long-run effects of this policy would be on private saving, public saving, and national saving.

   c. Use the *I,S* diagram to state and illustrate what the long-run impact of this program would be on national saving, investment, and the real interest rate.

5. Later on in the 1990s, the Reform party proposed cutting both government purchases and taxes.

   a. If both taxes and government purchases were cut by equal amounts (which was not true in the proposal of the official opposition), state and explain what the long-run effects of this policy would be on private saving, public saving, and national saving.

   b. Use the *I,S* diagram to state and illustrate what the long-run impact of this program would be on national saving, investment, and the real interest rate.

   c. Explain how the magnitude of the changes you depicted in Part b depends on the size of the marginal propensity to consume.

6. During and after the financial crisis of 2008, Canadians felt less secure and so began to save a greater portion of their incomes. Graphically illustrate what a permanent increase in saving would do to the level of investment.

7. The 2009 Federal Budget involved an increase in the annual deficit to its biggest value ever. Explain the effect of this policy on the real interest rate if it were to be maintained.

chapter 4

Money and Inflation

Fill-in Questions

Use the key terms below to fill in the blanks in the following statements. Each term may be used more than once.

central bank
classical dichotomy
commodity money
currency
deposits
disincentive for saving
double coincidence of wants
ex ante real interest rate
ex post real interest rate
Bank of Canada
fiat money
Fisher effect
Fisher equation
gold standard
hyperinflation
income velocity of money
inflation
medium of exchange
menu cost
monetary neutrality

monetary policy
money
money demand function
money supply
*M*1
*M*2
nominal interest rate
nominal variables
open-market operations
quantity equation
quantity theory
real interest rate
real money balances
real variables
seigniorage
shoe-leather cost
store of value
transactions velocity of money
unit of account

1. The overall increase in prices is called _____.

2. An episode of extraordinarily high inflation is known as a(n)

    _____.

3. _____ is the stock of assets used for transactions.
    It serves three functions: it is a(n) _____, a(n)
    _____, and a(n) _____.

4. In a barter economy, all trade requires the _____— the unlikely occurrence of two people each having a good that the other wants.

5. Money that has no intrinsic value is called _____ since it is established as money by government decree.

6. Gold is an example of _____ because it has some intrinsic value. An economy in which gold serves as money is said to be on a(n) _____.

7. The quantity of money available is called the _____. In many countries, the control of the money supply is delegated to a partially independent institution called the _____. In Canada this institution is called the _____.

8. The control of the money supply is called _____. In Canada, the primary way in which the _____ controls the supply of money is through _____—the purchase and sale of government bonds.

9. The most frequently used measure of the quantity of money— _____—includes _____, which consists of paper money and coins, and the funds that individuals hold in their chequing accounts. A somewhat broader measure of the quantity of money, called _____, includes all of the preceding items plus savings accounts.

10. The link between transactions and money is expressed in the equation $MV = PT$, which is called the _____. In this equation, V is called the _____. This equation can be turned into a useful theory— called the _____ of money—by making the additional assumption that V is constant.

11. Economists also use a similar equation, $MV = PY$, that replaces the number of transactions T with the total output of the economy Y. Because Y is also total income, the variable V in this equation is called the _____.

12. When analyzing the effects of money on the economy, it is often convenient to express the quantity of money in terms of the quantity of goods it can buy, M/P, which is called _____.

13. A(n) _____ is an equation that shows what determines the quantity of real money balances people wish to hold.

14. The revenue raised by the government through the printing of money is called _____.

15. The interest rate banks pay to depositors is called the _____. According to the _____, it is equal to the _____ plus the inflation rate. This one-for-one relation

between the inflation rate and the _____ is called the
_____.

16. The real interest rate that the borrowers and lenders expect when a loan is made is called the _____; the real interest rate actually realized is called the _____.

17. One cost of inflation, which is metaphorically called the _____ of inflation, is the inconvenience of reducing money holding. A second cost of inflation, which is called the _____, arises because high inflation causes firms to change their posted prices more often. A third cost is the _____.

18. Chapters 1–3 of the textbook focus on quantities and relative prices, which are called _____. Those variables that are expressed in terms of money, on the other hand, are called _____.

19. The phrase that macroeconomists use to describe the theoretical separation of real and nominal variables is the _____. It arises in models in which changes in the money supply do not influence _____. This irrelevance of money in determining _____ is called _____.

Multiple-Choice Questions

1. Money is:
   a. the stock of assets used for transactions.
   b. the number of dollars in the hands of the public.
   c. a store of value, a unit of account, and a medium of exchange.
   d. all of the above.

2. Barter economies require:
   a. the use of fiat money.
   b. the use of commodity money.
   c. a double coincidence of wants.
   d. money to serve as a store of value but not as a medium of exchange.

3. Fiat money:
   a. is backed by gold.
   b. is established as money by an Italian automobile manufacturer.
   c. includes currency and gold stored in bank vaults.
   d. is a type of money that has no intrinsic value.

4. The money supply necessarily increases when:
   a. there is an increase in government purchases.
   b. the Bank of Canada buys Treasury bills from the public.

    c. a private citizen buys a bond issued by General Motors.

    d. IBM sells stock to the public and uses the proceeds to finance the construction of a new factory.

5. All of the following are included in *M*2 EXCEPT:

    a. currency
                 c. savings deposits.

    b. demand deposits
        d. guaranteed investment certificates.

6. According to the Fisher equation, the nominal interest rate is:

    a. equal to the real interest rate plus inflation.

    b. equal to the real interest rate minus inflation.

    c. always greater than the real interest rate.

    d. constant.

7. According to the Fisher effect, a higher inflation rate leads to:

    a. higher real money balances
        c. a higher real interest rate.

    b. a higher nominal interest rate
     d. all of the above.

8. If inflation falls from 6 percent to 4 percent and nothing else changes, then, according to the Fisher effect: $i = r - \pi$

    a. both the nominal and the real interest rates fall by 2 percent.

    b. neither the nominal interest rate nor the real interest rate changes.

    c. the nominal interest rate falls by 2 percent and the real interest rate remains constant.

    d. the nominal interest rate does not change, but the real interest rate falls by 2 percent.

9. Expected inflation hurts:

    a. money holders.

    b. people who receive their pensions in fixed nominal terms and who bargained for their pensions before the inflation was expected.

    c. restaurant owners.

    d. all of the above.

10. Suppose that potatoes are the only product in the economy, and 1,000 kilograms of potatoes are sold in a given year at $0.15 per kilogram. The quantity of money in the economy is $50. The transactions velocity of money is:

    a. 5
                      c. 1.5.

    b. 3
                      d. 0.33.

11. If the nominal money supply rises by 6 percent, the price level rises by 4 percent, and output rises by 3 percent, then, according to the quantity equation, income velocity rises by:

    a. 13 percent
             c. 3 percent.
             $M \cdot h = P \cdot Y$

    b. 7 percent
              d. 1 percent.

                                          $106 \cdot h = 104 \cdot 103$

12. Suppose that the money supply increases by 1 percent in one year and then remains constant at this higher level thereafter. According to the quantity theory of money, the inflation rate:

    a. is 1 percent in the first year and thereafter.
    b. increases by 1 percent in the first year and remains constant at the higher level thereafter.
    c. increases by 1 percent in the first year and returns to its former value thereafter.
    d. is unaffected.

13. Suppose that the nominal interest rate equals 9 percent, the expected inflation rate is 5 percent, and actual inflation turns out to be 3 percent. In this case, the:

    a. *ex ante* real interest rate is 4 percent.
    b. *ex post* real interest rate is 4 percent.
    c. *ex ante* real interest rate is 6 percent.
    d. *ex post* real interest rate is 2 percent.

14. During a period of inflation, the cost of holding money equals:

    a. the nominal interest rate.
    b. the *ex ante* real interest rate plus the expected rate of inflation.
    c. both a and b.
    d. the *ex post* real interest rate.

15. The quantity of real money balances demanded depends on:

    a. the *ex ante* real interest rate
    b. the nominal interest rate
    c. real income.
    d. both b and c.

16. During periods of unexpected inflation, lenders are hurt while borrowers gain because the:

    a. *ex post* real interest rate exceeds the *ex ante* real interest rate.
    b. *ex post* real interest rate is lower than the *ex ante* real interest rate.
    c. real interest rate falls.
    d. nominal interest rate falls.

17. At the end of a period of hyperinflation, real money balances rise because the:

    a. central bank stops hyperinflation by printing more money.
    b. reduction in expected inflation decreases the nominal interest rate, and this raises the quantity of real balances demanded. This allows the real money supply to rise even as prices stabilize.
    c. reduction in inflation decreases the expected real interest rate, which increases the quantity of money demanded.
    d. real interest rate rises, so people put more of their assets into money.

18. If the money demand equation is $(M/P)^d = 0.4Y$, then:

    a. the income velocity of money is constant.
    b. money demand is unrelated to the interest rate.
    c. the income velocity of money equals 2.5.
    d. all of the above are true.

19. According to the classical dichotomy:

    a. the money supply does not affect any real variables.

    b. the price level and all other nominal variables are determined by the equilibrium in the money market.

    c. money is neutral.

    d. all of the above are true.

20. Almost all economists agree that the classical model is most relevant in discussions concerning:

    a. economic recessions
        c. the long run.

    b. the short run
          d. economic recoveries.

21. All of the following statements about credit cards are true EXCEPT:

    a. Credit card balances are included in $M2$ but not in $M1$.

    b. Credit card balances are not part of the money supply.

    c. Credit cards may affect the demand for money.

    d. Credit cards are a means of *deferring* payment, unlike debit cards.

Exercises

1. **The Quantity Equation and the Percentage Change Rule** *In this exercise, we examine the quantity equation and review the percentage change rule.*

    a. Income velocity V is the number of times per year an average dollar in the money supply changes hands in transactions involving final goods and services. It is equal to

$$V = PY/M \tag{4-1}$$

    Multiplying both sides of this equation by money M yields the quantity equation:

$$MV = PY \tag{4-2}$$

    In 2008, for example,

        real GDP = Y = \$1321 billion
        the GDP deflator = P = 1.211 (121.1/100)
        $M2$ = \$891.1 billion

    Consequently, the income velocity for $M2$ in 2008 was equal to $V = PY/M =$

    _____.

    b. Recall from Chapter 2 that the percentage change in the product of two variables is approximately equal to the sum of the percentage change in each of the variables. Applying this approximation to both sides of Equation 7-2 yields

$$\% \text{ Change in } M + \% \text{ Change in } V = \% \text{ Change in } P + \% \text{ Change in } Y \tag{4-3}$$

To confirm this approximation, consider the data in Table 4-1.

Table 4-1

(1)	(2)	(3) % Change in M	(4)	(5) % Change in V	(6)	(7) % Change in P	(8)	(9) % Change in Y
Period	M		V		P		Y	
1	100		2.0		1.0		200	
		_____		_____		_____		_____
2	104		2.02		1.03		204	

Fill in the blanks in Table 4-1. Verify that the percentage change version of the quantity equation is accurate to within two decimal places.

2. **The Quantity Theory and Long-Run Growth in GDP** *In this exercise, we examine the quantity theory when real GDP is rising at its trend rate of growth.*

   a. The simple quantity theory of money assumes that velocity is relatively constant and that real GDP increases at its long-run rate of growth—assumed to be 3 percent per year in this example. This 3 percent figure is the result of changes in population, resources, and technology, which are all typically viewed as exogenous. Substituting these values into the percentage change version of the quantity equation yields

   % Change in M + _____ = % Change in P + _____.

   Or, upon rearranging,

   % Change in P = % Change in M − _____%   (4-4)

   This equation indicates that, according to the quantity theory, the rate of inflation will be equal to the growth rate of the money supply minus the long-run rate of growth of output.

   b. Given the assumptions in Part a concerning velocity and real GDP growth, complete Columns 4, 5, 8, and 9 in Table 4-2 for four *successive* periods (the values for V and Y in Period 2 are already entered).

Table 4-2

(1)	(2)	(3) % Change in M	(4)	(5) % Change in V	(6)	(7) % Change in P	(8)	(9) % Change in Y
Period	M		V		P		Y	
1	100		2.0		1.0		200	
		3		0		_____		3
2	103		2.0		_____		206	
		_____		_____		_____		_____
3	97		_____		_____		_____	
		_____		_____		_____		_____
4	107		_____		_____		_____	

c. Use the data in Column 2 of Table 4-2 to complete Column 3. Now use Equation 4-4 to complete Column 7. Finally, use your approximations of the percentage changes in P in Column 7 to estimate the price levels in Column 6.

d. Using the exact quantity equation $MV = PY$ and the levels of M, V, and Y in Columns 2, 4, and 8, calculate the exact price level in each period and compare these answers with your estimates in Column 6. Note how the percentage change version of the quantity equation is a good approximation of the percentage changes in Table 4-2.

3. **Nominal Interest Rates, Real Interest Rates, and the Fisher Effect** *In this exercise, we analyze the distinction between nominal and real interest rates and discuss the Fisher effect.*

a. The real interest rate r is equal to the nominal interest rate i minus the inflation rate π, or

$$r = i - \pi \tag{4-5}$$

Use this equation to complete Table 4-3.

Table 4-3

(1) Real Interest Rate (%)	(2) Nominal Interest Rate (%)	(3) Inflation Rate (%)
_____	10	4
_____	10	8
_____	10	12
4	7	_____
−2	12	_____
3	_____	5
−2	_____	9

The Fisher equation is obtained by rearranging the preceding equation to obtain an equation expressing i, that is, by putting i on the left-hand side. Thus, the Fisher equation is

$$i = \text{_____}. \tag{4-6}$$

b. Recall from Exercise 2 that if the long-run annual growth of real output is 3 percent and velocity is constant, then the quantity equation implies that

$$\% \text{ Change in } P = \% \text{ Change in } M - \text{_____}\% \tag{4-7}$$

Since the percentage change in P is equal to the rate of inflation, this fact suggests that an increase in the rate of money growth of 1 percent causes a 1 percent increase in inflation. According to the Fisher equation, this 1 percent increase in inflation causes a 1 percent increase in the nominal interest rate i because the real interest rate r is presumed to be affected only by real variables. Use all of this information to complete Table 4-4.

Table 4-4

(1) % Change in P	(2) % Change in M	(3) Inflation Rate (%)	(4) Real Interest Rate (%)	(5) Nominal Interest Rate (%)
0	3	0	3	3
_____	4	_____	3	_____
_____	5	_____	3	_____
_____	2	_____	3	_____
_____	8	_____	3	_____

This one-for-one relation between the inflation rate and the nominal interest rate is called the *Fisher effect*. Almost all economists agree that the Fisher effect holds in the long run.

4. ***Ex Ante* versus *Ex Post* Real Interest Rates and Unexpected Inflation** *In this exercise, we introduce the distinction between the* ex ante *and* ex post *real interest rates and illustrate how unexpected inflation hurts lenders and benefits borrowers.*

a. Because the actual inflation rate during a year may be different from the inflation rate that was expected at the beginning of the year, the actual real interest rate during that year may turn out to be different from the real interest rate that was expected at the beginning of the year. To account for this difference, a distinction is made between the *ex ante* real interest rate and the *ex post* real interest rate. The *ex ante* real interest rate is the real interest rate that people expected to prevail at the beginning of the year. It is equal to $i - E\pi$, where $E\pi$ is equal to the expected rate of inflation. After the year ends, however, the rate of inflation is known, and people can calculate the *ex post* real interest rate—that is, the actual real interest rate during the year. The *ex post* real interest rate is equal to $i - \pi$, where π is equal to the actual rate of inflation. From this information, one can see that the *ex ante* real interest rate will equal the *ex post* real interest rate only if _____ = _____.

b. Use the information in Part a to complete Table 4-5.

Table 4-5

(1) Nominal Interest Rate (%)	(2) Expected Inflation (%)	(3) *Ex Ante* Real Interest Rate (%)	(4) Actual Inflation (%)	(5) *Ex Post* Real Interest Rate (%)
8	3	_____	3	_____
8	3	_____	5	_____
8	3	_____	1	_____
2	−1	_____	1	_____

c. Loan contracts are almost always written in terms of the nominal interest rate. The real cost of borrowing and lending, however, is the real interest rate. Unexpected inflation may change the real cost of the loan from what was expected by causing the *ex ante* real interest rate to differ from the *ex post* real interest rate. In Table 4-5, it is easy to see the following:

  i. When actual inflation is equal to expected inflation, the *ex post* real interest rate is equal to/higher than/lower than the *ex ante* real interest rate.

  ii. When actual inflation exceeds expected inflation (when there is unexpected inflation), the *ex post* real interest rate is equal to/higher than/lower than the *ex ante* real interest rate. Consequently, the real borrowing cost is equal to/higher than/lower than what was originally expected when the loan was made. Thus, unexpected inflation tends to help borrowers/lenders and hurt borrowers/lenders.

  iii. When actual inflation is less than expected inflation, the *ex post* real interest rate is equal to/higher than/lower than the *ex ante* real interest rate.

Consequently, the real borrowing cost is equal to/higher than/lower than what was originally expected when the loan was made. This tends to help borrowers/lenders and hurt borrowers/lenders.

5. **The Real Cost of Borrowing and the Real Interest Rate** *In this exercise, we see why the real cost of borrowing is equal to the real interest rate.*

    a. Since a borrower's actual dollar payments are based on the nominal interest rate, it is sometimes difficult to see why the real cost of borrowing is equal to the real interest rate. Consider a family that buys a new house for $300,000 and takes a mortgage loan equal to the full amount at 7 percent annual interest. The annual interest cost of the mortgage will equal $_____. Since the home is a real commodity, its nominal value will increase at the rate of inflation. If the expected rate of inflation is 4 percent, the home is expected to increase in value by about $_____ each year.
    Consequently, the expected real cost of the mortgage is equal to the difference between the annual mortgage payments and the expected appreciation of the home. This amount equals $_____ each year. Expressed as a percentage of the initial loan, this amount equals _____ percent. Thus, the expected real cost of the loan is equal to the *ex ante* real interest rate $i - E\pi =$ _____ percent.

    b. Suppose that there is unexpected inflation and the actual rate of inflation during the year is 6 percent. Since the mortgage loan was written in terms of the nominal interest rate prevailing at the time that the loan was made, the annual mortgage interest payment remains equal to $_____. The nominal value of the home, however, now increases by the actual rate of inflation, that is, by _____ percent, or by about $_____. Consequently, the real cost of the mortgage is equal to $_____ each year, or _____ percent of the initial loan. Thus, the actual real cost of the loan is equal to the *ex post* real interest rate, $i - \pi$, which equals _____ percent.

6. **The Money Demand Function** *In this exercise, we use the money demand function to derive the money demand curve.*

    a. The general money demand function can be written as

    $$(M/P)^d = L(i, Y) \qquad \text{(4-8)}$$

    One specific money demand function that fits Canadian data fairly well is

    $$(M/P)^d = i^{-0.1} \times Y \qquad \text{(4-9)}$$

    Note that this equation may be written as

    $$(M/P)^d = (1/i)^{1/10} \times Y \qquad \text{(4-10)}$$

Use a calculator to complete Table 4-6.

Table 4-6

(1) Nominal Interest Rate i	(2) $i^{-0.1}$	(3) Real Output Y	(4) Real Money Demand $(M/P)^d$
0.12 (= 12%)	_____	100	_____
0.08	_____	100	_____
0.05	_____	100	_____
0.03	_____	100	_____
0.01	_____	100	_____

The numbers in Column 4 of Table 4-6 indicate that the quantity of real money demanded <u>increases/decreases</u> when the nominal interest rate decreases, holding real output constant.

b. Plot the preceding points on Graph 4-1 and draw a curve connecting these points. Label your money demand curve L_1 ($Y = 100$).

Graph 4-1

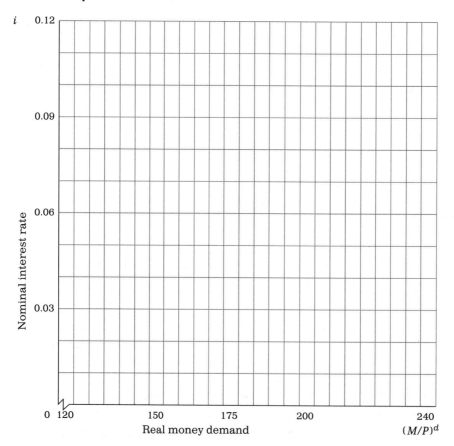

c. Now suppose the real output Y increases to 150. Use a calculator to complete Table 4-7.

Table 4-7

(1) Nominal Interest Rate i	(2) $i^{-0.1}$	(3) Real Output Y	(4) Real Money Demand $(M/P)^d$
0.12 (= 12%)	_____	150	_____
0.08	_____	150	_____
0.05	_____	150	_____
0.03	_____	150	_____
0.01	_____	150	_____

d. Plot the points from Columns 1 and 4 of Table 4-7 on Graph 4-1 and draw a curve connecting these points. Label your curve L_2 ($Y = 150$). Note that when real output Y increases, the money demand curve shifts to the right/left.

e. Conversely, if real output Y decreases, the money demand curve shifts to the right/left.

7. **Current Price Levels and Expected Future Money Growth** *In this exercise, we use the money demand function from Exercise 6 to illustrate how the current price level depends on the expected future money growth.*

a. Assume that the money demand function is the same as in Exercise 6—that is, $(M/P)^d = i^{-0.1} \times Y$. Also assume that real output and the nominal interest rate are initially equal to 100 and 3 percent, respectively. The quantity of real money demanded will then equal _____.

b. Assume further that expected inflation is initially 0 percent and the price level P is initially equal to 1.0. Consequently, the money market will be in equilibrium (money supply equals money demand) when the central bank sets the nominal money supply equal to _____.

c. Now assume that people believe that the central bank will soon increase the nominal money supply by 5 percent per year. This will increase inflationary expectations to 5 percent per year. According to the Fisher equation, the nominal interest rate will rise immediately to _____ percent. If real output remains constant, the quantity of real money demanded will fall to

_____.

d. Since the nominal money supply has not yet changed, the money market will remain in equilibrium only if the price level immediately changes to _____. Consequently, higher expected money growth in the future leads to an increase/no change/a decrease in the price level today.

8. **Inflation and the Real Return to Saving and Investment** *In this exercise, we illustrate how the taxation of nominal interest payments reduces the real return to saving and investment when there is inflation.*

CH

a. In Canada, people pay personal income taxes on nominal interest income and nominal capital gains. Because these provisions in the tax system are not indexed, inflation can affect the real return on saving and investment.

   i. If the real interest rate is equal to 2 percent and inflation is equal to 4 percent, according to the Fisher equation the nominal interest rate will equal _____ percent.

   ii. If inflation rises to 7 percent, the nominal interest rate will be _____ percent and the real interest rate will equal _____ percent.

b. The preceding formulation does not take into account taxation. In Canada, many families pay a marginal income tax rate of about one-third, or about 33.33 percent on nominal interest income. Thus, in Part a(i) of this exercise, these families pay one-third of the _____ percent nominal interest rate in taxes, leaving an after-tax nominal interest rate of _____ percent. The after-tax *real* interest rate will equal the after-tax nominal interest rate minus the rate of inflation. Thus, the after-tax real interest rate can be computed as _____ percent – _____ percent = _____ percent.

c. In Part a(ii), the (before-tax) nominal interest rate increases/stays constant/decreases, while the before-tax real interest rate increases/stays constant/decreases. Families, however, pay one-third of the _____ percent nominal interest rate in taxes, leaving an after-tax nominal interest rate of _____ percent. The after-tax real interest rate will equal the after-tax nominal interest rate minus the rate of inflation, or _____ percent – _____ percent = _____ percent.

d. Consequently, because the Canadian personal income tax system is *not* indexed in this respect (that is, it taxes nominal interest income rather than real interest income), inflation tends to increase/decrease the real return to savings even if the Fisher effect holds.

e. Similarly, consider an individual named Alice who purchased 100 shares of a company stock in 1998 for $1,500, or $15 per share. In 2008, Alice sold her stock for $1,800, or $18 per share. Her nominal capital gain is equal to the nominal value of the sale minus the nominal value of the purchase, or $_____ – $_____ = $_____. This gain represents _____ percent of the original purchase. With a tax rate of one-third of the nominal gain, Alice would pay $_____ in taxes, resulting in an after-tax nominal gain of $_____, or _____ percent of the original purchase.

f. Between 1998 and 2008, however, the GDP deflator rose from 92.3 (or 0.923) to 121.1 (or 1.211). Consequently, the real value of Alice's stock was $_____ in 1998 and $_____ in 2008. These amounts represented a *real* before-tax gain/loss of $_____, or _____ percent of the original real value of the purchase. Since taxes are paid on nominal gains, however, Alice's taxes on the sale of the stock remain equal to $_____. Thus, the real after-tax value of the stock sale was equal to the total receipts from the stock sale minus total taxes paid, divided by the GDP deflator, or $_____. Compared with the real value of the purchase in 1998, this amount represents a real after-tax gain/loss of $_____, or _____ percent of the original real value of the purchase. As a result of these distortions, many economists have recommended that the capital gains tax be indexed so that only real gains are taxed. (These calculations exclude the value of dividends that were paid between 1998 and 2008.)

Problems

Answer the following problems on a separate sheet of paper.

1. Which of the three functions of money is satisfied by each of the following?

    a. a $50 travelers' cheque.

    b. a $10 gift certificate at Chapters bookstores.

    c. a vacation home in the Caribbean.

2. In the absence of money, we would have a barter economy. In this type of economy, the price of each good X would be a ratio indicating the number of units of every other good in the economy for which one could trade one unit of good X. If there were two goods, X and Y, in the economy, we would have two price ratios. For example, if one can trade one unit of good X for three units of good Y, the price of good X is 3Y, and the price of good Y is (1/3)X.

    a. How many price ratios would there be in an economy with only three goods?

    b. How many price ratios would there be in an economy with only four goods?

    c. **CH** When the future mathematician Gauss was 10 years old, he derived the formula to determine the number of price ratios in an economy with any given number of goods. Letting *n* represent the number of goods, try to write that formula.

3. As a result of accelerated technological changes brought about by the Internet and wireless technology, some economists believe that the long-run rate of growth of real GDP in Canada may have risen to 4 percent per year. In addition, due to innovations in the finance industry, suppose the velocity of money is rising at about 2 percent per year. Use the quantity equation to illustrate what these developments imply about the exact noninflationary (i.e., zero inflation) long-run rate of growth of the money supply.

4. Inflation in Argentina between 1988 and 1989 was 3,078%. If a typical item in the Argentine GDP cost 100 australs (the Argentine currency) in 1988, how much did the typical item cost in 1989?

5. Suppose that money demand is represented by the equation $(M/P)^d = 0.25Y$. Use the quantity equation to calculate the income velocity of money.

6. a. What is the inflation tax?

   b. In what ways is the inflation tax a tax, and in what ways is it not a tax?

   c. Who pays for the inflation tax?

7. a. Take the (natural) logarithm of the quantity equation $MV = PY$.

   C b. Now totally differentiate this logarithmic version and derive the percentage change rule—% Change in M + % Change in V = % Change in P + % Change in Y—for small percentage changes.

   c. Use the percentage change rule to show that the quantity theory holds (approximately) if V is constant.

8. Suppose that money demand is represented by the equation $(M/P)^d = i^{-0.1}Y$.

   C a. Use calculus to compute the income elasticity of money demand, which is the elasticity of the quantity of money demanded with respect to output Y.

   b. Use calculus to compute the interest elasticity of money demand, which is the elasticity of the quantity of money demanded with respect to the interest rate i.

9. Recall that the exact formula for calculating the real interest rate is:

   $$1 + r = (1 + i)/(1 + \pi)$$

   Multiplying both sides by $(1 + \pi)$ and rearranging yields:

   $r = i - \pi - r\pi$, which is approximately $r = i - \pi$ when π is small.

   To understand this, suppose you start with $1 and earn an interest rate of 200 percent per year.

   a. How much money would you have at the end of the year?

   b. If inflation were 100 percent per year, and the initial price level were 1.0, what would the price level be at the end of the year?

   c. Calculate the real value of your wealth at the beginning and at the end of the year.

   d. Use these real values to calculate the real interest rate and use the equation at the beginning of this problem to verify your result.

10. Consider a monetary policy of zero inflation.

    ○ a. Ignoring (for now) the treatment of inflation within the Canadian tax code, what are the costs of expected inflation?

    b. Discuss how the way in which inflation is treated within the current tax laws on capital gains and interest income might lead to higher saving and investment if both actual and expected inflation were 0 percent rather than 5 percent. Briefly explain.

    c. If the long-run annual rate of growth of output is 3 percent, use the quantity equation (and any appropriate assumptions) to calculate the approximate eventual long-run growth rate of the money supply if zero inflation were achieved.

    d. If the Bank of Canada changed the growth rate of the money supply to this long-**CH** run growth rate immediately and people believed that it would persist, what would the immediate impact be on:

i. expected inflation?

ii. the nominal interest rate?

iii. real money demand?

iv. the price level? (Assume the nominal quantity of money *M* does not change.)

Data Questions

Locate the necessary economic data and apply them to answer the following data questions. For advice on how to access the data, see the Preface and the Economics Data on the Internet section on page xi.

1. **a.** Complete Table 4-8 with data about the various consumer price indices (CPI). The relevant Statistics Canada series are v41693271, v41693451, and v41693426. The CPI weights for Health and Personal Care and Transportation are .046 and .1896, respectively.

Table 4-8

(1) Year	(2) CPI All Items	(3) % Change	(4) Health and Personal Care	(5) % Change	(6) Transpor- tation	(7) % Change
1960	_____		_____		_____	
		_____		_____		_____
1970	_____		_____		_____	
		_____		_____		_____
1980	_____		_____		_____	
		_____		_____		_____
1990	_____		_____		_____	
		_____		_____		_____
2000	_____		_____		_____	

b. If a unit of medical care (for example, a visit to the physician) cost $50 in 2000, how much did it cost in 1960?

c. During which of the four intervals in Table 4–8 (1960–1970, 1970–1980, 1980–1990, 1990–2000) was the average *annual* rate of inflation for all items the highest? (Use simple averages if you don't know how to compute compound growth rates.)

d. During which of the four intervals in Table 4-8 was the average annual rate of inflation for all items the lowest?

2. Take annual data for the Consumer Price Index (Statistics Canada series v41693271) and *M*2 (Statistics Canada series v41552796) and calculate the average annual percentage increase over each of the following decades.

Table 4-9

Decade	Average Annual Percentage Increase in Money	Average Annual Percentage Increase in Prices
1960s	_____	_____
1970s	_____	_____
1980s	_____	_____
1990s	_____	_____

Are the entries in Table 4-9 consistent with the Quantity Theory of Money?

Questions to Think About

1. Many economists believe that a reduction in inflation might reduce GDP, at least temporarily. Each percentage point of real GDP in Canada now represents about $15 billion per year.

    a. How much would you be willing to pay in terms of percentage points of GDP in order to reduce the long-run rate of inflation from about 2 percent to 0 percent? Explain your answer.

    b. For how many years would you be willing to pay this price? Explain your answer.

2. According to Professor Shiller's survey, the public fears moderate rates of inflation much more than most economists do. Why do you think this is the case?

3. Ask a parent or friend what happened to her nominal wage (or earnings) in each of the last three years. Then ask what she thinks happened to her real wage (or earnings) during the same three years. Find data on the consumer price index to see if she is right about the latter.

chapter **5**

The Open Economy

Fill-in Questions

Use the key terms below to fill in the blanks in the following statements. Each term may be used more than once.

balanced trade

net capital outflow

net exports

nominal exchange rate

purchasing-power parity

real exchange rate

small open economy

trade balance

trade deficit

trade surplus

world interest rate

1. The total expenditure on domestic output is the sum of consumption, investment, government purchases, and ___*net exports*___.

2. ___*trade balance*___ indicates the amount domestic residents are lending abroad minus the amount foreigners are lending to us. It is equal to domestic saving minus domestic investment.

3. National accounting tells us that *S – I*, or ___*net capital outflow*___ must equal _____, where the latter is called the _____.

4. A ___*small open economy*___ is a small part of the world market and thus, by itself, can have only a negligible effect on the world interest rate.

5. If there is free access to world financial markets, investment in all small open economies will depend on the ___*world interest rate*___.

6. The ___*nominal exchange rate*___ is the relative price of the currency of two countries, such as 5 French francs per Canadian dollar.

7. The ___*purchasing power parity*___ is the rate at which one can trade the goods of one country for the goods of another. More specifically, it measures the number of foreign goods one can exchange for one comparable domestic good. It incorporates the relative price levels of the two countries as well as the _____.

8. According to the tenet of _____, a dollar (or any other currency) must have the same purchasing power in every country.

9. If a country's exports exceed its imports, it will have a(n) _____. If its imports exceed its exports, it will have a(n) _____. Finally, if its exports and imports are equal, it will have _____.

Multiple-Choice Questions

1. According to the national accounts identity, total expenditure on domestic output is the sum of:

   a. consumption of domestic goods and services, investment of domestic goods and services, government purchases of domestic goods and services, and exports of domestic goods and services.

   b. consumption, investment, government purchases, and net exports.

   c. both a and b.

   d. domestic spending on foreign goods and expenditures on imports.

2.. If national output $Y = 1,000$ and domestic spending on all domestic and foreign goods and services equals 900, net exports NX will equal:

   a. 100. c. 1,900.

   b. −100. d. 0.

3. The FALSE statement below is:

   a. net capital outflow is the excess of domestic saving over domestic investment.

   b. the trade surplus and net capital outflow must both equal zero.

   c. according to the national income accounts identity, net capital outflow must equal net exports.

   d. according to the national income accounts identity, capital outflow must equal the trade surplus (or the trade balance).

4. If domestic investment exceeds domestic savings, one would observe:

   a. borrowing from abroad. c. a trade deficit.

   b. a government budget deficit. d. both a and c.

5. With a constant world interest rate, full employment, and an initial trade surplus of zero, a tax cut in an open economy will result in:

   a. a trade deficit. c. negative net capital outflow.

   b. a reduction in national saving. d. all of the above.

6. Suppose that several large foreign countries decrease government spending, leading to a decrease in the world interest rate. In a small open economy, which of the following is most likely to happen?

   a. a decrease in saving

   b. a decrease in investment

   c. an increase in the trade deficit (or a reduction in the trade surplus)

   d. an increase in net capital outflow

7. If a computer costs $2,000 in Canada, how much will it cost in Germany if the nominal exchange rate is 0.8 euros per Canadian dollar?

   a. 2008 euros c. 1600 euros

   b. 2500 euros d. 1800 euros

8. Suppose that a comparable computer (or any other commodity) costs $5,000 in Canada and 3000 euros in Germany. If the nominal exchange rate is 0.8 euros per Canadian dollar, then the real exchange rate of the Canadian dollar (that is, the number of German computers that can be traded for one Canadian computer) is equal to:

   a. 0.6.   **c.** 1.25.

   b. 0.8.   **d.** 1.33.

9. As Canada's real exchange rate increases:

   a. foreign goods become cheaper to Canadian citizens.

   b. Canadian net exports fall.

   c. the Canadian trade surplus decreases.

   d. all of the above occur.

10. The correct relationship among net exports NX, the excess of saving over investment $S - I$, and the real exchange rate ε occurs in graph:

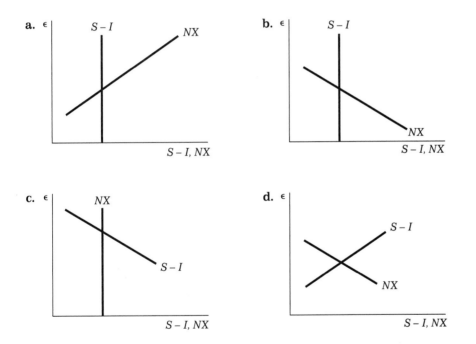

11. If the government of a small open economy increases personal income taxes, that country's:

    a. net exports increase.

    b. investment increases.

    c. equilibrium real exchange rate rises.

    d. consumption rises.

12. In a small open economy, a government policy of deficit reduction (I) leads to an increase in domestic investment spending if international bond-rating agencies respond by up-grading the country's debt, but (II) this policy leads to no change in domestic investment if there is no adjustment in the perceived risk differential.
    a. I is true; II is not.
    b. II is true; I is not.
    c. Both I and II are true.
    d. Neither I nor II is true.

13. If investment demand decreases in a small open economy:
    a. the equilibrium real exchange rate rises.
    b. net exports increase.
    c. national saving increases.
    d. net foreign investment decreases.

14. In the long run, if the German government places high tariffs on all imports:
    a. Germany's net exports rise.
    b. Germany's real foreign exchange rate increases.
    c. net foreign investment in Germany decreases.
    d. all of the above.

15. Slower growth in the Japanese money supply will lead to:
    a. an increase in inflation in Japan.
    b. a decrease in inflation in Canada.
    c. a depreciation of the dollar relative to the Japanese yen.
    d. all of the above.

16. According to purchasing-power parity, if a television set sells for $500 in Canada and 2,000 yuan in China, the nominal exchange rate, expressed in yuan per dollar, is:
    a. 2.5.
    b. 10.
    c. 4.
    d. 1.

17. If Canada has a bilateral trade deficit with China:
    a. China must have a bilateral surplus with each of its other trading partners.
    b. Canada must have a trade surplus with all the rest of its trading partners.
    c. Canada cannot have an overall trade surplus.
    d. none of the above statements is true.

18. All of the following may explain why capital is flowing to Canada from many poorer countries EXCEPT:
    a. property rights are enforced more fully in Canada.
    b. according to the Cobb-Douglas production function, additional capital will be more productive in countries with more capital per worker.
    c. Canada may have better access to advanced technology.
    d. corruption is less prevalent in Canada.

19. (I) when the long-run accumulation of debt service obligations is ignored, as in the
   A simplified analysis in the main text of Chapter 5, higher government spending raises the real exchange rate; but (II) when the accumulation of debt service obligations
   is not ignored, as in the Appendix to Chapter 5, higher government spending eventually reduces our real exchange rate.

   a. I is true; II is not.
   b. II is true; I is not.
   c. Both I and II are true.
   d. Neither I nor II is true.

20. Consider a small open economy whose demand for capital relationship is given by
   A $R = 30 - (1/2)K$, where K and R denote capital and its marginal product. Capital is
   perfectly mobile internationally, and this fact imposes $R = 10$ for this economy. The
   country's citizens own three quarters of the capital that is employed within the
   economy. (I) The country's *GDP* is 1200; (II) Labour's share of *GNP* is 57%.

   a. I is true; II is not.
   b. II is true; I is not.
   c. Both I and II are true.
   d. Neither I nor II is true.

Exercises

1. **National Accounting in an Open Economy** *In this exercise, we incorporate international trade into the national accounting identities in two alternative ways. The
   numbers involved are illustrative; they do not correspond to any particular year.*

   a. Total purchases by domestic households, businesses, and governments are
      equal to purchases of goods and services produced domestically plus purchases
      of goods and services produced in other countries. Using this knowledge, com-
      plete Table 5-1.

Table 5-1

(1) Group	(2) Purchases of Goods and Services Produced in Canada ($ in billions)	(3) Purchases of Goods and Services Produced Elsewhere ($ in billions)	(4) Total Purchases ($ in billions)
Canadian households	$C^d = \$310$	$C^f = \$40$	$C = \$$_____
Canadian businesses	$I^d = \$\ 60$	$I^f = \$$_____	$I = \$\ 80$
Canadian governments	$G^d = \$$_____	$G^f = \$10$	$G = \$100$
Total	$\$$_____	$\$$_____	$\$$_____

   b. Now examine the total of Column 2 of Table 5-1. $C^d + I^d + G^d$ is total domestic
      spending on domestic goods and services. It represents total purchases by

Canadian households, businesses, and governments of goods and services that are produced in Canada. In this example, total domestic spending on domestic goods is equal to $_____ billion.

c. The total of $C^f + I^f + G^f$ (Column 3 of Table 5-1) represents total purchases by Canadian households, businesses, and governments of goods and services that are produced in foreign countries. It is more commonly called total _____. In this example, this total is equal to $_____ billion.

d. The total of $C + I + G$ (Column 4 of Table 5-1) represents total purchases by Canadian households, businesses, and governments of all goods and services, both foreign and domestic. This is sometimes called total domestic spending. In this example, it is equal to $_____ billion.

e. Recall from Chapter 2 of the textbook that Y is equal to total national output (that is, the value of the goods and services produced in the economy). In the closed economy with no foreign trade, $Y = C + I + G$. In an open economy, however, national output is not merely equal to $C + I + G$ because they do not include foreign purchases of goods and services that are produced in Canada. These must be included in total Canadian output since they certainly represent Canadian production. On the other hand, $C + I + G$ includes purchases by Canadian households, businesses, and governments of foreign production, which should not be included in Canadian output and, therefore, must be subtracted. In Table 5-1, total imports into Canada equaled $_____ billion. If total exports equal $90 billion, Canadian output can be calculated as

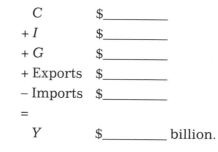

$$
\begin{array}{ll}
C & \$_____ \\
+\,I & \$_____ \\
+\,G & \$_____ \\
+ \text{Exports} & \$_____ \\
- \text{Imports} & \$_____ \\
= \\
Y & \$_____ \text{ billion.}
\end{array}
$$

f. In the national income accounts, exports minus imports is often called net exports NX. In this example, $NX = \$$_____ billion.

g. There is another way to calculate Y. Total Canadian production will equal total domestic spending on domestic goods and services plus Canadian exports:

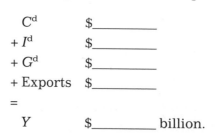

$$
\begin{array}{ll}
C^d & \$_____ \\
+\,I^d & \$_____ \\
+\,G^d & \$_____ \\
+ \text{Exports} & \$_____ \\
= \\
Y & \$_____ \text{ billion.}
\end{array}
$$

2. **Net Capital Outflow and the Trade Balance** *In this exercise, we introduce net foreign investment and the trade balance, and we emphasize how they must equal each other.*

a. According to the national accounts, net foreign investment, or $S - I$, must equal the trade balance NX. Thus, $S - I = NX$. Recall that S represents national saving, which is the sum of private saving $Y - T - C$ and public saving $T - G$. Japan's huge exports have led to a large Japanese trade surplus/deficit. Hence, in Japan, NX is positive/negative. Consequently, in Japan, $S - I$ is positive/negative. Therefore, the Japanese will borrow/lend the difference abroad, and we say that in Japan net capital outflow will be positive/negative. Note that net foreign investment is merely domestic purchases of foreign assets minus foreign purchases of domestic assets. Thus, Japanese purchases of foreign assets are greater/less than foreign purchases of Japanese assets.

b. For the past several years, the United States has had a trade deficit, implying that NX has been positive/negative. Consequently, in the United States, net capital outflow has been positive/negative. Thus, the United States is borrowing/lending abroad.

c. Now complete Table 5-2:

Table 5-2

					($ in billions)				
(1)	(2)	(3)	(4)	(5)	(6)	(7)	(8) Private Saving	(9) Public Saving	(10) National Saving
Case	Y	C	I	G	NX	T			
1	5,000	3,000	700	1,000	_____	900	_____	_____	_____
2	5,000	3,200	900	1,000	_____	900	_____	_____	_____
3	5,000	3,200	900	900	_____	1,000	_____	_____	_____

d. For each of the three preceding cases, calculate the trade balance and net foreign investment:

Case 1: Trade surplus = $_____ billion.

Net Capital outflow = $S - I$ = $ _____ billion.

Case 2: Trade surplus = $_____ billion.

Net Capital outflow = $S - I$ = $ _____ billion.

Case 3: Trade surplus = $_____ billion.

Net Capital outflow = $S - I$ = $ _____ billion.

e. Note in Case 2 above that a trade surplus of $_____ billion can also be expressed as a trade deficit of $_____ billion.

3. **National Saving and Investment in a Small Open Economy** *In this exercise, we discuss the effects of changes in national saving and investment in a small open economy if output is fixed at full employment.*

   a. Suppose that the economy is described by the following set of equations. These equations are identical to those in Exercise 6 of Chapter 3, except for the inclusion of international trade:

$$Y = \bar{Y} = F(\bar{K}, \bar{L}) = 1{,}200 \tag{5-1}$$
$$Y = C + I + G + NX \tag{5-2}$$
$$C = 125 + 0.75(Y - T) \tag{5-3}$$
$$I = I(r) = 200 - 10r \tag{5-4}$$
$$G = \bar{G} = 150 \tag{5-5}$$
$$T = \bar{T} = 100. \tag{5-6}$$

   If the real interest rate were equal to 10 percent, then $r = 10$ and:

   $C = $ _____

   $I = $ _____

   $G = $ _____

   and, thus,

   $NX = $ _____ .

   Consequently, the trade surplus would equal _____ .

   b. Conversely,

   disposable income = _____

   private saving = _____

   public saving = _____

   national saving $S = $ _____

   $S - I = $ _____

   and, thus, net capital outflow would equal _____ .

c. Draw the investment and saving curves on Graph 5-1, label them I_1 and S_1, and label the initial equilibrium Point A.

Graph 5-1

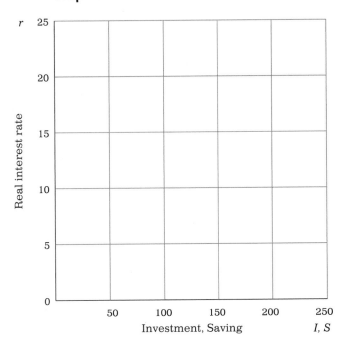

d. Now suppose that government purchases rose by 100 to 250. If Y remained equal to 1,200, this would shift the national saving curve to the <u>left/right</u> by _____. The investment curve would <u>shift left/not shift/shift right</u>. Draw the new curve(s) on Graph 5-1 and label them I_2 and S_2.

e. If this economy were a closed economy, investment would always have to equal saving. Thus, when saving fell to _____ in Part d, investment would also fall to _____. This would be accomplished by an increase in r to _____ percent. Label the new equilibrium for this closed economy Point B.

f. Now, however, suppose this is a small open economy and the world real interest rate r^* remains equal to 10 percent both before and after the increase of 100 in government purchases. Thus, investment remains equal to _____. Following the increase in domestic government purchases, net capital outflow $S - I$ changes to _____. Consequently, the trade surplus NX will change to _____. The change in net capital outflow indicates that domestic purchases of foreign assets minus foreign purchases of domestic assets will <u>rise/fall</u> by _____.

g. In the closed economy described in Chapter 3 of the textbook, a reduction in national saving leads to a(n) <u>increase/decrease</u> in the real interest rate and a(n) <u>increase/decrease</u> in investment. In a small open economy, however, a reduction in national saving raises/does not change/lowers the real interest rate. Consequently, investment increases/does not change/decreases. Instead, policies that decrease saving push net capital outflow up/down and the trade account toward surplus/deficit.

h. Now suppose that we start again at $G = 150$, $I = I_1$, $S = S_1$, and the world real interest rate $r^* = 10$ percent. If domestic investment in this small open economy rose by 50 at every level of the real interest rate, the investment curve would shift to the right/left by 50, while the national saving curve would shift to the right/not shift/shift to the left. Draw the new curve(s) on Graph 5-2 and label them I_3 and S_3.

Graph 5-2

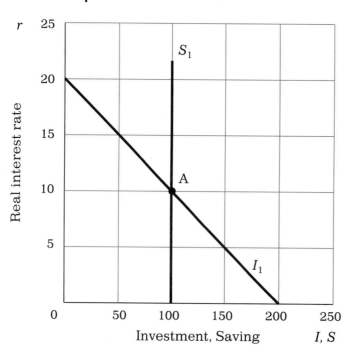

As a result of the autonomous increase in domestic investment, net capital outflow would now equal _____, while the trade surplus would now equal _____.

i. Finally, suppose we start again at Point A and the world real interest rate rises to 15 percent. This may have occurred as a result of a decline in world saving, which, in turn, may have resulted from changes in the fiscal policies of one or more large foreign countries. These changes in foreign fiscal policy that raise the world interest rate could include a(n) increase/decrease in foreign government purchases or a(n) increase/decrease in foreign government taxes. According to Equations 5-1 to 5-6, investment I would now equal _____. (Note that this represents a movement along I_1 rather than a shift in the curve.) National saving S would increase/not change/decrease. Consequently, net capital outflow $S - I$ would now equal

_____, while the trade surplus *NX* would equal
_____. Illustrate the extent of the new level of net capital
outflow on Graph 5-2 and label it $CF(r^* = 15)$.

4. **The Nominal Exchange Rate** *In this exercise, we introduce the nominal exchange rate. We show why net exports fall as the nominal exchange rate increases when we hold the price levels in the two countries constant.*

    Consider the trade of two mainframe computers between the United States and Germany. The IBM computer made in the United States sells for $10,000. A comparable computer made by Siemens in Germany sells for 15,000 euros. Although it is important to understand that net exports depend on the *real* exchange rate, in this exercise we assume that the price levels in both the United States and Germany remain constant. In this case, changes in the real exchange rate are reflected by changes in the nominal exchange rate.

    a. Complete Table 5-3.

    Table 5-3

(1) U.S. Nominal Foreign Exchange Rate (euros per dollar)	(2) Price of IBM Computer in the U.S.	(3) Price of IBM Computer in Germany	(4) Price of Siemens Computer in Germany	(5) Price of Siemens Computer in the U.S.
1.0	$10,000	_____	15,000 euros	_____
1.5	$10,000	_____	15,000 euros	_____
2.0	$10,000	_____	15,000 euros	_____

    b. Examining the numbers in Table 5-3, note that, as the U.S. nominal foreign exchange rate increases, the price of the IBM computer in Germany increases/decreases, while the price of the Siemens computer in Germany remains constant. Consequently, as the U.S. foreign exchange rate increases, U.S. exports of IBM computers will increase/decrease, assuming the price levels in both countries remain constant.

    c. Similarly, as the U.S. nominal foreign exchange rate increases, the price of the IBM computer in the United States increases/remains constant/decreases, while the price of the Siemens computer in the United States increases/remains constant/decreases. Consequently, as the U.S. foreign exchange rate increases, U.S. imports of Siemens computers will increase/decrease.

    d. Recall that net exports are calculated as exports/imports minus exports/imports. From Parts a–c we see that as the U.S. nominal foreign exchange rate increases, U.S. net exports increase/decrease, assuming the price levels in both countries remain constant.

e. As the U.S. nominal exchange rate of the dollar increases, it is said that the dollar has appreciated relative to the euro. Consequently, as the U.S. dollar appreciates, U.S. net exports increase/decrease.

5. **The Real Exchange Rate** *In this exercise, we allow the price levels in different countries to grow at different rates. We then show how these changes, along with changes in the nominal foreign exchange rate, are incorporated into the real exchange rate, and we illustrate its effects on net exports.*

a. Suppose that the United States now experiences 20 percent inflation while Germany's price level remains constant. As a result, the price of IBM computers in the United States rises to $12,000 while the price of Siemens computers remains equal to 15,000 euros. Complete Table 5-4.

Table 5-4

(1) U.S. Nominal Foreign Exchange Rate (euros per dollar)	(2) Price of IBM Computer in the U.S.	(3) Price of IBM Computer in Germany	(4) Price of Siemens Computer in Germany	(5) Price of Siemens Computer in the U.S.
1.5	$10,000	_____	15,000 euros	_____
1.5	$12,000	_____	15,000 euros	_____

b. Before U.S. inflation, at an initial U.S. nominal foreign exchange rate of 1.5 euros per dollar, the price of the IBM computer was greater than/equal to/less than the price of the Siemens computer in both Germany and the United States. After the U.S. price level rises by 20 percent, however, the price of the IBM computer becomes greater than/equal to/less than the price of the Siemens computer in both countries. Consequently, U.S. net exports would increase/not change/decrease.

c. Now suppose that at the same time the nominal exchange rate falls to 1.25 euros per dollar. Complete Table 5-5.

Table 5-5

(1) U.S. Nominal Foreign Exchange Rate (euros per dollar)	(2) Price of IBM Computer in the U.S.	(3) Price of IBM Computer in Germany	(4) Price of Siemens Computer in Germany	(5) Price of Siemens Computer in the U.S.
1.50	$10,000	_____	15,000 euros	_____
1.25	$12,000	_____	15,000 euros	_____

Note that the percentage change from 1.25 euros to 1.50 euros is _____ percent, while the percentage change from $10,000 to $12,000 is _____ percent. Therefore, if the U.S. nominal foreign exchange rate decreases by the same proportion as the domestic price level increases (holding the foreign price level constant), the price of the IBM computer will <u>increase above/remain equal to/decrease below</u> the price of the Siemens computer in both countries. Hence, net exports would <u>increase/not change/decrease</u>.

d. Whereas the nominal exchange rate indicates the amount of foreign currency a domestic resident gets (or a foreigner gives up) for one unit of domestic currency, the real exchange rate indicates the amount of foreign goods and services a domestic resident gets (or a foreigner gives up) for one equivalent domestic good or service. If an American sells one American good, he or she gets P, where P is the American price level. To buy German goods that person must trade these P into euros at the nominal foreign exchange rate of e, for example, 1.5 euros/$1. These $1.5 \times P$ euros will then buy $1.5P/P^*$ foreign (German) goods, where P^* equals the foreign (German) price level. The real exchange rate ε is the number of foreign goods the American can buy with one domestic good. Thus,

$$\varepsilon = 1.5P/P^* = e \times (P/P^*) \tag{5-7}$$

Use this formula to complete Table 5-6.

Table 5-6

(1) U. S. Nominal Foreign Exchange Rate (euros per dollar)	(2) U.S. Price Level	(3) German Price Level	(4) Real Foreign Exchange Rate
1.0	$10,000	15,000 euros	_____
1.5	$10,000	15,000 euros	_____
1.25	$12,000	15,000 euros	_____
1.5	$12,000	15,000 euros	_____
2.0	$10,000	15,000 euros	_____

e. Reexamining Parts a–d, we can see how net exports depend on the real foreign exchange rate. As the U.S. real foreign exchange rate rises, U.S. exports will <u>increase/decrease</u>, U.S. imports will <u>increase/decrease</u>, and U.S. net exports will <u>increase/decrease</u>. Remember that the real foreign exchange rate increases whenever the nominal exchange rate <u>increases/decreases</u>, the domestic price level <u>increases/decreases</u>, or the foreign price level <u>increases/decreases</u>.

6. **Determinants of the Real Exchange Rate in a Small Open Economy** *In this exercise, we discuss how the real exchange rate in a small open economy adjusts to equate net foreign investment and the trade surplus.*

a. The real exchange rate adjusts so that the trade surplus is equal to net foreign investment, $S - I$. Net capital outflow does not depend on the real exchange rate if the world real interest rate is constant and output remains equal to its full employment level. We have already seen, however, that the trade surplus NX increases/decreases as the real exchange rate increases.

b. Suppose that $S - I = 150$ and $NX = 250 - 100\varepsilon$. Draw these two curves on Graph 5-3 and label them $(S - I)_1$ and NX_1.

Graph 5-3

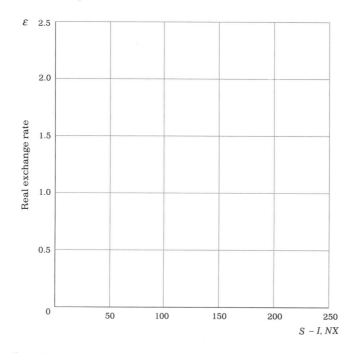

c. On Graph 5-3, net capital outflow equals _____.
Consequently, the trade surplus must equal _____, which will occur when ε equals _____. Label this initial equilibrium Point A on Graph 5-3.

d. Now suppose that the domestic government increases government purchases by 50. This will increase/decrease national saving by _____, while investment increases/remains the same/decreases, since the interest rate remains equal to the world real interest rate. Consequently, net capital outflow $S - I$ will increase/decrease by _____ to _____. This will shift the $S - I$ curve to the left/right by _____. Draw the new curve on Graph 5-3, label it $(S - I)_2$, and label the new equilibrium Point B. This implies that domestic purchases of foreign assets minus foreign purchases of domestic assets will increase/decrease as the domestic country increases its borrowing/lending abroad. Given the change in net capital outflow, the trade surplus must also increase/decrease by _____ to _____. This occurs at a new equilibrium real exchange rate of _____. Consequently, domestic fiscal expansion, via an increase in government purchases or a reduction in taxes, leads to a(n) increase/decrease in the equilibrium real exchange rate.

e. Let's start again at the initial equilibrium. Redraw NX_1, $(S - I)_1$, and Point A on Graph 5-4.

Graph 5-4

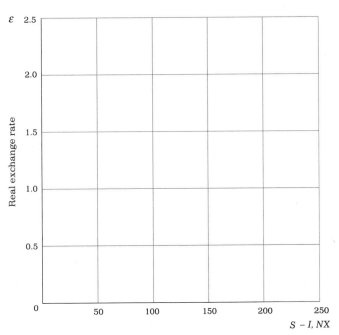

Some large foreign country now raises its taxes. This leads to a(n) increase/decrease in world saving and a(n) increase/decrease in the world real interest rate. Consequently, domestic investment would increase/decrease, $(S - I)$ would increase/decrease, and the $(S - I)$ curve would shift to the left/right. Draw the directional shift on Graph 5-4, label your new curve $(S - I)_3$, and label the new equilibrium Point B. This change would indicate a(n) increase/decrease in net capital outflow and a(n) increase/decrease in the trade surplus. To obtain this change in the trade surplus, the real exchange rate would have to rise/fall.

7. **The Nominal Foreign Exchange Rate and Purchasing-Power Parity** *In this exercise, we discuss the determinants of the nominal foreign exchange rate and purchasing-power parity.*

a. Recall that the equation for the real exchange rate is

$$\varepsilon = e \times (P/P^*) \tag{5-8}$$

If we multiply both sides of Equation 5-8 by P^*, we obtain

$$P^* \times \varepsilon = e \times P \qquad \text{(5-9)}$$

Using the percentage change rule from Chapter 2 of the textbook, we obtain

% Change in P^* + % Change in ε = % Change in e + % Change in P,   **(5-10)**

or, by rearranging,

% Change in e = % Change in ε + % Change in P^* – % Change in P **(5-11)**

Recall that the percentage change in the domestic price level is merely equal to the domestic rate of inflation π, while the percentage change in the foreign price level P^* is equal to the foreign rate of inflation π^*. Making these substitutions in Equation 5-11, complete the following equation:

% Change in e = _____.   **(5-12)**

Assuming that changes in the real exchange rate are relatively small, this equation implies that when the domestic rate of inflation exceeds the foreign rate of inflation, the nominal exchange rate will increase/decrease and the Canadian dollar will appreciate/depreciate. Conversely, when inflation is higher abroad, the nominal exchange rate tends to increase/decrease and the Canadian dollar appreciates/depreciates.

b. Suppose that two countries, Poland and Canada, produce only one commodity, vodka. Suppose that the Polish vodka sells in Poland for 100 zlotys per litre while the Canadian vodka sells in Canada for $20 per litre. If both countries trade on the world market and the vodkas are comparable, then their world prices must be comparable. In Canada, for example, Polish vodka must sell for $_____ per litre, while Canadian vodka must sell for _____ zlotys per litre in Poland. Consequently, for each country to continue producing vodka in the long run, the exchange rate must equal _____ zlotys per dollar. This illustrates the concept of purchasing-power parity, which states that a dollar (or any other currency) must have the same purchasing power in every country. In this example, purchasing power is defined in terms of buying a litre of vodka. Many economists believe that purchasing-power parity is a reasonable approximation of the real-world movements in exchange rates, especially in the long run.

c. Now suppose that the Canadian money supply doubles, leading to a doubling in the Canadian price level. Consequently, a litre of vodka will now sell for $_____ in Canada. In Poland, on the other hand, the price level remains constant so that the price of vodka remains equal to _____ zlotys. For trade to persist in the long run between the two countries, the foreign exchange rate must rise/fall to _____ zlotys per dollar.

d. Let's start over and now assume that the Polish price level doubles while Canadian prices remain constant. Consequently, a litre of vodka will sell for $20 per litre in Canada and _____ zlotys per litre in Poland. For trade to persist in the long run between the two countries, the foreign exchange rate must <u>increase/decrease</u> to _____ zlotys per dollar.

e. Use the data from Parts b–d to complete Table 5-7.

Table 5-7

(1) Long-Run Nominal Foreign Exchange Rate (zlotys per dollar)	(2) Canadian Price Level	(3) Polish Price Level	(4) Long-Run Real Foreign Exchange Rate
_____	20	100	_____
_____	40	100	_____
_____	20	200	_____

Note that purchasing-power parity implies that the real foreign exchange rate is _____. For this to be true, the net export curve must be <u>vertical/horizontal</u>.

f. In the case of purchasing-power parity, ε always equals _____, so the percentage change in ε equals _____, and, from Part a, the % Change in $e =$ _____. Thus, in this special case, <u>all/some/none</u> of the changes in the nominal exchange rate will reflect international differences in inflation rates.

Problems

Answer the following problems on a separate sheet of paper.

1. a. The saving rate in the United States is low compared with many of the countries with which the United States trades. If the United States were a closed economy, how would this affect U.S. investment relative to investment in their trading partners? Explain why.

   b. The United States, of course, is not a closed economy. Consequently, their low saving rate has resulted in national saving being substantially less than investment. What effects has this had on U.S. net capital outflow and the U.S. trade balance?

2. What does purchasing-power parity imply about:

   a. the nominal exchange rate between any two countries?

   b. the real exchange rate between any two countries?

   c. Explain your answers to both Parts a and b.

3. In Problem 9 of Chapter 4 in this workbook, you analyzed a zero inflation policy. If this policy were followed—forcing Canadian money growth to be less than money growth rates abroad, what would the *long-run* effect be on the:

    a. real Canadian foreign exchange rate? Use the appropriate theory to explain your answer.

    b. nominal Canadian foreign exchange rate? Use the appropriate equations and theories to illustrate and explain your answer.

4. Imagine that you are the governor of the Bank of Canada. Assume, further, that the money supply has been growing at 3 percent per year. You have been asked to explain the long-run effects of increasing the growth of the money supply to 10 percent per year. State and then *explain* the long-run effects of this change on each of the following (give numerical estimates when possible):

    a. the annual rate of inflation

    b. the real interest rate

    c. the nominal interest rate

    d. the real exchange rate

    e. the nominal exchange rate

    f. investment (ignore both taxes and uncertainty)

    g. real GDP

5. Suppose the price of a Big Mac hamburger is $4.09 in Canada and 12.50 yuan in China. Furthermore, suppose the nominal foreign exchange rate is 6.83 yuan per dollar.

    a. Calculate the real exchange rate.

    b. If the nominal prices of Big Macs remain unchanged in both countries, what would the purchasing-power parity theory predict would eventually be:

        i.   the real exchange rate. Explain.

        ii. the nominal exchange rate.

6. a. Many people think that the reunification of Germany created substantial investment opportunities in what was formerly East Germany. If this is true, what would the effects be on German net capital outflow, the German trade balance, and the German foreign exchange rate?

    b. At the same time, Germany had to increase its government spending dramatically to pay for the costs of reunification. How does this development affect your answers to Part a?

7. Given the record federal government budget deficit in 2009, after the recession is over, the government will embark on a deficit reduction program. For the purposes of this exercise, assume that both tax increases and spending cuts are involved, and that the tax increases are equal in magnitude to the spending cuts. Throughout this problem assume that the tax increases would be equal in magnitude to the cuts in government spending.

    a. Explain the long-run impact of such a deficit reduction program on private saving, public saving, and national saving.

   b. Suppose Canada was a closed economy. Use the *I,S* graph to illustrate what the long-run impact of this program would be on national saving, investment, and the real interest rate.

   c. Obviously, Canada is not a closed economy. Furthermore, Canada has a trade surplus. Illustrate this initial situation graphically using the *I,S* diagram.

   d. Treating Canada as a small open economy, use your graph from Part b to illustrate the long-run impact of these tax increases and (equal) cuts in government spending on national saving, investment, the real interest rate, and the trade surplus.

   e. On the appropriate graph, illustrate the effect of this program on the Canadian real exchange rate and net exports if Canada were a small open economy. First, simplify your analysis by ignoring long-run changes in foreign debt service obligations.

   f. Now repeat your answer for part e, this time extending the discussion to allow for the long-run changes in foreign debt-service obligations.

8. What does economic theory suggest is the long-run relationship between changes in a country's level of saving and its level of investment? Explain how your answer depends upon whether the country is a closed economy or a small open economy.

9. The Ontario Budget in 2000 involved tax cuts designed to stimulate investment.
A Using the analysis in the Appendix of Chapter 5, which highlights long-run changes in foreign debt service obligations, explain how this policy can be expected to affect Canada's real exchange rate.

10. a. In the 1980s, during the Reagan administration, the United States cut tax rates and increased defense spending, resulting in record budget deficits. State and explain what the effects were on:

   i. the levels of investment in Europe and Japan.

   ii. European and Japanese net capital outflow.

   iii. the European and Japanese trade balances.

   iv. the European and Japanese real exchange rates.

11. In 2005, *The Economist* reported that France's real exchange rate had increased relative to Germany's real exchange rate during the preceding two years. How can this be true if both France and Germany used the euro as their currency? Explain your answer using the formula for the real exchange rate and the percentage change rule.

12. Consider the *small open economy* of Chile. Assume Chile has a trade surplus and the real world interest rate is 3 percent.

   a. Indicate this initial situation on an appropriately labled *I,S* graph and then on an appropriately labeled *(S-I), NX* graph.

   Now, suppose foreigners develop a craving for Chilean wines. Consequently, the demand for Chilean exports increases.

   b. On the same graph you drew for Part a, illustrate the effect of this change in tastes on Chile's *NX* curve and its real exchange rate. As a result, what happens to Chile's trade surplus?

   c. In order to assist its other industries, the Chilean government wants to adjust taxes in order to maintain the real exchange rate at its initial level.

    i. In which direction should it change taxes? (First, read Part (ii) below.)

    ii. Use a second set of graphs for a small open economy to illustrate *and state* the effects on the amounts of saving, investment, net capital outflow, net exports, and the real interest rate if foreigners develop a craving for Chilean wine and the Chilean government responds as you indicated in Part (i) to keep the real exchange rate unchanged.

13. In 2009, the interest rate on 20-year bonds was 2 percent (per year) on Switzerland's government bonds and 3.5 percent on U.S. government bonds. Suppose the bonds for both countries were completely safe, the expected real interest rates were equal in both countries, and purchasing-power parity holds at every moment in the past, present, and future. Be as precise as you can and explain exactly what this difference in nominal interest rates (and these assumptions) implied about:

    a. expected changes in the U.S. real exchange rate vis-à-vis Switzerland.

    b. expected rates of inflation in the U.S. and Switzerland.

    c. expected changes in the U.S. nominal exchange rate vis-à-vis Switzerland.

Data Questions

Locate the necessary economic data and apply them to answer the following data questions. For advice on how to access the data, see the Preface and the Economics Data on the Internet Section on page xi.

1.   **a.** After visiting the Statistics Canada Web site, complete the following table.

Table 5-8

	1995	2008
Proportion of Canada's Exports to		
United States	_____	_____
European Union	_____	_____
Japan	_____	_____
Other OECD	_____	_____
Other Countries	_____	_____
Proportion of Canada's Imports from		
United States	_____	_____
European Union	_____	_____
Japan	_____	_____
Other OECD	_____	_____
Other Countries	_____	_____

    b. Has Canada's dependence on trade with the United States increased or decreased?

Unemployment

Fill-in Questions

Use the key terms below to fill in the blanks in the following statements. Each term may be used more than once.

discouraged workers
efficiency wage
employment insurance
frictional unemployment
insiders
labour force
natural rate of unemployment

outsiders
sectoral shift
steady state
structural unemployment
unemployment rate
wage rigidity

1. The unemployment rate is calculated as the percentage of the
_____ that is unemployed.

2. The labour market reaches a(n) _____ when the
_____ is constant and the flows into and out of unemployment are equal. This average rate of unemployment around which the economy
fluctuates is called the _____.

3. One of the causes of _____ is the change in the composition
of demand among firms, industries, or regions, which economists call a(n)
_____. One policy that increases
_____ is _____, a government pro-
gram in which unemployed workers can collect a fraction of their former wages for
a certain period of time after losing their jobs.

4. _____ occurs when the real wage fails to adjust until labour
supply equals labour demand. The resulting unemployment is called
_____.

5. The unemployment caused by unions and by the threat of unionisation is an in-
stance of conflict between two different groups of workers—_____,
such as senior union members, and _____, such as unemployed workers who would like a job in the unionized industry.

6. _____ theories, another cause of _____,
   suggest that high wages make workers more productive.

7. The official number of unemployed may underestimate the number of people
   who would like to work because it does not include those individuals, called
   _____, who may want a job but who, after an unsuccessful
   search, have given up looking.

Multiple-Choice Questions

1. Zero percent unemployment is an unrealistic and perhaps undesirable policy goal
   for all of the following reasons EXCEPT:
   a. it takes time to match jobs and workers.
   b. it would be inhumane to force the elderly to work.
   c. minimum wage laws restrict employment opportunities.
   d. some of the unemployed are unwilling to work at jobs that are available to them.

2. According to the theory of frictional unemployment, the main determinant of the
   natural rate of unemployment is the:
   a. rate of job separation and job finding.
   b. average period of unemployment.
   c. size of the labour force.
   d. quit rate.

3. Let L equal the size of the labour force, E the number of employed workers, and U
   the number of unemployed workers. The unemployment rate is equal to:
   a. $(L - E)/L$.
   b. U/L.
   c. $1 - (E/L)$.
   d. all of the above.

4. Let s denote the rate of job separation and f the rate of job finding. If the labour market is in a steady state, the natural rate of unemployment is equal to:
   a. $1/s$.
   b. $1/(s + f)$.
   c. $s/(s + f)$.
   d. $f/(s + f)$.

5. A government policy that will increase frictional unemployment is a(n):
   a. extension of job training programs.
   b. increase in employment insurance benefits.
   c. reduction in the minimum wage.
   d. dissemination of information about job vacancies.

6. Frictional unemployment occurs in each of the following cases EXCEPT when:
   a. there is a sectoral shift in the economy.
   b. certain firms go bankrupt.
   c. workers quit their current jobs to look for new ones in a different occupation.
   d. workers quit their current jobs and stop looking for work altogether.

7. Structural unemployment occurs when:

   a. wages are perfectly flexible.

   b. jobs are rationed.

   c. labour demand exceeds labour supply at the going wage.

   d. the labour market is perfectly competitive.

8. Economists believe that wage rigidity can be caused by:

   a. unions.

   b. minimum wage laws.

   c. efficiency wages.

   d. all of the above.

9. According to various efficiency wage theories, higher wages make workers more productive for all of the following reasons EXCEPT that higher wages:

   a. allow workers to afford more nutritious diets.

   b. attract higher-quality workers.

   c. may improve worker effort by increasing the cost of losing one's job.

   d. move people into higher tax brackets, so they have to work harder to have the same after-tax income.

10. The FALSE statement about unemployment is:

    a. when the nation's unemployment rate rises, most of the problem is that the average individual is unemployed for a longer time period; it is not that there is a corresponding increase in the number of individuals unemployed.

    b. the average unemployment rate rose in each succeeding decade during the second half of the 20th century.

    c. it is usual for the unemployment rate in Quebec to exceed that in the prairie provinces.

    d. technical change is hardest on individuals aged between 50 and 60 years; as a result, the unemployment rate for this age bracket is among the highest in Canada.

11. Compared with workers in Canada, Europeans typically:

    a. work fewer hours per year.

    b. are more likely to belong to a union.

    c. have higher tax rates.

    d. experience all of the above.

12. According to efficiency-wage theory, (I) the unemployment rate is higher, the higher is the level of payroll taxes; (II) the unemployment rate is higher, the more generous is employment insurance.

    a. I is true; II is not.

    b. II is true; I is not.

    c. Both I and II are true.

    d. Neither I nor II is true.

13. In a small open economy, (I) a tax on capitalists from which the revenue is used to make employment insurance more generous may raise labour's economic welfare;

(II) a tax on capitalists from which the revenue is used to cut payroll taxes may raise labour's economic welfare.

a. I is true; II is not.

b. II is true; I is not.

c. Both I and II are true.

d. Neither I nor II is true.

Exercises

1. **Labour-Force Movements and the Natural Rate of Unemployment** *In this exercise, we examine labour-force movements when the economy has reached its natural rate of unemployment.*

   a. The natural rate of unemployment is also the steady-state unemployment rate, the unemployment rate toward which the economy moves. Once the economy reaches this steady state, the unemployment rate tends to remain the same. Now consider the following example: Suppose that there are 2,300 employed people in the economy and 200 unemployed people. Suppose, further, that 23 percent, or 0.23, of the unemployed find jobs each month and that 2 percent, or 0.02, of the employed lose their jobs each month.

   i. During the next month, 23 percent of the 200 currently unemployed people, or $0.23 \times 200 =$ _____ people, will find a job.

   ii. During the next month, 2 percent of the 2,300 people now employed, or $0.02 \times 2,300 =$ _____ people, will lose their jobs and become unemployed.

   iii. Consequently, at the beginning of the next month, the total number of unemployed people U will equal 200 – _____ + _____ = _____, and the total number of employed people E will equal 2,300 + _____ – _____ = _____.

   iv. Why is this situation an example of a steady-state unemployment rate?

   b. Calculate the unemployment rate u in Part a. (Remember that the unemployment rate u expressed as a percent is equal to 100 multiplied by the number of unemployed people U divided by the labour force L or $100 \times U/L$.)

c. The number of people moving out of unemployment, fU, must equal the number of people moving into unemployment, sE, at the steady state. Since employment $E = L - U$:

$$fU = sE = s(L - U) \text{ or} \qquad\qquad \textbf{(6-1)}$$

$$fU = sL - sU. \qquad\qquad \textbf{(6-2)}$$

Bringing all terms involving U to the left-hand side of Equation 5-2 yields:

$$(s + f)U = sL. \qquad\qquad \textbf{(6-3)}$$

Dividing both sides of Equation 6-3 by $(s + f)L$ yields the formula for the steady-state unemployment rate:

$$\frac{U}{L} = \frac{s}{(s+f)}. \qquad\qquad \textbf{(6-4)}$$

Perform the necessary calculations to show that the steady-state unemployment rate derived using this formula (which is the same equation used in the textbook) is identical to the unemployment rate you calculated in Part a.

2. **The Transition to a New Natural Rate of Unemployment** *In this exercise, we examine the transition to a new natural rate of unemployment when the rates of job finding and job separation change.*

   a. We use the same numbers as in Exercise 1: there are 2,300 employed people and 200 unemployed people. Suppose that the government now increases the amount of unemployment benefits paid to employment insurance recipients. As the textbook suggests, an increase in employment insurance tends to decrease the probability of the unemployed finding a job and to increase the probability of job separation. Suppose that the rate of job finding falls to 20 percent per month, while the rate of job separation rises to 3 percent per month.

      i. Use calculations similar to the ones you performed in Exercise 1a to calculate how many of the 200 currently unemployed people will find a job during the first month following the change in employment-insurance benefits.

      ii. How many of the 2,300 people now employed will lose their jobs and become unemployed during the month?

    iii. Consequently, at the beginning of the next month, the total number of unemployed U will equal _____, and the total number of employed E will equal _____.

    iv. The unemployment rate at the beginning of the next month will equal $u = (U/L) \times 100 =$ _____ percent.

b. Suppose that the rates of job finding and job separation remain equal at 20 percent and 3 percent, respectively.

    i. During the second month following the change in employment-insurance benefits, how many unemployed people will find a job? (Use your answer from Exercise 2a(iii) as the initial number of unemployed and round off your answer to the nearest whole person.)

    ii. How many employed people will lose their jobs and become unemployed during the second month? (Again, use your answer from Exercise 2a(iii) as the initial number of employed and round off to the nearest whole person.)

    iii. Consequently, at the beginning of the third month, the total number of unemployed people U will equal _____ – _____ + _____ = _____, and the total number of employed people E will equal _____ + _____ – _____ = _____.

    iv. The unemployment rate at the beginning of the third month will equal $u = (U/L) \times 100 =$ _____ percent.

c. Use the formula $u = U/L = s/(s + f)$ to calculate the new steady-state natural rate of unemployment.

3. Demographics and the Natural Rate of Unemployment *In this exercise, we explore how a change in demographics can affect the natural rate of unemployment.*

It appears that the natural rate of unemployment rose from about 4 percent in the 1950s to at least 6 percent in the 1970s. Many economists cited the influx of women and teenagers into the labour force as one reason for this increase. In this exercise, we see how a change in the demographic composition of the labour force can affect the aggregate unemployment rate even if the unemployment rates for each demographic group remain constant.

a. The data in Table 6-1 depict a hypothetical economy that resembles in some important ways the experience of Canada between the 1950s and the 1970s. In Column 1, we see that the total labour force in the 1950s was 9 million, of which one-third, or 3 million, were female and two-thirds, or 6 million, were male. In the 1950s, 300 thousand women and 150 thousand men were unemployed, for a total number of unemployed of 450 thousand. Recalling that the unemployment rate u is equal to the number of unemployed U divided by the labour force L, the unemployment rate among women in the 1950s was $0.3/3.0 = 10$ percent. Use a similar calculation to complete the second and third lines of Column 3.

Table 6-1

	(1) Labour Force (in millions)	(2) Number of Unemployed (in millions)	(3) Unemployment Rate ($u = U/L$)
1950s			
Female	3	0.30	$u = U/L = 0.3/3.0 = 10\%$
Male	6	0.15	$u = \underline{\hspace{2cm}}$
Total	9	0.45	$u = \underline{\hspace{2cm}}$
1970s			
Female	4	0.40	$u = \underline{\hspace{2cm}}$
Male	6	0.15	$u = \underline{\hspace{2cm}}$
Total	10	—	$u = \underline{\hspace{2cm}}$

b. Note from the data in Table 6-1 that the unemployment rate for women was much higher than the unemployment rate for men. List several possible reasons for this situation.

c. By the 1970s, the total labour force in this economy had grown to 10 million because of a sharp increase in the number of women who wanted to work. At the same time, the number of unemployed had also increased, again solely among women. Now complete the remainder of Column 3 in Table 6-1.

d. What happened to the unemployment rates for females and males between the 1950s and the 1970s?

e. What happened to the total unemployment rate between the 1950s and the 1970s?

f. Explain how the total unemployment rate can change even while the unemployment rate for each group remains constant.

g. The Canadian economy is similar to our hypothetical economy in that the unemployment rate rose between the 1950s and the 1970s along with female labour-force participation. In addition, the unemployment rate for females was generally higher than the unemployment rate for males throughout most of this period. However, the difference between male and female unemployment rates largely disappeared in the 1980s. Some economists cite an increasing attachment to the labour force on the part of women, which would decrease the female unemployment rate. Others point to a decline in stable, high-paying, blue-collar manufacturing jobs that were typically held by men, which would increase the male unemployment rate. Consequently, the sharp rise in unemployment during the early 1980s can/cannot be attributed to the continuing increase in female labour-force participation.

h. In the 1990s, a similar phenomenon contributed to a significant reduction in the unemployment rate. Middle-age workers have lower unemployment rates than younger workers, in part because they are more committed to their jobs. As the baby-boom generation moved into their middle ages during the 1990s, middle-age workers became a greater portion of the labour force, just as women did after 1950. If we substitute "middle-age workers" and "younger workers" for "male" and "female" workers in Table 6-1, we find that the increase in the share of middle-age workers in the 1990s would increase/decrease the overall unemployment rate even if the unemployment rates of middle-age and younger workers, respectively, remained constant.

Problems

Answer the following problems on a separate sheet of paper.

1. **a.** In which two ways does employment insurance affect the natural rate of unemployment? Explain how each way changes the rate of unemployment.

   b. Despite its impact on the unemployment rate, the employment insurance program does have some beneficial effects.

      i. In which ways is the program perceived to increase overall equity (fairness)?

      ii. In which ways might the program increase overall efficiency (that is, increase real GDP)?

2. **a.** Explain how the elasticity of demand for low-wage workers determines the change in total wage income accruing to those workers following an increase in the minimum wage.

   b. Would policymakers be more or less likely to support higher minimum wages if economists found that the demand for low-wage workers was very inelastic? Explain.

   c. In 1991, the U.S. Congress passed a subminimum wage proposal whereby young **CH** workers could be paid less than the adult minimum wage for a limited period of time. Give reasons why minimum wage laws are thought to be more onerous and less essential for teenagers than for adults.

   d. Several economists and politicians have argued that subminimum wage laws for teenagers might reduce total adult employment.

      i. Explain why these economists take this position.

      ii. Why would the effect of subminimum wage laws for teenagers and adult unemployment depend on whether adults and teenagers are substitutes or complements in production?

3. During the 1950s and 1960s, most of the countries in Western Europe maintained **◻** very low rates of unemployment. In comparing the labour markets of North America and Western Europe, several economists discovered that there was considerably less mobility from employment to unemployment in Western Europe. This situation was partially the result of numerous laws in Western Europe that restricted companies' ability to lay off workers quickly.

   a. In Chapter 6 of the textbook, a theory of the natural unemployment rate for Canada was presented. In that model, the probability of job finding each month was 0.20, or 20 percent, and the probability of job separation was 0.01, or 1 percent. Suppose that these probabilities in Western Europe during the 1960s were 23.4 percent and 0.6 percent, respectively. Calculate the Western European natural rate of unemployment in the 1960s and compare it to the natural rate calculated in the textbook.

   b. Starting in the 1970s, several changes in Western Europe altered the rates of job finding and job separation considerably, and critics claimed that these countries suffered from a "disease" they called "Eurosclerosis." Calculate the new natural rate of unemployment in Europe if the probability of job finding decreases to 9.2 percent while the probability of job separation rises to 0.8 percent. (Note that the latter is still less than what is experienced in North America.)

4. This question concerns our theory of frictional unemployment.

C

   a. Differentiate the equation for the natural rate of unemployment with respect to *f*. Then show how an increase in *f* will affect that rate. Explain your answer.

   b. Now differentiate the equation for the natural rate of unemployment with respect to *s*. Then show how an increase in *s* will affect that rate. Explain your answer.

5. While it is very difficult to measure the natural rate of unemployment, the Canadian government publishes exact data every month on the overall rate of unemployment. Why do we care about the natural rate of unemployment if we have a much more precise estimate of the overall rate of unemployment?

6. In the federal government budget of 2007, the Canadian government introduced the

A Working Income Tax Benefit. This policy offers low-income Canadians a tax break on their employment earnings—a tax break that is not available when individuals receive employment insurance. The idea is to reward individuals when they work, not when they are not working (which is what EI does). In this question, you are to use the efficiency-wage model given in the Appendix to Chapter 6 (in the text) to analyze this proposal. In the text, it is assumed that EI receipts are not taxed. You are to consider two alternative situations. In Case I, assume that both employment earnings and EI receipts are taxed at rate *t*. Work out the expression for the unemployment rate. In Case II, assume that only EI receipts are taxed. Work out the expression for the unemployment rate in this case. Prove that unemployment must be lower in Case II—the situation that approximates the existence of the new policy—compared to Case I. To illustrate the magnitude of this unemployment effect, assume the following parameter values: $a = .03$, $c = .5$, and $t = .1$. By how much does the move from Situation I to II lower the structural unemployment rate?

7. Less than 30% of the Canadian labour force is unionized. Since wages for a large majority of workers are determined in nonunion markets, how can it still be said that unions increase the natural rate of unemployment?

8. The employment/population ratio is defined as the ratio of total employment to total population, expressed as a percentage, or $(E/P) \times 100$.

   a. Show the algebraic relationship among the employment/population ratio, the labour-force participation rate L/P, and the employment rate. The employment rate is equal to E/L, or 1 minus the unemployment rate u.

   b. Some economists believe that the employment/population ratio is a better measure of the economy's health than the unemployment rate. Give some reasons for supporting this position.

   c. On the other hand, many economists still believe that the unemployment rate is a better measure of the economy's health than the employment/population ratio. Give some reasons for supporting this position.

Data Questions

Locate the necessary economic data from the Statistics Canada Web site and apply them to answer the following data question. For advice on how to access the data, see the Preface and the Economics Data on the Internet section on p. xi.

1. Examine recent data on *unemployment*. Compare both levels of the unemployment rates across provinces, and the recent changes in employment and unemployment in various parts of the country. Can you offer reasons for these outcomes (for example, as in 2006, falling unemployment in the West due to booming resource industries and falling employment in Ontario due to the effects of a slowing U.S. economy and a rising Canadian dollar on manufacturing firms)? What proportion of the unemployed are long-term?

Questions to Think About

1. In what ways would you reform the employment insurance program to better achieve the dual goals of equity and efficiency?

2. Many economists favour the abolition of minimum wage laws. Do you? Why or why not?

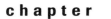

Economic Growth I

Fill-in Questions

Use the key terms below to fill in the blanks in the following statements. Each term may be used more than once.

Golden Rule level of capital accumulation
growth effect
level effect
Solow growth model
steady state

1. The _____ shows how saving, population growth, and technological progress affect the level of output and its growth over time.

2. In the absence of population growth, the _____ represents the long-run equilibrium of the economy, where the amount of investment equals the amount of depreciation, and the capital stock neither increases nor decreases.

3. A higher saving rate has a _____ because it affects the steady-state level of income per person but not its steady-state growth rate.

4. Polices that affect the steady-state growth rate of income per person are described as having a _____ .

5. The steady state with the highest consumption is called the
   _____.

Multiple-Choice Questions

1. The production function $Y = F(K, L)$ has constant returns to scale if:
   a. $F(zK, zL) = zY$.
   c. $zF(K, L) = Y$.
   b. $F(zK, zL) = Y$.
   d. $F(K + 1, L + 1) - F(K, L) = 1$.

2. If the production function $Y = F(K, L)$ has constant returns to scale, then:

    a. $F(zK, zL) = zY$.
    b. $F(K/L, 1) = Y/L$.
    c. $y = f(k)$, where y is output per worker and k is capital per worker.
    d. all of the above.

3. All of the following statements about the marginal product of capital MPK are true EXCEPT:

    a. $MPK = f(k + 1) - f(k)$.
    b. MPK tends to decline as k increases.
    c. when there is only a little capital, MPK is very small.
    d. MPK is equal to the slope of the production function $y = f(k)$.

4. The change in the capital stock is equal to:

    a. investment + depreciation.
    b. investment – depreciation.
    c. investment × depreciation.
    d. investment ÷ depreciation.

5. If capital lasts for an average of 50 years, and depreciation occurs at a constant rate, the depreciation rate is:

    a. 50 percent, or 0.5 per year.
    b. 2 percent, or 0.02 per year.
    c. 0.50 percent, or 0.005 per year.
    d. 0.02 percent, or 0.0002 per year.

6. In a steady state with no population growth:

    a. the amount of capital per worker remains constant over time.
    b. investment per worker equals depreciation per worker.
    c. saving per worker equals depreciation per worker.
    d. all of the above.

7. With no population growth, the steady-state level of capital per worker will increase whenever:

    a. the amount of investment per worker decreases.
    b. the depreciation rate increases.
    c. the saving rate increases.
    d. all of the above.

8. If $y = k^{1/2}$, $s = 0.4$, and the depreciation rate $\delta = 20$ percent (or 0.20), the steady-state level of the capital stock per worker is:

    a. 4.
    b. 8.
    c. 2.
    d. 16.

9. At the steady state described in Question 8, the amount of saving and investment per worker is:

    a. 0.8.
    b. 1.6.
    c. 10.
    d. 2.

10. Suppose that a country in a steady state implements policies to increase its saving rate. After the new steady state is reached:

    a. output per worker will grow more rapidly than before.
    b. the level of output per worker will be higher than before.
    c. the amount of capital per worker will be the same as before.
    d. all of the above.

11. The Golden Rule level of capital accumulation k^*_{gold} denotes the steady state with the highest:

    a. level of consumption per worker.
    b. level of output per worker.
    c. growth rate of consumption per worker.
    d. growth rate of output per worker.

12. Excluding population growth, at the Golden Rule level of capital accumulation k^*_{gold}:

    a. $f(k^*_{gold}) = \delta k^*_{gold}$.   c. $f(k)$ reaches a maximum.
    b. $MPK = \delta$.   d. all of the above.

13. If $y = k^{1/2}$, $\delta = 5$ percent $= 0.05$, and the Golden Rule level of capital accumulation $k^*_{gold} = 100$, then the saving rate associated with the Golden Rule level of capital accumulation is:

    a. 5 percent, or 0.05.   c. 20 percent, or 0.20.
    b. 10 percent, or 0.10.   d. 50 percent, or 0.50.

14. If the current steady-state level of capital per worker is less than the Golden Rule level and the government implements policies that increase the saving rate, consumption per worker will:

    a. initially fall below the original level but will eventually rise above it.
    b. continuously rise above the original level.
    c. initially rise far above the original level and then gradually fall back toward it.
    d. continuously fall below the original level.

15. If the current steady-state level of capital per worker is greater than the Golden Rule level and the saving rate falls, consumption per worker will:

    a. initially fall below its original level but will eveunally rise above it.
    b. continuously rise above its original level until the level of capital per worker reaches the Golden Rule level.
    c. initially rise far above its original level and then gradually fall until the level of capital per worker reaches the Golden Rule level.
    d. continuously fall below its original level.

16. "Break-even" investment is the amount of investment:

    a. at which economic profits are maximized.
    b. required to keep the capital stock per worker constant.
    c. at which economic profits are zero.
    d. at which the marginal product of capital is equal to its price.

17. In the Solow growth model with population growth n, the change in capital per worker is equal to:

    a. $sf(k) + (\delta + n)k$.   **c.** $sf(k) - (\delta + n)k$.

    b. $sf(k) + (\delta - n)k$.   **d.** $sf(k) - (\delta - n)k$.

18. An increase in the rate of population growth n will:

    a. increase the steady-state level of capital per worker.

    b. decrease the steady-state level of capital per worker.

    c. have no effect on the steady-state level of capital per worker.

    d. decrease the steady-state level of capital per worker if $\delta < n$ and increase the steady-state level if $\delta > n$.

19. The Solow growth model predicts that countries with higher population growth rates will have:

    a. lower steady-state levels of output per worker.

    b. lower steady-state growth rates of output per worker.

    c. both a and b.

    d. higher steady-state growth rates of output per worker.

20. A decrease in the rate of population growth n, like an increase in the saving rate:

    a. increases the steady-state growth rate of income per person.

    b. increases the steady-state level of income per person.

    c. decreases the steady-state growth rate of income per person.

    d. decreases the steady-state level of income per person.

21. At the Golden Rule level of capital per person with population growth:

    a. the marginal product of capital is equal to the rate of population growth.

    b. the marginal product of capital is equal to the rate of depreciation minus the rate of population growth.

    c. the marginal product of capital is equal to the rate of depreciation plus the rate of population growth.

    d. the marginal product of capital is equal to the saving rate.

22. Malthus's prediction that mankind would forever live in poverty turned out to be wrong because:

    a. Malthus did not foresee the massive technological advances in farming.

    b. Malthus did not foresee how birth control could allow people to satisfy their sexual desires without increasing the population.

    c. Malthus did not foresee that people might want to reduce the size of their families.

    d. all of the above.

23. According to Michael Kremer:

    a. Malthus will turn out to be correct after all.

    b. rapid population growth may increase economic growth.

    c. rapidly growing civilizations will eliminate each other in wars.

    d. all of the above are true.

Exercises

1. **The Accumulation of Capital** *In this exercise, we use a Cobb-Douglas production function to introduce the Solow growth model. You will need a calculator with a square-root key.*

   a. Consider the simple production function:

   $$Y = K^{1/2} L^{1/2}. \tag{7-1}$$

   For numerical simplicity, the same production function as in Chapter 7 of the textbook is used, although most of the other parameters are different. Recall from Chapter 3 of the textbook that this production function displays constant returns to scale because when all inputs double, output doubles/falls by half/remains constant.

   b. Now divide Equation 7-1 by L and complete Equation 7-2, where y represents output per worker:

   $$y = \frac{Y}{L} = K^{1/2} \left(\frac{L^{1/2}}{L} \right) = K^{1/2}(L)^{\underline{\quad}} = \left(\frac{K}{L} \right)^{\underline{\quad}} = k^{\underline{\quad}}, \tag{7-2}$$

   where $k = K/L$ = the amount of capital per worker.

   c. Use Equation 7-2 for y to complete Column 2 in Table 7-1.

   ### Table 7-1

(1) Capital per Worker k	(2) Output per Worker $y = k^{1/2}$	(3) Consumption per Worker c	(4) Investment per Worker i	(5) Depreciation per Worker δk	(6) Change in Capital per Worker Δk
0	_____	_____	_____	_____	_____
4	_____	_____	_____	_____	_____
12	_____	_____	_____	_____	_____
16	_____	_____	_____	_____	_____
20	_____	_____	_____	_____	_____
36	_____	_____	_____	_____	_____

d. Plot and graph the data from Table 7-1, Columns 1 and 2, on Graph 7-1 and label the curve $f(k)$.

Graph 7-1

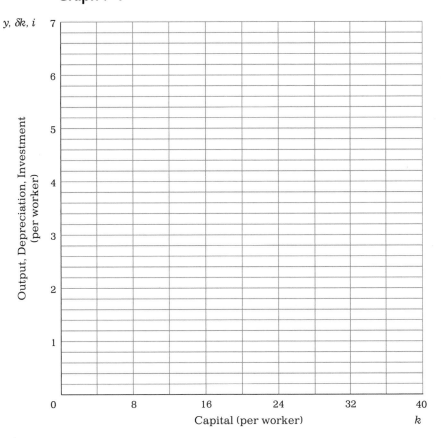

Note that the slope of this production function indicates how much extra output per worker is obtained from an extra unit of capital per worker. This amount is called the _____.

e. As in Chapter 7 of the textbook, assume that output per worker is divided between consumption per worker c and investment per worker i:

$$y = c + i. \tag{7-3}$$

Assume also that consumption per worker is a constant fraction of output per worker:

$$c = (1 - s)y, \tag{7-4}$$

where $s =$ the saving rate. If $s = 0.20$, households save _____ percent of their income. Alternatively, if $s = 0.20$, $c = ($_____$)y$, and households consume _____ percent of their income. Use this value of s to complete Column 3 of Table 7-1.

f. Substitute Equation 7-4 in Equation 7-3 to obtain:

$$y = (1 - s)y + i.$$ (7-5)

Now solve Equation 7-5 for i.

$i =$ _____.

If $s = 0.20$, $i =$ _____ y. Use Equation 7-5 to complete Column 4 of Table 7-1. Plot and graph these points on Graph 7-1 and label the curve $sf(k)$.

g. Although investment creates new capital per worker, part of the existing capital stock is used up or becomes obsolete each year as a result of depreciation. Let δ represent the fraction of the capital stock that wears out each year. If capital lasts for an average of 25 years, $\delta = 1/25 = 0.04$. Assume that capital lasts for an average of 20 years, so that $\delta = 1/$_____ $=$ _____.
The amount of depreciation per worker will then equal the rate of depreciation multiplied by the amount of capital per worker, or δk. Use this second value of δ to complete Column 5 of Table 7-1. Plot and graph these points on Graph 7-1, and label the curve δk.

h. The total change in the capital stock will be equal to the additions resulting from investment minus the amount worn out because of depreciation:

$$\Delta k = i - \delta k = sf(k) - \delta k,$$ (7-6)

if $s = 0.20$, $sf(k) = 0.20k^{1/2}$. If capital lasts for an average of 20 years so that $\delta =$ _____, use Equation 7-6 to solve for the change in the capital stock.

$\Delta k =$ _____ $-$ _____.

Use this expression for Δk to complete Column 6 of Table 7-1.

i. In the steady state, the amounts of capital per worker, output per worker, and consumption per worker remain constant from one year to the next. The amount of capital per worker remains constant when $\Delta k = $ _____, which occurs when $i = sf(k) = \delta k$. Locate this point on Graph 7-1 and label it k^*. At the steady-state level of capital per worker, $k^* = $ _____. Consequently, output per worker $= (k^*)^{1/2} = $ _____ consumption per worker $= $ _____, and saving per worker $= $ _____. To the right of k^* (that is, when $k > k^*$), investment is greater than/less than depreciation, so the amount of capital per worker rises/falls until it equals k^*. To the left of k^*, investment is greater than/less than depreciation, so the amount of capital per worker rises/falls until it equals k^*.

j. We can also solve for k^* algebraically, as in Chapter 7 of the textbook. In the steady state, $\Delta k = 0$, so $0 = sf(k^*) - \delta k^*$. Substitute the production function from Part b and the values for s and δ from Part h and solve for k^*.

$k^* = $ _____.

k. If households began to save a greater fraction of their incomes, s would rise. If s rises, the saving (and investment) curve on Graph 7-1 would shift upward/downward. At the old steady-state level of k^*, investment would then be greater than/less than depreciation. As a result, the amount of capital per worker would rise/fall, and the steady-state level of k^* would rise/fall. This change in k^* would increase/decrease the amount of output per worker in the steady state. Thus, a higher saving and investment rate will lead to a higher/lower steady-state level of output per worker. Once the economy reaches this new steady state, however, output per worker will increase/decrease/remain constant. Therefore, in the long run, an increase in the saving rate will increase/decrease/have no effect on an economy's growth rate. Conversely, a lower saving and investment rate will lead to a higher/lower steady-state level of output per worker but will increase/decrease/have no effect on the long-run growth rate.

2. **Moving to the Steady State** *Table 7-2 in the textbook illustrates how an economy approaches the steady state when the initial level of capital is smaller than the steady-state level. In this exercise we illustrate how it approaches the steady state if the initial level of capital is larger than the steady-state level.*

   a. Suppose the production function and relevant parameters are the same as in Exercise 1, i.e., $y = f(k) = k^{1/2}$; $c = (1 - s)y = 0.8y$; $i = sy = 0.2y$; and $\delta = 0.05$. For simplicity, assume that the population growth rate $n = 0$. Suppose, furthermore, that the initial level of k is 25. Recall that the change in k, $\Delta k = i - \delta k$. Use these data to comple the first row of Table 7-2.

Table 7-2

(1) Year	(2) Capital per Worker k	(3) Output per Worker y	(4) Consumption per Worker c	(5) Investment per Worker i	(6) Depreciation per Worker δk	(7) Change in k Δk
1	25	_____	_____	_____	_____	_____
2	_____	_____	_____	_____	_____	_____
3	_____	_____	_____	_____	_____	_____
•						
•						
•						
30	_____	_____	_____	_____	_____	_____
31	_____	_____	_____	_____	_____	_____
•						
•						
•						
100	_____	_____	_____	_____	_____	_____
101	_____	_____	_____	_____	_____	_____
•						
•						
•						
∞	_____	_____	_____	_____	_____	_____

   b. The amount of capital per worker in year 2 will be equal to the amount of capital per worker in year 1 plus the change in capital per worker in year 1. Using the data from Columns 2 and 7 in Table 7-2, the amount of capital per worker in year 2 will equal _____ – _____ = _____. Use this number and the information in Part a to complete the second and third rows of Table 7-2. Round off to three decimal places.

   c. Obviously, the amount of capital per worker will fall as long as depreciation per worker exceeds investment per worker. Using these data, the amount of capital per worker in year 30 will equal 20.063. Enter this number in Table 7-2 and complete the rows corresponding to years 30 and 31.

d. Similarly, the amount of capital per worker in year 100 will equal 16.657. Enter this number in Table 7-2 and complete the rows for years 100 and 101.

e. Eventually we read the steady-state level of $k^* = 16$. Enter this in the last row of Table 7-2 and complete the row. When we reach the steady state, $i = \delta k$, so that $\Delta k =$ _____, which is the definition of the steady state.

f. Recall that we can calculate the steady-state level of k directly since $sf(k^*) = \delta k^*$. Thus, $k^*/f(k^*) = s/\delta$. Use $f(k) = k^{1/2}$, $s = 0.2$, and $\delta = 0.05$ to solve for k^*.

$k^* =$ _____

3. **The Golden Rule Level of Capital Accumulation** *In this exercise, we use the production function and parameters from Exercise 1 to derive and illustrate the conditions for the Golden Rule level of capital accumulation.*

a. One goal among policymakers might be to choose the steady-state capital stock with the highest level of consumption per worker, denoted by k^*_{gold}. Although the rate of depreciation δ is typically assumed to be exogenous (that is, fixed by external technological factors), policymakers may be able to affect the saving rate s in order to change k^*. As we saw in Exercise 1, as s increases, the steady-state level of capital per worker increases/decreases. If only steady states are considered, recall that:

$$c = y - i = f(k^*) - i = f(k^*) - \delta k^*. \tag{7-7}$$

In Equation 7-7 $\Delta k = 0$ in the steady state is used so that investment equals depreciation and $i = \delta k^*$. As in Exercise 1, assume that $Y = K^{1/2}L^{1/2}$, divide Y by L, and derive the exponent on k in the equation for $y = f(k)$.

$y = f(k) = (k)^{\overline{}}$.

If k^* merely denotes certain values of k, then $f(k^*) = (k^*)^{1/2}$.

b. If it again is assumed that capital lasts an average of 20 years, $\delta = 1/20 =$ _____. Use the information from Parts a and b to complete Columns 2–4 in Table 7-3.

Table 7-3

(1) Capital per Worker k^*	(2) Output per Worker $f(k^*) = k^{*1/2}$	(3) Depreciation per Worker δk^*	(4) Consumption per Worker $c^* = f(k^*) - \delta k^*$	(5) Saving per Worker $sf(k^*) = sk^{*1/2}$
0	_____	_____	_____	_____
4	_____	_____	_____	_____
16	_____	_____	_____	_____
36	_____	_____	_____	_____
64	_____	_____	_____	_____
100	_____	_____	_____	_____
121	_____	_____	_____	_____
144	_____	_____	_____	_____

c. Plot and graph the points in Column 2 on Graph 7-2 and label the curve $f(k^*)$. Plot and graph the points in Column 3 on Graph 7-2 and label the curve δk^*. Finally, plot and graph the points in Column 4 on Graph 7-2 and label the curve c^*. Note from Graph 7-2 that consumption per worker c^* is maximized when $k^* =$ _____. Thus, the Golden Rule level of the capital stock $k^*_{gold} =$ _____.

Graph 7-2

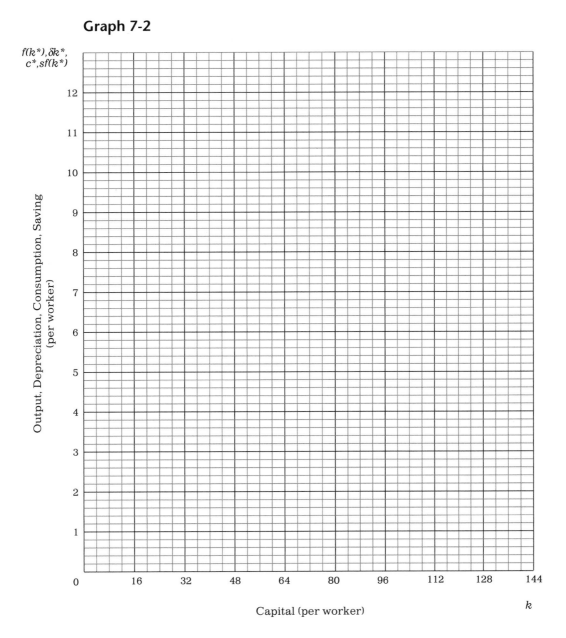

$f(k^*), \delta k^*, c^*, sf(k^*)$

Output, Depreciation, Consumption, Saving (per worker)

Capital (per worker)

k

d. At this level of k^*_{gold}, depreciation equals $\delta k^*_{\text{gold}} = $ _____ and output per worker $f(k^*_{\text{gold}}) = (k^*_{\text{gold}})^{1/2} = $ _____. Since this is a steady state, $\Delta k = 0$ and investment and saving must both equal depreciation. Consequently:

$$i = sy = sf(k^*_{\text{gold}}) = \delta k^*_{\text{gold}}.$$

Substitute the values of k^*_{gold}, $f(k^*_{gold})$, and δ, and calculate the Golden Rule level of s:

$s =$ _____ .

Compared with the saving rate in Exercise 1 of 0.20, policymakers would have to <u>increase/decrease</u> the saving rate in order to achieve the Golden Rule level of capital accumulation.

e. Note that, at the Golden Rule level of k^*_{gold}, neither capital per worker nor output per worker typically is maximized. From Graph 7-2, we can see that at any level of k^* above k^*_{gold}, the amount of depreciation δk^* is <u>higher/lower</u> than at k^*_{gold}. Hence, in the steady state, investment is <u>higher/lower</u> than at k^*_{gold}. Although output at this point is <u>greater/less</u> than at k^*_{gold}, there is <u>more/less</u> output remaining for consumption.

f. As Chapter 7 of the textbook suggests, there is an alternative way of calculating k^*_{gold}, which is easier if one knows calculus (see Problem 3 for an example). Examining Graph 7-2, consumption per worker is equal to the difference between $f(k^*)$ and δk^*. Consequently, c^* will be maximized when this difference is maximized. When k^* increases by 1 unit, δk^* increases by δ units, or by _____ . When k^* increases by 1 unit, $f(k^*)$ increases by MPK units, where MPK is the marginal product of capital. At small values of k^* the slope of the $f(k^*)$ curve, which is equal to MPK, is obviously <u>greater/less</u> than the slope of the δk^* curve. Consequently, at small values of k^*, c^* <u>increases/de-creases</u> as k^* is increased. At large values of k^*, the slope of the $f(k^*)$ curve is <u>greater/less</u> than the slope of the δk^* curve. Consequently, for large values of k^*, c^* <u>increases/decreases</u> as k^* is increased. Starting again at a small value of k^*, consumption per worker continues to increase as long as the slope of the $f(k^*)$ curve is <u>greater/less</u> than the slope of the δk^* curve. Consequently, c^* reaches a maximum when the slopes of the two curves are equal. This point occurs when $MPK = \delta$. Since $\delta =$ _____ , when $k = k^*_{gold}$, $MPK =$ _____ .

g. Let us verify the preceding result that $MPK =$ _____ when $k = k^*_{gold} =$ _____ . MPK is defined as the change in output per worker when k increases by 1 unit. When $k = k^*_{gold} =$ _____ , $y = (k^*_{gold})^{1/2} =$ _____ . When k in-

creases by 1 unit to _____, $y = (k)^{1/2} = $ _____, so $MPK = $ _____.
Hence, the values of MPK and δ are close. The small difference is the result of our taking a discrete (whole-unit) change in k.

h. As you discovered in Part d, the saving rate s that yielded the Golden Rule level of capital and consumption per worker in this model was
_____. Use this value of s to complete Column 5 in Table 7-3, graph these points in Graph 7-2, and label your curve $sf(k^*)$. Note that at k^*_{gold}, saving per worker (which is equal to investment per worker) is greater than/equal to/less than the amount of depreciation per worker. Thus, k^*_{gold} represents a steady-state level of the capital stock.

i. If the saving rate were higher than the rate in Part h, the $sf(k^*)$ curve would shift up/down and the steady-state capital stock would be too high/low. If the saving rate were lower than the rate in Part h, the $sf(k^*)$ curve would shift up/down and the steady-state capital stock would be too high/low.

4. Changing the Saving Rate to Reach the Golden Rule Level of Consumption *We use the results of Exercises 1 and 3 to illustrate what happens when an economy changes its saving rate to reach the Golden Rule level of consumption.*

a. As in Exercises 1 and 3, suppose the production function is $y = k^{1/2}$. If the rate of depreciation $\delta = 0.05$, we showed in Exercise 3 that the Golden Rule level of the saving rate $s = $ _____, the Golden Rule level of the capital stock per worker $k^*_{gold} = $ _____, the Golden Rule level of output per worker $y = (k^*_{gold})^{1/2} = $ _____, and the Golden Rule level of consumption per worker $c = (1 - s)y = $ _____.

b. In Exercise 1, we used the same production function and rate of depreciation and found that when the saving rate was 0.2, the steady-state level of capital per worker $k^* = $ _____, and the steady-state level of output per worker $y = (k^*)^{1/2} = $ _____. Consequently, the level of consumption per worker at this steady state would be $c = (1 - s)y = (1 - 0.2)$ _____ = _____. In order to increase consumption per worker to the Goden Rule level, policymakers would therefore have to increase/decrease the saving rate.

c. Suppose we begin at the steady state in Exercise 1 (and Part b above), and policymakers suddenly increase the saving rate from 0.2 to 0.5. Consumption per worker will eventually rise from its initial steady-state level of _____ to the Golden Rule level of _____.

d. The transition to the Golden Rule level, however, will be uncomfortable. If output per worker y initially equals 4.0 and policymakers increase the saving rate s to 0.5, the amount of consumption per worker $c = (1 - s)y$ will immediately change from 3.2 to $(1 - 0.5)4 = $ _____. Thus, immediately after the increase in s, consumption per worker will rise/fall.

e. After the immediate increase/decrease in consumption, however, the higher
    saving rate will increase both k and y. In the period in which the saving rate
    rises to 0.5, for example, both investment and saving per worker will increase
    from $i = sy = 0.2(4) =$ _____ to $0.5(4) =$ _____. Since depreciation per worker
    $\delta k = 0.05(16) =$ _____, capital per worker will increase in the next period from its
    initial value of 16 to $16 + i - \delta k = 16 +$ _____ $-$ _____ $=$ _____. Consequently,
    in the following period, output per worker $y = k^{1/2}$ will equal _____, and con-
    sumption per worker $(1 - s)y$ will increase from 2 to $(1 - 0.5)$_____ $=$ _____.
    As k and y continue to increase in subsequent periods, consumption per worker
    will also increase until it reaches its Golden Rule level.

f. Parts c–e illustrate that when the saving rate is intially below the Golden Rule
    saving rate and policymakers increase it to its Golden rule value, consumption
    per worker will initially rise/fall because the saving rate has risen but the
    amount of capital per worker has not yet increased by enough to raise con-
    sumption. Over time, however, the higher saving rate will increase/decrease the
    amounts of capital and output per worker, and the level of consumption per
    worker will gradually rise/fall until it reaches the higher Golden Rule level of
    consumption, as shown in Figure 7-10 in the textbook.

g. If, on the other hand, the saving rate is initially above its Golden Rule value, the
    transition to the Golden Rule level of consumption is more comfortable. In that
    case a reduction in the saving rate to its Golden Rule level of 0.5 will immediate-
    ly increase/decrease the level of consumption per worker. Since the initial lev-
    els of capital per worker and output per worker are greater than the Golden
    Rule levels, the level of consumption immediately after the decrease in s will
    also be greater/less than the Golden Rule level. The economy, however, is no
    longer in a steady state. Over time, the levels of capital per worker and output
    per worker will rise/fall to their Golden Rule levels, along with consumption.

h. As an extreme example, suppose the saving rate is initially 1.0. In the steady
    state, $sf(k^*) = \delta k^*$, so that

$$1.0(k^*)^{1/2} = 0.05k^*.$$

Squaring both sides of this equation yields

$$k^* = 0.0025(k^*)^2$$

Calculate the initial steady-state value of k^*:

$k^* =$ _____. Thus, the initial value of output per worker $y = (k^*)^{1/2} =$ _____, the initial level of saving per worker $sy = 1.0y =$ _____, and the initial level of consumption per worker $c = (1 - s)y =$ _____. Because society is saving (and investing) all of its output, there is nothing left over to consume. (This also illustrates how the saving rate can be too high.) If policymakers reduce the saving rate from 1.0 to the Golden Rule level of 0.5, consumption per worker at the initial level of output will immediately jump to $(1 - 0.5)y =$ _____. Note that this value is higher/lower than both the initial level of consumption and the Golden Rule level. It is not, however, a steady state. Over time, the reduction in s will lead to a higher/lower level of capital and output per worker. Consequently, after the initial increase/decrease in consumption, consumption per worker will rise/fall toward its Golden Rule level.

i. Thus, if the saving rate is initially above the Golden Rule saving rate and policymakers reduce it to the Golden Rule value, consumption will immediately rise/fall by a substantial amount. Thereafter, however, consumption per worker will gradually rise/fall until it reaches the Golden Rule level. At all times during the transition to the Golden Rule level, however, consumption will be higher/lower than its initial level, as shown in Figure 7-9 in the textbook.

5. **Population Growth** *In this exercise, we add population growth to the Solow growth model and derive the new conditions for the steady state.*

a. Recall that k is the ratio K/L. Furthermore, recall from Exercise 4 in Chapter 2 that the percentage change of a ratio is approximately equal to the percentage change in the numerator minus the percentage change in the denominator. Suppose the amount of capital K remains constant over time (so that its percentage change equals 0), but the number of workers L grows at $n = 0.02 = 2$ percent per year. Using the ratio rule for percentage changes, the percentage change in k will then be about $0 -$ _____ $=$ _____ percent. Consequently, k will fall by about _____ percent per year because the same amount of capital must now be spread over an increasing number of workers. If investment i is added and it is assumed, as before, that the rate of depreciation $\delta = 0.05$, the change in the capital stock per worker will now be:

$$\Delta k = i - \delta k - nk = i - 0.05k - 0.02k. \tag{7-8}$$

Note in Equation 7-8 that if i and δ both equal 0, k falls by _____ percent per year.

b. Recall that investment per worker is assumed to be a constant fraction s of output per worker. As in Exercise 1, assume that $s = 0.2$. Substituting s into Equation 7-8 yields

$$\Delta k = sf(k) - \delta k - nk = sf(k) - (\delta + n)k = 0.2f(k) - 0.07k. \tag{7-9}$$

Assume that $f(k) = (k)^{1/2}$. Use these values for s, δ, and n to complete Table 7-4.

Table 7-4

(1) Capital per Worker k	(2) Output per Worker $f(k) = k^{1/2}$	(3) Investment per Worker $sf(k)$	(4) Break-even Investment per Worker $(\delta + n)k$	(5) Change in Capital per Worker $sf(k) - (\delta + n)k$
0	_____	_____	_____	_____
4	_____	_____	_____	_____
8	_____	_____	_____	_____
16	_____	_____	_____	_____
36	_____	_____	_____	_____

c. Plot and graph Columns 2, 3, and 4 of Table 7-4 on Graph 7-3 and label the curves $f(k)$, $sf(k)$, and $(\delta + n)k$, respectively.

Graph 7-3

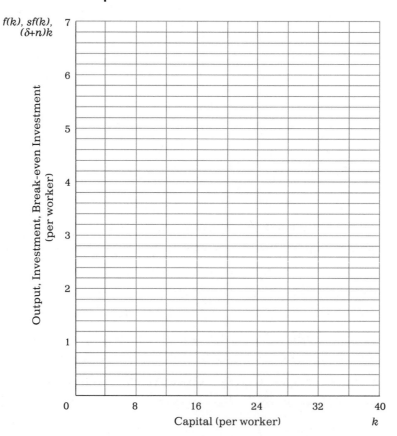

d. In the steady state, the change in the capital stock per worker equals
_____. Consequently, rearranging Equation 7-9, in the
steady state, $sf(k) =$ _____. Locate the steady-state level
of k^* on Graph 7-3 and label it Point A. Use the preceding values of s, δ, and n to
calculate k^* to within two decimal places:

$k^* =$ _____.

e. If the population growth rate increased to 3 percent per year, the $(\delta + n)k$ curve
on Graph 7-3 would shift up/shift down/not shift, while the $sf(k)$ curve would
shift up/shift down/not shift. Consequently, the steady-state capital stock per
worker would increase/decrease/remain constant. Thus, the Solow growth
model predicts that economies with higher population growth have high-
er/lower levels of capital per worker and therefore higher/lower levels of output
per worker.

f. Population growth also affects the Golden Rule level of capital accumulation.
Recall that consumption per worker can be computed as

$$c = y - i. \tag{7-10}$$

Output per worker is equal to $f(k)$, and in the steady state $\Delta k = 0$, so $i = (\delta + n)k$.
Substituting $f(k)$ and $(\delta + n)k$ into Equation 7-10 yields

$$c = f(k) - (\delta + n)k. \tag{7-11}$$

As in Exercise 3, consumption per worker is maximized when the slope of the
$f(k)$ curve, which is equal to MPK, is equal to the slope of the $(\delta + n)k$ curve, which
is equal to _____. Consequently, the Golden Rule level of
k^*_{gold} is the level of k at which the following occurs:

$MPK =$ _____ + _____. (7-12)

As n increases, the MPK at which the Golden Rule level is achieved increas-
es/decreases. Since MPK increases/decreases as k increases, this relationship
implies that an increase in n will increase/decrease the Golden Rule level of
capital per worker.

Problems

Answer the following problems on a separate sheet of paper.

1. Suppose that the production function is $Y = 10(K)^{1/4}(L)^{3/4}$ and capital lasts for an average of 50 years so that 2 percent of capital wears out every year. Assume that the rate of growth of population equals 0. If the saving rate $s = 0.128$, calculate the steady-state level of capital per worker, output per worker, consumption per worker, saving and investment per worker, and depreciation per worker.

2. Consider an economy in a steady state with population growth rate n and a rate of capital depreciation δ.

   a. At the steady state $\Delta k = 0$, what condition must be met for this to hold?

   b. What is maximized at the Golden Rule level of k?

   c. What other condition must be met at the Golden Rule level of k?

3. Assume that an economy is initially in a steady state, that population growth and the rate of technological change are both zero, but that capital depreciates at rate δ. Use the appropriate graphs to illustrate *and explain* how an increase in the saving rate would affect all of the following:

   a. the steady-state capital stock per worker.

   b. the steady-state level of output per worker.

   c. the steady-state rate of growth of output per worker.

   d. the Golden Rule capital stock per worker.

   e. the rate of growth of output per worker during the transition from the initial steady state to the final steady state.

4. Assume that the rate of growth of population equals 0. Suppose that there is a sudden increase in the rate at which capital depreciates. The production function remains unchanged.

   a. On a graph, illustrate the effects of this change on the steady-state level of capital per worker if the saving rate remains unchanged.

   b. Describe the effect of this change on the Golden Rule level of capital per worker, and explain your answer.

5. Consider an economy in which the rate of depreciation of capital is δ and there is no population growth. Starting from an initial steady state, suppose it experienced a long-run decline in both its saving rate and rate of depreciation.

   a. Use the appropriate graphs to illustrate what would happen to the steady-state level of capital per worker.

   b. What would happen to the Golden Rule level of capital accumulation k^*_{gold}?

6. **C** In Chapter 3 of the text, the marginal product of capital was defined as the amount by which total output changes when capital rises by 1 unit, or $MPK = dY/dK$. In Chapter 7 of the text MPK is equal to amount by which output per worker rises when capital per worker rises by 1 unit, or $MPK = df(k)/dk = f'(k)$, where $k = K/L$. Use calculus and the chain rule to show that the two definitions are the same.

7. Suppose that the production function is $Y = 10(K)^{1/4}(L)^{3/4}$ and that capital lasts for an average of 50 years. Assume that the rate of growth of population equals 0.

   a. As Chapter 7 of the textbook states, in the steady state $c = f(k^*) - \delta k^*$. Use calculus to find the Golden Rule level of capital per worker.

   b. Now calculate the level of output per worker at this Golden Rule level, the amount of depreciation per worker, the level of investment per worker, the rate of saving per worker, and the level of consumption per worker.

8. Totally differentiate the capital-labour ratio K/L to prove that the change in the ratio, dk, is equal to $i - \delta k - nk$ (where i, δ, and n represent investment per worker, the rate of depreciation, and the population growth rate, respectively).

9. Assume that the current steady-state level of capital per worker is less than the Golden Rule level.

   a. What must happen to the saving rate in order to achieve the Golden Rule level?

   b. If the indicated change in the saving rate in Part a is achieved, what will happen to consumption per worker in both the short run and the long run?

   c. What kind of policies might be implemented in order to achieve this change in the saving rate?

10. Suppose that a country is initially operating at a steady-state level of capital per worker. If a birth-control campaign is successful in significantly reducing the country's population growth, what will happen to the growth *rates* of capital per worker, output per worker, and total output on the path to the new steady state? At the new steady state, how will each of these three growth rates compare with their initial steady-state values?

11. Suppose a country has a production function that exhibits constant returns to scale. Starting from an initial steady state with population growth rate n and a rate of capital depreciation δ, the country is devasted by an epidemic (like AIDS or the Black Plague) that quickly kills half of its population without affecting its capital stock.

   a. According to the Solow growth model, what would be the immediate impact of this epidemic on total output? Explain.

   b. Explain what the Solow model implies would be the immediate impact of this epidemic on total output per worker.

   c. If the saving rate is unchanged and the population regains its pre-epidemic growth rate, the economy will eventually return to its initial steady-state level of k^*. Draw three graphs with time on the horizontal axis (like the one on the next page) to illustrate the time paths of capital per worker k, consumption per worker c, and output per worker y in the initial steady state (to the left of line A), after the epidemic strikes but before the new steady state is reached (between lines A and B), and after the final steady state is reached (to the right of line B).

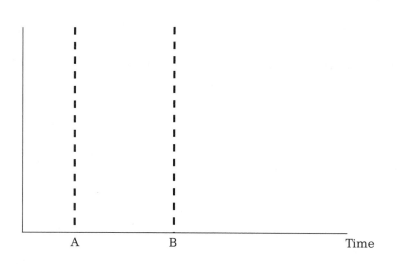

Data Question

Locate the necessary economic data and apply them to answer the following data question. All of the relevant data may be found in (the back of) the Economic Report of the President *or at http://www.gpoaccess.gov/eop/.*

1. Calculate for each of the following periods the *average annual* growth rate of real GDP for Canada, the United States, Japan, Germany, China, India, and all of Africa (for the most recent period, calculate the arithmetic average):

    a. 1990–1999.

    b. 2000–2008.

    c. According to Table 7-1 in the texbook, GDP per capita was $45,790 in the United States in 2007 and $5,345 in China. If real GDP per capita continues to grow at about 2.5 percent per year in the United States and 10 percent per year in China, when will China's real GDP per capita surpass the United States?

Economic Growth II

Fill-in Questions

Use the key terms below to fill in the blanks in the following statements. Each term may be used more than once.

effective workers
efficiency of labour
endogenous growth theory
human capital

labour-augmenting technological
  progress
technological externality

1. To introduce technological change, the Solow growth model assumes
   _____, which causes the _____ to
   grow over time.

2. The variable measuring the _____ in the production func-
   tion depends on the health, education, skill, and knowledge of the labour force.

3. The number of _____ takes into account the number of
   workers and the efficiency of each worker. It is equal to the number of workers multiplied by the _____.

4. According to the Solow growth model, in the steady state, output per effective
   worker grows at the same rate as _____.

5. _____ is the knowledge and skills that workers acquire
   through education and training.

6. Although the capital variable in the Solow growth model measures only physical
   capital, and the rate of _____ is usually taken as exogenous,
   research indicates that differences in _____ are at least as
   important as differences in physical capital in explaining international differences
   in standards of living.

7. A(n) _____ exists when capital accumulation by one firm
   results in technological advances that other firms can freely use to benefit themselves and society.

8. According to _____, the rate of technological progress is not exogenous. Many of its adherents believe that the economy can exhibit constant returns to capital, as long as capital is broadly defined to include knowledge.

Multiple-Choice Questions

1. The Solow growth model predicts that countries with higher population growth rates will have:
   a. lower steady-state levels of output per worker.
   b. lower steady-state growth rates of output per worker.
   c. both a and b.
   d. higher steady-state growth rates of output per worker.

2. In the Solow growth model with population growth n and labour-augmenting technological progress g, the change in capital per effective worker is equal to:
   a. $sf(k) + (\delta + n + g)k$.
   b. $sf(k) + (\delta - n - g)k$.
   c. $sf(k) - (\delta + n + g)k$.
   d. $sf(k) - (\delta - n - g)k$.

3. In the Solow growth model with population growth and technological progress, the steady-state growth rate in output per *effective* worker is equal to:
   a. zero.
   b. the rate of technological progress g.
   c. the growth rate of population n plus the rate of technological progress g.
   d. the saving rate s.

4. In the Solow growth model with population growth and technological progress, the steady-state growth rate in output per worker is equal to:
   a. zero.
   b. the rate of technological progress g.
   c. the growth rate of population n plus the rate of technological progress g.
   d. the saving rate s.

5. In the Solow growth model, persistent increases in standards of living are due to:
   a. technological progress, which leads to sustained growth in output per worker.
   b. a high saving rate, which leads to sustained high rates of growth.
   c. a high rate of population growth, which leads to a larger labour force.
   d. all of the above.

6. The capital stock in the Canadian economy is well below the Golden Rule level because the net marginal product of capital, $MPK - \delta$, is:

   a. greater than the long-run growth rate of real GNP.
   b. greater than the sum of the long-run rates of population growth and technological progress.
   c. both a and b.
   d. none of the above.

7. If the capital stock in a country is initially below the Golden Rule level of capital, the country can move toward the Golden Rule steady state by:

   a. increasing the rate of saving.
   b. reducing government expenditures on noninvestment items.
   c. providing tax incentives that reward new investment.
   d. all of the above.

8. Technological progress is encouraged by:

   a. the patent system.
   b. tax incentives for research and development.
   c. government subsidies for research.
   d. all of the above.

9. Evidence concerning convergence among different countries' standards of living indicates that:

   a. unadjusted incomes per capita are not converging.
   b. incomes per capita among countries with similar cultures and policies are converging.
   c. countries with different savings rates, population growth rates, and education levels appear to be converging to different steady states.
   d. all of the above.

10. When the steady state has been reached:

    a. real wages grow at the rate of technological progress.
    b. the real rental cost of capital grows at the rate of technological progress.
    c. the number of effective workers grows at the rate of technological progress.
    d. all of the above.

11. Researchers have found that countries that permit free international trade tend to:

    a. grow more rapidly.
    b. grow more slowly.
    c. have more severe business cycles.
    d. be located near the equator.

12. Institutions that economists believe foster economic growth include:

    a. courts that uphold legal protections for shareholders and creditors.
    b. developed capital markets that facilitate borrowing and lending.
    c. governments that do not tolerate corruption.
    d. all of the above.

13. Countries that lie closer to the equator tend to:

    a. discourage free international trade.

    b. grow less rapidly than other countries.

    c. have more severe business cycles than other countries.

    d. have higher inflation rates than other countries.

14. Which of the following reasons would theoretically justify a government technology policy that encouraged investment in certain areas:

    a. a decline in the rate of investment.

    b. the identification and measurement of technological externalities in capital accumulation.

    c. a decline in the real interest rate.

    d. all of the above.

15. The worldwide slowdown in economic growth from the early 1970s to the late 1990s may be explained by:

    a. the entrance of the "baby boomers" into the workforce, which has lowered the average level of experience.

    b. the depletion of the planet's natural resources.

    c. the decline in oil prices in the 1990s.

    d. all of the above.

16. In the Solow growth model, the rate of technological progress is:

    a. exogenous.   c. 3 percent.

    b. endogenous.   d. 0 percent.

17. Acceptance of endogenous growth theory implies:

    a. additional saving and investment can lead to persistent growth.

    b. capital may not be subject to diminishing returns if knowledge is viewed as a type of capital.

    c. the rate of technical change is endogenous.

    d. all of the above.

18. Empirical research indicates that the social rate of return to investment in research is:

    a. less than the private rate of return to investment in physical capital.

    b. about equal to the private rate of return to investment in physical capital.

    c. greater than the private rate of return to investment in physical capital.

19. The Solow residual is:

    A a. the change in total factor productivity.

    b. the change in output that cannot be explained by changes in inputs.

    c. an often-used measure of technological progress.

    d. all of the above.

20. Empirical studies indicate that the unusually high growth rates in Hong Kong,
   Ⓐ Singapore, South Korea, and Taiwan from 1966–1990 were due to unusually large
   increases in all of the following EXCEPT:

   a. labour force participation.   **c.** total factor productivity.

   b. the capital stock.   **d.** educational attainment.

Exercises

1. **Technological Progress** *In this exercise, we incorporate technological progress into the Solow growth model.*

   a. Now assume that each worker becomes more productive over time. To do this, we now measure the number of effective workers $L \times E$, where E grows at some constant rate g. Thus,

   $$Y = F(K, L \times E) \tag{8-1}$$

   E measures the productive abilities of labour, which depend upon health, experience, and knowledge. Recall from Exercise 4 in Chapter 2 that the percentage change of a product of two variables is approximately equal to the sum of the percentage changes in each of the variables. Thus, if the percentage change (i.e., the growth rate) in L is n and the percentage change (i.e., the growth rate) in E is g, then the percentage change in $L \times E$ (and hence the growth in the number of effective workers) is approximately equal to _____ + _____.

   b. We now analyze the economy in terms of quantities per effective worker. Let $k = K/(L \times E)$ stand for capital per effective worker, and $y = Y/(L \times E)$ represent output per effective worker. Thus, we can again write $y = f(k)$. Note that we can also write k as $k = (K/L)/E$. Suppose the amount of capital per worker K/L (as opposed to capital per effective worker) remains constant over time and the efficiency of labor grows by 1 percent per year. According to the percentage change approximation for a ratio, the percentage change in $k = (K/L)/E$ will then equal _____ – _____ = _____. Thus, the amount of capital per effective worker k will fall by about _____ percent per year because the same amount of capital per worker must now be spread over an increasing number of effective workers. If investment i is added and it is assumed, as before, that the rate of depreciation $\delta = 0.05$ and the rate of population growth $n = 0.02$, the change in the capital stock per effective worker will now be:

   $$\Delta k = i - \delta k - nk - gk = i - 0.05k - 0.02k - 0.01k. \tag{8-2}$$

   Note in Equation 8-2 that if i, δ, and n all equal 0, k falls by _____ percent per year.

c. Investment per effective worker is assumed to be a constant fraction s of output per worker. Assume that $s = 0.2$. Substituting s into Equation 8-2 yields:

$$\Delta k = sf(k) - \delta k - nk - gk = sf(k) - (\delta + n + g)k = 0.2f(k) - 0.08k. \qquad \textbf{(8-3)}$$

Assume that $f(k) = (k)^{1/2}$. Use these values for s, δ, and n to complete Table 8-1.

Table 8-1

(1) Capital per Effective Worker k	(2) Output per Effective Worker $f(k) = k^{1/2}$	(3) Investment per Effective Worker $sf(k)$	(4) Break-even Investment per Effective Worker $(\delta + n + g)k$	(5) Change in Capital per Effective Worker $sf(k) - (\delta + n + g)k$
0	_____	_____	_____	_____
4	_____	_____	_____	_____
6	_____	_____	_____	_____
8	_____	_____	_____	_____
16	_____	_____	_____	_____
36	_____	_____	_____	_____

d. Plot and graph Columns 1, 2, 3, and 4 of Table 8-1 on Graph 8-1 and label the curves $f(k)$, $sf(k)$, and $(\delta + n + g)k$, respectively.

Graph 8-1

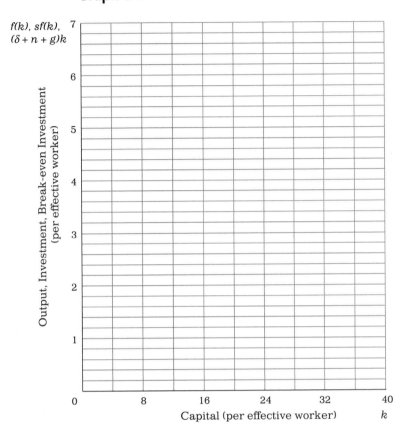

e. In the steady state, the change in the capital stock per effective worker equals _____. Consequently, rearranging Equation 8-3, in the steady state, $sf(k)$ = _____. Locate the steady-state level of k^* in Graph 8-1, and label it Point A. Use the preceding values of s, δ, n, and g to calculate k^* to within two decimal places.

$$k^* = \text{_____}.$$

f. In the steady state, capital per effective worker is constant—that is, $\Delta k = 0$, and $sf(k) = (\delta + n + g)k$. Similarly, output per effective worker is constant. Since the number of effective workers per worker is growing at rate g, however, output per worker will grow at rate _____. Thus, in the Solow growth model, steady-state growth in output per worker depends solely on the rate of <u>saving/depreciation/technological change</u>.

g. Since the number of workers is growing at rate n, total output will grow at the rate of _____ + _____.

2. **The Golden Rule with Technological Change.** *In this exercise, we see how technological change affects the Golden Rule level of capital.*

   a. Technological change also affects the Golden Rule level of capital accumulation. In a world with technological progress, population growth, and capital depreciation, the Golden Rule level of capital accumulation is defined as the steady-state level of capital per effective worker of labour that maximizes consumption per effective worker of labour. Recall that consumption per effective worker can be computed as:

   $$c = y - i \tag{8-4}$$

   Output per effective worker is equal to $f(k)$, and, in the steady state $\Delta k = 0$, so $i = sf(k) = (\delta + n + g)k$. Substituting $f(k)$ and $(\delta + n + g)k$ into Equation 8-4 yields:

   $$c = f(k) - (\delta + n + g)k \tag{8-5}$$

   As in Chapter 7, consumption per effective worker is maximized when the slope of the $f(k)$ curve, which is equal to MPK, is equal to the slope of the $(\delta + n + g)k$ curve, which is equal to _____. Consequently, the Golden Rule level of k^*_{gold} is the level of k at which the following occurs:

   $$MPK = \underline{\hspace{1.5cm}} + \underline{\hspace{1.5cm}} + \underline{\hspace{1.5cm}}. \tag{8-6}$$

   b. Equation 8-6 can also be written as:

   $$MPK - \delta = \underline{\hspace{1.8cm}} + \underline{\hspace{1.8cm}}. \tag{8-7}$$

   Recall that the term on the left-hand side of Equation 8-7 is called the net marginal product of capital, and the sum of the two terms on the right-hand side is equal to the growth rate of total output in the steady state.

   c. Suppose the economy reaches a steady state in which the net marginal product of capital exceeds the growth rate of total output. Recall that the marginal product of capital increases/decreases as we add capital. Thus, in order to decrease the net marginal product of capital and attain the Golden Rule level of consumption, we can increase/decrease the steady-state amount of capital per effective worker by increasing/decreasing the saving rate.

   d. Similarly, if the economy reaches a steady state in which the net marginal product of capital is less than the growth rate of total output, we can attain the Golden Rule level of consumption by increasing/decreasing the steady-state amount of capital per effective worker. This can be accomplished by increasing/decreasing the saving rate.

3. **Endogenous Growth** *In this exercise, we examine a simple one-sector model to illustrate the idea of endogenous growth.*

   a. Consider the simple production function:

   $$Y = AK \qquad \text{(8-8)}$$

   where Y is total output, K is the total capital stock, and A is a constant. Dividing both sides of Equation 8-8 by K indicates that A is equal to _____, or the amount of output produced for each unit of capital.

   b. Recall that the percentage change in the product of two variables is approximately equal to the sum of the percentage changes in each of the variables. Applying this rule to Equation 8-8 yields:

   $$\% \text{ Change in } Y = \% \text{ Change in } A + \% \text{ Change in } K. \qquad \text{(8-9)}$$

   Since A is a constant,

   $$\% \text{ Change in } Y = \text{_____}. \qquad \text{(8-10)}$$

   Insofar as the percentage change in any variable X is calculated as $\Delta X/X$, we can rewrite Equation 8-10 as:

   $$\text{_____} = \text{_____}. \qquad \text{(8-11)}$$

   c. As before, let s be the fraction of total income that is saved and invested and let δ be the rate at which capital depreciates. Consequently, the change in the capital stock

   $$\Delta K = sY - \delta K \qquad \text{(8-12)}$$

   Making this substitution for the numerator of the right-hand side of Equation 8-11 yields:

   $$\Delta Y/Y = (sY - \delta K)/K = \text{_____} - \text{_____}. \qquad \text{(8-13)}$$

   d. Recall from rearranging Equation 8-8 that $Y/K = $ _____. Making this substitution in Equation 8-13 yields:

   $$\Delta Y/Y = sA - \delta. \qquad \text{(8-14)}$$

   e. Equation 8-14 can be used to illustrate the idea behind endogenous growth theory. Note that the growth rate of output $\Delta Y/Y$ will be positive, and output will grow indefinitely, as long as _____ is greater than _____. This occurs because the production function in Equation 8-8 exhibits constant, rather than diminishing, returns to capital. Advocates of endogenous growth theory believe that this assumption is reasonable if the capital stock is interpreted more broadly to include knowledge as a type of capital because knowledge may not be subject to diminishing returns. Consequently, economies that are more successful in producing knowledge may be able to sustain higher rates of economic growth, even in the long run.

4. **A Two-Sector Endogenous Growth Model** *In this exercise, we develop a simple two-sector model with endogenous growth.*

   a. Consider the following Cobb-Douglas production function:

   $$Y = F(K, (1 - u)LE) = K^{1/2}[1 - u)LE]^{1/2} \qquad (8\text{-}15)$$

   where

   Y = output in manufacturing

   K = the physical capital stock

   $(1 - u)$ = the fraction of the labour force employed in manufacturing

   L = the labour force, and

   E = the efficiency of labour

   If $u = 0.10$, then $(1 - u) = $ _____ .

   If, in addition, $K = 4$, $L = 8$, and $E = 2$, then

   $Y = K^{1/2}[(1 - u)LE]^{1/2} = $ _____ $^{1/2}[$ _____ $\times$ _____ $\times$ _____ $]^{1/2}$

   Solve for manufacturing output Y.

   $Y = $ _____ .

   b. Now, suppose that knowledge is the output of a second sector, called the university sector. Changes in the efficiency of labour E are determined by changes in the level of knowledge, which are determined by the fraction of the labour force that is employed in universities and the existing stock of knowledge:

   $$\Delta E = g(u)E = uE. \qquad (8\text{-}16)$$

   If, for example, $u = 0.10$, then $\Delta E = $ _____ E and the growth rate of knowledge $\Delta E/E = $ _____ $ = $ _____ percent per year. In this model, the growth rate of the efficiency of labour is therefore endogenously determined by the fraction of the labour force employed in universities.

c. In Part a, the number of effective workers in manufacturing is equal to $(1 - u)EL$ = _____. Suppose both the number of effective workers in manufacturing $(1 - u)EL$ and the physical capital stock double to _____ and _____, respectively. Calculate the new level of manufacturing output:

Y = _____.

d. Compare your results in Parts a and c. Since the production in Equation 8-15 exhibits constant returns to scale, when both the amount of physical capital and the number of effective workers in manufacturing doubled, output <u>quadrupled/doubled/remained constant.</u>

e. Note that the number of effective workers in manufacturing $(1 - u)EL$ will double whenever we <u>quadruple/triple/double</u> any *one* of the following: the fraction of workers in manufacturing $(1 - u)$, knowledge E, or the labour force L.

f. If we interpret capital broadly to include both physical capital K and knowledge E, then when we double all capital (i.e., both K and E) output in both the manufacturing and university sectors will <u>quadruple/double/remain constant.</u> Consequently, this economy exhibits <u>increasing/constant/diminishing</u> returns to capital, broadly defined.

g. As in the Solow model, the steady-state growth of output per worker will be equal to the rate of change of the efficiency of labour, which, in this model, is the rate at which knowledge accumulates. In Part b, we found that the growth rate of E is equal to the fraction of the labour force employed in universities, or u = _____ percent. Consequently, technological growth is determined endogenously in this model. Persistent growth in output per worker occurs because the creation of knowledge in universities never slows down. Furthermore, if u increases and a greater fraction of the labour force becomes employed in universities, the rate at which knowledge accumulates will <u>increase/decrease /remain constant,</u> and the steady-state growth of output per worker will <u>increase/decrease/remain constant.</u>

5. **Growth Accounting** *In this exercise, we use a Cobb-Douglas production function and an extension of the percentage change rule that is discussed in Chapter 2 of the textbook to derive the formula for the growth in total factor productivity.*

   a. Consider the following Cobb-Douglas production function:

$$Y = AK^\alpha L^{1-\alpha} = AK^{0.3} L^{0.7}. \tag{8-17}$$

An extension of the percentage change rule presented in Chapter 2 of the textbook can be used to derive an equation for the approximate percentage change in Y:

$$\% \text{ Change in } Y = \% \text{ Change in } A + \alpha \times (\% \text{ Change in } K) +$$
$$(1 - \alpha) \times (\% \text{ Change in } L) =$$
$$\% \text{ Change in } A + \underline{\hspace{2cm}} \times (\% \text{ Change in } K) + \hspace{1cm} \text{(8-18)}$$
$$\underline{\hspace{2cm}} \times (\% \text{ Change in } L).$$

The first term on the right-hand side of Equation 8-18, % Change in A, is commonly called the *percentage change in total factor productivity*. It measures increases in Y that occur over time even if the amounts of capital and labour remain constant. Equation 8-18 states that the percentage change in output over time is equal to the percentage change in total factor productivity plus 0.3 times the percentage change in capital plus 0.7 times the percentage change in labour. The coefficients on the changes in capital and labour are precisely equal to their exponents in the Cobb-Douglas production function.

b. Invert Equation 8-18 to solve for total factor productivity growth if $\alpha = 0.3$:

% Change in A = _____.

c. Now use these results along with the following historical data to estimate annual total factor productivity growth for Canada between 1960 and 1985. In this period, the annual growth rates of GDP, capital, and labour were 3.1, 3.2, and 1.9 percent, respectively. Consequently, the estimated annual growth rate of total factor productivity during this period was % Change in A = _____ – _____ – _____ = _____ percent.

Problems

Answer the following problems on a separate sheet of paper.

1. Suppose that the production function is $Y = 10(K)^{1/4}(EL)^{3/4}$ and capital lasts an average of 10 years, so that 10 percent of capital wears out every year. Assume that the rate of growth of population is 4 percent, the rate of technological growth is 2 percent and the saving rate $s = 0.128$.

a. Derive the equation for output per effective worker $y = Y/EL = f(k)$, where k equals the amount of capital per effective worker.

b. Calculate the steady-state levels for each of the following: capital per effective worker, output per effective worker, consumption per effective worker, saving and investment per effective worker, and depreciation per effective worker.

c. Now calculate the steady-state growth rates of capital per worker, output per worker, saving and investment per worker, and consumption per worker.

d. Finally, calculate the steady-state growth rates of capital, output, saving and investment, and consumption.

2. Suppose that output per effective worker assumed the following values:

Period 1:   100

Period 2:   100

Period 3:   100

Period 4:   120

Period 5:   132

Period 6:   138.8

Period 7:   138.8

Period 8:   138.8

a. Draw a graph with Periods 1–8 on the horizontal axis and the value of output per effective worker in each period on the vertical axis.

b. Assume that the data refer to the value of output per worker at the beginning of that period. Draw a second graph with Periods 1–7 on the horizontal axis and the growth rate of output per effective worker during each period on the vertical axis.

3. Consider an economy in a steady state with population growth rate n, a rate of capital depreciation δ, and a rate of labour-augmenting technological progress g.

a. At the steady state $\Delta k = 0$, where k equals capital per effective worker. What condition must be met for this to hold? Describe the condition in words as well as symbols.

b. Describe in words what is maximized at the Golden Rule level of k.

c. What other condition must be met at the Golden Rule level of k?

4. Suppose the production function is $Y = 10(K)^{1/4}(EL)^{3/4}$ and capital lasts an average of 10 years. Assume that the rate of growth of population is 4 percent and the rate of technological growth is 2 percent. The marginal product of capital can be expressed as $MPK = 2.5\,(k)^{-3/4}$ where k is the level of capital per effective worker.

a. Derive the equation for output per effective worker $y = Y/EL = f(k)$, where k equals the amount of capital per effective worker.

b. Calculate the Golden Rule level of capital per effective worker and the saving rate associated with this steady state.

c. Calculate all of the following at their Golden Rule levels: output per effective worker, saving and investment per effective worker, and consumption per effective worker.

5. As in Problems 1 and 4, suppose the production function is $Y = 10(K)^{1/4}(EL)^{3/4}$ and
capital lasts an average of 10 years. Assume once more that the rate of growth of
population is 4 percent and the rate of technological growth is 2 percent.

    a. Derive the equation for output per effective worker $y = Y/EL = f(k)$, where k
equals the amount of capital per effective worker.

    b. Use calculus to derive the marginal product of capital $MPK = f'(k)$.

    c. In the steady state consumption per effective worker

$$c = f(k) - (\delta + n + g)k.$$

    Use calculus to derive the condition for the Golden Rule level of k and solve.

6. Totally differentiate the ratio of capital to effective labour $k = K/(E \times L)$ to prove that
the change in the ratio dk is equal to $i - \delta k - nk - gk$, where i, δ, n, and g represent
investment per effective worker, the rate of depreciation, the population growth
rate, and the rate of technological progress, respectively.

7. Consider an economy in a steady state with population growth rate n, a rate of capital depreciation δ, and a rate of labour-augmenting technological progress g.

    a. Use the appropriate graphs to illustrate and explain how an increase in the sav-
ing rate would affect the steady-state capital stock per effective worker.

    b. Draw three graphs with time on the horizontal axis (like the one below) to illus-
trate the time paths of capital per effective worker k, output per effective worker
y, and consumption per effective worker, c. In each case, show the initial steady
state (to the left of line A), after the saving rate is increased but before the new
steady state is reached (between lines A and B), and after the final steady state is
reached (to the right of line B).

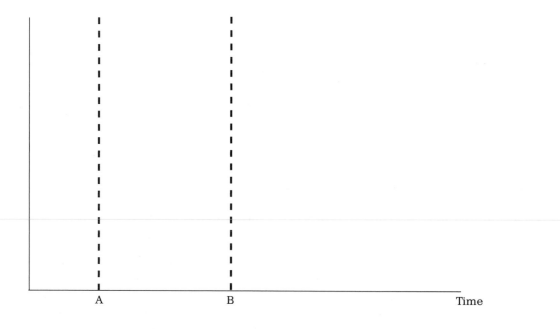

8. Suppose that a country is initially operating at a steady-state level of capital per worker and is able to double its rate of labour-augmenting technological progress.

   a. What will happen to its steady-state level of capital per effective worker?

   b. Consequently, what can one say about the growth rates of capital per effective worker and output per effective worker on the path to the new steady state?

   c. At the new steady state, what can we say about the growth rates of capital per effective worker, consumption per effective worker, and output per effective worker?

   d. Comparing the initial and final steady states, what happens to the growth rates of capital, output, and consumption *per worker*?

9. In each of the following cases determine whether the level of the capital stock per effective worker is above, below, or at the Golden Rule steady state:

   a. The country of Ferilia has a population growth rate of 4 percent and a rate of technological progress of 3 percent. Capital income is 30 percent of GDP, the depreciation of capital is 12 percent of GDP, and the capital stock is 3 times one year's GDP.

   b. The country of Begonia has a steady-state growth rate of real GDP of 4 percent per year. Capital typically lasts for 20 years, and the marginal product of capital is 9 percent of the value of each unit of capital.

10. Suppose that the production function is $Y = AK^{0.3}L^{0.7}$.

    A

    a. If total factor productivity grows at 2 percent per year and both the capital stock and the number of workers grow at 1 percent per year each, calculate the growth rate of output.

    b. If the rate of capital accumulation doubles to 2 percent per year, calculate the new growth rate of output.

11. In Chapter 3 of the textbook, the marginal product of capital was defined as the amount by which total output changes when capital rises by 1 unit, or $MPK = dY/dK$.

    C In Chapter 8 of the text, MPK is equal to the amount by which output per effective worker rises when capital per effective worker rises by 1 unit, or $MPK = df(k)/dk = f'(k)$, where $k = K/EL$. Use calculus and the chain rule to show that the two definitions are the same.

Questions to Think About

1. Can countries differ in their rates of technological progress over long periods of time? Why can't lagging countries simply adopt the more advanced technologies?

2. In the Solow growth model with technological progress, the Golden Rule criterion maximizes the level of consumption per efficiency unit. Is this the ethically correct criterion for policymakers? If the capital stock is now below the Golden Rule steady state, reaching the Golden Rule requires a sacrifice by current generations for the benefit of future generations. Technological progress, however, will automatically make future generations richer because each person will be born with more efficiency units. Should policymakers ask current generations to sacrifice some of their consumption to benefit their richer descendants?

3. There were several proposed solutions to the crisis concerning public pensions. The government opted for increases in payroll taxes. Consider the effects of this decision, and of the other proposals the government rejected, on the budget deficit, economic growth, and income distribution. Which proposal do you prefer?

4. How would one measure the "stepping on toes" and "standing on shoulders" effects?

chapter 9

Introduction to Economic Fluctuations

Fill-in Questions

Use the key terms below to fill in the blanks in the following statements. Each term may be used more than once.

aggregate demand

aggregate supply

demand shock

stabilization policy

stagflation

sticky wages and prices

supply shock

1. According to the classical model, in the long run wages and prices are perfectly flexible and monetary policy affects only nominal variables, not real variables. In the short run, however, monetary policy appears to have a potent effect on output and employment because of _____.

2. The _____ curve depicts a relationship between the quantity of output demanded and the aggregate price level.

3. In the long run, output is determined by technology and the amount of capital and labour. Consequently, in the long run, the _____ curve is vertical, and shifts in _____ affect the price level but do not affect output or employment.

4. _____ occurs when output falls and prices rise simultaneously.

5. When the Bank of Canada changes the money supply to offset an adverse supply or demand shock and to keep output and employment at their natural levels, this is an example of a(n) _____.

6. A sharp, sudden increase in the price of oil is an example of a(n) _____. The expanded availability of credit cards may be viewed as a(n) _____.

Multiple-Choice Questions

1. The FALSE statement about economic fluctuations is:

   a. real GDP in Canada has generally increased over time, but it fluctuates around its average rate of growth.

   b. economists sometimes call the fluctuations in output and employment the *business cycle*.

   c. the fluctuations in output and employment are regular and predictable.

   d. during the recession in the early 1990s, real GDP fell and the unemployment rate rose.

2. Economists generally believe that:

   a. wages and prices are flexible in the long run.

   b. wages and prices are sticky in the short run.

   c. output moves toward its full employment level in the long run.

   d. all of the above are true.

3. The FALSE statement about the aggregate demand curve is:

   a. for a fixed money supply, the quantity equation yields a negative relationship between the price level P and output Y.

   b. the aggregate demand curve has a negative slope.

   c. when the Bank of Canada increases the money supply, the economy moves along a stationary aggregate demand curve, real output increases, and the price level decreases.

   d. the money supply is held constant as the economy moves along a stationary aggregate demand curve.

4. The graph that shows the effect of a decrease in the money supply is:

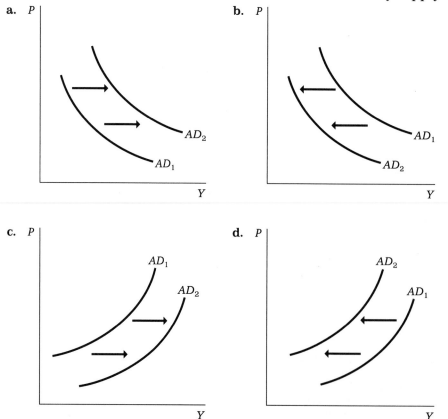

5. The long-run effects of an increase in the money supply include:

   a. an increase in the price level but no change in output.

   b. an increase in output but no change in the price level.

   c. an increase in both the price level and output.

   d. no change in either the price level or output.

6. If prices and wages are fixed in the short run but perfectly flexible in the long run, then:

   a. the long-run aggregate supply curve will be vertical.

   b. the short-run aggregate supply curve will be horizontal.

   c. changes in the money supply will affect output in the short run but not in the long run.

   d. all of the above are true.

7. In the short run, suppose that *all* prices are stuck at some predetermined level. The effect of a reduction in the money supply in the short run can be seen in graph:

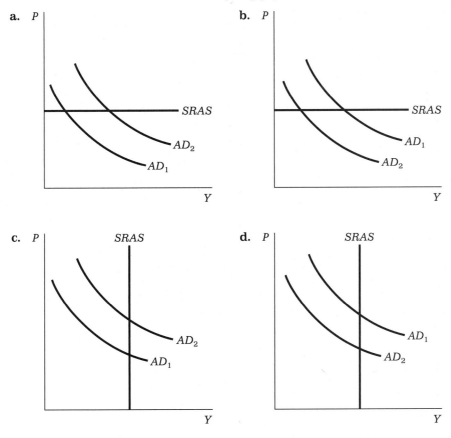

8. If the economy is originally at its long-run equilibrium level and then its aggregate demand curve shifts to the left, the path of the economy is shown in graph:

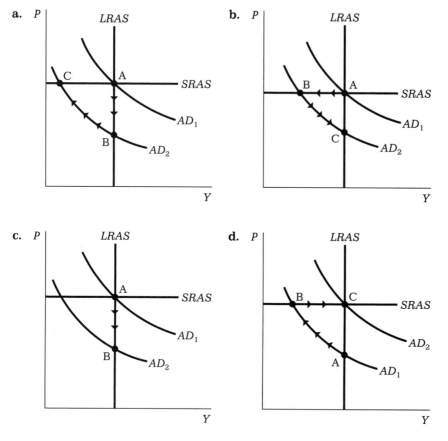

9. The introduction of credit cards results in all of the following EXCEPT a(n):

   a. increase in money demand.

   b. increase in the velocity of money.

   c. shift to the right in the aggregate demand curve.

   d. increase in output in the short run.

10. If there is an unusually good harvest and food prices fall, we will experience a(n):

    a. adverse supply shock.

    b. upward shift in the short-run aggregate supply curve.

    c. increase in output and a decrease in the aggregate price level.

    d. shift in the aggregate demand curve.

11. When the Bank of Canada uses stabilization policy to offset the decline in output following an adverse supply shock, the point on the following graph at which the economy will stabilize is:

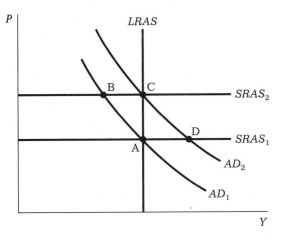

    a. A

    b. B

    c. C

    d. D

Exercises

1. **The Quantity Equation and the Aggregate Demand Curve** *In this exercise, we use the quantity equation to derive the aggregate demand curve. We then illustrate how changes in the money supply and the velocity of money affect the aggregate demand curve.*

    a. The quantity equation is $MV = PY$, where M equals the money supply, V equals the velocity of money, P is the aggregate price level, and Y is real GDP. Assume the money supply is fixed at $M = 1{,}000$ and the velocity of money is fixed at $V = 2.0$, and complete Table 9-1.

Table 9-1

(1) M	(2) V	(3) PY	(4) P	(5) Y
1,000	2.0	_____	2.0	_____
1,000	2.0	_____	1.5	_____
1,000	2.0	_____	_____	2,000
1,000	2.0	_____	0.8	_____
1,000	2.0	_____	_____	4,000

b. Plot on Graph 9-1 the data in Columns 4 and 5 of Table 9-1. Draw the aggregate demand curve that results when $M = 1,000$ and $V = 2.0$, and label your curve AD_1.

Graph 9-1

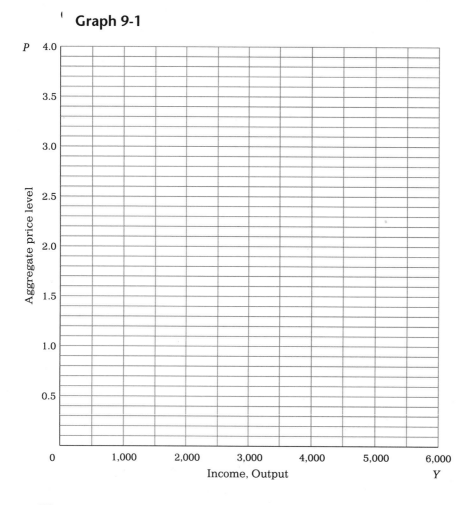

c. The aggregate demand curve depicts the relationship between the quantity of output demanded and the aggregate price level. As the price level falls, the quantity of output demanded rises/falls, holding the quantity of money and the velocity of money constant.

d. Suppose that the money supply increases to 1,500, while velocity remains equal to 2.0. Complete Table 9-2.

Table 9-2

(1) M	(2) V	(3) P	(4) Y
1,500	2.0	2.0	_____
1,500	2.0	1.5	_____
1,500	2.0	1.0	_____
1,500	2.0	0.8	_____
1,500	2.0	0.5	_____

e. Plot the data in Columns 3 and 4 of Table 9-2 on Graph 9-1. Draw the aggregate demand curve that results when $M = 1,500$ and $V = 2.0$, and label your curve AD_2.

f. Suppose that the money supply remained at its original level of 1,000, but the velocity of money increased to 3.0. The numbers in Columns 3 and 4 of Table 9-2 would then be greater/the same/smaller. Thus, either an increase in the money supply or a(n) increase/decrease in the velocity of money shifts the aggregate demand curve to the right/left.

g. Suppose that the money supply fell to 500 while velocity remained equal to 2.0. Complete Table 9-3.

Table 9-3

(1) M	(2) V	(3) P	(4) Y
500	2.0	2.0	_____
500	2.0	1.5	_____
500	2.0	1.0	_____
500	2.0	0.8	_____
500	2.0	0.5	_____

h. Plot on Graph 9-1 the data in Columns 3 and 4 of Table 9-3. Draw the aggregate demand curve that results when $M = 500$ and $V = 2.0$, and label your curve AD_3.

i. Suppose that the money supply remained at its original level of 1,000, but the velocity of money decreased to 1.0. The numbers in Columns 3 and 4 of Table 9-3 would be greater/the same/smaller. Thus, either a decrease in the money supply or a(n) increase/decrease in the velocity of money shifts the aggregate demand curve to the right/left.

2. **The Long-Run Aggregate Supply Curve** *In this exercise, we introduce the long-run aggregate supply curve and discuss the long-run effects of shifts in aggregate demand.*

a. Suppose that the economy is operating at its natural rate (that is, at full employment) when $Y = 2,000$. In the long run, wages and prices are completely flexible and the economy achieves its natural-rate level of output. Consequently, in the long run, we know that $Y =$ _____ but that the aggregate price level can take on any value, depending on monetary policy. Plot this relationship on Graph 9-2 and label it *LRAS*.

Graph 9-2

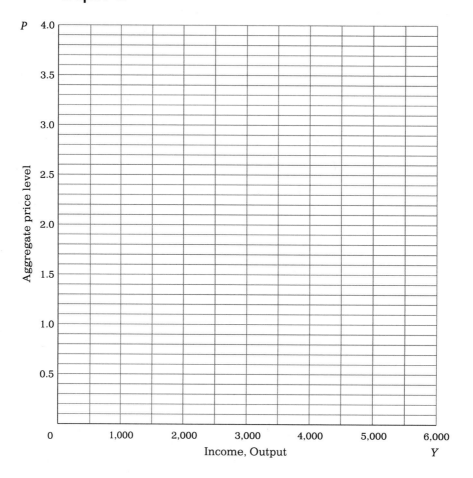

b. Redraw the aggregate demand curve AD_1 from Exercises 1a and 1b on Graph 9-2, and label the initial equilibrium levels of output and prices Y_1 and P_1, respectively.

c. Suppose that the money supply increases to 1,500, as in Exercise 1d. This will shift the aggregate demand curve to the <u>right/left</u>. Draw AD_2 from Exercise 1d on Graph 9-2 and label the new long-run equilibrium levels of output and prices Y_2 and P_2, respectively.

d. The long-run aggregate supply curve is <u>horizontal/upward sloping/vertical</u>. Consequently, increases in the money supply or in the velocity of money will <u>increase/not change/decrease</u> the aggregate price level in the long run, while they will <u>increase/not change/decrease</u> real GDP in the long run. This occurs because, in the long run, wages and prices increase or decrease in order to maintain output at its natural-rate level. In Exercise 1d, the increase in the money supply to $M = 1,500$ would <u>increase/decrease</u> the price level to $P =$ _____ in the long run.

e. Now suppose that the money supply decreases to 500, as in Exercise 1g. This will shift the aggregate demand curve to the right/left. Draw AD_3 from Exercise 1h on Graph 9-2 and label the new long-run equilibrium levels of output and prices Y_3 and P_3, respectively.

f. A decrease in the money supply or a(n) increase/decrease in the velocity of money will increase/not change/decrease the aggregate price level in the long run, while it will increase/not change/decrease real GDP in the long run. Once again, this occurs because, in the long run, wages and prices increase or decrease in order to maintain output at its natural-rate level.

3. **The Short-Run Aggregate Supply Curve and the Transition to the Long Run** *In this exercise, we introduce the short-run aggregate supply curve and discuss both the short-run and long-run effects of shifts in aggregate demand.*

a. Suppose that the economy is operating at its natural rate when $Y = 2,000$, as in Exercise 2. In the long run, wages and prices are completely flexible, and $Y =$

_____. Redraw the long-run aggregate supply curve on Graph 9-3.

Graph 9-3

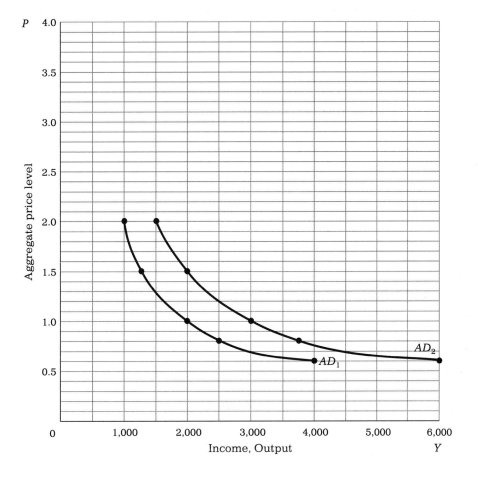

b. In the short run, output may deviate from its natural-rate level because short-run wages and prices are sticky/flexible. Chapter 9 of the textbook describes the extreme example in which all prices are completely rigid in the short run. For simplicity, assume that the price level is fixed in the short run at $P = 1.0$, regardless of the level of output. This means that firms will supply whatever amount of output is demanded at a constant price in the short run. Draw this short-run aggregate supply curve on Graph 9-3 and label it $SRAS_1$.

c. In Graph 9-3 we have also drawn AD_1 and AD_2 from Exercises 1 and 2. (We have smoothed the edges of these curves to make them more accurate.) Locate the initial equilibrium on AD_1 and label it Point A.

d. Now suppose that the money supply increases to $M = 1,500$, while V remains equal to 2.0. As before, the aggregate demand curve shifts right/left to AD_2.

e. In the short run, the price level is fixed at $P = 1.0$ and the economy moves along $SRAS_1$. Consequently, in the short run, an increase in the money supply will increase/not change/decrease output and increase/not change/decrease the price level. Label this first short-run equilibrium following the increase in the money supply Point B. At Point B, $Y = $ _____ and $P = $ _____.

f. At Point B, output exceeds/is equal to/is less than its natural-rate level. Consequently, over time, wages and prices will increase/not change/decrease. Suppose that the price level then rises to 1.2, regardless of the level of output. Draw this new short-run aggregate supply curve on the graph, label it $SRAS_2$, and label this second short-run equilibrium Point C. At Point C, $Y = $ _____ and $P = $ _____.

g. At point C, output exceeds/is equal to/is less than its natural-rate level. Consequently, over time, wages and prices will increase/not change/decrease. As this occurs, the short-run aggregate supply curve will shift upward/not shift/shift downward. The price level will continue to rise until $Y = $ _____. This occurs when $P = $ _____. Draw the final short-run aggregate supply curve on Graph 9-3, label it $SRAS_F$ (for final), and label the final equilibrium Point F. Note that, like Point A, Point F represents both a short-run and a long-run equilibrium.

h. If we started again at Point A and decreased the money supply, output would increase/not change/decrease in the short run and the aggregate price level would increase/not change/decrease. Over time, however, the price level would increase/decrease as long as output remained greater than/equal to/less than its natural-rate level. This would gradually shift the $SRAS$ curve upward/downward until the economy reached long-run equilibrium at $Y = $ _____. The initial shift in the aggregate demand curve would also occur if velocity increased/decreased.

i. Thus, in the short run, a shift in the aggregate demand curve will primarily affect output/the price level. In the long run, a shift in the aggregate demand curve will primarily affect output/the price level.

4. **Supply Shocks** *In this exercise, we introduce supply shocks and analyze the short-run effects of stabilization policy.*

a. As stated in the textbook, events that change costs and prices irrespective of demand are called *supply shocks*. Droughts and OPEC oil price increases are examples of adverse supply shocks. Starting from the initial equilibrium depicted below, an adverse supply shock would shift the short-run aggregate supply curve upward/downward. Draw this new curve on Graph 9-4 and label it $SRAS_2$. Locate the new short-run levels of output and prices if no change in economic policy is enacted, and label them Y' and P', respectively.

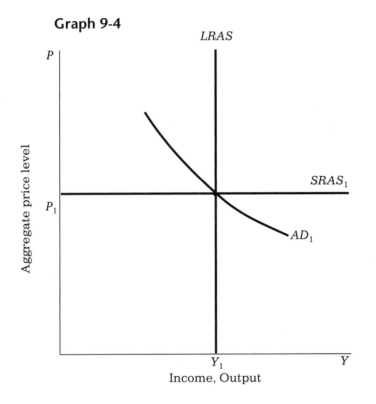

Graph 9-4

b. If no change in economic policy is enacted, an adverse supply shock will increase/not change/decrease output and increase/not change/decrease the aggregate price level in the short run, a phenomenon that is sometimes called

_____.

c. If, on the other hand, the Bank of Canada wishes to keep output from changing, it can increase/decrease the money supply and shift the aggregate demand curve to the right/left. This is called *accommodating policy*. Illustrate this option on Graph 9-4 by drawing the appropriate aggregate demand curve and labeling it AD_2.

d. The advantage of this option is that output will be higher/lower than it would have been if the Bank of Canada had done nothing. The drawback is that the price level will be permanently higher/lower than it would have been if the Bank of Canada had done nothing.

e. In the event of a beneficial supply shock such as a(n) increase/decrease in oil prices or a good harvest, we have the best of both worlds in the short run even if the Bank of Canada doesn't respond: a(n) higher/unchanged/lower price level and a(n) higher/unchanged/lower level of output.

Problems

Answer the following problems on a separate sheet of paper.

1. **a.** During the Depression, the U.S. central bank, the Federal Reserve, enacted policies that *reduced* the money supply. Sketch a graph and on it indicate what this would do to the aggregate demand and aggregate supply curves in the short run if output were originally at its natural rate. What would happen to output and the aggregate price level in the short run?

   b. On the same graph, indicate what would happen to the short-run aggregate supply and aggregate demand curves over time if there were no further reductions in the money supply. Consequently, what would happen to output and the price level over time?

   c. What is the effect of this policy on output and the price level in the long run?

2. Totally differentiate the quantity equation and derive the slope of the aggregate demand curve.

3. Almost all economists agree that wages and prices are flexible in the long run and that real GDP moves toward its natural rate. The speed with which this occurs, however, is a subject of considerable debate. Some economists believe that sticky wages and prices make the movement back to the natural rate a long, protracted process, while others believe that wages and prices are sufficiently flexible to move the economy rapidly to its natural rate. What do you suppose economists who believe that the natural-rate level is achieved very slowly think about the importance of stabilization policies? Why? What do you suppose economists who believe that the natural rate is achieved rapidly think about stabilization policies? Why?

4. Suppose the OPEC suddenly collapsed and oil prices plummeted. Indicate what would happen to the short-run aggregate supply and aggregate demand curves, output, and the aggregate price level.

5. **a.** Suppose velocity is stable. What would the Bank of Canada need to know in order to keep output at its natural-rate level following a supply shock?

   b. Assume that velocity is unstable and unpredictable. How would this complicate the Bank of Canada's ability to stabilize the economy following a supply shock?

Questions to Think About

1. **a.** In what kinds of markets and for what kinds of commodities do you think prices are very sticky in the short run?

    b. In what kinds of markets and for what kinds of commodities do you think prices are fairly flexible in the short run?

2. Who benefits from wage and price stickiness? Who is harmed? Why?

Aggregate Demand I

Fill-in Questions

Use the key terms below to fill in the blanks in the following statements. Each term may be used more than once.

actual expenditure   *LM* curve
IS curve   multiplier
Keynesian cross   planned expenditure
liquidity preference theory

1. _____ is the amount households, firms, and the government spend on goods and services. _____ is the amount households, firms, and the government would like to spend on goods and services. In equilibrium, the two are equal.

2. In the _____ model, the equilibrium level of income is determined by the intersection of the planned expenditure curve and the actual expenditure curve.

3. In the _____ model, every $1 increase in government purchases increases equilibrium income by $1 times the government-purchases _____.

4. The _____ shows the relationship between the interest rate and the level of income at which planned expenditure is equal to actual expenditure.

5. The _____ illustrates the combinations of income and interest rates at which real money supply is equal to real money demand.

6. A change in fiscal policy will shift the _____; a change in monetary policy will shift the _____.

7. According to the _____, people wish to hold a smaller quantity of real money balances when the interest rate increases.

Multiple-Choice Questions

1. If investment, taxes, and government purchases are held constant, the planned expenditure curve:
    a. slopes upward and its slope is equal to the *MPC*.
    b. slopes downward and its slope is equal to the *MPC*.
    c. is a 45-degree line.
    d. is a vertical line.

2. In the Keynesian cross model, the 45-degree line indicates that:
    a. GDP rises whenever consumption rises.
    b. actual expenditure is always equal to income.
    c. the equilibrium level of income increases whenever actual income increases.
    d. all of the above.

3. At the equilibrium level of income:
    a. unintended inventory accumulation is equal to zero.
    b. planned expenditure is equal to actual expenditure.
    c. there is no tendency for GDP to change.
    d. all of the above.

4. If income exceeds planned expenditure, firms will cut back production because unplanned inventory accumulation will be:
    a. positive.
    b. negative.
    c. zero.
    d. indeterminate.

5. If the consumption function is $C = 100 + 0.8(Y - T)$, the government-purchases multiplier is:
    a. 0.8.
    b. 1.25.
    c. 4.
    d. 5.

6. If the consumption function is $C = 100 + 0.8(Y - T)$ and taxes decrease by $1, the equilibrium level of income will:
    a. decrease by $5.
    b. decrease by $4.
    c. increase by $5.
    d. increase by $4.

7. If the consumption function is $C = 100 + 0.8(Y - T)$ and both taxes and government purchases increase by $1, the equilibrium level of income will:
    a. remain constant.
    b. increase by $3.
    c. increase by $1.
    d. decrease by $4.

8. The FALSE statement below is:

   a. a decrease in the interest rate increases planned investment.

   b. a decrease in the interest rate shifts the planned expenditure curve upward.

   c. a decrease in the interest rate shifts the *IS* curve to the right.

   d. as the interest rate falls, planned expenditure is equal to actual expenditure at a higher level of income.

9. An increase of $1 in government purchases will:

   a. shift the planned expenditure curve upward by $1.

   b. shift the IS curve to the right by $[1/(1 - MPC)]$.

   c. not shift the *LM* curve.

   d. all of the above.

10. According to the loanable funds interpretation of the *IS* curve:

    a. firms want to invest more as their income rises.

    b. banks want to lend more as the interest rate rises.

    c. an increase in income raises saving and lowers the interest rate that equilibrates the supply of and demand for loanable funds.

    d. all of the above.

11. A decrease in taxes will shift the planned expenditure curve _____ and the *IS* curve to the _____.

    a. upward; left

    b. upward; right

    c. downward; left

    d. downward; right

12. The following statement about the *LM* curve is TRUE:

    a. the *LM* curve slopes upward and it is drawn for a given level of income.

    b. the *LM* curve slopes downward and an increase in price shifts it upward.

    c. the *LM* curve slopes upward and it is drawn for a given supply of real money balances.

    d. along the *LM* curve, actual expenditure is equal to planned expenditure.

13. An increase in the money supply shifts the:

    a. *LM* curve upward (to the left).

    b. *LM* curve downward (to the right).

    c. *IS* curve to the right.

    d. *IS* curve to the left.

14. According to the quantity equation $MV = PY$, if velocity is constant, the:

    a. *LM* curve will slope upward.

    b. *LM* curve will slope downward.

    c. *LM* curve will be horizontal.

    d. *LM* curve will be vertical.

15. A normal *LM* curve can be derived from the quantity equation if it is assumed that:

    a. a higher interest rate reduces money demand and raises velocity.

    b. a higher interest rate reduces both money demand and velocity.

    c. velocity is constant.

    d. the price level is constant.

16. At the intersection of the IS and LM curves:

    a. actual expenditure is equal to planned expenditure.

    b. real money supply is equal to real money demand.

    c. the levels of Y and r satisfy both the goods market equilibrium condition and the money market equilibrium condition.

    d. all of the above.

17. Tax cuts do all of the following EXCEPT:

    a. stimulate aggregate demand by raising households' disposable income.

    b. reduce the government budget deficit.

    c. stimulate aggregate supply by improving workers' incentives.

    d. increase output in the short run.

18. Chapters 4 and 10 indicate that an increase in the money supply:

    a. reduces the nominal interest rate in the short run.

    b. increases the nominal interest rate in the long run.

    c. does not affect the real interest rate in the long run.

    d. does all of the above.

Exercises

1. **The Keynesian Cross** *In this exercise, we illustrate the Keynesian cross using a simple model of a closed economy.*

    a. Consider the following model of the economy (in billions of dollars):

    $$Y = C + I + G. \tag{10-1}$$

    $$C = C(Y - T) = 125 + 0.75(Y - T). \tag{10-2}$$

    $$I = \bar{I} = 100. \tag{10-3}$$

    $$G = \overline{G} = 150. \tag{10-4}$$

    $$T = \overline{T} = 100. \tag{10-5}$$

    The *MPC* is defined as _____.

    The value of the *MPC* in this model = _____. If consumption were graphed as a function of disposable income $(Y - T)$, as is done in Chapter 3 of the textbook, the *y* intercept, which is the value of the variable depicted on the vertical axis when the value of the variable depicted on the horizontal axis is 0, would equal _____. The slope of the curve would equal

    _____.

b. Now, however, consumption will be graphed as a function of Y, rather than of $(Y - T)$. Substituting $T = 100$ into the equation, we obtain

$$C = 125 + 0.75\ (Y - 100),\ \text{or}$$
$$C = \underline{\hspace{1.5cm}} + \underline{\hspace{1.5cm}} Y.$$

Use this information to plot and draw the consumption expenditure curve on Graph 10-1 and label it C.

Graph 10-1

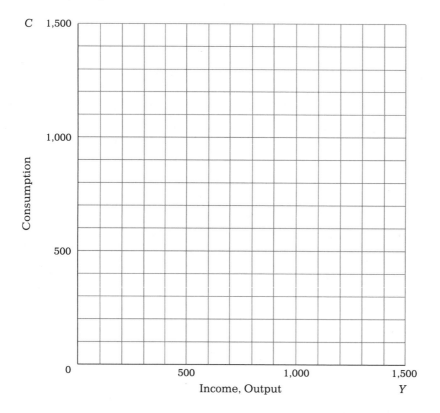

The y intercept of this consumption expenditure curve, which is the value of consumption when income $Y = 0$, is _____, and the slope is _____. When we draw consumption as a function of income Y, note that the y intercept differs from when we draw consumption as a function of disposable income $Y - T$, as you can see by comparing your answers to those in Parts a and b. When $Y = 0$ and $T = 100$, $(Y - T) = $ _____, which is <u>greater than/less than/equal to</u> zero.

c. In this simple model, both planned investment and government purchases are constant and independent of the level of Y, that is, they are exogenous. Use the information from Part a to draw the relationship between planned investment and Y on Graph 10-2, and label it I. Draw the relationship between government purchases and Y on Graph 10-3 and label it G.

Graph 10-2

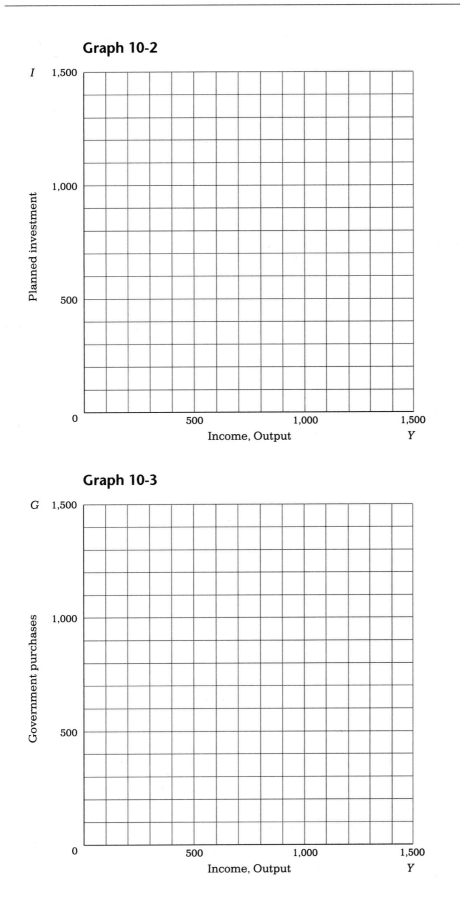

Graph 10-3

d. Recall that total planned expenditure *PE* is equal to $C + I + G$. Use the information from Graphs 10-1, 10-2, and 10-3 to draw the planned expenditure curve on Graph 10-4. Label your curve *PE*.

Graph 10-4

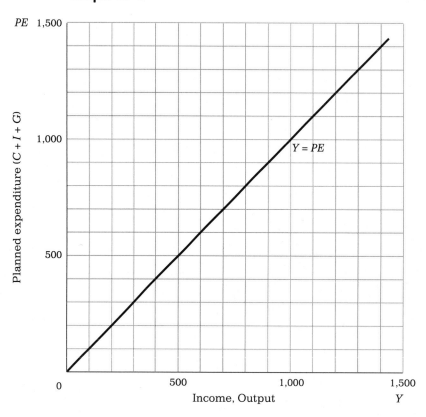

e. The value of the *y* intercept on Graph 10-4 is equal to the level of planned expenditure when $Y = 0$. This value is equal to the level of consumption when $Y = 0$, plus the level of planned investment when $Y = 0$, plus the level of government purchases when $Y = 0$. This value is equal to _____ + _____ + _____ = _____. Similarly, the numerical value of the slope of the planned expenditure curve on Graph 10-4 is equal to the slope of the consumption function curve, plus the slope of the planned investment curve, plus the slope of the government-purchases curve, or _____ + _____ + _____ = _____.

f. Since $E = C + I + G$, the equation for the planned expenditure curve can be derived by adding together the equations for C, I, and G. Thus,

$$PE = 125 + 0.75(Y - T) + I + G. \qquad \text{(10-6)}$$

Substituting the exogenous values of T, I, and G into this equation, we get

$$PE = 125 + 0.75(Y - 100) + 100 + 150.$$

This equation can be simplified to

$$PE = \underline{\hspace{1.5cm}} + \underline{\hspace{1.5cm}} Y. \qquad \text{(10-7)}$$

g. Equation 10-7 will yield values of planned expenditure PE for any value of Y. The equilibrium, however, occurs only along the 45-degree line labeled $Y = PE$ on Graph 10-4. Only along this curve will income (or output) equal planned expenditure. The slope of this 45-degree line is \underline{\hspace{4cm}}. Solve for the equilibrium level of income in this model by setting $Y = PE = 300 + 0.75Y$ and solving for Y.

$Y = $ \underline{\hspace{5cm}}.

On Graph 10-4, label this initial equilibrium Y_1.

h. If income (output) exceeds planned expenditure, there will be unplanned investment in the form of unplanned inventory accumulation. For example, if $Y = 1,600$, planned expenditure PE will equal $300 + 0.75(1,600) = $ \underline{\hspace{4cm}}. Consequently, the level of unplanned inventory accumulation will equal $Y - PE = 1,600 - $ \underline{\hspace{4cm}} $=$ \underline{\hspace{4cm}}. As inventories increase, firms will <u>hire/lay off</u> workers and <u>increase/decrease</u> production. As a result, Y will <u>rise/fall</u> until equilibrium is reached at $Y = $ \underline{\hspace{4cm}}. When this equilibrium is reached, unplanned inventory investment will equal \underline{\hspace{4cm}}.

i. Conversely, when Y is less than planned expenditure, inventories will fall. For example, if $Y = 1,000$, planned expenditure PE will equal $300 + 0.75(1,000) =$ _____. Consequently, the level of unplanned inventory accumulation will equal $Y - PE = 1,000 -$ _____ $=$ _____. As inventories decrease, firms will <u>hire more/lay off</u> workers and <u>increase/decrease</u> production. As a result, Y will <u>rise/fall</u> until an equilibrium is reached at $Y =$ _____. When this equilibrium is reached, unplanned inventory investment will equal _____.

2. **The Government-Purchases Multiplier** *In this exercise, we derive and graphically illustrate the government-purchases multiplier.*

Assume the same information as in Exercise 1 (again, in billions of dollars):

$$Y = C + I + G \tag{10-8}$$
$$C = C(Y - T) = 125 + 0.75(Y - T) \tag{10-9}$$
$$I = \bar{I} = 100 \tag{10-10}$$
$$G = \bar{G} = 150 \tag{10-11}$$
$$T = \bar{T} = 100. \tag{10-12}$$

The initial equilibrium is depicted on Graph 10-5.

Graph 10-5

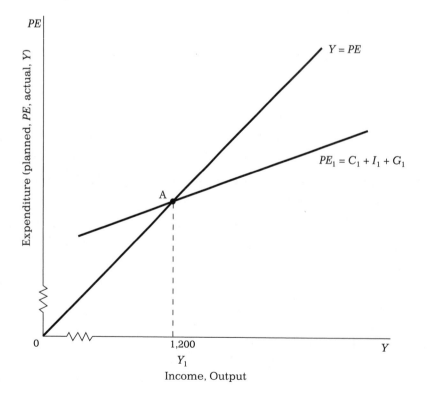

a. The initial level of government purchases is _____. This is illustrated by the curve G_1 on Graph 10-6.

Graph 10-6

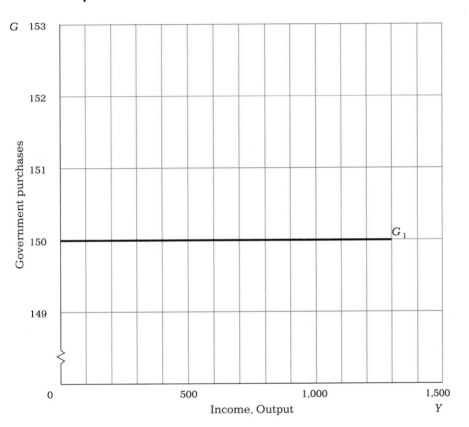

Suppose that the government decides to purchase two new aircraft at a total cost of $1 billion. Consequently, government purchases G will rise at all levels of Y to _____. This will shift the whole government purchases curve on Graph 10-6 upward by _____. Plot and draw this new curve on Graph 10-6 and label it G_2.

b. Since taxes T and planned investment I have not changed, the consumption and investment functions on Graphs 10-1 and 10-2 in Exercise 1 will not shift. Consequently, the planned expenditure curve $PE = C + I + G$ will shift upward by _____. Plot and draw the new planned expenditure curve on Graph 10-5 and label it PE_2.

c. As in Exercise 1f, the equation for the new planned expenditure curve PE_2 can be derived by adding together the equations for C, I, and G. Thus,

$$PE_2 = 125 + 0.75(Y - T) + I + G_2.$$

Substituting the same values of T and I but the new value of G into this equation, we get

$$PE_2 = 125 + 0.75(Y - 100) + 100 + 151.$$

This can be simplified to

$$PE_2 = \underline{\hspace{5cm}} + \underline{\hspace{5cm}} Y.$$

d. It is tempting to say that the $1 billion increase in government purchases will increase the equilibrium level of income by $1 billion, but this would be incorrect. As government purchases increase, Y increases. This, in turn, increases disposable income and the level of consumption. Consequently, Y will increase by more than $1 billion. Recall that in equilibrium, planned expenditure is equal to income (that is, $PE = Y$). Calculate the new equilibrium level of income by setting the equation for PE_2 in Part c equal to Y and solving for Y.

$$PE_2 = \underline{\hspace{4cm}} + \underline{\hspace{4cm}} Y = Y.$$

$$Y = \underline{\hspace{4cm}}.$$

On Graph 10-5, label the equilibrium Point B and label the new equilibrium level of output Y_2.

e. From Part d we see that an increase in government purchases of $1 billion leads to a $_____ billion increase in national income and output. This value is equal to the increase in government purchases multiplied by the government-purchases multiplier, where the latter is defined as $\Delta Y/\Delta G$. In this model, the multiplier equals $1/(1 - MPC)$.

f. The theory behind the government-purchases multiplier can be seen by completing Table 10-1 (sometimes called the *round-by-round story*).

Table 10-1

	Change in $Y = C + I + G$
Round 1	
G rises by $1 billion as the government purchases new aircraft. Y rises immediately by . . .	+ $1 billion
Round 2	
The total disposable income of workers, suppliers, and owners at Boeing Corporation (the producer of the aircraft) rises by $1 billion. Consequently, their total consumption rises by $MPC \times$ ($1 billion). As new goods (Chevrolet automobiles, for example) are produced to meet this increase in consumption demand, Y rises by . . .	+ $$MPC$ billion
Round 3	
The total disposable income of workers, suppliers, and owners at General Motors Corporation rises by $$MPC$ billion. Thus, their total consumption rises by $MPC(MPC \times$ $1 billion$) = $$_____ billion. As new goods (for example, Levi's jeans) are produced, Y rises by . . .	+ $ _____ billion
Round 4	
The total disposable income of workers, suppliers, and owners at Levi Strauss & Co. rises by $$MPC^2$ billion. Consequently, their total consumption rises by $MPC($$MPC^2 \times$ $1 billion$) = $$_____ billion. As new goods are produced, Y rises by . . .	+ $_____ billion

The total change in Y is equal to the sum of all the changes resulting from each round. Since $MPC < 1$, the increase in Y from each successive round becomes smaller and smaller and eventually approaches zero. The sum of all of these increments is equal to $1 + MPC + MPC^2 + MPC^3 + MPC^4 + MPC^5 + . . . = 1/(1 - MPC)$. Since the MPC in our model = _____, the government-purchases multiplier = $1/(1 -$ _____$) =$ _____.

3. **The Tax Multiplier** *In this exercise, we derive and graphically illustrate the tax multiplier and, in Part g, the balanced-budget multiplier.*

Assume the same information as in Exercise 2 (again in billions of dollars): The initial equilibrium is illustrated on Graph 10-7.

$$Y = C + I + G \tag{10-13}$$

$$C = C(Y - T) = 125 + 0.75(Y - T) \tag{10-14}$$

$$I = \bar{I} = 100 \tag{10-15}$$

$$G = \bar{G} = 150 \tag{10-16}$$

$$T = \bar{T} = 100. \tag{10-17}$$

Graph 10-7

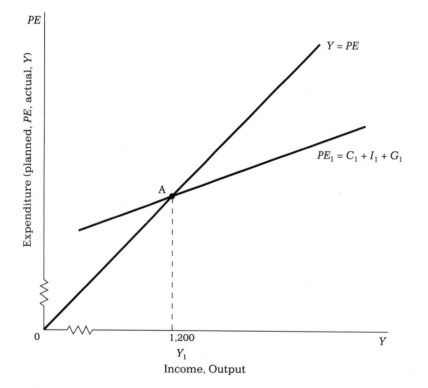

a. Suppose that the government decides to decrease taxes by $1 billion by decreasing tax revenues or by increasing transfer payments. Since disposable income equals $Y - T$, this tax decrease will increase the level of disposable income at every level of Y by $1 billion. Consequently, consumption will increase by $MPC \times$ $1 billion at each level of Y. (Reread the last two sentences carefully.) As a result, the consumption expenditure curve on Graph 10-8 will shift upward from C_1 to C_3 by $$MPC$ billion. Since MPC = _____, the consumption expenditure curve will shift up by $_____ billion.

Graph 10-8

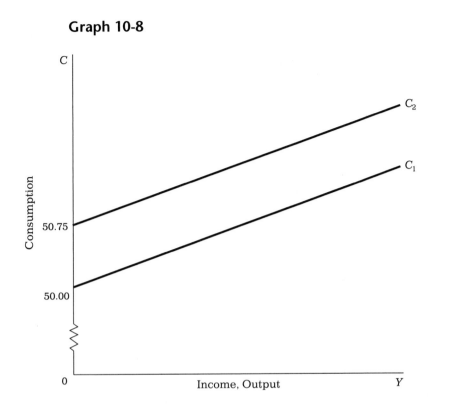

Neither government purchases nor planned investment has changed, so the I and G curves will be the same as in Graphs 10-2 and 10-3. Since $PE = C + I + G$ and $MPC = 0.75$, the \$1 billion tax reduction will shift the planned expenditure curve upward by \$ _____ billion. Plot and draw the new planned expenditure curve on Graph 10-7 and label it PE_3.

b. Once again, the equation for the new planned expenditure curve PE_3 can be derived by adding together the equations for C, I, and G. Thus,

$$PE_3 = 125 + 0.75(Y - T) + I + G.$$

Substituting the same values of I and G but the new value of T into this equation, we get

$$PE_3 = 125 + 0.75(Y - 99) + 100 + 150.$$

This can be simplified to

$PE_3 =$ _____ + _____ Y.

c. Calculate the new equilibrium level of income by setting the equation for PE_3 in Part b equal to Y and then solving for Y.

$PE_3 =$ _____ + _____$Y = Y.$

$Y =$ _____. On Graph 10-7, label the new equilibrium Point C and label the new equilibrium level of output Y_3.

d. From Part c, we see that a $1 billion reduction in taxes leads to a

$\$$_____ billion increase in national income and output. This is equal to the decrease in taxes ($1 billion) multiplied by the tax multiplier, where the latter is equal to $MPC/(1 - MPC)$.

e. Complete Table 10-2 to see the rationale behind the tax multiplier.

Table 10-2

	Change in $Y = C + I + G$
Round 1 T falls by $1 billion. Disposable income rises by $1 billion and consumption rises by $MPC \times \$1$ billion. As new goods (Chevrolet automobiles) are produced, Y rises by . . .	$+ \$MPC$ billion
Round 2 The total disposable income of workers, suppliers, and owners at General Motors Corporation rises by $\$MPC$ billion. Thus, their total consumption rises by $MPC(MPC \times \$1$ billion$) = \$$_____ billion. As new goods (Levi's jeans) are produced, Y rises by . . .	$+ \$$_____ billion
Round 3 The total disposable income of workers, suppliers, and owners at Levi Strauss & Co. rises by $\$MPC^2$ billion. Consequently, their total consumption rises by $MPC(\$MPC^2$ billion$) = \$$_____. As new goods are produced, Y rises by . . .	$+ \$$_____ billion

---

The total change in Y is equal to the sum of all the changes resulting from each round. As Chapter 10 of the textbook illustrates, the sum of all these increments is equal to $MPC + MPC^2 + MPC^3 + MPC^4 + MPC^5 + . . . = MPC/(1 - MPC)$. Since the MPC in our model = _____, $MPC/(1 - MPC) =$

_____$/(1 -$ _____$) =$

_____.

f. Compare the algebraic expression for the tax multiplier in Part e with the algebraic expression for the government-purchases multiplier in Exercise 2f. Note that the tax multiplier is equal to the government-purchases multiplier minus 1, which equals

$[1/(1 - MPC)] - 1 = [1 - (1 - MPC)]/(1 - MPC) = $ _____.

Examine the two round-by-round stories in Tables 10-1 and 10-2. Note that the only difference between the effects of an increase in government purchases and the effects of an equal decrease in taxes on Y is that the (direct) Round 1 effect of the increase in government purchases does not occur when taxes are reduced.

g. Now suppose that both government purchases and taxes were simultaneously increased by $1 billion. Since the government budget surplus would remain unchanged, this policy is sometimes called a *balanced-budget change* in G and T. The $1 billion increase in G would shift the planned expenditure curve upward/downward by $_____ billion, while the $1 billion increase in T would shift the planned expenditure upward/downward by $_____ billion. Consequently, the combined policy changes would shift the planned expenditure curve upward/downward by $_____ billion, and the equilibrium level of Y would rise/fall/remain constant. This occurs because an increase in G has a larger/smaller effect on Y than an equal reduction in taxes, just as Tables 10-1 and 10-2 indicated. In Exercise 2, an increase in government expenditures of $1 billion increased the equilibrium level of Y by $_____ billion. In Exercise 3, a reduction in taxes of $1 billion increased the equilibrium level of Y by $_____ billion. Reversing this second result, a $1 billion increase in taxes would increase/decrease the equilibrium level of Y by $_____ billion. Thus, a simultaneous increase in both G and T by $1 billion will increase/decrease the equilibrium level of Y by $_____ billion.

4. **The IS Curve** *In this exercise, we use a simple model of the economy to derive the IS curve and we discuss the parameters that affect its slope.*

Consider the following model of the economy (in billions of dollars):

$$Y = C + I + G \qquad\qquad\qquad\qquad \text{(10-18)}$$
$$C = C(Y - T) = 125 + 0.75(Y - T) \qquad \text{(10-19)}$$
$$I = 200 - 10r \qquad\qquad\qquad\qquad \text{(10-20)}$$
$$G = \overline{G} = 150 \qquad\qquad\qquad\qquad \text{(10-21)}$$
$$T = \overline{T} = 100. \qquad\qquad\qquad\qquad \text{(10-22)}$$

a. Note that this model is identical to the one used in Exercises 1–3, except that planned investment now depends on the interest rate. For each percentage point increase in the real interest rate r, planned investment falls by
_____. Now use the new investment equation to complete Column 2 in Table 10-3. Plot the data from Columns 1 and 2 on Graph 10-9, draw this investment curve, and label it I.

Table 10-3

(1) Interest Rate (%)	(2) Planned Investment	(3) Equilibrium Level of Income
0	_____	_____
5	_____	_____
10	100	1,200
15	_____	_____
20	_____	_____

Graph 10-9

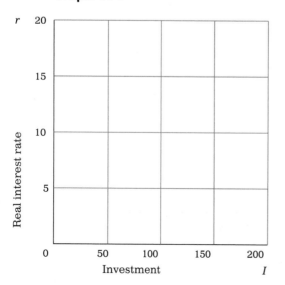

b. From Table 10-3, note that when $r = 10$, $I = 100$, and the equilibrium level of Y is the same as in Exercise 1. The equilibrium level of Y can be computed for other values of the interest rate in two ways. First, recall that total planned expenditure PE is equal to $C + I + G$. Now use the new equation for investment, along with the initial levels of T and G (which have not changed), and solve for PE in terms of Y and r:

$$PE = 125 + 0.75(Y - 100) + (200 - 10r) + 150.$$

$PE = $ _____ + _____ $Y - $

_____ r.

c. Next, recall that the equilibrium level of Y is defined as the level of Y at which income Y is equal to total planned expenditure PE. Calculate the new equilibrium level of income by setting the equation for PE in Part b equal to Y and solving for Y. Note that the equilibrium Y will be a function of r:

$PE = $ _____ + _____ $Y - $

_____ $r = Y$.

$Y = $ _____ $-$ _____ r.

Use this equation to complete Column 3 of Table 10-3.

d. Alternatively, the remaining equilibrium values of Y can be computed using the multiplier analysis derived in Exercise 2. The initial equilibrium is illustrated on Graph 10-10. When $r = 10$ percent, $I =$ _____, the planned expenditure curve is PE_1, and $Y =$ _____.

Graph 10-10

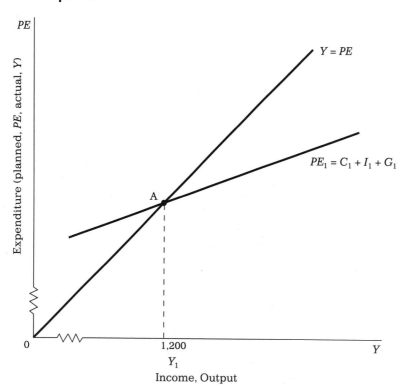

e. If r falls by 5 percentage points to 5 percent, I increases by $5(10) =$ _____. As a result, the planned expenditure curve PE would shift upward by _____. Draw the new planned expenditure curve on Graph 10-10 and label it PE_2. Since this shift is the same as one that would follow an increase in government purchases of _____, the multiplier effects on consumption will be the same, and the government-purchases multiplier can be used to calculate the change in Y. Thus, the change in Y will equal the increase in investment multiplied by the government-purchases multiplier, or

$$\text{Change in } Y = \underline{\quad\quad} \times 1/(1 - MPC).$$

Since $MPC =$ _____, the numerical value for the

Change in $Y =$ _____ $\times 1/(1 -$ _____$) =$ _____.

This should be the same as the change indicated in Table 10-3.

f. The *IS* curve depicts the relationship between the interest rate *r* and the equilibrium value of income from the investment function and the Keynesian cross. (This is sometimes called the equilibrium in the goods market.) Reexamine Table 10-3 and note that as the interest rate falls, the level of planned investment falls/rises/remains the same. This shifts the planned expenditure curve upward/downward by the same amount as the increase in planned investment. Finally, the equilibrium level of income *Y* rises by the increase in planned investment multiplied by the government-purchases multiplier. This shift occurs because *Y* rises by the initial increase in investment plus the multiplier effects on consumption.

g. Use the data in Columns 1 and 3 of Table 10-3 to plot and draw the *IS* curve on Graph 10-11 (label the curve *IS*). Reread Part f to make sure that you understand how the *IS* curve is derived.

Graph 10-11

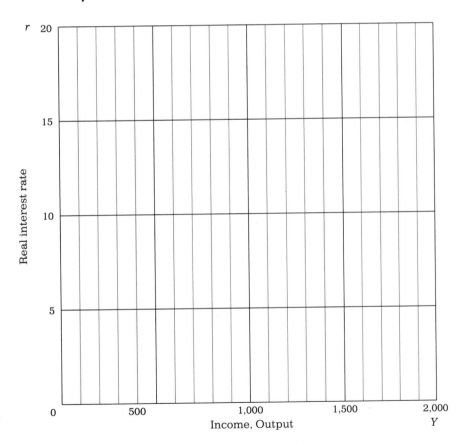

5. **Fiscal Policy and the *IS* Curve** *In this exercise, we show how changes in fiscal policy shift the* IS *curve.*

a. Consider the same model of the economy as in Exercise 4 (in billions of dollars), in which planned investment depends on the interest rate:

$$Y = C + I + G \tag{10-23}$$
$$C = C(Y - T) = 125 + 0.75(Y - T) \tag{10-24}$$
$$I = 200 - 10r \tag{10-25}$$
$$G = \overline{G} = 150 \tag{10-26}$$
$$T = \overline{T} = 100. \tag{10-27}$$

As we saw in Exercise 4, when $r = 10$, $I =$ _____ and $Y =$ _____. This original equilibrium is illustrated on Graphs 10-12 and 10-13.

Suppose that government purchases now increase by $1 billion to $151 billion, as in Exercise 2. If the interest rate remains equal to 10 percent, then investment is unchanged, the planned expenditure curve shifts upward by $1 billion, and the equilibrium level of Y rises by $1 billion multiplied by the government-purchases multiplier, which equals $1 billion $\times 1/(1 - MPC)$.

Thus, if the interest rate remains equal to 10 percent and $MPC = 0.75$, the equilibrium level of Y rises by $1 billion $\times 1/(1 -$ _____ $) =$ $ _____ billion. The new equilibrium level of $Y =$ _____.

b. Draw the new planned expenditure curve on Graph 10-12, label it $PE_2(r = 10)$, and illustrate the change in Y if r remains constant. Note that the scales of the x and y axes have been broken so that a small shift in the expenditure curve and a small change in Y will be noticeable.

c. This change can also be depicted on Graph 10-13 by a shift in the *IS* curve to the <u>right/left</u>. The amount of the horizontal shift measures the change in Y if r remains constant. Given the answer to Part b, the horizontal shift in the *IS* curve must equal $1 billion $\times 1/(1 - MPC) =$ $_____ billion. Draw the new *IS* curve on Graph 10-13, and label it IS_2.

d. Thus, an increase in government purchases will shift the *IS* curve to the <u>right/left</u> by the change in government purchases multiplied by the government-purchases multiplier. Conversely, a decrease in government purchases will shift the *IS* curve to the <u>right/left</u> by the change in government purchases multiplied by the _____.

Graph 10-12

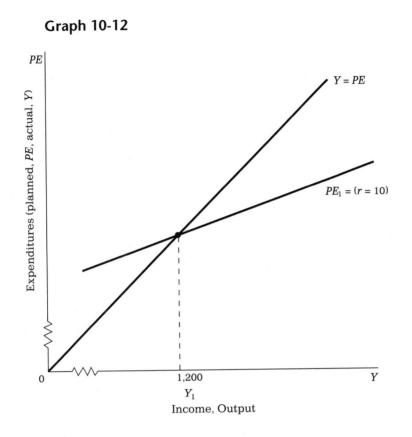

Graph 10-13

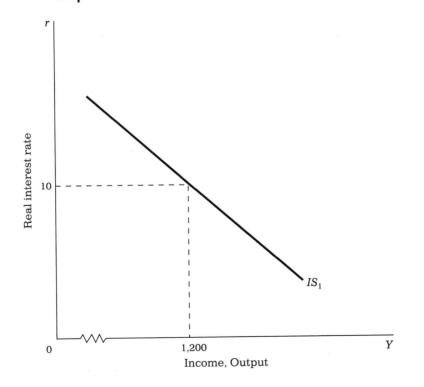

e. The government-purchases multiplier equals $1/(1 - MPC)$. As the MPC gets larger, the denominator gets larger/smaller and the value of the multiplier gets larger/smaller. Consequently, as the MPC gets larger, the horizontal shift in the IS curve following a change in government purchases gets larger/smaller. Therefore, as the MPC gets larger, the round-by-round multiplier effects depicted in Table 10-1 become larger/smaller, and the change in the equilibrium level of Y becomes larger/smaller.

f. Now assume that $G = 150$ and that taxes fall by $1 billion. In Exercises 3a and d, it was shown that the planned expenditure curve would shift upward by $MPC billion, and Y would increase by the reduction in taxes ($1 billion) multiplied by the tax multiplier $MPC/(1 - MPC)$, or by $MPC/(1 - MPC) billion. Thus, if the interest rate remains equal to 10 percent and $MPC = 0.75$, the equilibrium level of Y rises by $_____ billion $\times$ _____/(1 - _____) = _____ billion. The new equilibrium level of $Y = $ _____.

Draw the new planned expenditure curve on Graph 10-14, label it PE_3 $(r = 10)$, and indicate the change in Y if r remains constant.

g. This change can be depicted on Graph 10-15 by a shift in the IS curve to the right/left. The amount of the horizontal shift measures the change in Y if r remains constant. Given your answer to Part f, the horizontal shift in the IS curve must equal $1 billion $\times MPC/(1 - MPC)$. If $MPC = 0.75$, this is equal to $_____ billion. Draw the new IS curve on Graph 10-15 and label it IS_3.

h. Thus, a decrease in taxes (resulting from either a reduction in taxes or an increase in government transfers) will shift the IS curve to the right/left by the decrease in taxes multiplied by the tax multiplier. Conversely, an increase in taxes will shift the IS curve to the right/left by the change in taxes multiplied by the _____.

i. The tax multiplier equals $MPC/(1 - MPC)$. As the MPC gets larger, the numerator gets larger/smaller and the denominator gets larger/smaller. Consequently, the tax multiplier gets larger/smaller. Thus, as the MPC gets larger, the horizontal shift in the IS curve following a change in taxes would get larger/smaller. As the MPC gets larger, the round-by-round multiplier effects depicted in Table 10-2 become larger/smaller, and the change in the equilibrium level of Y becomes larger/smaller. Consequently, a larger MPC implies a flatter/steeper IS curve.

Graph 10-14

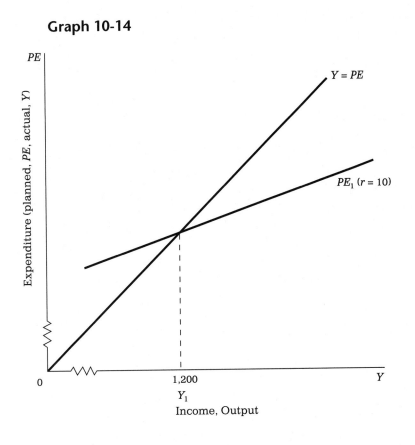

Graph 10-15

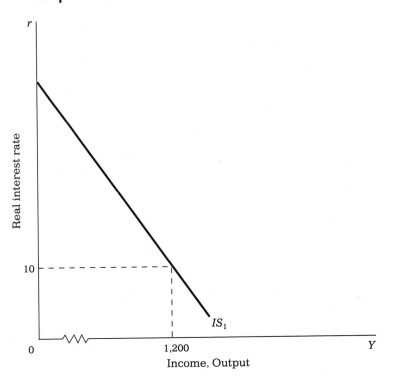

6. **The *LM* Curve** *In this exercise, we use the money supply/money demand diagram to derive the* LM *curve.*

a. Suppose that the following equation (in billions of dollars) describes the supply of real money balances:

$$(M^s/P) = \overline{M}/\overline{P} = 800/1.0 = 800. \tag{10-28}$$

This equation states that the Bank of Canada has fixed the nominal money supply at $M = 800$, and the price level is fixed at $\overline{P} = 1.0$. Since the supply of real money balances is independent of the interest rate, it will be depicted as a vertical line. Draw this line on Graph 10-16 and label it $\overline{M}/\overline{P}$.

Graph 10-16

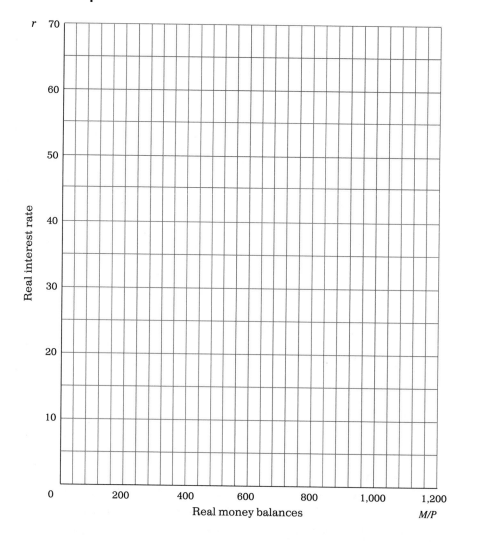

b. Suppose that the following equation describes the demand for real money balances:

$$(M/P)^d = L(r, Y) = 0.8Y - 16r. \qquad \textbf{(10-29)}$$

This equation states that the demand for real money balances depends on the level of real income Y and the interest rate r. (In Chapter 10 of the textbook, footnote 5 notes that money demand actually depends on the nominal interest rate i, rather than on the real interest rate r, and that this difference will be explored more fully in Chapter 11.) Using Equation 10-29, complete Table 10-4.

Table 10-4

(1) Real Income Y	(2) Interest Rate r (%)	(3) Real Money Demand $(M/P)^d = 0.8Y - 16r$
1,100	55	_____
1,100	25	_____
1,100	10	_____
1,100	5	_____
1,100	0	_____

Plot these points on Graph 10-16, draw the resulting money demand curve, and label it $L(r, Y = 1,100)$.

c. From Graph 10-16 and Table 10-4, it can be seen that if real income $Y = 1,100$, the supply of real money balances is equal to the demand for real money balances when $r =$ _____ percent.

d. Now suppose that real income increases to $Y = 1,200$. Complete Table 10-5.

Table 10-5

(1) Real Income Y	(2) Interest Rate r (%)	(3) Real Money Demand $(M/P)^d = 0.8Y - 16r$
1,200	60	_____
1,200	50	_____
1,200	25	_____
1,200	10	_____
1,200	5	_____

Plot these points on Graph 10-16, draw the resulting money demand curve, and label it $L(r, Y = 1,200)$. When Y increases, the real money supply curve remains unchanged at $M/P = 800$, but the real money demand curve shifts to the left/right. Consequently, the interest rate at which the supply of real money balances is equal to the demand for real money balances rises/falls to $r =$ _____ percent.

e. Finally, suppose that real income increases to $Y = 1,400$. Complete Table 10-6.

Table 10-6

(1) Real Income Y	(2) Interest Rate r (%)	(3) Real Money Demand $(M/P)^d = 0.8Y - 16r$
1,400	70	_____
1,400	50	_____
1,400	25	_____
1,400	10	_____
1,400	0	_____

Plot these points on Graph 10-16, draw the resulting money demand curve, and label it $L(r, Y = 1,400)$. When Y increases again, the real money supply curve remains unchanged at $M/P = 800$, but the real money demand curve again shifts to the left/right. Consequently, the interest rate at which the supply of real money balances is equal to the demand for real money balances rises/falls to $r =$ _____.

f. The LM curve depicts the combinations of r and Y for which a given supply of real money balances is equal to real money demand. Throughout Exercise 6, the supply of real money balances has been fixed at $M/P =$ _____.
From Table 10-4, we learned that when $Y = 1,100$, real money supply equals real money demand at $r =$ _____. From Table 10-5, we learned that when $Y = 1,200$, real money supply equals real money demand at $r =$ _____. And from Table 10-6 and Graph 10-16, we learned that when $Y = 1,400$, real money supply equals real money demand at $r =$ _____. Plot and draw a curve for these three points on Graph 10-17 and label it LM_1.

g. Along each LM curve, a constant real money supply is equal to real money demand. As Y increases, real money demand will increase/decrease if the interest rate remains constant. Since the real money supply has remained unchanged, the interest rate must rise/fall to keep real money demand equal to the unchanged real money supply.

Graph 10-17

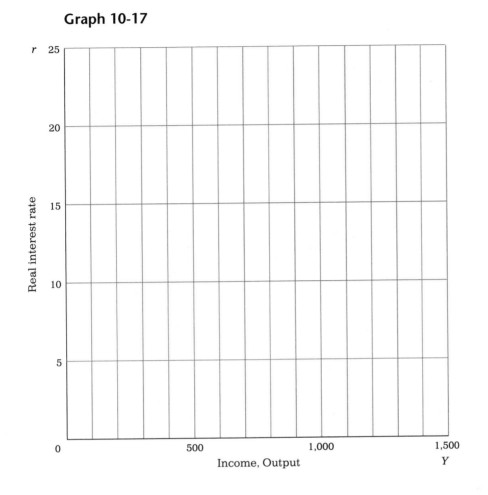

h. Now let us derive the equation for our *LM* curve. Along the LM_1 curve, the real money supply equals _____ and this value is equal to real money demand. Thus, along the LM_1 curve,

$$\overline{M}/\overline{P} = \text{_____} = 0.8Y - 16r.$$

Since *r* appears on the vertical axis on Graph 10-17, it is useful to rearrange this equation and solve for *r*.

$r =$ _____ + _____ Y.

The *y* intercept of this *LM* curve is _____ and the slope of the *LM* curve is _____ .

7. **Monetary Policy and the *LM* Curve** *In this exercise, we show how changes in monetary policy shift the LM curve.*

a. Refer to the initial money supply and money demand equations:

$$(M^s/P) = \overline{M}/\overline{P} = 800/1.0 = 800 \qquad \textbf{(10-30)}$$

$$(M/P)^d = 0.8Y - 16r. \qquad \textbf{(10-31)}$$

By setting money supply equal to money demand and solving for r, the equation for the *LM* curve in Exercise 6h can be derived:

$$r = \underline{\hspace{5cm}} + \underline{\hspace{5cm}} Y.$$

Draw the curve for this equation on Graph 10-18 and label it LM_1.

Graph 10-18

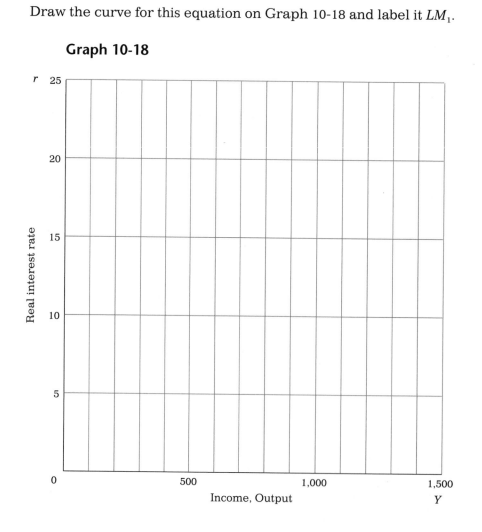

b. Following the example given in Chapter 10 of the textbook, suppose that the central bank decreased the money supply to $(M^s/P) = 640$. Set this new money supply equal to the money demand equation, Equation 10-31, and solve for r to derive the equation for the new LM curve.

$r =$ _____ $+$ _____ Y.

Plot and draw the new LM curve from this equation on Graph 10-18 and label it LM_2. The slope of LM_2 is <u>greater than/less than/equal to</u> the slope of LM_1. The y intercept of LM_2 is <u>greater than/less than</u> the y intercept of LM_1. (Be careful about your signs.) Consequently, a reduction in the real money supply will shift the LM curve to the <u>right (downward)/left (upward)</u>.

c. For the money market to remain in equilibrium, a reduction in the real money supply must be matched by an equal reduction in money demand. This match can be accomplished by a(n) <u>increase/decrease</u> in r at each level of Y and/or a(n) <u>increase/decrease</u> in Y at each level of r. Consequently, a decrease in the real money supply will shift the LM curve to the <u>right (downward)/left (upward)</u>. Conversely, an increase in the real money supply will shift the LM curve to the <u>right (downward)/left (upward)</u>.

8. **The Short-Run Equilibrium** *In this exercise, we use the models developed in the preceding exercises to illustrate the short-run IS-LM equilibrium.*

   a. Consider the model of the economy from Exercise 4, in which planned investment depends on the interest rate:

   $$Y = C + I + G. \tag{10-32}$$
   $$C = C(Y - T) = 125 + 0.75(Y - T). \tag{10-33}$$
   $$I = 200 - 10r. \tag{10-34}$$
   $$G = \overline{G} = 150. \tag{10-35}$$
   $$T = \overline{T} = 100. \tag{10-36}$$

   As we saw in Exercise 4, the equation for the *IS* curve can be derived by setting total planned expenditure, *PE* = *C* + *I* + *G*, equal to *Y* and solving for *r*:

   $$PE = 125 + 0.75(Y - 100) + (200 - 10r) + 150 = Y. \tag{10-37}$$

   $$r = \underline{\hspace{5cm}} - \underline{\hspace{5cm}} Y.$$

Plot and draw the *IS* curve from this equation on Graph 10-19 and label it IS_1.

Graph 10-19

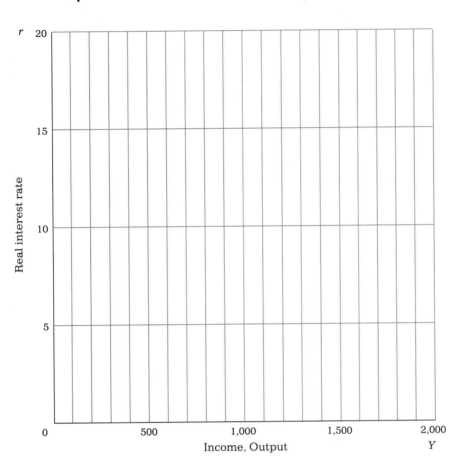

b. In Exercise 6, we derived the equation for the *LM* curve by setting the money supply equation equal to the money demand equation and solving for *r*:

$$(\overline{M}/\overline{P}) = 800 = (M/P)^d = 0.8Y - 16r$$

$$800 = 0.8Y - 16r.$$

(10-38)

$r = $ _____ + _____ Y.

Plot and draw the *LM* curve for this equation on Graph 10-19 and label it LM_1.

c. The equilibrium of the economy occurs at the intersection of the *IS* curve and the *LM* curve. This point gives the interest rate *r* and the level of income *Y* at which actual expenditure equals planned expenditure, and the supply of real money balances equals the demand for real money balances. Compute the equilibrium values of *Y* and *r* by setting the equation for the *IS* curve equal to the equation for the *LM* curve and solving for *Y* and *r*.

The equilibrium value of $Y =$ _____ and the equilibrium value of $r =$ _____ percent. Locate these values on Graph 10-19 and label them Y_1 and r_1, respectively.

Problems

Answer the following problems on a separate sheet of paper.

1. Assume the following model of the economy:
$$C = 180 + 0.8(Y - T)$$
$$I = 190$$
$$G = 250$$
$$T = 150.$$

   a. What is the value of the *MPC* in this model?

   b. Draw the planned expenditure curve and indicate its slope and *y* intercept.

   c. Compute the equilibrium level of income.

   d. Calculate the level of unplanned inventory accumulation when $Y = 3,000$.

2. Consider the same model as in Problem 1:
$$C = 180 + 0.8(Y - T)$$
$$I = 190$$
$$G = 250$$
$$T = 150.$$

   a. Compute the initial equilibrium level of income.

b. If government purchases were to increase by 10 to 260, what would happen to each of the following? State the amount as well as the direction of the changes.

  i.   the planned expenditure curve

  ii. the equilibrium level of income

  iii. the level of consumption

  iv. the government budget deficit

c. Starting over again at $G = 250$, suppose that taxes increased by 10 to 160. What would happen to each of the following? State the amount as well as the direction of the changes.

  i.   the planned expenditure curve

  ii. the equilibrium level of income

  iii. the level of consumption

  iv. the government budget deficit

d. Starting over one last time at $G = 250$ and $T = 150$, suppose that government expenditures and taxes were both increased by 10 to 260 and 160, respectively. What would happen to each of the following? This time, draw the consumption, government purchases, and planned expenditure graphs to indicate the amount as well as the direction of the changes.

  i.   the planned expenditure curve

  ii. the equilibrium level of income

  iii. the level of consumption

  iv. the government budget deficit

3. Consider the following model of the economy:
$$C = 170 + 0.6(Y - T)$$
$$I = 250$$
$$G = 300$$
$$T = 200.$$

a. What is the value of the marginal propensity to consume?

b. What is the value of the government budget *deficit*?

c. Calculate the equilibrium level of GDP.

d. What is the value of the government-purchases multiplier?

e. Use your answer to Part d to calculate the amount by which government purchases of goods and services would have to rise in order to increase the equilibrium level of GDP by 50.

4. Consider the following model of the economy:
$$C = 20 + 0.75(Y - T)$$
$$I = 380$$
$$G = 400$$
$$T = 0.20Y$$
$$Y = C + I + G$$

a. What is the value of the *MPC* in this model?

b. The equation for taxes indicates that when Y rises by \$100, taxes rise by \$20. Consequently, when Y rises by \$100, disposable income $Y - T$ rises by \$80 and consumption rises by 0.75(80) = \$60. Draw the consumption and planned expenditure curves as a function of Y and label their slopes and y intercepts.

c. Compute the equilibrium level of income.

d. At the equilibrium level of income, what is the value of the government budget surplus?

e. Increase G by 10 to 410, calculate the government-purchases multiplier, and explain why it no longer equals $1/(1 - MPC)$.

5. Suppose that the following equations describe an economy. (C, I, G, T, and Y are measured in billions of dollars, and r is measured as a percent; for example, $r = 10$ = 10%):

$$C = 170 + 0.6(Y - T)$$
$$T = 200$$
$$I = 100 - 4r$$
$$G = 350$$
$$(M/P)^d = L = 0.75Y - 6r$$
$$M^s/P = M/P = 735.$$

a. Derive the equation for the IS curve. (*Hint:* It is easier to solve for Y here.)

b. Derive the equation for the LM curve. (*Hint:* Again, it is easier to solve for Y.)

c. Now express both the IS and LM equations in terms of r. Graph both curves and calculate their slopes.

d. Use the equations from Parts a and b to calculate the equilibrium levels of real output, the interest rate, planned investment, and consumption.

e. At the equilibrium level of real output, calculate the value of the government budget surplus.

6. **a.** Rather than being independent of changes in Y, suppose that planned investment increases as real income Y rises and decreases as Y falls. Briefly explain why this situation might occur. Then draw the planned investment curve.

b. Compared to the case in which investment is independent of Y, how would the situation in Part a affect each of the following?

   i. the slope of the planned expenditure curve

   ii. the government-purchases multiplier

   iii. the shapes of the IS and/or LM curves

7. Suppose that there is a sudden increase in the demand for money—that is, at the same levels of r and Y people want to hold more money. What would happen to the money demand curve and the LM curve?

8. How would each of the following changes affect the shape of the IS curve?

a. the MPC gets bigger

b. investment becomes more sensitive to changes in the interest rate (for example, investment now rises by a bigger amount whenever the interest rate falls by one percentage point)

Data Question

Consult the Web site of the Department of Finance in Ottawa (http://www.fin.gc.ca).

1. Click on "Budgets," then the most recent Budget, and finally on "Budget in Brief." For example, for the 2009 Budget, you can read about the government's "Action Plan" for dealing with the recession. Use the *IS-LM* model to interpret the Department's explanation. Is the reasoning presented consistent with the model? Does knowledge of the model help you understand this reasoning?

Questions to Think About

1. Which definition of the money supply, *M*1 or *M*2, is more appropriate to use to derive the *LM* curve?

2. Banks pay interest on chequing deposits, although the interest rates they pay are usually less than those paid on government bonds. Given this, does the liquidity preference theory of money still make sense? If so, what variable should appear on the vertical axis of the money demand and *LM* curves?

3. Many companies do not need to borrow in order to invest because they have ample retained earnings from past profits. Why will their investment decisions still depend on the interest rate?

Aggregate Demand II

Fill-in Questions

Use the key terms below to fill in the blanks in the following statements. Each term may be used more than once.

debt-deflation theory   Pigou effect

liquidity trap

1. A lower price level implies higher real money balances. According to the _____, consumers then feel wealthier and, therefore, spend more.

2. According to the _____, unexpected deflation hurts debtors and benefits creditors. Consequently, national income will fall if debtors have a higher propensity to spend than creditors.

3. Some economists believe that interest rates fell so low in the 1930s and again in 2008 and 2009 that many countries, including Canada and Japan, may have been in a _____, in which expansionary monetary policy was unable to stimulate the economy.

Multiple-Choice Questions

1. An increase in government purchases will shift the:
   a. *IS* curve to the left and decrease both the interest rate and the level of income.
   b. *IS* curve to the right and increase both the interest rate and the level of income.
   c. *IS* curve to the right and increase the level of income but decrease the interest rate.
   d. *LM* curve downward (to the right) and increase the level of income but decrease the interest rate.

2. An increase in taxes will shift the:
   a. *IS* curve to the left and decrease both the interest rate and the level of income.
   b. *IS* curve to the right and increase both the interest rate and the level of income.
   c. *IS* curve to the right and increase the level of income but decrease the interest rate.
   d. *LM* curve downward (to the right) and increase the level of income but decrease the interest rate.

3. An increase in the money supply will shift the:
   a. *IS* curve to the left and decrease both the interest rate and the level of income.
   b. *LM* curve downward (to the right) and increase both the interest rate and the level of income.
   c. *IS* curve to the right and increase the level of income but decrease the interest rate.
   d. *LM* curve downward (to the right) and increase the level of income but decrease the interest rate.

4. If real income rose and the interest rate fell following an increase in government purchases, the:
   a. *IS* curve must be vertical.
   b. *LM* curve must be vertical.
   c. Bank of Canada must have increased the money supply at the same time.
   d. Bank of Canada must have decreased the money supply at the same time.

5. If the Bank of Canada decreases the money supply at the same time as taxes increase, the:
   a. interest rate will definitely rise.
   b. interest rate will definitely fall.
   c. equilibrium level of income will definitely rise.
   d. equilibrium level of income will definitely fall.

6. The *IS* curve will shift to the right if:
   a. consumer confidence in the economy improves.
   b. firms become more optimistic about the economy and decide to invest more at each interest rate.
   c. the government increases transfer payments.
   d. all of the above.

7. If people suddenly wish to hold more money at each interest rate:
   a. the money demand curve will shift to the right.
   b. the *LM* curve will shift upward (to the left).
   c. real income will fall.
   d. all of the above.

8. Which of the following statements explains why the aggregate demand curve is downward-sloping?
   a. A lower price level increases real balances. Consequently, the *LM* curve shifts downward (to the right) and the level of income increases.
   b. A lower price level forces the Bank of Canada to increase the money supply. Consequently, the *LM* curve shifts down (to the right) and the level of income increases.
   c. A lower price level induces the government to reduce taxes. Consequently, the *IS* curve shifts to the right and the level of income increases.
   d. all of the above.

9. As we move along a stationary aggregate demand curve, one factor that is held constant is:

    a. real income.
    b. the aggregate price level.
    c. the (nominal) money supply.
    d. real money balances.

10. All of the following will shift the aggregate demand curve to the right EXCEPT a(n):

    a. increase in government purchases.
    b. reduction in transfer payments.
    c. increase in the (nominal) money supply.
    d. reduction in taxes.

11. The FALSE statement below is:

    a. the classical assumption that output reaches its natural rate is best used to describe the long run.
    b. in the short run, output may deviate from its natural rate.
    c. in the *IS-LM* model, the price level is assumed to be sticky in the short run.
    d. in the *IS-LM* model, aggregate demand is never equal to the natural rate of output even in the long run.

12. If income is initially less than the natural rate of output, the price level:

    a. will gradually fall, shifting the *LM* curve downward (to the right).
    b. will gradually rise, shifting the *LM* curve upward (to the left).
    c. will fall, shifting the *IS* curve to the right.
    d. is stuck at this level even in the long run.

13. According to adherents of the money hypothesis, the Great Depression in the United States was caused by a:

    a. sharp decline in the money supply.
    b. decline in business confidence.
    c. decline in consumer confidence.
    d. sharp decline in real money balances.

14. According to adherents of the spending hypothesis, the Great Depression in the United States was caused by:

    a. a reduction in business and consumer confidence.
    b. a contractionary (leftward) shift in the *IS* curve.
    c. the stock market crash.
    d. all of the above.

15. According to the Pigou effect:

    a. for a given supply of money, a lower price level shifts the *LM* curve outward, which leads to a higher level of income.
    b. since consumers will buy more of a good as its price falls, real output will rise during a depression.
    c. as prices fall and real balances rise, consumers will feel wealthier and spend more.
    d. all of the above.

16. According to the debt-deflation theory, unexpected deflation hurts debtors and benefits creditors. Consequently, national income will fall if:

    a. both groups have the same spending propensities.
    b. debtors have a higher propensity to spend than creditors.
    c. creditors have a higher propensity to spend than debtors.
    d. the *MPC* for both groups is less than 1.

17. The following statement is FALSE:

    a. money demand depends on the nominal interest rate.
    b. investment demand depends on the real interest rate.
    c. *IS-LM* analysis is unable to incorporate changes in expected inflation.
    d. an expected deflation causes the real interest rate to rise at each level of the nominal interest rate, which leads to a contractionary (leftward) shift of the *IS* curve.

18. Most economists believe that a Great Depression in the United States is less likely today than it was during the 1930s because:

    a. their knowledge of monetary and fiscal stabilization policies has improved.
    b. their system of federal deposit insurance makes widespread bank failures less likely.
    c. they now have more automatic stabilizers, such as the income tax.
    d. all of the above.

19. From 1996 to 2006, housing prices in the United States doubled. When prices fell by 20 percent during the next two years, however, which of the following repercussions contributed to the recession that began in 2008?

    a. a rise in mortgage defaults and home foreclosures
    b. large losses at the financial institutions that owned mortgage-backed securities
    c. a decline in consumer confidence, due partly to increased volatility in the stock market
    d. All of the answers are correct.

20. If an economy is in a liquidity trap, then:

    a. the interest rate is so low that fiscal policy cannot stimulate the economy.
    b. the interest rate is so low that monetary policy cannot stimulate the economy.
    c. the budget deficit is so high that fiscal policy cannot stimulate the economy.
    d. all of the above.

21. Here are two propositions about monetary policy. (I) If the central bank fixes the nominal money supply, the aggregate demand curve is steeper when the *MPC* is larger; (II) If the central bank adjusts the interest rate to pursue a target price level, the aggregate demand curve is steeper when the *MPC* is larger.

    a. I is true; II is not.
    b. II is true; I is not.
    c. Both I and II are true.
    d. Neither I nor II is true.

22. Here are two propositions about monetary policy. (I) The more aggressively the central bank adjusts the interest rate trying to achieve price stability, the smaller is the temporary recession that is caused by a drop in aggregate demand; (II) The more aggressively the central bank adjusts the interest rate trying to achieve price stability, the smaller is the temporary recession that is caused by an adverse supply shock.

   a. I is true; II is not.
   b. II is true; I is not.
   c. Both I and II are true.
   d. Neither I nor II is true.

23. If the central bank could adjust the interest rate so that it maintained perfect price stability:

   a. the aggregate demand curve would be vertical.
   b. the aggregate demand curve would be horizontal.
   c. the short-run aggregate supply curve would be vertical.
   d. the short-run aggregate supply curve would be horizontal.

Exercises

1. **Shifts in the *IS* and *LM* Curves and Short-Run Changes in the Equilibrium Level of Income** *In this exercise, we review the policy and nonpolicy changes that shift the IS and LM curves, and we graphically illustrate the short-run changes in the equilibrium level of income. A review of Exercises 4 and 7 in Chapter 10 would be very helpful.*

a. Examine the initial equilibrium shown at Point A on Graph 11-1.

Graph 11-1

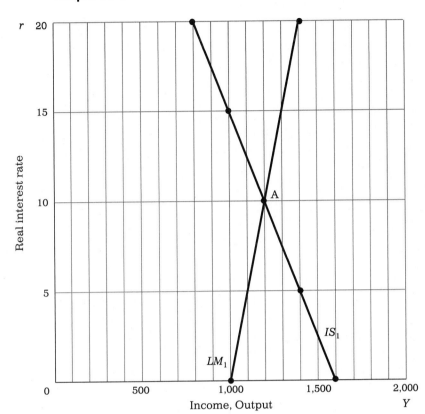

Recall that the *IS* curve depicts the relationship between the interest rate *r* and the equilibrium value of income that results from the investment function and the Keynesian cross. The *LM* curve depicts the combinations of *r* and *Y* for which a given supply of real money balances is equal to real money demand. At the initial situation illustrated in Graph 11-1, the initial equilibrium level of income equals _____, and the initial equilibrium interest rate equals _____ percent. This occurs at Point A.

b. Starting from the initial equilibrium illustrated on Graph 11-1, suppose that government purchases increase by $100 (billion). As a result, the planned expenditure curve (which is not shown) will shift <u>upward/downward</u> by $_____ billion. If the *MPC* equals 0.75, the *IS* curve will shift to the <u>right/left</u> by $100 billion × the government-purchases multiplier, or by $_____ billion. Draw this *IS* curve on Graph 11-1 and label it *IS*₂.

c. As income rises, money demand <u>rises/falls</u>. To keep real money demand equal to a constant real money supply, any increase in income must be accompanied by a(n) <u>increase/decrease</u> in the interest rate. As a result of this change in the interest rate, firms will <u>increase/decrease</u> investment, which partially offsets the effect of the increase in government purchases. Consequently, the equilibrium level of income rises by <u>more/less</u> than the horizontal shift in the *IS* curve. Locate the new equilibrium on Graph 11-1 and label it Point B.

d. Starting again from Point A, suppose that taxes increased by $100 billion. If the $MPC = 0.75$, the expenditure curve will shift <u>upward/downward</u> by $_____ billion, and the *IS* curve will shift to the <u>right/left</u> by $_____ billion. Draw this curve on Graph 11-1 and label it IS_3.

e. As income falls, money demand <u>rises/falls</u>. To keep real money demand equal to a constant real money supply, any decrease in income must be accompanied by a(n) <u>increase/decrease</u> in the interest rate. This, in turn, leads to a(n) <u>increase/decrease</u> in investment, which partially offsets the effect of the increase in taxes. Consequently, the equilibrium level of income falls by <u>more/less</u> than the horizontal shift in the *IS* curve. Locate the new equilibrium on Graph 11-1 and label it Point C.

f. Now examine Graph 11-2, which again illustrates the initial equilibrium.

Graph 11-2

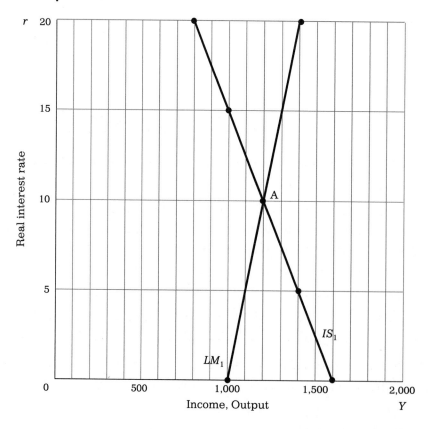

If the Bank of Canada were to increase the money supply, the *LM* curve would shift upward (to the left)/downward (to the right). Draw this shift on Graph 11-2. Label the new curve *LM*$_2$ and the new equilibrium Point D. As a result of this increase in the money supply, the equilibrium interest rate would rise/fall and the equilibrium level of income would rise/fall. When the Bank of Canada increases the money supply, at the initial interest rate people have more money than they want to hold. Consequently, they start depositing the extra money in banks or buy more bonds, which tends to raise/lower the interest rate until people want to hold all the extra money created by the Bank of Canada. This change in the interest rate increases/decreases planned investment, which increases/decreases planned expenditure and the equilibrium level of income. If, instead, the Bank of Canada reduced the money supply, the *LM* curve would shift upward (to the left)/downward (to the right), the equilibrium interest rate would rise/fall, and the equilibrium level of income would rise/fall.

g. Nonpolicy changes can also shift the *IS* and/or *LM* curves. If firms suddenly feel more optimistic about the future and decide to invest more at every interest rate, the *IS/LM* curve would shift _____, the equilibrium level of income would rise/fall, and the equilibrium interest rate would rise/fall. If households became more pessimistic about the future and decided to consume less at every level of disposable income, the *IS/LM* curve would shift _____, the equilibrium level of income would rise/fall, and the equilibrium interest rate would rise/fall. Finally, if the amount of real money demanded increases substantially at each interest rate and level of income, the money demand curve will shift to the right/left and the *IS/LM* curve would shift _____. Consequently, the equilibrium level of income would rise/fall and the equilibrium interest rate would rise/fall.

2. **The Aggregate Demand Curve** *In this exercise, we examine the changes in the* IS-LM *equilibria as the price level varies and derive the aggregate demand curve.*

   a. Graph 11-3 illustrates the initial equilibrium in the basic model presented in the exercises for Chapter 10 of this workbook.

   The real money supply initially is equal to $800 billion, and the initial equilibrium is at Point A. If the real money supply increases to $1,040 billion, the *LM* curve will shift upward (to the left)/downward (to the right). Locate the appropriate curve on Graph 11-3, label it *LM*$_2$, and label the new equilibrium Point B.

   b. If, on the other hand, the real money supply falls to $560 billion, the *LM* curve will shift upward (to the left)/downward (to the right). Locate this curve on Graph 11-3, label it *LM*$_3$, and label the corresponding equilibrium Point C.

   c. The aggregate demand curve can now be derived using Graphs 11-3 and 11-4. As we saw in Part a, the *LM* curve will shift downward (to the right) whenever there

Graph 11-3

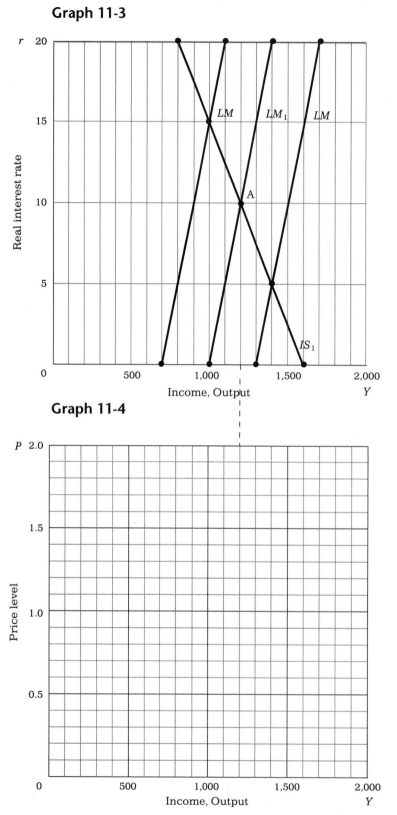

Graph 11-4

is an increase in the real money supply. This can be accomplished if the Bank of Canada increases the nominal money supply M, holding the aggregate price level P constant. It can also be accomplished by reducing P, while holding M constant. Using this information, a more general and realistic aggregate demand curve than the one introduced in Chapter 9 can be derived. This aggregate demand curve plots the relationship between the price level and the level of income that arises from the *IS-LM* model. On Graph 11-3, Point A represents the *IS-LM* equilibrium when the real money supply equals $800 billion. If the nominal money supply $M = \$800$ billion and the real money supply equals M/P, the aggregate price level $P =$

_____. From Graph 11-3, note that real income Y at Point A =

_____. Use this information to plot one point on what will become the aggregate demand curve on Graph 11-4 and label this Point A.

d. Similarly, Point B on Graph 11-3 represents the *IS-LM* equilibrium when the real money supply equals 1,040. If M remains equal to 800, this occurs as a result of a change in the price level. Thus, $M/P = 800/P = 1{,}040$. Calculate P (round off to two decimal places).

$P =$ _____.

Real income at Point B on Graph 11-3 = _____. Use this information about P and Y to plot another point on the aggregate demand curve on Graph 11-4 and label this Point B.

e. Finally, Point C on Graph 11-3 represents the *IS-LM* equilibrium when the real money supply equals 560. If, instead of a decrease in the nominal money supply, this situation occurs as a result of a change in the price level, then $M/P = 800/P = 560$. Calculate P (round off to two decimal places).

$P =$ _____.

Real income at Point C = _____. Use this information about P and Y to plot another point on the aggregate demand curve on Graph 11-4, and label this Point C. Now connect all three points on Graph 11-4 to draw the aggregate demand curve.

f. Summarizing Parts a–e, the aggregate demand curve slopes downward because as the aggregate price level falls, real money balances increase/decrease. This shifts the *IS/LM* curve _____, increases/decreases the interest rate, and increases/decreases planned investment. As a result, the equilibrium level of income at the intersection of the *IS* and *LM* curves increases/decreases. Note that, as we move along a stationary aggregate demand curve, government purchases, taxes, and the nominal money supply all remain constant.

3. **Fiscal Policy and the Aggregate Demand Curve** *In this exercise, we show how changes in fiscal policy shift the aggregate demand curve.*

On Graphs 11-5 and 11-6, the aggregate demand curve is derived for arbitrary *IS-LM* curves.

Graph 11-5

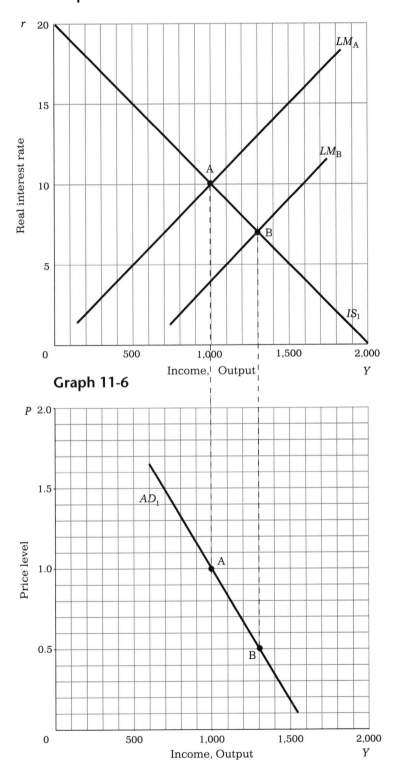

Graph 11-6

a. Assume that LM_A is drawn for a nominal money supply equal to 800 (billion dollars) and a price level equal to 1.0. Thus, at the initial equilibrium Point A, $P =$ _____ and $Y =$ _____. (Find Y from Graph 11-5.) Point A is also depicted on Graph 11-6. If the price level fell to 0.5, the real money supply would increase to $M/P = 800/0.5 =$ _____. This is reflected on Graph 11-5 by a shift in the LM curve to LM_B. The goods and money markets reach a new equilibrium at Point B, at which $Y =$ _____. This change is also reflected on Graph 11-6 by a movement along AD_1 to Point B.

b. Start again at Point A with $M/P = 800/1.0 = 800$, and let government purchases rise by 100. If the marginal propensity to consume equals 0.75 (or 3/4), the government-purchases multiplier $= 1/(1 - MPC) =$ _____. Consequently, if government purchases rise by 100, the IS curve shifts to the right/left by _____. Draw this new IS curve on Graph 11-5 and label it IS_2.

c. Because the LM curve has a positive slope, Y would rise by more/less than the horizontal shift in the IS curve. Starting at Point A on Graph 11-5, find the new equilibrium level of income if P remains equal to 1.0 and label it Point C. Find the corresponding point on Graph 11-6 and also label it Point C. (It will no longer lie on AD_1.)

d. Now start at Point B on Graph 11-5, with $M/P = 800/0.5 = 1,600$. Find the new equilibrium level of income if P remains equal to 0.5 after government purchases rise by 100 and label it Point D. Find the corresponding point on Graph 11-6 and also label it Point D. (It will no longer lie on AD_1.)

e. Connect Points C and D on Graph 11-6 to draw the new aggregate demand curve and label it AD_2. Compare Points C and A in both graphs. At Point C, real income is higher than/lower than/equal to real income at Point A, and the price level at Point C is higher than/lower than/equal to the price level at Point A. Now compare Points D and B. At Point D, real income is higher than/lower than/equal to real income at Point B, and the price level is higher than/lower than/equal to the price level at Point B.

f. Consequently, an increase in government purchases will shift the IS curve to the right/left and the aggregate demand curve to the right/left. A reduction in taxes will shift the IS curve to the right/left and the aggregate demand curve to the right/left.

4. **Monetary Policy and the Aggregate Demand Curve** *In this exercise, we show how changes in monetary policy shift the aggregate demand curve.*

On Graphs 11-7 and 11-8, the aggregate demand curve is derived for arbitrary *IS-LM* curves.

Graph 11-7

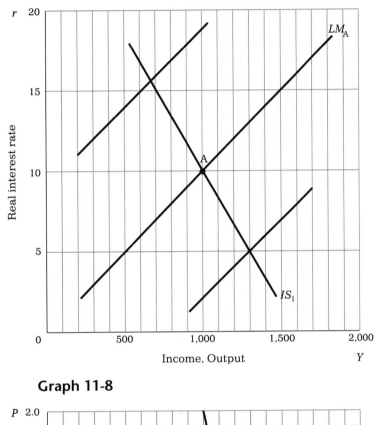

Graph 11-8

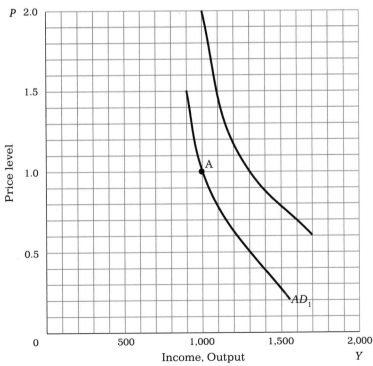

a. Assume that LM_A is drawn for a (nominal) money supply equal to 800 (billion dollars) and a price level equal to 1.0. Thus, at the initial equilibrium Point A, $P =$ _____ and $Y =$ _____. (Find Y from Graph 11-7.) Point A is also illustrated on Graph 11-8.

b. If the Bank of Canada were to double the nominal money supply to 1,600 and the price level remained constant, the real money supply would rise to $M/P =$ $1,600/1.0 =$ _____. This would shift the LM curve on Graph 11-7 upward (to the left)/downward (to the right). Locate the new LM curve on Graph 11-7 and label it LM_E. Locate the point on Graph 11-7 at which the goods and money markets reach a new equilibrium and label it Point E. Find the corresponding point on Graph 11-8 and also label it Point E (Point E does *not* lie on AD_1).

c. Note that, at Point E on Graph 11-8, real income is higher than/lower than/equal to real income at Point A, whereas the price level at Point E is higher than/lower than/equal to the price level at Point A. Consequently, an increase in the nominal money supply will shift the aggregate demand curve to the right/left. Conversely, a decrease in the nominal money supply will shift the aggregate demand curve to the right/left.

d. Finally, suppose that the nominal money supply remained equal to 1,600 while the price level rose to 2.0. The real money supply would then equal $M/P =$ $1,600/2.0 =$ _____. Consequently, the LM curve would shift all the way back to LM_A, and Y would equal _____ (even though the price level is now 2.0). Locate the new equilibrium points on both Graphs 11-7 and 11-8 and label them Points F. Note that Point F is the same as Point A on Graph 11-7 but not the same as Point A on Graph 11-8. This situation occurs because an increase in the nominal money supply will shift the aggregate demand curve, but the LM curve is affected only by changes in real money balances.

5. **The *IS-LM* Model in the Short Run and the Long Run** *In this exercise, we start from an IS-LM equilibrium level of income that is lower than the long-run equilibrium level and illustrate how reductions in the aggregate price level will shift the LM curve toward the long-run equilibrium.*

   a. Assume the following equation for an economy's *IS* curve:

$$r = 40 - 0.025Y.$$

   Plot and draw this curve on Graph 11-9 and label it IS_1.

   Graph 11-9

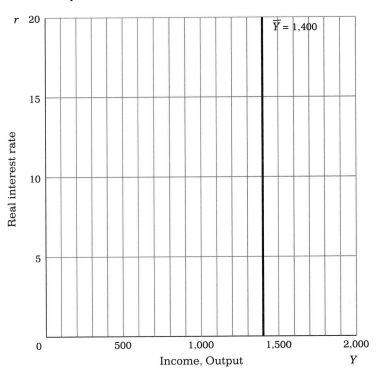

   b. Assume the following money demand curve for this economy:

   $M/P = 0.8Y - 16r.$

   If $M = 800$ and $P = 1.0$, derive the equation for the economy's *LM* curve by setting real money balances equal to real money demand and solving for *r*.

$r = $ _____ + _____ $Y.$

Plot and draw this curve on Graph 11-9 and label it $LM(P_1 = 1.0)$.

c. Solve the *IS* and *LM* equations simultaneously. The initial equilibrium level of income and the initial interest rate are:

$Y =$ _____ ; $r =$ _____ .

Label the initial equilibrium Point A on Graphs 11-9 and 11-10. Remember that the initial price level is assumed to be 1.0.

Graph 11-10

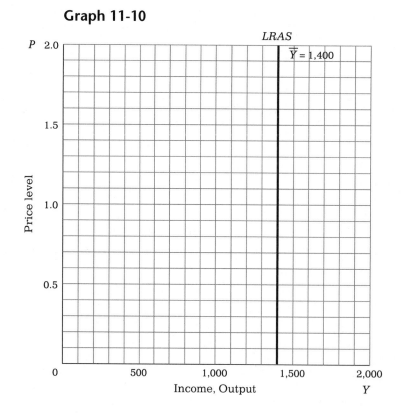

d. As you can see from Graphs 11-9 and 11-10, the natural rate of output $\overline{Y}$, which is also the long-run equilibrium level of income, is assumed to equal 1,400. Consequently, the initial level of income is <u>more/less</u> than the long-run equilibrium level of income. Point A is a short-run equilibrium level because the price level is assumed to be <u>sticky/flexible</u> in the short run, leading to a <u>horizontal/vertical</u> short-run aggregate supply curve.

e. In the long run, however, prices are sticky/flexible. Thus, as time goes by, the price level will rise/fall. This change will increase/decrease the real money supply, thereby shifting the *LM* curve upward (to the left)/downward (to the right) until it intersects the *IS* curve at the natural rate of output. Draw the long-run position of the *LM* curve on Graph 11-9 and label it $LM(P_2)$. Label the final equilibrium Point B on both Graphs 11-9 and 11-10.

f. The final price level can be computed in the following way. In the long run, $Y =$
CH 1,400, and we lie on the original *IS* curve. Substitute $Y = 1,400$ into the *IS* equation and solve for r.

$r =$ _____.

Given our long-run values for Y and r, use the money demand equation to compute real money demand.

$M/P =$ _____.

Since M is still equal to 800, this increase in M/P must come from a decrease in the price level. Solve the preceding equation for P (round off to two decimal places).

$P =$ _____.

g. Conversely, if the initial *IS-LM* equilibrium level of income were higher than the natural rate of output, over time the aggregate price level would rise/fall, thereby shifting the *IS/LM* curve _____ until the *IS* and *LM* curves intersected at the long-run equilibrium.

6. **Changes in Expected Inflation in the *IS-LM* Model** *In this exercise, we illustrate how a change in expected inflation will change the* IS-LM *equilibrium.*

   a. Investment is a function of the real interest rate r, whereas money demand is a function of the nominal interest rate i. Consequently, the *IS* curve should be drawn as a function of r, and the *LM* curve should be drawn as a function of i. Assume that the equations for the *IS* and *LM* curves are:

$$IS \text{ curve: } r = 40 - 0.025Y \text{ and}$$
$$LM \text{ curve: } i = -50 + 0.05Y.$$

   Recall that $r = i - E\pi$. Assume that expected inflation equals zero so that $r = i$, and it does not matter which variable we put on the vertical axis. We'll put the nominal interest rate i on the vertical axis. Draw these two curves on Graph 11-11, label them IS_1 and LM_1, and label the initial equilibrium Point A.

   Graph 11-11

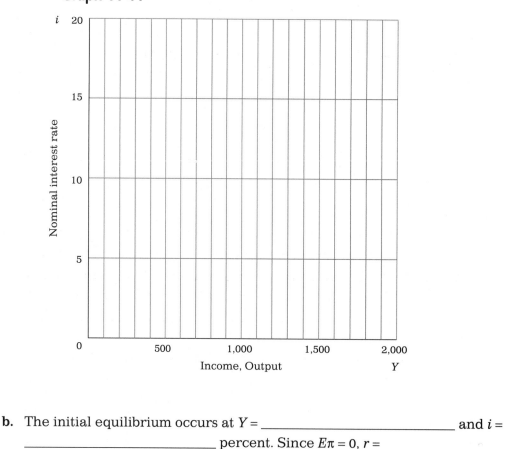

   b. The initial equilibrium occurs at $Y = $ _____ and $i = $ _____ percent. Since $E\pi = 0$, $r = $ _____ percent.

c. Now suppose that we have deflation, and expected inflation falls to –7.5 percent. As a result of this decrease in expected inflation, the real interest rate at the initial value of the nominal interest rate will rise to $r = i - E\pi =$

_____ $- (-7.5) =$ _____.

Consequently, at each level of i, r will now be higher/lower than it was before the expected deflation. Since the LM curve is a function of the nominal interest rate, it will not shift. The IS curve, on the other hand, is a function of the real interest rate. From the IS equation, it is known that $Y = 1,200$ when $r =$ _____.

When $E\pi = 0$, this value of r occurs when $i =$ _____. Now that $E\pi = -7.5$ percent, this level of r will occur when $i = r + E\pi =$

_____ + _____ =

_____ percent.

Thus, the same level of investment will occur only if i falls by _____ percentage points. Consequently, the IS curve shifts upward/downward by

_____ percentage points. Draw the new IS curve on Graph 11-11, label it IS_2, and label the new equilibrium Point B.

d. The equation for the new IS curve when $E\pi = -7.5$ percent is $i = 32.5 - 0.025Y$. Set this equal to the equation for the LM curve, and compute the new equilibrium values of Y and i:

$Y =$ _____; $i =$ _____.

e. The decrease in expected inflation leads to a(n) increase/decrease in Y and a(n) increase/decrease in i. The real interest rate $r = i - E\pi$ was initially equal to

_____ $-$ _____ $=$ _____

but now equals _____ $-$ _____ $=$

_____. Consequently, the real interest rate rises/falls.

Problems

Answer the following problems on a separate sheet of paper.

1. (Parts a–e of this problem are the same as Problem 5 in Chapter 10 of this workbook.) Suppose that the following equations describe an economy (C, I, G, T, and Y are measured in billions of dollars, and r is measured in percent; for example, $r = 10$ means $r = 10\%$):

$$C = 170 + 0.6(Y - T)$$
$$T = 200$$
$$I = 100 - 4r$$
$$G = 350$$
$$(M/P)^d = L = 0.75Y - 6r$$
$$M^s/P = \overline{M}/\overline{P} = 735.$$

   a. Derive the equation for the *IS* curve. (*Hint:* It is easier to solve for real output Y here.)

   b. Derive the equation for the *LM* curve. (*Hint:* Again, it is easier to solve for real output Y.)

   c. Now express both the *IS* and *LM* equations in terms of r. Plot and graph both curves and calculate their slopes.

   d. Use the equations from Parts a and b to calculate the equilibrium levels of real output Y, the interest rate r, planned investment I, and consumption C.

   e. At the equilibrium level of real output Y, calculate the value of the government budget surplus.

   f. Suppose that G increases by 36 to 386. Derive the new *IS* and *LM* equations and plot and draw these curves on the graph you drew for Part c.

   g. What is the horizontal shift in the *IS* curve and/or the *LM* curve in Part f (that is, if r remains constant, by how much does Y increase on each curve)?

   h. Refer to the *IS* and *LM* equations you derived in Part f. With Y on the left-hand side of the equations, calculate the new equilibrium levels of real output Y, the interest rate r, planned investment I, and consumption C.

   i. Instead of increasing G, suppose that the Bank of Canada sought to achieve the
   CH equilibrium level of real output Y in Part h through expansionary monetary policy alone. By how much would the Bank of Canada have to increase the money supply? (*Hint:* Start by drawing the appropriate shifts in the *IS* curve and/or the *LM* curve in Parts f and g.)

   j. Compare the equilibrium levels of consumption C, government spending G, and planned investment I in Parts h and i. Based on this comparison, why might some economists prefer expansionary fiscal policy while others prefer expansionary monetary policy?

2. As a result of the dramatic events in Eastern Europe in the 1990s, many citizens in Western countries now feel less threatened by Russia and have called for massive reductions in their defense budgets as "peace dividends."

   a. Suppose that our defense budget were cut by $1 billion. If no other policy changes are enacted, use the *IS-LM* model to analyze what would happen to real GDP and the interest rate. Illustrate the changes that would occur by graphing the *IS* and *LM* curves and indicating their shift(s).

   b. Now suppose that defense spending were cut by the same $1 billion, but government transfers were raised by the same amount ($1 billion) to alleviate poverty and subsidize education and day care. Draw the appropriate shifts in the *IS* and/or *LM* curves on your graph for Part a and predict what would happen to real GDP and the interest rate.

   c. Compare the sizes of the changes in Parts a and b.

   d. Finally, start over and suppose that defense spending were cut by $1 billion and the government used the money to give unrestricted grants to the struggling economies of Eastern Europe. Assuming that this action does not change the money supply, what does the *IS-LM* model predict would be the change in Canadian GDP relative to the changes described in Parts a and b? Explain briefly.

3. Many economists believe that consumption expenditures depend on household wealth in addition to disposable income.

   a. If this were true, how would the stock market crash in October 1987 have affected the consumption expenditure curve and the planned expenditure curve?

   b. Draw representative *IS* and *LM* curves on a graph and illustrate the consequent shift(s) in the *IS* curve and/or the *LM* curve. Indicate the predicted (directional) changes in real output *Y* and the interest rate *r*.

4. In the 1990s, many governments proposed reducing their budget deficits by increasing net taxes and reducing government spending. Some economists claimed that this policy would reduce interest rates and increase real GDP as well as cut the deficit.

   a. Draw *IS-LM* graphs to analyze the effects of this mix of fiscal policies on the deficit, interest rates, and real GDP. (Assume that taxes are lump sum, that is, taxes are an absolute amount that is unrelated to the level of income.) Are these results consistent with the economists' predictions?

   b. Most economists who believe that an increase in taxes and a reduction in government spending would both increase GDP and cut the deficit implicitly assume that the country's monetary policy would change if this deficit-reduction plan were enacted. Draw *IS-LM* graphs on a separate sheet of paper to show what kind of monetary policy must accompany this mix of fiscal policy changes in order to decrease the deficit and interest rates, while increasing GDP.

   c. What happens to the aggregate demand curve in Parts a and b?

5. Suppose two countries differ only in the size of their *MPC*. In Country A, the *MPC* is large, and in Country B, the *MPC* is small.

   a. Draw representative *IS* and *LM* curves for each country and label them IS^A and LM^A for Country A and IS^B and LM^B for Country B. Compare the shapes of the *IS* and *LM* curves in the two countries and explain your results.

   b. In which country will an increase in the money supply be more effective in changing real output? Illustrate using the graph you drew in Part a.

6. Suppose that private spending (for example, *C* or *I*) is volatile and unpredictable. This situation implies that the *IS* curve would frequently shift to the right and to the left.

   a. Assume that the central bank decided to keep the real money supply constant. Draw *IS-LM* curves to illustrate how real output *Y* would respond to the instability in private spending.

   b. Now suppose that the central bank tried to keep the interest rate constant at its initial level even if this required frequent changes in the real money supply. Draw a money supply and demand diagram to show what the central bank would have to do to the real money supply when *Y* increases (because of a shift in the *IS* curve to the right). What would this monetary response do to the *IS* curve and/or *LM* curve?

   c. Similarly, if the central bank tried to keep the interest rate *r* constant, what would the central bank have to do to the real money supply when the *IS* curve shifts to the left and *Y* falls? What would this response do to the *IS* curve and/or *LM* curve?

   d. Using your answers to Parts b and c, explain which of the two policies (keeping *M/P* constant or keeping *r* constant) would stabilize the economy better (by minimizing the fluctuations in real GDP) if the main source of instability in the economy were fluctuations in private spending.

7. a. In 2009, our federal government enacted its "Action Plan" to address the recession. It involved both increases in government spending and tax cuts. Draw the appropriate graphs to indicate what happened to the *IS*, *LM*, aggregate demand, and short-run aggregate supply curves in Canada at that time, and indicate any short-run changes in the equilibrium levels of *r*, *I*, *C*, *G*, *Y*, and *P* that would have happened if the Bank of Canada had not changed any of its policies.

   b. During this period, the Bank of Canada actually pursued expansionary monetary policy and kept interest rates constant. Redraw your diagrams from Part a and indicate what actually happened to the *IS* curve, *LM* curve, aggregate demand curve, short-run aggregate supply curve, and the levels of *r*, *I*, *C*, *G*, *Y*, and *P*. How do they compare with the levels in Part a?

8. Suppose policymakers want to raise investment but keep real GDP constant. Use the *IS-LM* model to describe and illustrate what *mix* of monetary and fiscal policies would achieve this goal.

9. In addition to depending on disposable income, suppose household consumption were also a function of the interest rate. In particular, assume that households consume more (i.e., save less) when the interest rate falls.

    a. Explain how this situation would influence the shapes of the *IS* and/or *LM* curves relative to the case in which consumption is not a function of the interest rate.

    b. Now use *IS-LM* curves to illustrate how this situation would influence the short-run effectiveness of monetary policy.

    c. What, if anything, would this modification do to the shape of the aggregate demand curve?

10. a. Suppose the economy were initially in long-run and short-run equilibrium. Illustrate this position by drawing an *IS-LM* graph and, directly below it, the aggregate supply-aggregate demand graph.

    b. Now suppose that oil prices increase dramatically. On the same graphs that you drew in Part a, illustrate what happens in both the short run and the long run to the *IS* curve, *LM* curve, short-run aggregate supply curve, long-run aggregate supply curve, and the equilibrium levels of Y and P. Explain the changes depicted in the graphs.

11. Draw *IS-LM* curves using the nominal interest rate on the vertical axis and illustrate the initial equilibrium. Now illustrate the effects of a change in expected inflation from 0 percent to 10 percent on the *IS* curve and the *LM* curve, and the equilibrium levels of i, Y, and r.

12. a. Draw an *IS* curve and an *LM* curve using the real interest rate r on the vertical axis, assuming that expected inflation is 0 percent.

    b. Illustrate how the *IS* and/or *LM* curves you drew in Part a would shift if expected inflation fell to –10 percent. What happens to Y, r, and i? Compare your answer to the analysis presented in the textbook.

13. Some economists believe that the money supply M tends to increase as the interest rate increases. Draw a money-supply, money-demand graph, and, next to it, derive the *LM* curve to illustrate how this tendency would affect the slope of the *LM* curve.

14. Some economists believe that the Japanese economy entered a liquidity trap in the late 1990s as interest rates fell almost to zero. One proposed solution was an announced, long-term expansionary monetary policy that increased both the nominal money supply and inflationary expectations. Draw *IS-LM* curves using the nominal interest rate on the vertical axis and illustrate how a successful implementation of this policy would affect the equilibrium levels of i, Y, and r.

Data Questions

Consult the Web site of the Bank of Canada.

1. Click on "Monetary Policy" and then "Why Monetary Policy Matters: A Canadian Perspective" to learn more about the history of the Bank and how it operates.

2. Try to restate some of these discussions in the section on "the transmission mechanism of monetary policy" by adding explicit reference to the *IS-LM* model as part of each explanation.

3. From the home page, click on "Media Room" and then "Press Releases." Look for a recent item such as "Overnight Rate Raised by 1/4 Percentage Point." Use your knowledge of the *IS-LM* model to help you interpret what you read.

4. From "Media Room," click on "Monetary Policy Report." Use your knowledge of the *IS-LM* model to make your understanding of the Report more explicit.

Questions to Think About

1. Based on the discussion presented in Chapter 11 of the textbook, do you think the Great Depression in the United States was caused primarily by a shock to the *LM* curve or a shock to the *IS* curve? What evidence do you find most convincing and why?

2. What does the experience of the Great Depression imply about the downward flexibility of prices and the speed with which the economy moves to the natural rate of output after an aggregate demand shock?

3. Does a more aggressive targeting of price stability by the Bank of Canada keep real output more or less insulated from demand and supply shocks?

chapter 12

The Open Economy Revisited: The Mundell-Fleming Model and the Exchange-Rate Regime

Fill-in Questions

Use the key terms below to fill in the blanks in the following statements. Each term may be used more than once.

currency board
devaluation
dollarization
fixed exchange rate
floating exchange rate

impossible trinity
Mundell-Fleming model
revaluation
speculative attack

1. Under a _____ regime, the exchange rate is allowed to fluctuate freely in response to changing economic conditions.

2. Under a _____ regime, a central bank buys or sells the domestic currency for foreign currencies at a predetermined price.

3. Under a _____ regime, monetary policy is dedicated to the single goal of keeping the exchange rate at the announced level. Consequently, one argument in favour of a _____ is that they allow monetary policy to be used for other purposes.

4. In a fixed-exchange-rate regime, a reduction in the value of the domestic currency is called a(n) _____; an increase in the value of the domestic currency is called a(n) _____.

5. In the _____, a(n) _____ shifts the *LM** curve to the right, whereas a(n) _____ shifts the *LM** curve to the left.

6. Proponents of _____ argue that this policy reduces some of the uncertainty in international business transactions.

7. A _____ occurs when there is a change in investors' perceptions that makes the maintenance of a _____ impossible.

8. A(n) _____ is an arrangement by which the central bank holds enough foreign currency to back each unit of the domestic currency.

9. _____ occurs when a foreign country adopts the U.S. dollar as its domestic currency.

10. According to the _____, a country cannot have all of the following: free capital flows, an independent monetary policy, and a _____.

Multiple-Choice Questions

1. The exchange rate is defined as the amount of foreign currency needed to buy one unit of domestic currency (for example, 100 yen per dollar). A higher exchange rate:
   a. makes domestic goods less expensive relative to foreign goods.
   b. stimulates exports and depresses imports.
   c. leads to a decrease in net exports.
   d. leads to higher income.

2. In the conventional *IS-LM* model, real income Y and the real interest rate r appear on the axes. When the exchange rate increases:
   a. investment increases and the *IS* curve shifts to the right.
   b. net exports increase and the *IS* curve shifts to the right.
   c. investment decreases and the *IS* curve shifts to the left.
   d. net exports decrease and the *IS* curve shifts to the left.

3. All of the following statements about the Mundell-Fleming model drawn with aggregate income Y and the exchange rate e on the axes are true EXCEPT:
   a. the interest rate is fixed at the world interest rate.
   b. the *LM** curve is vertical because the exchange rate does not enter the money demand or money supply equations.
   c. the *IS** curve slopes downward because a lower exchange rate stimulates investment.
   d. the intersection of the *IS** and *LM** curves determines the equilibrium exchange rate.

4. In a small open economy with a floating exchange rate, fiscal policy will be ineffective because:
   a. monetary policy will completely offset it.
   b. the exchange rate will remain constant.
   c. a fall in net exports will offset any increases in government purchases or consumption.
   d. the exchange rate will rise by the same amount as the interest rate.

5. In a small open economy with a floating exchange rate, monetary expansion does all of the following EXCEPT:

    a. lower the interest rate.

    b. increase the equilibrium income level.

    c. decrease the exchange rate.

    d. cause net exports to rise.

6. Trade restrictions have no effect on income under floating exchange rates because:

    a. net exports increase but investment decreases.

    b. the exchange rate rises to offset the initial increase in net exports.

    c. the fall in imports equals the rise in exports.

    d. all of the above.

7. If the current yen-to-dollar exchange rate (for example, 200 yen per dollar) is above a fixed exchange rate set by the Bank of Canada (for example, 150 yen per dollar), arbitragers can make profits by:

    a. buying yen in foreign exchange markets and selling them to the Bank of Canada.

    b. buying yen from the Bank of Canada and selling them in foreign exchange markets.

    c. buying dollars in foreign exchange markets and selling them to the Bank of Canada.

    d. none of the above.

8. The profit-making actions described in Question 7 will cause the money supply to:

    a. rise, thereby shifting the LM^* curve to the left.

    b. rise, thereby shifting the LM^* curve to the right.

    c. fall, thereby shifting the LM^* curve to the left.

    d. fall, thereby shifting the LM^* curve to the right.

9. If the current yen-to-dollar market exchange rate (for example, 100 yen per dollar) is below a fixed exchange rate set by the Bank of Canada (for example, 150 yen per dollar), arbitragers can make profits by:

    a. buying yen from the Bank of Canada and selling them in foreign exchange markets.

    b. buying dollars in foreign exchange markets and selling them to the Bank of Canada.

    c. buying dollars from the Bank of Canada and selling them in foreign exchange markets.

    d. both a and b.

10. The profit-making actions described in Question 9 will cause the money supply to:

    a. rise, thereby shifting the LM^* curve to the left.

    b. rise, thereby shifting the LM^* curve to the right.

    c. fall, thereby shifting the LM^* curve to the left.

    d. fall, thereby shifting the LM^* curve to the right.

11. Under a gold standard, if the Bank of Canada sells an ounce of gold for $100, and the Bank of England sells an ounce of gold for 50 pounds, then the equilibrium exchange rate would be fixed at:

    a. 2 pounds per dollar.   **c.** 1.5 pounds per dollar.
    b. 0.5 pounds per dollar.   **d.** 5 pounds per dollar.

12. An expansionary fiscal policy under fixed exchange rates will:

    a. force the Bank of Canada to increase the money supply in order to prevent the exchange rate from falling.
    b. increase real income.
    c. eventually lead the IS^* and LM^* curves to shift to the right.
    d. all of the above.

13. If the Bank of Canada tries to increase the money supply under fixed exchange rates:

    a. national income will be unaffected.
    b. the initial increase in the money supply will be offset if the Bank of Canada maintains the original fixed exchange rate.
    c. the LM^* curve on a $Y - e$ graph will shift first to the right and then to the left, back to its original position.
    d. all of the above.

14. If the value of the currency is reduced via a devaluation, the:

    a. LM^* curve shifts to the right, and both net exports and income rise.
    b. LM^* curve shifts to the right, net exports fall, and income rises.
    c. LM^* curve shifts to the left, and both net exports and income fall.
    d. IS^* and LM^* curves both shift to the right.

15. A restrictive trade policy under a fixed exchange rate will:

    a. have the same effect as under a floating exchange rate.
    b. raise the equilibrium level of national income.
    c. shift the IS^* curve to the right and the LM^* curve to the left on a $Y - e$ graph.
    d. lead to a devaluation of the currency.

16. In the Mundell-Fleming model:

    a. both fiscal and monetary policy will have greater effects on national income if the exchange rate is fixed rather than flexible.
    b. both fiscal and monetary policy will have greater effects on national income if the exchange rate is flexible rather than fixed.
    c. fiscal policy will have a greater effect on national income if the exchange rate is fixed rather than flexible, whereas monetary policy will be more potent if the exchange rate is flexible.
    d. fiscal policy will have a greater effect on national income if the exchange rate is flexible rather than fixed, whereas monetary policy will be more potent if the exchange rate is fixed.

17. The risk premium in a country's interest rate will rise if:

    a. people expect the country's exchange rate to fall.
    b. fears arise that the government may not pay all of its debt.
    c. the country's foreign exchange reserves are quickly being depleted.
    d. all of the above.

18. An increase in a country's perceived risk premium will:

    a. shift its *IS** and *LM** curves to the right, resulting in an appreciation of its exchange rate.
    b. shift its *IS** and *LM** curves to the left, resulting in a depreciation of its exchange rate.
    c. shift its *IS** curve to the left and its *LM** curve to the right, resulting in a depreciation of its exchange rate.
    d. shift its *IS** curve to the right and its *LM** curve to the left, resulting in an appreciation of its exchange rate.

19. An argument in favour of floating exchange rates is that they:

    a. reduce uncertainty and promote international trade.
    b. allow monetary policy to be used for purposes other than maintaining exchange rates.
    c. reduce the volatility of exchange rates.
    d. all of the above.

20. Countries with currency boards:

    a. typically have flexible exchange rates.
    b. restrict capital mobility.
    c. are more likely to have speculative attacks on their currency.
    d. are less likely to have speculative attacks on their currency.

21. Dollarization by a foreign country is an extreme form of maintaining:

    a. a balance of trade with the United States.
    b. a fixed exchange rate with the United States.
    c. a floating exchange rate with the United States.
    d. the impossible trinity.

22. According to the *impossible trinity,* it is impossible for a nation to have:

    a. a balanced budget, free capital flows, and a fixed exchange rate.
    b. free capital flows, a fixed exchange rate, and independent fiscal policy.
    c. free capital flows, a floating exchange rate, and independent monetary policy.
    d. free capital flows, a fixed exchange rate, and independent monetary policy.

23. Suppose the initial level of income is less than the long-run equilibrium level. Then, in the Mundell-Fleming model with a changing price level, the price level will:

    a. fall, shifting the IS^* curve to the right.
    b. rise, shifting the IS^* curve to the left.
    c. rise, shifting the LM^* curve to the left.
    d. fall, shifting the LM^* curve to the right.

24. When the Mundell-Fleming model is extended to allow the consumer price index to depend directly on the exchange rate, (I) fiscal policy has no lasting effect on real output under flexible exchange rates, and (II) the LM^* locus is no longer vertical.

    a. I is true; II is not.
    b. II is true; I is not.
    c. Both I and II are true.
    d. Neither I nor II is true.

25. Consider the Mundell-Fleming model when it is extended to allow the consumer price index to depend directly on the exchange rate, and for real-wage rigidity. In that case, (I) fiscal policy has no lasting effect on the real output under flexible exchange rates, and (II) monetary policy has no lasting effect on real output under flexible exchange rates.

    a. I is true; II is not.
    b. II is true; I is not.
    c. Both I and II are true.
    d. Neither I nor II is true.

Exercises

1. **The Effect of the Exchange Rate on the *IS* Curve** *In this exercise, we add net exports to the planned expenditure curve and illustrate the effects of changes in the exchange rate on the planned expenditure and IS curves.*

    a. Consider the following model of the economy:

    $$PE = C + I + G + NX \tag{12-1}$$
    $$C = 125 + 0.75(Y - T) \tag{12-2}$$
    $$I = 200 - 10r \tag{12-3}$$
    $$G = 100 \tag{12-4}$$
    $$T = 100 \tag{12-5}$$
    $$NX = 150 - 50e. \tag{12-6}$$

    This model is very similar to the one presented in the Student Guide exercises for Chapters 10 and 11, except that net exports NX are now included. As in Chapter 12 of the textbook, NX is negatively related to the nominal exchange rate e. Since both the domestic and foreign price levels are held fixed in Chapter 12 of the textbook, changes in the nominal exchange rate e are proportional to changes in the real exchange rate ε, so we can focus on changes in e.

b. Suppose that the nominal exchange rate e is initially equal to 2.0 (for example, 2 euros per dollar). Consequently, $NX = 150 - 50($_____$) =$ _____. Substitute this value of net exports NX into Equation 12-1, along with Equations 12-2 to 12-5, and simplify to obtain the equation for aggregate planned expenditure PE in terms of the interest rate r and aggregate income Y:

$PE =$ _____ $+$ _____ $Y -$ _____ $r.$

c. Recall that, in equilibrium, $PE = Y$. Derive the equation for the IS curve by setting the preceding expenditure equation equal to Y and solving for r.

$r =$ _____ $-$ _____ $Y.$

Graph this equation on Graph 12-1 and label it $IS(e = 2)$.

Graph 12-1

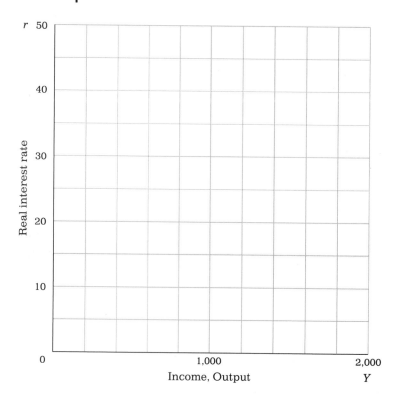

d. Now suppose that the exchange rate falls to $e = 1.0$ (for example, 1 euro per dollar). This exchange rate reflects a(n) appreciation/depreciation of the dollar relative to the euro. As a result, Canadian net exports would rise/fall to $NX = 150 - 50(\underline{\hspace{1cm}}) = \underline{\hspace{1cm}}$. Substitute this new value of net exports NX, along with Equations 12-2 to 12-5, into Equation 12-1, set the result equal to Y, and derive the equation for the new IS curve.

$r = \underline{\hspace{1cm}} - \underline{\hspace{1cm}} Y$.

Graph this equation on Graph 12-1 and label the curve $IS(e = 1)$.

e. Summarizing the results, we see that a reduction in the exchange rate reflects a(n) appreciation/depreciation of the dollar, which will increase/decrease net exports. This reduction shifts the aggregate expenditure curve upward/downward and thereby shifts the IS curve to the right/left. In this example, the reduction in the exchange rate e from 2 to 1 increases net exports NX by \underline{\hspace{3cm}}. This increase in NX shifts the expenditure curve upward/downward by \underline{\hspace{3cm}} and shifts the IS curve to the left/right by the shift in the expenditure curve multiplied by the (government purchases) multiplier, or by _____ × _____ = _____. Conversely, an increase in the exchange rate reflects a(n) appreciation/depreciation of the dollar, which will increase/decrease net exports. This change shifts the aggregate expenditure curve upward/downward and thereby shifts the *IS* curve to the left/right.

2. **The Mundell-Fleming Model on a *Y* − *e* Graph** *In this exercise, we derive the Mundell-Fleming model on a graph with aggregate income* Y *and the exchange rate* e *on the axes.*

   a. On Graph 12-1, each *IS* curve represents the combinations of the interest rate *r* and aggregate income *Y* for which the goods market is in equilibrium, holding the exchange rate *e* fixed. As Chapter 12 of the textbook indicates, one can also draw an *IS* curve, called *IS**, which represents the combinations of the exchange rate *e* and aggregate income *Y* for which the goods market is in equilibrium, holding the interest rate *r* fixed at the world interest rate *r**. Consider the same model utilized in Exercise 1:

   $$PE = C + I + G + NX \qquad \text{(12-7)}$$
   $$C = 125 + 0.75(Y - T) \qquad \text{(12-8)}$$
   $$I = 200 - 10r \qquad \text{(12-9)}$$
   $$G = 100 \qquad \text{(12-10)}$$
   $$T = 100 \qquad \text{(12-11)}$$
   $$NX = 150 - 50e. \qquad \text{(12-12)}$$

   Suppose that $r* = 10$ percent. If $e = 2.0$, then $NX =$ _____. An examination of Graph 12-1 reveals that the goods market will be in equilibrium when $Y =$ _____. Locate this point on Graph 12-2 and label it Point A.

   b. Now suppose that *e* falls to 1.0. Graph 12-1 shows that when $e = 1.0$ and $r = 10$, the goods market is in equilibrium when $Y =$ _____. Locate this point on Graph 12-2 and label it Point B. Connect Points A and B and label the resulting curve *IS**($r = 10$). Intuitively, as the exchange rate falls, net exports rise/fall, the aggregate expenditure curve shifts upward/downward, and the level of income increases/decreases.

Graph 12-2

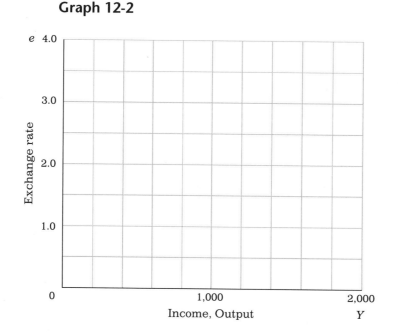

c. The *LM* curve is unaffected by changes in *e* because neither money demand nor money supply depends on the exchange rate. Alternatively, there is only one level of income for which the *LM* curve intersects the $r = r^*$ curve, regardless of the level of *e*. Suppose that when $r^* = 10$, the money market is in equilibrium when $Y = 1,200$. Draw a vertical *LM** curve on Graph 12-2 at this level of *Y*.

d. Graph 12-2 now illustrates the combinations of *e* and *Y* for which the goods market is in equilibrium (along the *IS** curve), and the combinations of *e* and *Y* for which the money market is in equilibrium (along the *LM** curve), assuming that $r^* = 10$. The levels of *e* and *Y* at which both the goods and money markets are in equilibrium are at *e* = _____ and *Y* = _____.
This equilibrium occurs at Point _____ on Graph 12-2.

3. **The Small Open Economy with a Floating Exchange Rate** *In this exercise, we explore the effects of fiscal and monetary policies for a small open economy with a flexible exchange rate.*

a. Graph 12-3 depicts an initial equilibrium using the *IS** and *LM** curves introduced in Exercise 2.

The *IS** and *LM** curves indicate that the initial equilibrium levels of the exchange rate *e* and aggregate income *Y* are at *e* = _____ and *Y* = _____. Locate this point on Graph 12-3 and label it Point A.

Graph 12-3

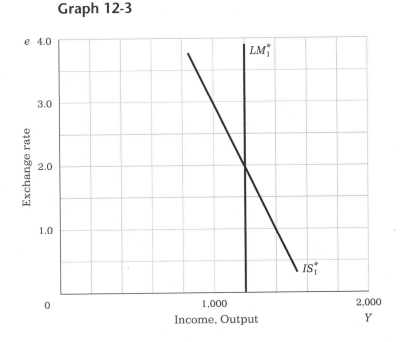

b. Now suppose that the government pursues an expansionary fiscal policy either by increasing/decreasing government purchases G or by increasing/decreasing taxes T. If the exchange rate e is held constant, this policy will increase/decrease aggregate income Y. Thus, the IS^* curve will shift to the left/right. Draw the new IS^* curve on Graph 12-3 and label it IS_2^*. Locate the point on the IS_2^* curve at which $e = 2.0$ and label it Point B.

c. At Point B on Graph 12-3, the demand for money is greater than/less than/equal to the supply of money. Since money demand is unrelated to the exchange rate e, equilibrium can be achieved in the money market only if aggregate income Y increases/decreases/remains constant from Point B. This situation is achieved through a(n) increase/decrease in e. As e rises/falls, net exports NX increase/decrease, and the economy moves along the IS_2^* curve until the new equilibrium is achieved when money demand once again equals the initial money supply. Locate this point on Graph 12-3 and label it Point C. The upward pressure on e occurs because expansionary fiscal policy tends to increase/decrease the interest rate. Yet, whenever the domestic interest rate rises above/falls below the world interest rate, Canadian and foreign investors buy more Canadian assets, which increases/decreases the exchange rate e. This assumption of perfect capital mobility (from Chapter 8) results in a constant real world interest rate r^*.

d. Comparing Points A and C on Graph 12-3, note that in a small open economy with a flexible exchange rate, expansionary fiscal policy increases/decreases/has no effect on the equilibrium level of aggregate income Y and increases/decreases/has no effect on the equilibrium exchange rate e. Consequently, net exports NX will rise/fall/remain constant. Conversely, contractionary fiscal policy increases/decreases/has no effect on the equilibrium level of Y and increases/decreases/has no effect on e.

e. The results in Part d occur because the LM* curve is vertical; only one level of income will equilibrate the money market as long as the money supply is unchanged. Now start again at Point A on Graph 12-4.

Graph 12-4

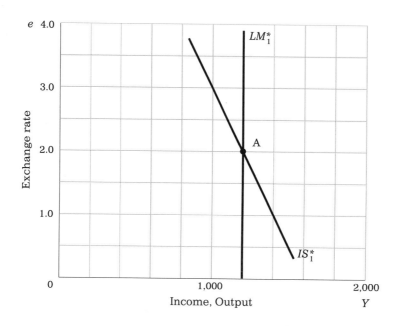

An increase in the money supply will shift the conventional LM curve drawn with r and Y on the axes to the left (upward)/right (downward). If the interest rate r is constant at the real world interest rate r*, then the level of aggregate income Y at which this higher money supply equals money demand will rise/fall. As a result, the LM* curve on Graph 12-4 will shift to the left/right. Draw a new LM* curve on Graph 12-4 and label it LM_2^*. Obviously, the equilibrium level of income increases/decreases/remains constant and the equilibrium exchange rate e increases/decreases/remains constant. Thus, net exports NX will rise/fall/remain constant.

f. In both a closed economy and a small open economy with a flexible exchange rate, expansionary monetary policy will lead to a(n) increase/decrease in the equilibrium level of national income. There are, however, some important differences. In a closed economy, an increase in the money supply increases investment (and, hence, GDP) by reducing _____. In a small open economy with a flexible exchange rate, the interest rate remains fixed at the world interest rate. As soon as the domestic interest rate falls a little, capital flows into/out of the domestic economy. This causes the exchange rate to appreciate/depreciate, which increases/decreases net exports and, hence, GDP.

4. Managing a Fixed Exchange-Rate System *In this exercise, we illustrate how the maintenance of a fixed exchange rate requires adjustments in the money supply.*

a. Graph 12-5 depicts a hypothetical situation in which the IS^* and LM^* curves intersect at an equilibrium exchange rate of $e = 3$ at Point A. This situation implies, for example, that people could exchange 3 euros per dollar on the international currency markets.

Graph 12-5

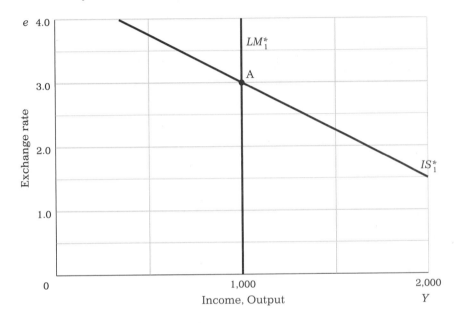

Suppose that Canada committed itself to maintaining a fixed exchange rate of $e = 2$, or _____ euros per dollar. Draw a horizontal line on Graph 12-5 to show this exchange rate, and label it e_{Fixed}. The Bank of Canada would establish this exchange rate by holding a reserve of euros and selling them for 2 euros per dollar. It would also commit itself to buying euros for 2 euros per dollar. It is *critical* to note that whenever these transactions occurred, the Bank of Canada would be changing the Canadian money supply by buying or selling dollars.

b. In Part a, note that the initial equilibrium exchange rate is <u>greater than/less than</u> the fixed exchange rate. As Chapter 12 of the textbook indicates, this situation cannot prevail for long because it creates opportunities for arbitrage. At $e = 3$, people would profit by buying euros on the international currency markets and selling them to the Bank of Canada at its fixed exchange rate. For example, at $e = 3$, people would trade \$1 for _____ euros on the international currency markets. They would then sell these _____ euros to the Bank of Canada and receive \$1 for every 2 euros or

[\$1/(2 euros)] × _____ euros = _____.

They would continue to profit by this kind of arbitrage as long as the equilibrium exchange rate exceeded the fixed exchange rate.

c. In Part b, the Bank of Canada buys euros with newly created dollars. This action increases/decreases the Canadian money supply and shifts the LM^* curve to the left/right. The LM^* curve will continue to shift until $e = e_{Fixed}$. Draw the final LM^* curve on Graph 12-5 and label it LM_2^*. Label the final equilibrium Point B. Consequently, under a fixed-exchange-rate regime, whenever $e > e_{Fixed}$, the domestic money supply will increase/decrease, and the LM^* curve will shift to the left/right until $e = e_{Fixed}$.

d. Now suppose that the equilibrium exchange rate is 1.0, while the Bank of Canada continues to maintain an official fixed exchange rate of 2. This initial situation is depicted on Graph 12-6 at Point C. Draw a horizontal line on Graph 12-6 at $e = 2$ and label it e_{Fixed}.

Graph 12-6

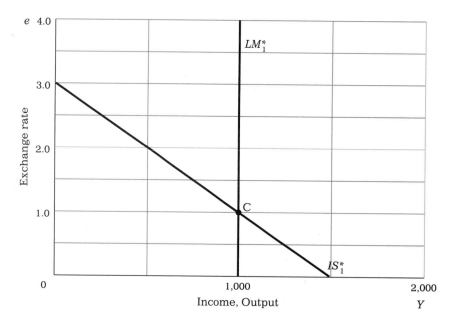

On Graph 12-6, the initial equilibrium exchange rate is greater than/less than the fixed exchange rate. This situation, too, creates opportunities for arbitrage. At $e = 1$, people would profit by buying dollars on the international currency markets and selling them to the Bank of Canada at its fixed exchange rate of $e_{Fixed} = 2$. For example, at $e = 1$, people would trade 1 euro for \$_____ on the international currency markets. They would then sell the \$_____ to the Bank of Canada at its fixed exchange rate and receive _____ euros. They would continue to profit by this kind of arbitrage as long as the fixed exchange rate exceeded the equilibrium exchange rate.

e. When the Bank of Canada is buying dollars in Part d, these dollars are retired from circulation and the Canadian money supply increases/decreases. This situation, in turn, shifts the LM^* curve to the left/right. The LM^* curve will continue to shift until $e = e_{Fixed}$. Draw the final LM^* curve on Graph 12-6, label it LM_3^*, and label the final equilibrium Point D. Consequently, under a fixed-exchange-rate regime, whenever $e < e_{Fixed}$, the domestic money supply will increase/decrease and the LM^* curve will shift to the left/right until $e = e_{Fixed}$.

5. **The Small Open Economy with a Fixed Exchange Rate** *In this exercise, we explore the effects of fiscal and monetary policies for a small open economy with a fixed exchange rate.*

   a. Graph 12-7 depicts a situation in which the equilibrium exchange rate is equal to the fixed exchange rate of 2. Draw a horizontal line on Graph 12-7 at $e = 2$ and label it e_{Fixed}.

Graph 12-7

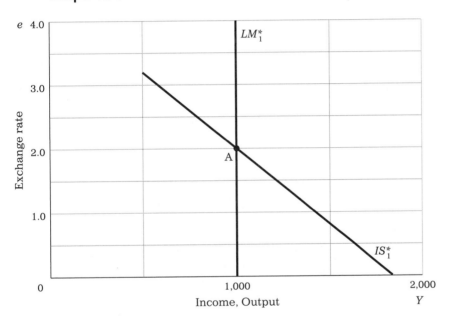

Starting from Point A, suppose that the government pursued expansionary fiscal policy. As in Exercise 3, this policy would shift the IS^* curve to the left/right. Draw the new IS^* curve on Graph 12-7 and label it IS_2^*.

   b. In Exercise 3, we found that under a flexible-exchange-rate regime, expansionary fiscal policy will increase/decrease/have no effect on real output Y and increase/decrease/have no effect on the exchange rate e. If, on the other hand, the exchange rate is fixed, as we saw in Exercise 4, the Bank of Canada will have to increase/decrease the money supply, shifting the LM^* curve to the left/right until $e = e_{Fixed} = $ _____. Draw the new LM^* curve on Graph 12-7, label it LM_2^*, and label the new equilibrium Point B. Thus, under a fixed-exchange-rate regime, expansionary fiscal policy will <u>increase/decrease/</u> <u>have no effect on</u> real output Y and <u>increase/decrease/have no effect on</u> the exchange rate e. This situation occurs because the Bank of Canada will be forced to change the money supply in order to maintain the fixed exchange rate at $e = 2$.

c. Now start again at Point A on Graph 12-8 with $e = e_{\text{Fixed}}$.

Graph 12-8

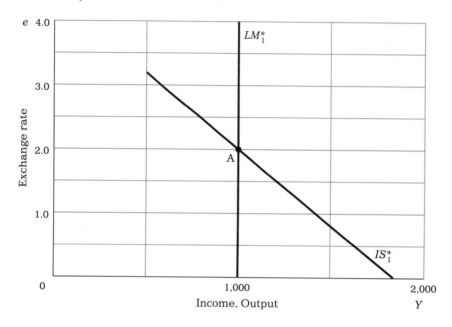

Expansionary monetary policy will initially shift the LM^* curve to the <u>left/right</u>. Draw this new LM^* curve on Graph 12-8 and label it LM_3^*. In Exercise 3 we found that under a flexible-exchange-rate regime, expansionary monetary policy will <u>increase/decrease/have no effect on</u> real output Y and <u>increase/decrease/have</u> <u>no effect on</u> the exchange rate e. If, on the other hand, the exchange rate is fixed, as the equilibrium exchange rate <u>rises above/falls below</u> the fixed exchange rate, the Bank of Canada will find itself <u>buying/selling</u> euros and <u>buying/selling</u> dollars. This activity will <u>increase/decrease</u> the money supply and will shift the LM^* curve to the <u>left/right</u> until $e = e_{\text{Fixed}} =$ _____. Draw the final LM^* curve on Graph 12-8, label it LM_4^*, and label the new equilibrium Point C. (Note the relationship between LM_1^* and LM_4^*.) Thus, under a fixed-exchange-rate regime, expansionary monetary policy will <u>increase/decrease/have no effect on</u> real output Y and will <u>increase/decrease/have no effect on</u> the exchange rate. This situation occurs because the final money supply will be <u>greater than/less</u> <u>than/equal to</u> the initial money supply. The normal power of monetary policy to change income is lost because the money supply is dedicated to maintaining the fixed exchange rate. Finally, since the exchange rate does not change, net exports NX will <u>rise/fall/remain constant</u>.

d. Starting over once again at Point A on Graph 12-8, suppose that Canada devalued the dollar by reducing the fixed exchange rate from 2 to 1. If the initial equilibrium exchange rate were 2, the Bank of Canada would find itself <u>buying/selling</u> euros and <u>buying/selling</u> dollars. This activity would <u>increase/decrease/have no effect on</u> the money supply and would shift the LM^* curve to the <u>left/right</u> until $e = 1$. As a result, Y would <u>increase/decrease/remain constant</u>. Conversely, a revaluation of the dollar to $e = 3$ would shift the LM^* curve to the <u>left/right</u>, and Y would <u>increase/decrease/remain constant</u>.

6. **Incorporating Risk Premiums in the Mundell-Fleming Model** *In this exercise, we use the Mundell-Fleming model to analyze the effects of changes in a country's perceived risk premium.*

a. Real interest rates may differ among countries for a variety of reasons. One reason is that assets in one country (for example, government bonds) may be viewed as riskier than similar assets in another country if the first country is politically or economically unstable. To induce international investors to purchase their assets, the domestic interest rate in countries that are seen as more risky will be <u>higher/lower</u>.

Graph 12-9

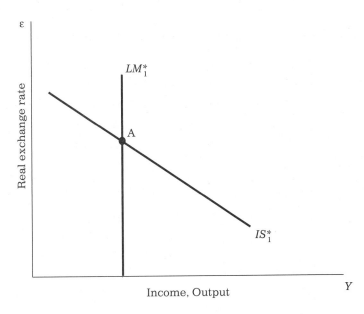

b. Point A in Graph 12-9 depicts an initial equilibrium in a small open economy. If new political turmoil raises this country's perceived risk, its domestic interest rate r <u>rises/falls</u>. This change in the interest rate would <u>increase/decrease</u> investment and thereby shift the IS^* curve to the <u>left/right</u>. Draw this new IS^* curve in Graph 12-9 and label it IS_2^*.

c. This change in the interest rate would also increase/decrease the demand for money. Because this allows a higher level of income for any given money supply, the *LM** curve would shift to the left/right. Draw the new *LM** curve in Graph 12-9, label it LM_2^*, and label the new equilibrium Point B.

d. Comparing Points A and B, we see that an increase in a country's perceived risk premium will lead to a(n) appreciation/depreciation of its exchange rate and a(n) increase/decrease in its real income.

e. Even though higher domestic interest rates reduce investment, national income rises because the change in the exchange rate increases/decreases net exports by an even greater amount. In those countries that have experienced perceived increases in risk, however, national income has often declined for one of several reasons. First, the central banks have occasionally reduced the money supply in order to counteract the exchange rate depreciation, which shifts the *IS*/LM** curve to the left/right. Second, the depreciation causes the price of imported goods to rise, which may increase the domestic price level *P*. This would increase/decrease the real money supply and shift the *IS*/LM** curve to the left/right. Finally, domestic residents may increase their demand for money because money is a liquid and relatively safe asset. This would shift the *IS*/LM** to the left/right.

7. **The Mundell-Fleming Model with a Changing Price Level** *In this exercise, we show how the long-run price adjustments that move the economy toward its long-run equilibrium operate within the Mundell-Fleming model's flexible-exchange-rate regime.*

a. In Chapter 9 of the textbook, we saw how shifts in the aggregate supply curve move the economy toward its long-run equilibrium. The same phenomenon also occurs in the Mundell-Fleming model, although the aggregate demand curve is somewhat different. Points A in Graphs 12-10 and 12-11 depict an initial equilibrium at which output is greater than/equal to/less than the long-run natural rate of output $\overline{Y}$.

Note that the vertical axis in Graph 12-10 now measures the real exchange rate ε. Recall that $\varepsilon = e(P/P^*)$, where *e* represents the nominal exchange rate and P/P^* represents the ratio of domestic to foreign prices. It was not necessary to make this adjustment in Exercises 2–5 because the price levels there were assumed to increase/remain constant/decrease. Since ε is on the vertical axis in Graph 12-10, however, a change in *P* will not shift the *IS** curve.

b. When the short-run equilibrium level of output is less than *Y*, the short-run aggregate supply *SRAS* curve will shift upward/downward over time, just as in a closed economy. (Although the *SRAS* curve is depicted as a horizontal line in Graph 12-11, one can derive the same results from a positively sloped *SRAS* curve.) As this *SRAS* curve shifts, the domestic price level *P* will rise/fall and output will rise/fall. Draw the final *SRAS* curve in Graph 12-11, label it $SRAS_2$, and label the long-run equilibrium Point Z.

Graph 12-10

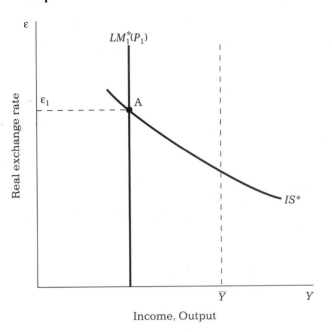

Income, Output

Graph 12-11

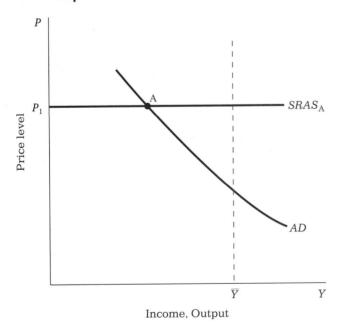

Income, Output

c. Returning to Graph 12-10, the reduction in the domestic price level will
increase/decrease real money supply/demand. This will shift the *IS*/LM** curve
to the right/left since the exchange rate is flexible. Hence, the real exchange
rate will rise/fall and net exports will rise/fall. Draw the final *LM** curve, label it

LM$_2^*$, and label the final equilibrium Point Z. Comparing Points Z and A, output rises/falls/remains the same and net exports rise/fall/remain the same. Investment rises/falls/remains the same because the real interest rate rises/falls/remains the same.

Problems

Answer the following problems on a separate sheet of paper.

1. Explain why a monetary contraction for a small open economy under fixed exchange rates will have no effect on real income.

2. During the fall of 1992, Great Britain decided to leave the European Monetary System (EMS), in which members agreed to limit fluctuations in the exchange rates among their currencies. Describe the advantages and disadvantages of such a move.

3. Not all countries in Europe are currently participating in the single European currency, called the euro.

   a. How does monetary unification change the ability of each country that is currently a participant to conduct independent countercyclical monetary and fiscal policy?

   b. How does the introduction of the euro and monetary unification change the ability of each European country that is not a participant (but typically has a floating exchange rate) to conduct independent countercyclical monetary and fiscal policy?

4. If a small open economy with a flexible exchange rate is experiencing a recession, what will automatically happen over time to its trade balance, foreign exchange rate, and national output?

5. Suppose the government in a small developing economy places restrictions on agricultural exports in order to increase the domestic food supply and lower food prices. Use the Mundell-Fleming model to analyze the short-run effects of this policy on the exchange rate and real GDP if the country has a:

   a. flexible exchange rate.

   b. fixed exchange rate.

6. Use the Mundell-Fleming model to illustrate the short-run effects of the Mexican crisis in a small open economy with a fixed exchange rate.

7. In 1997, 1998, and 1999, the risk premiums associated with several countries in Southeast Asia and Latin America (notably Brazil) rose dramatically. By the year 2000, many of these countries had regained economic stability by reducing their foreign debt burdens and more efficiently managing their economies. Use the Mundell-Fleming model to illustrate the effects of renewed stability on these countries' domestic interest rates, exchange rates, and real GDP under a regime of flexible exchange rates.

8. As the textbook states, Argentina introduced a currency board in the early 1990s. Under this arrangement the Argentine central bank held one U.S. dollar for every outstanding Argentine peso and maintained a fixed dollar-peso exchange rate of 1:1. Although the Argentine economy initially responded well to this innovation, it ran into severe difficulties by the late 1990s and was forced to abandon the currency board in 2002. One of the reasons for its difficulties was the fact that many of Argentina's major trading partners, most notably Brazil, allowed their currencies to fall in value relative to the U.S. dollar during the late 1990s. Because Argentina maintained a fixed dollar-peso exchange rate, the devaluation of Brazil's and other neighbors' currencies essentially shifted the Argentine net export curve to the left below:

Graph 12-12

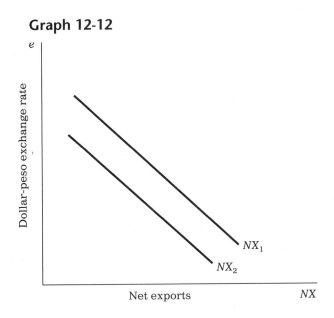

a. Treating Argentina as a small, open economy, use the Mundell–Fleming model to illustrate the effects of this de-facto shift in its net export curve on Argentina's domestic interest rate and real GDP if Argentina adhered to its fixed exchange rate relative to the dollar. (This is largely what happened.)

b. Now use the appropriate graphs to show what the effects of this shift in net exports would have been on Argentina's dollar-peso exchange rate and real GDP if Argentina had allowed its dollar-peso exchange rate to float freely following Brazil's devaluation. (While many economists believe this is what Argentina should have done, others believe that earlier abandonment of the currency board would have created other difficulties by reducing the credibility of Argentina's central bank.)

9. Suppose you are about to enter a debate on whether it is advisable for the central bank in a small open economy to "lean against the wind," that is, to adopt a floating exchange rate policy but to limit the short-run variations in the exchange rate. What arguments would you have ready for the debate?

10. Consider the Mundell-Fleming model extended in two ways; let the consumer price index depend directly on the exchange rate, and let the price of domestic goods be a positive function of the level of real output (an upward-sloping short-run aggregate supply curve). Assume that the central bank pegs the overall consumer price index. Draw a diagram in e-Y space that allows you to determine whether an increase in foreign interest rates causes a domestic recession.

Questions to Think About

1. Would you advise the leader of a small open economy in Africa to adopt a fixed or floating exchange rate? Would your answer be different if the country were in Europe? Why or why not?

2. Why do policymakers in small open countries with floating exchange rates pursue countercyclical fiscal policies?

3. Would the world economy be better off with just one currency? Why or why not?

Aggregate Supply and the Short-Run Tradeoff Between Inflation and Unemployment

Fill-in Questions

Use the key terms below to fill in the blanks in the following statements. Each term may be used more than once.

adaptive expectations

cost-push inflation

demand-pull inflation

hysteresis

imperfect-information model

NAIRU

natural-rate hypothesis

Phillips curve

rational expectations

sacrifice ratio

sticky-price model

1. The _____ assumes that firms do not instantly adjust the prices they charge in response to changes in demand. It states that the slope of the short-run aggregate supply curve depends on the proportion of firms in the economy that have flexible prices.

2. The _____ assumes that all markets clear, but that short-run and long-run aggregate supply curves differ because of short-run misperceptions about prices. Therefore, when prices unexpectedly rise, suppliers infer that their relative prices have risen, which induces them to produce more output.

3. According to both the _____ and the _____ models, when aggregate output is equal to the natural level of output and there are no supply shocks, the actual price level will be equal to the expected price level.

4. The graph of the negative relationship between inflation and unemployment, holding expected inflation constant, is called the _____.

5. When the Phillips curve is written as $\pi = \pi_{-1} - \beta(u - u^n) + v$, the natural rate of unemployment is sometimes called the _____.

6. According to the _____, when unemployment falls below the natural rate, inflation tends to rise. This type of inflation is called _____.

7.   Rising inflation due to an adverse supply shock is called _____.

8.   According to the assumption of _____, people form their expectations of inflation based solely on recently observed inflation.

9.   According to the assumption of _____, people form their expectations by optimally using all of the available information, including information about current policies, to forecast the future.

10.   The _____ is the number of percentage points of a year's real GDP that must be foregone to reduce inflation by 1 percentage point. It will tend to be lower if people have _____ rather than

_____.

11.   According to the _____, the economy returns in the long run to the levels of output, employment, and unemployment described by the classical model. In the short run, however, output and unemployment are affected by fluctuations in aggregate demand.

12.   _____ is the term used to describe the long-lasting influence of history on the natural rate of unemployment. For example, a recession can have permanent effects on output and unemployment if it eventually reduces the skills of those who become unemployed.

Multiple-Choice Questions

1.   In the sticky-price model, prices are sticky in the short run because:

    a. some prices are set by long-term contracts and cannot be changed in the short run.

    b. once a firm has printed and distributed its catalog or price list, it is costly to change prices.

    c. firms base their prices on the costs of production, which include labour costs, and wages may be sticky because they depend on social norms that evolve slowly over time.

    d. All of the above are true.

2.   In the sticky-price model:

    a. all firms adjust prices instantly in response to changes in demand.

    b. no firms adjust prices instantly in response to changes in demand.

    c. some firms adjust prices instantly in response to changes in demand while others do not.

    d. output is constant.

3.   If all firms in the economy have fixed prices in the short run:

   a.   the short-run and long-run aggregate supply curves will be identical.

   b.   the short-run aggregate supply curve will be vertical.

   c.   the short-run aggregate supply curve will be horizontal.

   d.   none of the above will be true.

4.   In the sticky-price model, the equation $p = P + a(Y - \overline{Y})$ describes the behaviour of:

   a.   a firm with flexible prices in the short run.

   b.   a firm with sticky prices in the short run.

   c.   all firms in the short run.

   d.   all firms in the long run but no firms in the short run.

5.   In the sticky-price model, the equation $p = EP + a(EY - E\overline{Y})$ describes the behaviour of:

   a.   a firm with flexible prices in the short run.

   b.   a firm with sticky prices in the short run.

   c.   all firms in the short run.

   d.   all firms in the long run but no firms in the short run.

6.   In the sticky-price model, the equation $Y = \overline{Y} + \alpha(P - EP)$ describes the behaviour of:

   a.   each and every firm in both the short run and the long run.

   b.   the overall economy in both the short run and the long run.

   c.   both a and b.

   d.   small firms but not large firms.

7.   According to the imperfect-information model, when prices unexpectedly rise, suppliers infer that their relative prices have _____, which induces them to _____ output.

   a.   increased; increase

   b.   decreased; decrease

   c.   increased; decrease

   d.   decreased; increase

8.   Both the sticky-price and the imperfect-information models can explain why countries with variable aggregate demand have short-run aggregate supply curves that are:

   a.   flat.

   b.   steep.

   c.   horizontal.

   d.   vertical.

9. According to the sticky-price model, countries with higher rates of inflation will have a:

   a. steeper short-run aggregate supply curve.

   b. flatter short-run aggregate supply curve.

   c. vertical short-run aggregate supply curve.

   d. horizontal long-run aggregate supply curve.

10. Both models of aggregate supply discussed in Chapter 13 of the textbook predict:

    a. an upward-sloping *SRAS* curve.

    b. a vertical *LRAS* curve.

    c. that the actual level of output is equal to its natural rate in the long run.

    d. all of the above.

11. According to the Phillips curve, the inflation rate depends on:

    a. expected inflation.

    b. the difference between the actual and natural rates of unemployment.

    c. supply shocks.

    d. all of the above.

12. When unemployment is below the natural rate and inflation rises, it is characterized as:

    a. demand-pull inflation.

    b. cost-push inflation.

    c. a supply shock.

    d. stagflation.

13. Compared with the assumption of adaptive expectations, the assumption of rational expectations implies that the transition to the new long-run equilibrium following a credible change in monetary or fiscal policy will take:

    a. less time.

    b. more time.

    c. the same amount of time.

    d. any of the above.

14. The Phillips curve immediately shifts upward whenever:

    a. inflation rises.

    b. unemployment falls.

    c. an adverse supply shock, such as an oil price increase, occurs.

    d. all of the above.

15. Assume that a typical estimate of the sacrifice ratio is about 5. Thus, if the inflation rate were to be lowered by 2 percentage points, the amount of one year's GDP we must give up is:

    a. 2 percent.

    b. 2.5 percent.

    c. 5 percent.

    d. 10 percent.

16. According to the hypothesis of unemployment hysteresis, a prolonged recession will:

    a. increase the natural rate of unemployment.

    b. decrease the natural rate of unemployment.

    c. have no effect on the natural rate of unemployment.

    d. never occur.

17. Hysteresis also:

    a. increases the sacrifice ratio.

    b. decreases the sacrifice ration.

    c. increases the sacrifice ratio when inflation is high but decreases the sacrifice ratio when inflation is low.

    d. has no effect on the sacrifice ratio.

18. Recent work on imperfect information models:

    a. stresses the increasingly limited availability of information.

    b. stresses the limited ability of individuals to incorporate information about the economy into their decisions.

    c. has found that people do not make forecasts about relative prices.

    d. stresses all of the answers.

Exercises

1. **The General Short-run Aggregate Supply Curve** *In this exercise, we discuss the general short-run aggregate supply equation that is derived later from four different models. We graph this equation and discuss the changes that will shift the aggregate supply curve.*

    a. All three models of aggregate supply discussed in Chapter 13 of the textbook result in an aggregate supply equation of the following form:

    $$Y = \overline{Y} + \alpha(P - EP),$$

    where Y is output, $\overline{Y}$ is the natural rate of output, P is the price level, and EP is the expected price level. This equation implies that output will be at its natural rate when the actual price level is <u>greater than/less than/equal to</u> the expected price level. Output exceeds its natural rate $(Y > \overline{Y})$ only when the actual price level is <u>greater than/less than/equal to</u> the expected price level.

    b. It is easier to graph this equation if we isolate P on the left-hand side. Subtracting $\overline{Y}$ from both sides of the equation and rearranging yields

    $$\alpha P - \alpha EP = Y - \overline{Y},$$
    $$\alpha P = \alpha EP + (Y - \overline{Y}), \text{or}$$
    $$P = EP + \left(\frac{1}{\alpha}\right)(Y - \overline{Y}).$$

    (13-1)

Equation 13-1 indicates that when $Y = \overline{Y}$, $P = EP$. Graph this equation on Graph 13-1, label the curve *AS,* and label the slope of the line.

Graph 13-1

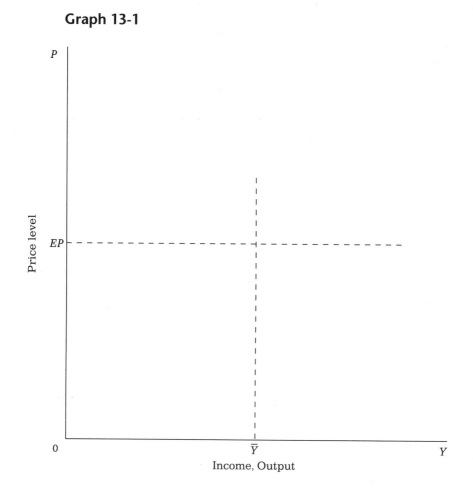

c.   Equation 13-1 and Graph 13-1 indicate that an increase in the expected price level will shift the aggregate supply curve <u>upward (to the left)/downward (to the right)</u>. An increase in the natural rate of output will shift the aggregate supply curve <u>upward (to the left)/downward (to the right)</u> because the level of Y at which output will equal its natural rate (and P will equal EP) will <u>increase/ decrease</u>. The next four exercises illustrate how we can derive this aggregate supply curve from three different models of aggregate supply.

2.   **The Sticky-Price Model** *In this exercise, we derive the aggregate supply curve using the sticky-price model.*

a.   In the sticky-price model, the prices of some firms or products may be sticky because of long-term contracts or because of the way that markets are structured. The prices of other firms or products, however, will be flexible. As a result, the slope of the aggregate supply curve, reflecting the degree of price stickiness in the entire economy, will depend on the proportion of firms (or products) that have sticky prices.

$$p = P + a(Y - \overline{Y}).$$

b. Let us first consider a firm with flexible prices. This firm will set its price p so that: If the aggregate price level P rises, this firm's costs will <u>rise/fall</u>, and it will <u>raise/lower</u> its own price p. If aggregate income rises above its natural rate, the demand curve for the firm's product will also <u>increase/decrease</u>, resulting in a(n) <u>increase/decrease</u> in price.

c. The firms with sticky prices have to set their prices before the aggregate price level and level of income become known. Therefore, they must set their prices according to their expectations of these variables:

$$p = EP + a(EY - E\overline{Y}).$$

If s represents the fraction of all firms with sticky prices, and $(1 - s)$ represents the fraction with flexible prices, then the overall price level will be a weighted average of the prices of flexible and sticky-price firms:

$$P = s[EP + a(EY - E\overline{Y})] + (1 - s)[P + a(Y - \overline{Y})].$$

Now suppose that aggregate income is expected to be at its natural rate—that is, $EY = E\overline{Y}$. Consequently, $EY - E\overline{Y} = $ _____, and

$$P = sEP (1 - s)[P + a(Y - \overline{Y})], \text{ or}$$
$$P = sEP + P - sP + [(1 - s)a(Y - \overline{Y})], \text{ or}$$
$$sP = sEP + [(1 - s)a(Y - \overline{Y})], \text{ or}$$
$$P = EP + [(1 - s)a/s](Y - \overline{Y}).$$

(13-2)

Equation 13-2 indicates that income will equal its natural rate, that is, $Y = \overline{Y}$, whenever the aggregate price level is <u>greater than/less than/equal to</u> the expected price level. Output (income) will exceed its natural rate only if the aggregate price level is <u>greater than/less than/equal to</u> the expected price level. As the proportion of firms with sticky prices rises, s rises. The rise in s <u>increases/decreases</u> the numerator of the coefficient of Y and <u>increases/decreases</u> the denominator. Consequently, the coefficient of Y <u>increases/decreases</u>. This <u>increases/decreases</u> the slope of the aggregate supply curve; hence, the aggregate supply curve becomes <u>flatter/steeper</u>. In Chapter 9 of the textbook, for example, the short-run aggregate supply curve was <u>horizontal/vertical</u>, the implicit value of s was _____, and <u>all/no</u> firms were assumed to have sticky prices in the short run.

3. **The Imperfect-Information Model** *In this exercise, we develop the aggregate supply curve using the imperfect-information model.*

a. In the imperfect-information model, all markets clear, and output again deviates from its natural rate whenever prices deviate from their expected levels. Following the simple example presented in Chapter 13 of the textbook, consider a wheat farmer in an imperfectly competitive wheat market. This wheat farmer will increase her production of wheat only if she thinks that the price of wheat relative to all other goods and services—that is, P_{wheat}/P—has increased. Although the farmer can easily see when the price of wheat rises, she does not immediately get information about the aggregate price level. Consequently, she makes a forecast of the aggregate price level EP. As a result, the production of wheat will be positively related to P_{wheat}/EP. This relationship is graphed on Graph 13-2.

Graph 13-2

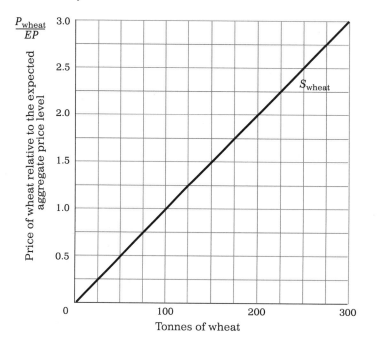

b. Assume that the equilibrium price of wheat equals $1. If the expected aggregate price level $EP = 1.0$, and the actual price of wheat $P_{wheat} = \$1$, then the expected relative (or real) price of wheat $= P_{wheat}/EP =$

_____/_____ = _____.

From Graph 13-2, we see that the quantity of wheat produced will equal

_____ tonnes. Label this Point A.

c. Suppose for the moment that the expected price level remains equal to 1.0, but that the farmer suddenly finds that the price of wheat has risen to $3. As a result, the farmer thinks that the relative price of wheat has risen to $P_{wheat}/EP =$

$_____/_____ = _____.

From Graph 13-2, we see that the quantity of wheat produced will rise/fall to

_____ tonnes. Label this Point B.

d. In the imperfect-information model, however, farmers realize that part of the increase in the price of wheat probably reflects an increase in the aggregate price level. Thus, they respond to the increase in the price of wheat by increasing both the quantity of wheat produced and EP. On Graph 13-3, Point A reflects the situation in which $P_{wheat} = \$1$ and $EP = 1.0$. Thus, at Point A, the expected relative price of wheat = $P_{wheat}/EP =$ _____ / _____ = _____. From Graph 13-2, we see that when this occurs, the quantity of wheat supplied will equal _____ tonnes.

Graph 13-3

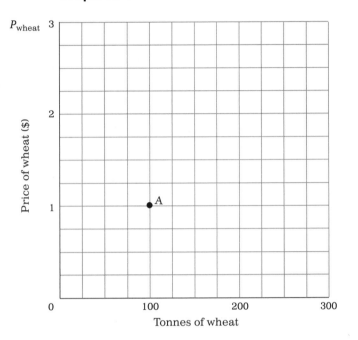

e. Starting from $1, suppose that the farmer again finds that the price of wheat has risen to $3. This represents an increase in P_{wheat} of _____ percent. Now, however, the farmer estimates that half of this percentage increase represents an increase in the aggregate price level. Consequently, her estimate of EP rises by $0.5 \times$ _____ percent = _____ percent, that is, EP rises from 1.0 to _____. The new expected relative price of wheat is now $P_{wheat}/EP = \$3/$ _____ = _____. From Graph 13-2, we see that at this expected relative price, the quantity of wheat supplied will equal _____ tonnes. Label this Point C on Graph 13-2. Locate the point on Graph 13-3 that corresponds to this quantity and price of wheat ($3) and also label it Point C. Connect Points A and C on Graph 13-3 and label the curve AS_1. (In reality, of course, GDP includes more than just wheat.)

f. Extending this story to the entire economy, each producer will increase production only if she thinks that the price of the commodity she produces has risen relative to the aggregate price level. The price of all commodities taken together is merely the aggregate price level P. In long-run equilibrium, $P = EP$, so that P/EP = _____, and output will be at its equilibrium or natural rate. If $P > EP$, output will be greater/less than its natural rate, and if $P < EP$, output will be greater/less than its natural rate. These conditions result in an upward-sloping short-run aggregate supply curve.

g. Now suppose that there has been a great deal of inflation in the recent past. **CH** Consequently, when P_{wheat} rises from \$1 to \$3, or by _____ percent, our farmer assumes that 70 percent of this increase represents an increase in the aggregate price level. Thus, the farmer's EP rises by $0.70 \times$ _____ percent = _____ percent, that is, from $EP = 1.0$ to EP = _____. The new expected relative price of wheat is now $P_{wheat}/EP = \$3/$_____ = _____. From Graph 13-2, we see that at this expected relative price, the quantity of wheat supplied will equal _____ tonnes. Locate this quantity and this price of wheat (\$3) on Graph 13-3 and label it Point D. Connect Points A and D on Graph 13-3 and label your curve AS_2. AS_2 is flatter/steeper than AS_1. Thus, if firms believe that most of any increase in the price of their output is the result of general inflation, the aggregate supply curve will be relatively flat/steep. In the extreme case in which all increases in P_{wheat} are assumed to result from general inflation, P_{wheat}/EP will always equal _____, the quantity of wheat supplied will always equal _____ tonnes, and the aggregate supply curve will be horizontal/vertical.

4. **The Short-Run and Long-Run Effects of an Increase in Aggregate Demand** *In this exercise, we link the aggregate supply and aggregate demand curves developed in Chapters 10 and 11 of the textbook with the long-run aggregate supply curve presented in Chapter 9 of the textbook.*

a. On Graph 13-4, we put the aggregate supply and aggregate demand curves together to depict an initial equilibrium at Point A.

Graph 13-4

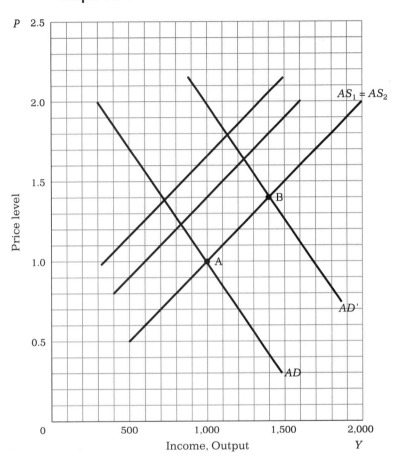

Recall that the aggregate demand curve slopes downward because as the aggregate price level falls, real money balances increase/decrease. This change in real money balances shifts the *IS/LM* curve _____.
Consequently, the equilibrium level of income at the intersection of the *IS* and *LM* curves increases/decreases. The short-run aggregate supply curve slopes upward because output increases above its natural rate only if the price level rises above/falls below the expected price level. Finally, the long-run aggregate supply curve is vertical because in the long run all prices and wages are sticky/flexible, and in the long run output will always be greater than/less than/equal to its natural rate, regardless of the price level.

b. At Point A, output is equal to the natural rate of output, which we arbitrarily set equal to 1,000. Consequently, the aggregate price level *P* must be greater than/equal to/less than its expected level *EP*. If *EP* does not change, it must therefore equal _____ all along the short-run aggregate supply curve AS_1.

c. Now suppose that the aggregate demand curve shifts to the right, to AD', in the second period. This shift could result from a(n) increase/decrease in government purchases, a(n) increase/decrease in taxes, a(n) increase/decrease in the money supply, or a variety of other reasons. If the expected price level does not change (this is an important assumption), it will remain equal to

_____. Consequently, in the second period, the short-run aggregate supply curve will not immediately shift (and, as on Graph 13-4, $AS_1 = AS_2$), and we will move to Point B. At Point B, output $Y =$

_____ and $P =$ _____. (These numbers must be read from the graph itself.)

d. If the policy change is a one-time, permanent change, the aggregate demand curve will not shift again. Nevertheless, the economy will not stay at Point B forever because, at Point B, the actual price level is greater than/less than/equal to the expected price level. Consequently, in the next period, the expected price level will increase/remain the same/decrease.

e. Suppose that the expected price level in any period is equal to the last period's actual price level—that is, $EP = P_{-1}$. Since the actual price level P in Period 2 =

_____, the expected price level in Period 3 will equal

_____. This change will shift the short-run aggregate supply curve upward/downward because, in Period 3, output will equal its natural rate only if $P = EP =$ _____. Label as AS_3 the curve on Graph 13-4 that depicts the short-run aggregate supply curve in Period 3.

f. Consequently, in Period 3 the economy moves to the intersection of AD' (since AD' remains stationary) and AS_3. Label this Point C on Graph 13-4. At Point C,

$Y =$ _____ and $P =$ _____. (Again, read these data from the graph; round off if necessary.) Between Periods 2 and 3, output has risen/fallen, whereas the price level has risen/fallen.

g. At Point C, the actual price level is greater than/less than/equal to the expected price level. Consequently, in the next period, the expected price level will increase/remain the same/decrease. If $EP = P_{-1}$ and the actual price level in Period 3 = _____, then the expected price level in Period 4 will rise to _____. This rise in EP will shift the short-run aggregate supply curve upward/downward so that, in Period 4, output will equal its natural rate only if $P = EP =$ _____. Label as AS_4 the curve on Graph 13-4 that depicts the short-run aggregate supply curve in Period 4. Label as Point D the point that represents the short-run equilibrium in Period 4.

h. At Point D on Graph 13-4, the actual price level is greater than/less than/equal to the expected price level. Consequently, in the next period, the expected price level will increase/remain the same/decrease, and this change will shift the short-run aggregate supply curve upward/downward. The short-run aggregate supply curve will continue to shift in each successive period as long as $P > EP$.

This shift will occur as long as actual output is greater than/less than the natural rate of output. The short-run aggregate supply curve will stop shifting when $P = EP$, which occurs when $Y = \overline{Y}$. At this point, the short-run aggregate supply curve will intersect the aggregate demand curve at a point along the long-run aggregate supply curve. Label the long-run equilibrium on Graph 13-4 Point F. At Point F, $Y =$ _____ and $P =$ _____. Draw the short-run aggregate supply curve that corresponds to this long-run equilibrium on Graph 13-4 and label it AS_F. At Point F, the expected price level $EP =$ _____, and this is equal to the actual price level. The equilibrium level of output Y is also equal to the natural rate of output $\overline{Y}$. Consequently, there are no forces pushing the economy away from Point F.

i.   Comparing Points A and F, the long-run effects of the increase in aggregate demand were an increase/no change/a decrease in output and an increase/no change/a decrease in the price level.

j.   Now suppose that we start again at Point A, and the aggregate demand curve once again shifts to AD'. Since this shift occurred unexpectedly, the economy would move to Point B. In Period 3, however, people (particularly those who have taken an intermediate macroeconomics course) may begin to realize that prices will continue to rise. Consequently, they may try to revise their expectations of the future price level to take this into account. If they did, the expected price level would rise more rapidly than indicated in Parts e through h, and the short-run aggregate supply curve would shift upward more/less rapidly, provided that wages and prices could change as rapidly as price expectations. As a result, the economy would reach its long-run equilibrium more/less rapidly.

5.   **The Phillips Curve** *In this exercise, we use the Phillips curve to analyze the short-run and long-run effects of changes in macroeconomic policies.*

a.   The Phillips curve is an alternative way to analyze the interactions between aggregate supply and aggregate demand. The Phillips curve equation is

$$\pi = E\pi - \beta(u - u^n) + v, \qquad\qquad (13\text{-}3)$$

where π equals the actual inflation rate, $E\pi$ equals expected inflation, u and u^n equal the actual and natural rates of unemployment, v represents the effects of supply shocks that shift the Phillips curve, and β is greater than zero. According to Equation 13-3, when the unemployment rate exceeds the natural rate of unemployment and there are no supply shocks, $\beta(u - u^n)$ is positive/negative. Thus, actual inflation, $\pi = E\pi - \beta(u - u^n)$, will be greater/less than expected inflation.

b.   Suppose that the Phillips curve equation was

$$\pi = E\pi - 0.4(u - u^n) + v.$$

Suppose, in addition, that expected inflation was 8 percent, the natural rate of unemployment was 5 percent, and there were no supply shocks. Consequently, the Phillips curve equation corresponding to this situation would be

$$\pi = 8 - 0.4(u - 5). \qquad \textbf{(13-4)}$$

Solve this equation for π.

$\pi =$ _____ $-$ _____ u.

Note that in Equation 13-4, inflation and unemployment are expressed as percentages rather than decimals. Plot and draw Equation 13-4 on Graph 13-5 and label it PC_1.

Graph 13-5

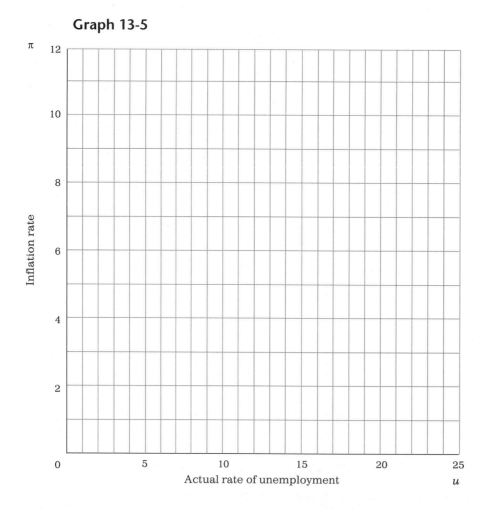

Note that on Graph 13-5, when $u = u^n$, actual inflation is <u>greater than/less than/equal to</u> the expected inflation rate of 8 percent.

c. Suppose that the economy was initially at the natural rate of unemployment. Find the point along PC_1 on Graph 13-5 at which the unemployment rate is equal to the natural rate of unemployment and label it Point A. If the Bank of Canada and the government thought that inflation must be reduced, they could decrease aggregate demand in the second period by increasing/decreasing government purchases, increasing/decreasing taxes, and/or increasing/decreasing the money supply. If expected inflation does not change (this is an important assumption), it will remain equal to _____ percent. Consequently, in the second period, the Phillips curve will not shift, and we will move along PC_1 to the left/right. Since the Phillips curve did not shift, change the label of PC_1 on Graph 13-5 to $PC_1 = PC_2$.

d. Suppose that these policies increased the unemployment rate to 10 percent. Find this point on your Phillips curve on Graph 13-5 and label it Point B. At Point B, $u =$ _____ percent and $\pi =$ _____ percent.

e. At Point B, actual inflation is greater than/less than/equal to expected inflation. Consequently, in the next (third) period, expected inflation will rise/fall and the Phillips curve will shift upward/downward.

f. Suppose that expected inflation in any period was equal to actual inflation during the preceding period, that is,

$$E\pi = \pi_{-1}.$$

In Period 2, we found that $\pi =$ _____ percent.
Consequently, in Period 3, $E\pi =$ _____ percent. This value will change the Phillips curve equation to

$$\pi = E\pi - 0.4(u - 5) = \text{_____} - 0.4(u - 5). \qquad \textbf{(13-5)}$$

Solve this equation for π.

$\pi =$ _____ $-$ _____ $u.$

Plot and draw Equation 13-5 on Graph 13-5 and label the curve PC_3.

g. In Period 3, suppose that the government and the Bank of Canada continued their policies and kept the unemployment rate at 10 percent. Find this point on PC_3 on Graph 13-5 and label it Point C. At Point C, $u =$ _____ percent and $\pi =$ _____ percent.

h. At Point C, actual inflation is <u>greater than/less than/equal to</u> expected inflation. Consequently, in the next (fourth) period, expected inflation will <u>rise/fall</u> and the Phillips curve will shift <u>upward/downward</u>. Since actual inflation in Period 3 = _____ percent, expected inflation in Period 4 will equal _____ percent. Once again, this value will change the Phillips curve equation to

$$\pi = E\pi - 0.4(u - 5) = \text{\underline{\hspace{4cm}}} - 0.4(u - 5). \qquad \textbf{(13-6)}$$

Solve this equation for π.

$$\pi = \text{\underline{\hspace{4cm}}} - \text{\underline{\hspace{4cm}}} \, u.$$

Plot and draw Equation 13-6 on Graph 13-5 and label the curve PC_4.

i. In Period 4, suppose that the government and the Bank of Canada eased their policies and allowed the unemployment rate to resume its natural rate of 5 percent. Find this point on PC_4 on Graph 13-5 and label it Point D. At Point D, $u =$ _____ percent, $\pi =$ _____ percent, and actual inflation is <u>greater than/less than/equal to</u> expected inflation. Consequently, in the next (fifth) period, expected inflation will <u>rise/stay the same/fall</u>, and the Phillips curve will <u>shift upward/remain stationary/shift downward</u>. Thus, Point D represents a new long-run equilibrium.

j. In this exercise, it took two periods of excess unemployment to reduce inflation from 8 percent to _____ percent. If each period lasted for one year, it took two years of unemployment that exceeded the natural rate by $10 - 5 =$ _____ percentage points, or a total of $2 \times$ _____ = _____ percentage-point years of cyclical unemployment, to reduce inflation by $8 -$ _____ _____ = _____ percentage points. For each percentage-point reduction in inflation, it took _____ percentage-point years of cyclical unemployment. According to Okun's law (see Chapter 2 of the textbook), each percentage-point year of cyclical unemployment represents 2 percentage points in lost GDP. Consequently, in our example, it took _____ percentage points in lost GDP to reduce inflation by 1 percentage point. This is called the _____ ratio.

k. Now suppose that we start over at Point A, and unemployment again rises to 10 percent. Since this rise occurs unexpectedly, the economy would move to Point

B. In Period 3, however, people may realize that inflation will continue to fall. As a result, they may try to revise their expectations of future inflation to take this into account. If they did, expected inflation would fall more rapidly than indicated in Parts c through i, and the Phillips curve would shift downward more/less rapidly, provided that wages and prices could change as rapidly as inflationary expectations. As a result, the economy would reach its long-run equilibrium more/less rapidly and the sacrifice ratio would be higher/lower than in Part j.

l. The path depicted in Parts c through i is only one of several ways to reduce inflation, even if expected inflation changes slowly. On Graph 13-6, the initial Phillips curve and the initial equilibrium have been redrawn.

Graph 13-6

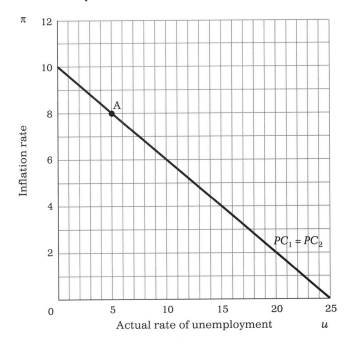

At Point A, $E\pi = 8$, $u = $ _____ percent, and $\pi = $ _____ percent. Now suppose that the Bank of Canada and the government thought it necessary to reduce inflation more rapidly than in Part c. Consequently, they pursued more restrictive policies and increased unemployment to 15 percent in the second period. Find this point on the Phillips curve on Graph 13-6 and label it Point B. At Point B, $u = $ _____ percent and $\pi = $ _____ percent. (Note that $E\pi$ has not yet changed.) If expected inflation in the third period is equal to actual inflation in the second period, $E\pi$ would fall to _____ percent. Consequently, the Phillips curve equation would change to

$$\pi = E\pi - 0.4(u - 5) = \underline{\hspace{4cm}} - 0.4(u - 5).$$ **(13-7)**

Solve this equation for π.

$\pi =$ _____ $-$ _____ u.

Plot and draw Equation 13-7 on Graph 13-6 and label the curve PC_3. In Period 3, suppose that the government and the Bank of Canada eased their policies and allowed the unemployment rate to resume its natural rate of 5 percent. Find this point on PC_3 on Graph 13-6 and label it Point C. At Point C, $u =$ _____ percent, $\pi =$ _____ percent, and actual inflation is <u>greater than/less than/equal to</u> expected inflation. Consequently, Point C represents a new long-run equilibrium. This situation shows that inflation could be reduced more quickly if a more restrictive policy were enacted that increased unemployment more drastically. Note, however, that it took _____ percentage-point years of cyclical unemployment here to reduce inflation by _____ percentage points, which is <u>more than/less than/equal to</u> the amount it took in Parts c through i.

m. Finally, suppose that we start again at Point A on Graph 13-6 and that there is an adverse supply shock, such as a substantial increase in oil prices. In this case, the Phillips curve would <u>shift upward/remain stationary/shift downward</u> even if expected inflation did not change.

6. **A Nonlinear Short-Run Phillips Curve** *In this exercise, we use a nonlinear short-run Phillips curve to analyze the costs of a temporary bout of inflation.*

a. Consider an economy with the following Phillips curve:

$$\pi = -\beta(u - u^n) + \pi_{-1}.$$

Because of the relative downward rigidity of the wage adjustment process, β is greater when unemployment is less than the natural rate, than it is when unemployment exceeds the natural rate. In particular, assume that $\beta = 1.0$ when $u < u^n$ and $\beta = 0.5$ when $u > u^n$.

Suppose the central bank picks the time path for inflation given in Table 13-1.

Table 13-1

(1) Time Period	(2) Inflation	(3) Excess Unemployment $(u - u^n)$
1	0%	0%
2	0%	_____
3	3%	_____
4	6%	_____
5	6%	_____
6	3%	_____
7	0%	_____
8	0%	_____

b. Fill in the third column in Table 13-1.

c. Compare the average unemployment and inflation rates in the time periods 3 and 4 interval, to what occurs in the interval involving periods 1 and 2.

d. Compare the average unemployment and inflation rates in the interval involving periods 2 through 7, to what occurs in the first two periods.

e. What do your calculations suggest about a tradeoff between inflation and unemployment?

Problems

Answer the following problems on a separate sheet of paper.

1. Use the sticky-price model of aggregate supply to explain how the ability of monetary and fiscal policy to change the real GDP would be affected by the fraction of firms in the economy that have flexible prices.

2. Suppose that the economy is initially at the natural rate of output, and the expected price level in any period is equal to the actual price level in the preceding period. If the Bank of Canada makes a credible, permanent reduction in the money supply, draw a graph to illustrate the path of the economy in both the short run and the long run, using aggregate supply and aggregate demand curves.

   a. Explain how your answer to Problem 2 would be different if expectations were rational.

   b. Explain how your answer to Problem 2 would depend on the fraction of firms that have flexible prices.

3. If the economy is initially at the natural rate of output and inflation rises, what additional macroeconomic data would enable one to determine whether the inflation was demand-pull or cost-push? Explain.

4. In the sticky-price model, the equation for the short-run aggregate supply curve is:

$$P = EP + [(1 - s)a/s](Y - \overline{Y})$$

where s is the fraction of firms with sticky prices and $a > 0$. The slope of this curve dP/dY is $(1 - s)a/s$. Calculate the derivative of this expression with respect to s, and discuss what this tells us about how the fraction of firms with sticky prices affects the steepness of the short-run aggregate supply curve. (You may treat both EP and $\overline{Y}$ as constants.)

5. Suppose the economy has the Phillips curve:

$$\pi = E\pi - 0.25(u - 0.04)$$

   a. What is the natural rate of unemployment in this economy?

   b. Graph the short-run Phillips curve if the expected rate of inflation is 3 percent, or 0.03.

   c. What is the sacrifice ratio in this economy?

6. a. Draw an appropriately labeled Phillips curve and illustrate the current position of the Canadian economy. Somewhere in your graph clearly indicate each of the following: the current actual unemployment rate, the (approximate) natural rate of unemployment, the actual rate of inflation, and the (approximate) expected rate of inflation.

7. Canadian monetary policy is based on keeping the inflation rate between 1 and 3 percent each year. When the inflation target was introduced, the target band was higher, and it was gradually reduced to the 1–3 percent range over several years.

   a. Use aggregate supply and aggregate demand curves to illustrate the short-run and long-run effects on real GDP if this policy had been adopted in such a way that it involved an immediate reduction in the money supply.

   b. How would the speed with which the economy moves to the new long-run equilibrium depend on the following factors—rational expectations, wage and price flexibility, and policy credibility?

8. What does the hysteresis theory of unemployment imply about the effects of a recession on the long-run aggregate supply curve? Briefly explain.

Data Questions

Locate the necessary economic data and apply them to answer the following data questions. For advice on how to access the data, see the Preface, and the Economic Data on the Web section on page xi.

1. a. The case study on the sacrifice ratio in the textbook focused on the disinflation of the early 1980s. This question invites you to extend this discussion to the later disinflation. Use data for the GDP price deflator or the CPI to calculate the average inflation rate over the 1992–1999 period. By how much is this average inflation rate below the inflation rate in 1988? This difference represents the amount of disinflation accomplished by the Bank of Canada during the 1988–1991 period.

b. Using the analysis near the end of chapter 13 in the textbook as a guide, esti-mate the sacrifice ratio involved with the 1988–1991 disinflation. Assume a natur-al unemployment rate of 7.5 percent, and compare the unemployment rate to this number. Calculate the excess of the actual over the natural unemployment rate for each year during the 1988 to 1999 period. Add these numbers together. Divide by two—to assume that contractionary monetary policy caused only one half of this excess unemployment.

c. Assume an Okun's Law coefficient of 2. What is the total loss of output as a result of this disinflation? What is the sacrifice ratio? How does this sacrifice ratio com-pare to that estimated in the text—for disinflation over a higher inflation range? Does this comparison support the hypothesis that the short-run Phillips curve is flatter at lower inflation rates?

Questions to Think About

1. Some economists have criticized the imperfect information model because the expansion of the Internet must have shortened the period of time during which sup-pliers are uncertain about whether an increase in the price of the product they pro-duce represents an increase in relative prices or a general increase in all prices. As your text states, recent work on imperfect information models of aggregate supply focus on the limited ability of people to absorb and process information that is wide-ly available. As a result, price setters may respond slowly to macroeconomic news. Consider the wheat farmer introduced in the text and describe the difficulties he would have absorbing new price and other macroeconomic information. It might be useful to read the references cited in Footnote 3 in the textbook.

2. How could one defend the fact that Canadian authorities have adopted a 2 percent inflation target rather than a 0 percent inflation target?

chapter 14

A Dynamic Model of Aggregate Demand and Supply

Fill-in Questions

Use the key terms below to fill in the blanks in the following statements. Each term may be used more than once.

impulse response function
natural rate of interest
predetermined variable

random variable
Taylor Principle
Taylor rule

1. The _____ is the real interest rate at which, in the absence of any shock, the demand for goods and services equals the natural level of output.

2. A _____ is a variable whose values are determined by chance.

3. According to the _____, used by the Federal Reserve in the United States, the real federal funds rate equals 2 percent when inflation is 2 percent and GDP is at its natural level.

4. A(n) _____ is a variable that was endogenous in an earlier period but is treated as essentially exogenous in the current period.

5. A(n) _____ is a graph of the time path of an endogenous variable after a shock.

6. According to the _____, the central bank must respond to an increase in inflation with an even greater increase in the nominal interest rate in order to keep inflation stable.

7. According to the _____, the central bank must respond to an increase in inflation by increasing the real interest rate in order to keep inflation stable.

Multiple-Choice Questions

1. The dynamic aggregate demand, aggregate supply, or *DAD-DAS*, model:

    a. focuses on how output and inflation respond over time to exogenous changes in the economic environment.

    b. explicitly incorporates the response of monetary policy to economic conditions.

    c. better exemplifies the macroeconomic models used by economists at the research frontier than models in previous chapters.

    d. All of the answers are correct.

2. In the aggregate demand equation $Y_t = \overline{Y}_t - \alpha(r_t - \rho) + \varepsilon_t$, the term ε_t:

    a. represents a random variable that fluctuates over time but equals zero, on average.

    b. can capture non-permanent changes in fiscal policy that affect the demand for goods and services.

    c. can capture a variety of exogenous influences on the demand for goods and services.

    d. All of the answers are correct.

3. The natural rate of interest ρ is the real interest rate at which:

    a. the inflation rate is equal to zero.

    b. the unemployment rate is equal to zero if there are no shocks.

    c. the demand for goods and services equals the natural level of output if there are no shocks.

    d. All of the answers are correct.

4. The amount of aggregate demand falls as the real interest rate r rises because:

    a. firms engage in fewer investment projects.

    b. consumers save more and spend less.

    c. the dollar might appreciate causing net exports to fall.

    d. All of the answers are correct.

5. In the expression $E_t \pi_{t+1}$:

    a. $E_t \pi_{t+1}$ represents the expectation formed in period t of inflation in period $t + 1$.

    b. $E_t \pi_{t+1}$ represents the expected change in inflation between periods t and $t + 1$.

    c. $E_t \pi_{t+1}$ is equal to zero when output is at its natural level.

    d. All of the answers are correct.

6. In the Fisher equation $r_t = i_t - E_t \pi_{t+1}$, r_t represents the:

    a. natural rate of interest.

    b. *ex post* real interest rate.

    c. *ex ante* real interest rate.

    d. expected change in the real interest rate.

7. In the augmented Phillips curve equation $\pi_t = E_{t-1}\pi_t + \varphi(Y_t - \overline{Y}_t) + v_t$:

   a. inflation depends on expected inflation because some firms set prices in advance. When firms expect high inflation, they anticipate higher costs and raise their own prices.

   b. inflation rises when actual output rises because firms experience increasing marginal costs.

   c. the term v_t is a random supply shock, such as a temporary oil price shock.

   d. All of the answers are correct.

8. In the monetary policy rule $i_t = \pi_t + \rho + \theta_\pi(\pi_t - \pi_t^*) + \theta_Y(Y_t - \overline{Y}_t)$:

   a. π_t^* is the central bank's target for the inflation rate in period t.

   b. a large value of θ_π means that the central bank will raise interest rates more vigorously when actual inflation rises.

   c. a large value of θ_Y means that the central bank will raise interest rates more vigorously when actual output rises.

   d. All of the answers are correct.

9. According to the Taylor rule, the nominal federal funds rate (which is the American equivalent of the Bank of Canada's overnight lending rate) is:

   a. equal to 2 percent if inflation is 2 percent and real GDP is at its natural level.

   b. equal to 3 percent if inflation is 4 percent and real GDP is at its natural level.

   c. equal to 5 percent if inflation is 2 percent and real GDP exceeds its natural level by 2 percent.

   d. All of the answers are correct.

10. According to the Taylor rule, used by the central bank in the United States, the *real* federal funds rate is:

    a. equal to 2 percent if inflation is 2 percent and real GDP is at its natural level.

    b. equal to 3 percent if inflation is 4 percent and real GDP is at its natural level.

    c. equal to 3 percent if inflation is 2 percent and real GDP exceeds its natural level by 2 percent.

    d. All of the answers are correct.

11. In long-run equilibrium:

    a. both output and the real interest rate are at their natural values.

    b. both inflation and expected inflation are at the target rate of inflation.

    c. the nominal interest rate is equal to the natural rate of inflation plus the target rate of inflation.

    d. All of the answers are correct.

12. One difference between the conventional aggregate supply model developed in Chapter 13 and the dynamic aggregate supply model developed in this chapter is that:

    a. in the dynamic aggregate supply model, inflation replaces the price level as the variable measured on the vertical axis.

    b. in the dynamic aggregate supply model, the rate of growth of output replaces the level of output as the variable measured on the vertical axis.

    c. supply shocks no longer shift the dynamic aggregate supply model.

    d. All of the answers are correct.

13. The dynamic aggregate supply curve shifts when:

    a. the natural level of output changes.

    b. there is a supply shock.

    c. the rate of inflation in the preceding period changes.

    d. All of the answers are correct.

14. One difference between the conventional aggregate demand model developed in Chapters 10–12 and the dynamic aggregate demand model is that:

    a. in the dynamic aggregate demand model, inflation replaces the price level as the variable measured on the vertical axis.

    b. in the dynamic aggregate demand model, the rate of growth of output replaces the level of output as the variable measured on the vertical axis.

    c. changes in fiscal policy no longer shift the dynamic aggregate demand curve.

    d. All of the answers are correct.

15. The dynamic aggregate demand curve is downward sloping because:

    a. when inflation falls, goods and services become cheaper, so people buy more.

    b. when inflation falls, the central bank responds by decreasing the real interest rate, which increases the quantity of goods and services demanded.

    c. when inflation falls, the central bank decreases the money supply, which increases output.

    d. All of the answers are correct.

16. The dynamic aggregate demand curve shifts when:

    a. the natural level of output changes.

    b. the inflation target changes.

    c. there is a change in the demand shock ε_t.

    d. All of the answers are correct.

17. An increase in government spending or a reduction in taxes:

    a. shifts the *DAD* curve downward (to the left).

    b. results in a movement along a stationary *DAD* curve upward and to the left.

    c. shifts the *DAD* curve upward (to the right).

    d. results in a movement along a stationary *DAD* curve downward and to the right.

18. An increase in the central bank's inflation target:

    a. shifts the *DAD* curve upward (to the right).
    b. results in a movement along a stationary *DAD* curve downward and to the right.
    c. may result in either a. or b., depending on whether the money supply changes.
    d. shifts the *DAD* curve downward (to the left).

19. If the short-run equilibrium level of output lies below the natural level, the

    a. *DAD* curve will shift upward (to the right).
    b. *DAD* curve will shift downward (to the left).
    c. *DAS* curve will shift downward (to the right).
    d. *DAS* curve will shift upward (to the left).

20. If the natural level of output increases, the:

    a. *DAD* curve and the *DAS* curve both shift to the right.
    b. *DAD* curve and the *DAS* curve both shift to the left.
    c. *DAD* curve shifts to the right and the *DAS* curve shifts to the left.
    d. *DAD* curve shifts to the left and the *DAS* curve shifts to the right.

21. Starting at the natural level of output, if there is an adverse supply shock in period t such that υ_t is positive for one period and subsequently returns to zero, then:

    a. in period t, the *DAS* curve shifts upward by the exact size of the shock.
    b. in period $t + 1$, the *DAS* curve starts to shift back down toward its initial position.
    c. the *DAD* curve does not shift.
    d. All of the answers are correct.

22. Starting at the natural level of output, if there is an adverse supply shock in period t such that υ_t is positive for one period and subsequently returns to zero, then:

    a. output falls in period t but subsequently returns gradually to its natural level.
    b. the real interest rate rises in period t but subsequently returns gradually to its natural rate.
    c. inflation rises in period t but subsequently returns gradually to its target rate.
    d. All of the answers are correct.

23. Impulse response functions are graphs of the time paths of the:

    a. expected future shocks.
    b. economic variables before a shock.
    c. economic variables after a shock.
    d. pulse rates of the Bank of Canada governing council members after a shock.

24. Starting from the natural level of output, a positive shock to aggregate demand (like expansionary fiscal policy) in period t that lasts for five periods and then returns to zero will:

    a. shift the *DAD* curve to the right for five periods and then shift it back.
    b. lead to a series of upward shifts in the DAS curve, starting in period $t + 1$.
    c. increase both output and inflation in the short run.
    d. All of the answers are correct.

25. In the periods following a positive shock to aggregate demand, the *DAS* curve starts to shift upward because the:

    a. shock increases inflation, which, in turn, increases expected future inflation.
    b. shock leads to a series of additional supply shocks.
    c. central bank raises its target rate of inflation.
    d. central bank reduces its target rate of inflation.

26. If the central bank reduces its inflation target permanently:

    a. the *DAD* curve shifts downward by the change in the target and both output and inflation fall in the short run.
    b. the *DAD* curve shifts upward by the change in the target and both output and inflation rise in the short run.
    c. the *DAS* curve starts to shift upward in later periods.
    d. output remains permanently below its natural level.

27. If expectations are formed rationally rather than adaptively, then:

    a. inflation will always be zero.
    b. future inflation will always equal expected inflation.
    c. people may respond to announcements of new policy by altering their expectations of inflation more rapidly and output will return to its natural level more quickly.
    d. All of the answers are correct.

28. If the central bank responds strongly to inflation and weakly to output:

    a. the central bank will raise interest rates a lot in response to a supply shock.
    b. the *DAD* curve will be very flat.
    c. a supply shock will have a big effect on output and a small effect on inflation.
    d. All of the answers are correct.

29. Compared with the Federal Reserve in the United States, the European Central Bank seems to:

    a. give more weight to output stability and less weight to inflation stability.
    b. give more weight to inflation stability and less weight to output stability.
    c. lower interest rates more during recessions.
    d. allow inflation to fluctuate more than the Fed.

30. According to the Taylor Principle, in order for inflation to be stable, the central bank must respond to an increase in inflation by:

    a. increasing its inflation target.
    b. increasing the nominal interest rate by more than the increase in inflation.
    c. decreasing the real interest rate.
    d. All of the answers are correct.

31. According to real-business-cycle theory, real GDP is always:

    a. greater than the natural rate of output.

    b. equal to the natural rate of output.

    c. less than the natural rate of output.

    d. less than or equal to the natural rate of output.

32. All of the following are characteristics of real-business-cycle theory EXCEPT:

    a. prices are sticky.

    b. the economy behaves according to the assumptions of the classical model.

    c. all unemployment is voluntary.

    d. all real wages are flexible.

33. In the Robinson Crusoe parable, changes in real GDP were due to:

    a. changes in aggregate demand, such as changes in the money supply.

    b. changes in aggregate supply, such as technology shocks and the weather.

    c. changes in neither aggregate demand nor aggregate supply.

    d. inflation.

34. According to real-business-cycle theory, output rises when the real interest rate increases because of:

    a. changes in technology.

    b. the intertemporal substitutions of labour.

    c. changes in the amount of real money balances.

    d. price and wage stickiness.

35. A new classical economist might explain that the reduction in output during a recession is caused by:

    a. a low real interest rate, which causes workers to choose leisure now and post-pone working until some future period.

    b. a deterioration in the available production technology.

    c. an increase in emplopyment insurance benefits, which leads workers to choose more leisure.

    d. All of the answers are correct.

36. According to real-business-cycle theory, the positive relationship between real GDP and the money supply is probably caused by:

    a. increases in the money supply that lead to reductions in the real interest rate, increases in investment, and increases in output.

    b. increases in output that lead to increases in money demand and accommodating increases in money supply.

    c. increases in the money supply that lead to inflation, lower real wages, and increases in the quantity of labour demanded and GDP.

    d. All of the answers are correct.

Exercises

1. **The Dynamic Aggregate Demand Curve** *In this exercise, we derive the dynamic aggregate demand curve and discuss the variables that make it shift.*

The dynamic aggregate demand curve (which we shall call the *DAD* curve) is the intertemporal analogue of the aggregate demand curve derived in Chapter 11 of the text. It is based on the demand for goods and services, the Fisher equation (which was introduced in Chapter 4), and a monetary policy rule set by the central bank. The demand for goods and services is given by the equation:

$$Y_t = \overline{Y}_t - \alpha(r_t - \rho) + \varepsilon_t, \tag{14-1}$$

where Y_t is the total output of goods and services in the current period, which we call period t, $\overline{Y}_t$ is the natural level of output in period t, r_t is the real interest rate in period t, and ε_t is a random variable representing a shock to demand in period t. Both α and ρ are parameters greater than zero. The parameter ρ represents the natural rate of interest. This is defined as the real interest rate at which, in the absence of any demand shocks, the demand for output equals the natural level of output.

a. Equation 14-1 indicates that the demand for output rises along with the natural level of output. As a country becomes richer over time, its demand for goods and services increases proportionately. The second term on the right-hand side of Equation 4-1 indicates that, when the real interest rate rises, the demand for output will <u>rise/fall/remain constant</u>. The reasoning is similar to that in earlier chapters. When the real interest rate rises, borrowing becomes more expensive and saving is more rewarding. Consequently, firms' investment falls and consumers save more and spend less, both of which reduce the demand for output. The larger the value of the parameter α, the <u>more/less</u> the demand for goods and services falls in response to a given increase in the real interest rate.

b. The second building block of the dynamic aggregate demand curve is the Fisher equation, according to which the (*ex ante*) real interest rate in period t is equal to the nominal interest rate in period t minus the expected rate of future inflation:

$$r_t = i_t - E_t \pi_{t+1}. \tag{14-2}$$

The last term in Equation 14-2, $E_t \pi_{t+1}$, represents the expectation of what the inflation rate will be in period _____ (the subscript on π) based on information available in period _____ (the subscript on E).

c. The third building block of the *DAD* curve is the way in which people form their expectations. The text assumes that inflation expectations are adaptive, which means that the expectation of next period's inflation is equal to the current rate of inflation. This is represented by the equation:

$$E_t\pi_{t+1} = \pi_t. \tag{14-3}$$

Thus, if the current rate of inflation is 2 percent, people expect next period's inflation rate will be _____ percent. This is an admittedly simple way of forming expectations, and we shall discuss a more sophisticated alternative in a later exercise.

d. The fourth building block is the monetary policy rule, which determines the nominal interest rate. The monetary policy rule reflects the behaviour of the central bank and the way in which it responds to inflation and output gaps:

$$i_t = \pi_t + \rho + \theta_\pi(\pi_t - \pi_t^*) + \theta_Y(Y_t - \overline{Y}_t). \tag{14-4}$$

In Equation 14-4, π_t^* is the central bank's target for the inflation rate in period _____. The parameter θ_π represents the responsiveness of the central bank to high inflation. Similarly, the parameter θ_Y represents the responsiveness of the central bank to higher levels of output. Both θ_π and θ_Y are assumed to be greater than zero.

e. The monetary policy rule can also be seen as the way in which the central bank controls the real interest rate. According to Equation 14-2, the real interest rate is $r_t = i_t - E_t\pi_{t+1}$. Furthermore, if inflationary expectations are adaptive, $E_t\pi_{t+1}$ is equal to _____. Substituting this into the preceding equation yields $r_t = i_t - \pi_t$. If we subtract π_t from both sides of Equation 14-4, we obtain:

$$i_t - \pi_t = [\pi_t + \rho + \theta_\pi(\pi_t - \pi_t^*) + \theta_Y(Y_t - \overline{Y}_t)] - \pi_t, \text{ or}$$
$$r_t = \rho + \theta_\pi(\pi_t - \pi_t^*) + \theta_Y(Y_t - \overline{Y}_t). \tag{14-5}$$

Consequently, whenever inflation rises above the inflation target, the central bank responds by increasing/decreasing the real interest rate. This will tend to increase/decrease investment and consumption and push inflation back toward its target. Similarly, whenever output rises above its natural level, the central bank responds by increasing/decreasing the real interest rate. This will tend to increase/decrease investment and consumption and increase/decrease output, pushing it back toward its natural level. Equation 14-5 also indicates that, when $\pi_t = \pi_t^*$ and $Y_t = \overline{Y}_t$, the central bank will set the real interest rate equal to _____, the natural rate of interest.

f.   Our final step in deriving the *DAD* curve involves the substitution of Equation 14-5 for r_t in Equation 14-1 to obtain:

$$Y_t = \overline{Y}_t - \alpha[\rho + \theta_\pi(\pi_t - \pi_t^*) + \theta_Y(Y_t - \overline{Y}_t) - \rho] + \varepsilon_t, \text{ or}$$

$$Y_t = \overline{Y}_t - \alpha[\theta_\pi(\pi_t - \pi_t^*) + \theta_Y(Y_t - \overline{Y}_t)] + \varepsilon_t. \qquad \textbf{(14-6)}$$

Equation 14-6 indicates that, whenever inflation rises, output <u>rises/falls</u>. This occurs because the central bank responds to higher inflation by increasing the real interest rate, which <u>increases/decreases</u> investment and consumption and thereby <u>increases/decreases</u> output.

g.   Now, expand the second term within the brackets of Equation 14-6 to obtain:

$$Y_t = \overline{Y}_t - \alpha\theta_\pi(\pi_t - \pi_t^*) - \alpha\theta_Y Y_t + \alpha\theta_Y \overline{Y}_t + \varepsilon_t. \qquad \textbf{(14-7)}$$

The *DAD* equation in the text may be derived by collecting the terms involving Y_t on the right-hand side of Equation 14-7, bringing all the terms involving Y_t to the left-hand side of the equation and solving for Y_t to obtain:

$Y_t = $ _____.   **(DAD)**

(Make sure you check your answer with the equation in the text or in the answer section of the Study Guide before proceeding.)

h. Since all the parameters in the first bracket in the *DAD* equation are positive and the brackets are preceded by a minus sign, the equation indicates that there is an inverse relationship between inflation and output along the *DAD* curve. Holding the other variables constant, when inflation rises, output <u>rises/falls</u>. Furthermore, if there is no demand shock (i.e., $\varepsilon_t = 0$) and output is equal to its natural level so that $Y_t - \overline{Y}_t = 0$, the *DAD* equation indicates that inflation will be <u>greater than/equal to/less than</u> its target. Assume that the inflation target is initially 2 percent. Locate the point in Graph 14-1 where $\pi_t = \pi_t^*$ and $Y_t = \overline{Y}_t$ and label it Point A. Then, draw a negatively sloped curve in Graph 14-1 through Point A and label it *DAD* ($\pi_t^* = 2\%$; $\varepsilon_t = 0$).

Graph 14-1

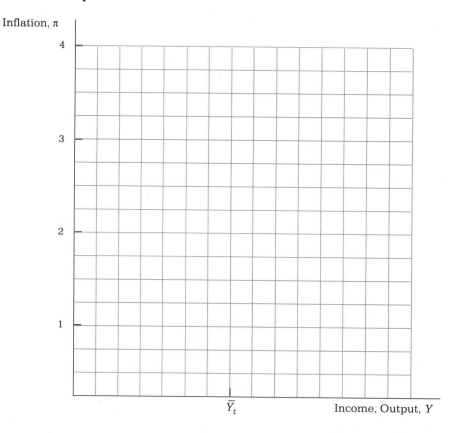

i. The *DAD* equation also suggests three events that will shift the *DAD* curve. First, suppose there is a demand shock and $\varepsilon_t > 0$. The demand shock could be caused by temporary consumer or business optimism or by an increase in government spending or a decrease in net taxes. The *DAD* equation indicates that the level of output Y_t will then <u>rise/fall</u>, even if inflation doesn't change. This means that the entire *DAD* curve will shift <u>upward (to the right)/downward (to the left)</u>. Secondly, a change in the central bank's inflation target will also shift the *DAD* curve. Since π_t^* is preceded by two minus signs in the *DAD* equation, an increase in π_t^* will <u>increase/decrease</u> the level of output Y_t if inflation doesn't change.

Consequently, the *DAD* curve will shift <u>upward (to the right)/downward (to the left)</u>. Finally, if we begin again at Point A in Graph 14-1 and both actual output and the natural level of output rise by the same amount, then $Y_t - \overline{Y}_t$ will still equal zero. If there is no demand shock, the *DAD* equation indicates that inflation will then be <u>greater than/equal to/less than</u> its target. In this case, the entire *DAD* curve will shift to the right by the amount of the increase in the natural level of output.

2. **The Taylor Rule** *We introduce the Taylor rule and illustrate how the central bank might use it to conduct monetary policy.*

Recall the monetary policy rule presented in Exercise 1:

$$i_t = \pi_t + \rho + \theta_\pi(\pi_t - \pi_t^*) + \theta_Y(Y_t - \overline{Y}_t).$$

(14-4)

After examining the behaviour of the federal funds rate set by the Federal Reserve in the United States over time, John Taylor developed a modified version of the monetary policy rule, which has become known as the Taylor rule:

(14-8)

Nominal Federal Funds Rate = Inflation + 2% +
0.5(Inflation − 2%) − 0.5(GDP gap)

where the GDP gap is equal to the percentage by which the actual level of GDP lies below the natural level of GDP. Because the Taylor rule tracked the actual behaviour of the federal funds rate so closely, Taylor suggested that the Federal Reserve may have implicitly been following it in conducting monetary policy. Related studies suggest that the Bank of Canada conducts monetary policy in a similar manner, although our central bank places somewhat more weight on its inflation target.

a. Comparing Equations 14-8 and 14-4, the Taylor rule implies that the natural rate of interest is _____ percent and the Fed's inflation target is _____ percent.

b. When actual GDP is equal to its natural level, the GDP gap is _____ percent. Therefore, according to the Taylor rule, when actual GDP is equal to its natural level and actual inflation is 2 percent, the Fed sets the nominal federal funds rate equal to _____ + 2 + 0.5(_____ − 2) − 0.5(_____) = _____ percent. In accordance with the general monetary policy rule, the Fed increases the nominal federal funds rate whenever the actual inflation rate <u>rises/falls</u>.

c. If the actual level of GDP is 99 and the natural level of GDP is 100, the actual level of GDP is _____ percent below the natural level, and the GDP gap is 1 percent. Whenever actual GDP falls further below the natural level, the GDP gap <u>rises/falls</u>, and the Fed <u>increases/decreases</u> the nominal federal funds rate in order to stimulate the economy.

d. Use the Taylor rule to complete Columns 4 and 5 of the following table.

Table 14-1

(1) Inflation (%)	(2) Actual GDP $ billions	(3) Natural Level of GDP $ billions	(4) GDP gap (%)	(5) Nominal Federal Funds Rate (%)	(6) Real Federal Funds Rate (%)
2	100	100	_____	_____	_____
3	100	100	_____	_____	_____
2	94	100	_____	_____	_____
2	106	100	_____	_____	_____
4	96	100	_____	_____	_____

e. Recall that the real federal funds rate is equal to the nominal federal funds rate plus/minus the actual rate of inflation and complete Column 6 in Table 14-1.

f. Finally, examine the first two rows of Table 14-1. When inflation rose by 1 percentage point, the Fed increased the nominal federal funds rate by _____ percentage points so that the real federal funds rate rose/fell by _____ percentage points.

3. **The Dynamic Aggregate Supply Curve** *In this exercise, we derive the dynamic aggregate supply curve, compute its slope, and discuss what factors shift it.*

a. The dynamic aggregate supply (*DAS*) curve is the intertemporal analogue of the short-run aggregate supply curve derived in Chapter 13 of the text. It is based on the expectations-augmented Phillips curve with exogenous supply shocks, according to the equation:

$$\pi_t = E_{t-1}\pi_t + \varphi(Y_t - \overline{Y}_t) + \upsilon_t.$$

(14-9)

In Equation 14-9, inflation in period t depends on $E_{t-1}\pi_t$, which is what people in period _____ expected inflation to be in period _____. This term reflects the fact that some firms set their prices in advance. When expected inflation rises, these firms expect their costs will rise, too, so they raise their own prices.

b. Inflation in period t also depends on the deviation of output from its natural level, $Y_t - \overline{Y}_t$. In Chapter 13, the Phillips curve was expressed in terms of the deviation of the unemployment rate from the natural rate of unemployment, but it was derived from Equation 14-9 using one form of Okun's law. When output rises above its natural level, the unemployment rate rises above/falls below its natural rate. Firms then experience increasing marginal costs and raise prices. The parameter φ reflects how quickly firms raise prices in response to the higher marginal costs. It is assumed to be greater than zero.

c. Finally, as in Chapter 13, inflation in period t depends on a supply shock v_t. This supply shock is an exogenous random variable. Although its average value is zero, it can be positive or negative in any particular period. One example is an oil shock in which oil prices rise temporarily because of a supply disruption in the Middle East. In this case, v_t would be positive during the disruption and then return to zero when the disruption ends. Supply shocks can be positive or negative. If good weather results in an abundant harvest, v_t would be positive/negative during the bountiful period in which food prices fell, and it would return to zero in the following period.

d. As in Exercise 1, we assume expectations are adaptive, in which case the current expectation of next period's inflation rate is merely the current rate of inflation. Similarly, last-period's expectation of this period's inflation is equal to last period's actual rate of inflation. This is represented by the equation:

$$E_{t-1}\pi_t = \pi_{t-1}. \tag{14-10}$$

If we substitute Equation 14-10 into Equation 14-9, we obtain the equation for the dynamic aggregate supply curve, which we shall henceforth call the *DAS* curve:

$$\pi_t = \pi_{t-1} + \varphi(Y_t - \overline{Y}_t) + v_t. \tag{DAS}$$

Use the *DAS* equation to complete Table 14-2.

Table 14-2

(1) $\pi_{t-1}(\%)$	(2) φ	(3) Y_t	(4) $\overline{Y}_t$	(5) v_t	(6) $\pi_t(\%)$
2	0.25	100	100	0	_____
2	0.25	101	100	0	_____
2	0.25	99	100	0	_____
2	0.25	100	100	1	_____
2	0.25	101	100	1	_____

e. In the first row of Table 14-2, output is equal to its natural level of 100 and there is no supply shock (i.e., $v_t = 0$). Consequently, inflation in period t will be equal to inflation in period $t - 1$, or $\pi_t = \pi_{t-1} = $ _____ percent. Find this point in Graph 14-2 and label it Point A. In the second row of Table 14-3, last period's inflation is 2 percent, there is no supply shock, and output exceeds its natural level by _____ unit(s). Thus, in the second row, which is not meant to be one period later than the first row, inflation in period t will be _____ percent. Find this point in Graph 14-2 and label it Point B. And in the third row of Table 14-3, note that, when last period's inflation is 2 percent, there is no supply shock, and output falls below its natural level by _____, then inflation in period t will be _____ percent. Find this point in Graph 14-2, label it Point C. Now, connect Points A, B, and C in Graph 14-2 and label the curve $DAS(\pi_{t-1} = 2\%; v_t = 0)$.

f. The slope of the *DAS* curve in Graph 14-2 is _____, which we can see from the *DAS* equation is equal to the parameter _____. Thus, if marginal costs and prices rise more rapidly in response to increases in output, the value of φ will rise/fall, the slope of the *DAS* curve will become bigger/smaller, and the curve itself will become steeper/flatter.

g. In Rows 4 and 5 of Table 14-2, we see how a supply shock affects the *DAS* curve. In these rows, a temporary supply shock increases the value of v_t to 1. If actual output remains equal to 100, inflation in period *t* rises to _____ percent. If, on the other hand, output rises to 101, inflation in period t rises to _____ percent. Find these points in Graph 14-2 and label them Points D and E, respectively, and draw the corresponding *DAS* curve and label it $DAS(\pi_{t-1} = 2\%; v_t = 1)$. Comparing the two *DAS* curves, note that, when there is a supply shock that increases v_t to 1, the *DAS* curve shifts upward/downward by _____ percentage point(s).

h. Now, let's explore two other changes that will shift the *DAS* curve. Complete Table 14-3.

Table 14-3

(1) $\pi_{t-1}(\%)$	(2) φ	(3) Y_t	(4) $\overline{Y}_t$	(5) v_t	(6) $\pi_t(\%)$
3	0.25	100	100	0	_____
3	0.25	101	100	0	_____
3	0.25	110	110	0	_____

The only difference between the first two rows of Table 14-3 and Table 14-2 is that inflation in period *t* – 1 has now risen to 3%. As a result, if the level of output is 100, inflation in period *t* is _____ percent, and if output rises to 101, inflation in period *t* rises to _____ percent. Find these points in Graph 14-3 and label them Points F and G, respectively, and draw the corresponding dynamic aggregate supply curve and label it $DAS(\pi_{t-1} = 3\%; v_t = 0)$. Compare the new *DAS* curve with the original curve, which is already drawn in Graph 14-3. Note that, when inflation in period *t* – 1 rises by 1 percentage point, the *DAS* curve shifts upward/downward by _____ percentage point(s). Similarly, if inflation in period *t* – 1 were to fall, the *DAS* curve would shift upward (to the left)/downward (to the right).

Graph 14-2

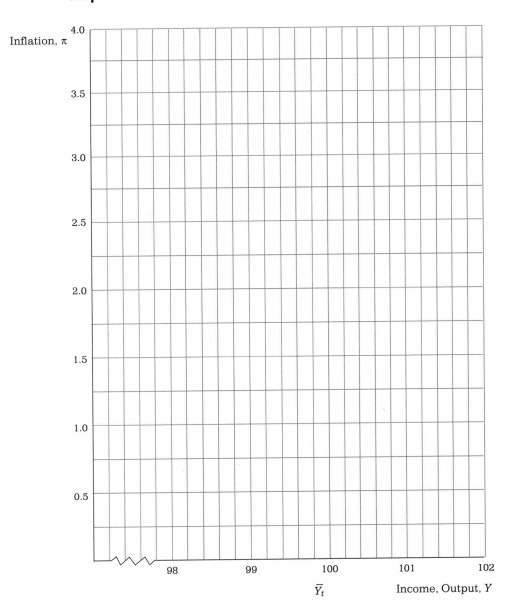

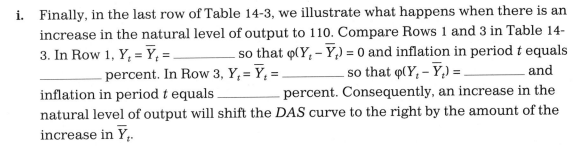

i.   Finally, in the last row of Table 14-3, we illustrate what happens when there is an increase in the natural level of output to 110. Compare Rows 1 and 3 in Table 14-3. In Row 1, $Y_t = \overline{Y}_t =$ _____ so that $\varphi(Y_t - \overline{Y}_t) = 0$ and inflation in period t equals _____ percent. In Row 3, $Y_t = \overline{Y}_t =$ _____ so that $\varphi(Y_t - \overline{Y}_t) =$ _____ and inflation in period t equals _____ percent. Consequently, an increase in the natural level of output will shift the *DAS* curve to the right by the amount of the increase in $\overline{Y}_t$.

4. **Long-run Equilibrium** *In this exercise, we derive the long-run equilibrium conditions for the dynamic aggregate supply, aggregate demand model.*

   a. In order to derive the long-run equilibrium conditions for the *DAS-DAD* model, it is useful to repeat some of the basic equations from Exercises 1 and 3:

   $$Y_t = \overline{Y}_t - \alpha(r_t - \rho) + \varepsilon_t, \tag{14-1}$$

   $$i_t = \pi_t + \rho + \theta_\pi(\pi_t - \pi_t^*) + \theta_Y(Y_t - \overline{Y}_t) \tag{14-4}$$

   $$Y_t = \overline{Y}_t - [\alpha\theta_\pi/(1+\alpha\theta_Y)](\pi_t - \pi_t^*) + [1/(1+\alpha\theta_Y)]\varepsilon_t \tag{DAD}$$

   $$\pi_t = \pi_{t-1} + \varphi(Y_t - \overline{Y}_t) + \upsilon_t. \tag{DAS}$$

   b. In long-run equilibrium, there are no shocks ($\varepsilon_t = \upsilon_t = 0$) and inflation remains constant over time ($\pi_t = \pi_{t-1}$). When these two conditions are substituted into the *DAS* equation, we are left with the first long-run condition $Y_t =$ _____. Thus, like the earlier aggregate supply, aggregate demand model of Chapter 13, output returns to its natural level in the long run.

   c. Equation 14-1 indicates that, at long-run equilibrium when $Y_t = \overline{Y}_t$ and $\varepsilon_t = 0$, the real interest rate $r_t =$ _____. This is a reflection of the fact that the natural interest rate is the real interest rate at which, in the absence of any shocks, output is equal to its natural level.

   d. If we set output equal to its natural level in the *DAD* equation and set $\varepsilon_t = 0$, we obtain the result $\pi_t =$ _____. Thus, in the long run, inflation eventually equals the _____. Furthermore, if inflation is stable in the long run and expectations are adaptive, then $E_t\pi_{t+1} = \pi_t =$ _____. Thus, in long-run equilibrium expected inflation is also equal to the _____ rate of inflation.

   e. Finally, making these substitutions in Equation 14-4 yields the long-run condition that $i_t = \pi_t + \rho$. If inflation in the long run is equal to its target, then it = _____ + ρ, and the nominal interest rate is equal to the _____ plus the natural rate of interest.

Graph 14-3

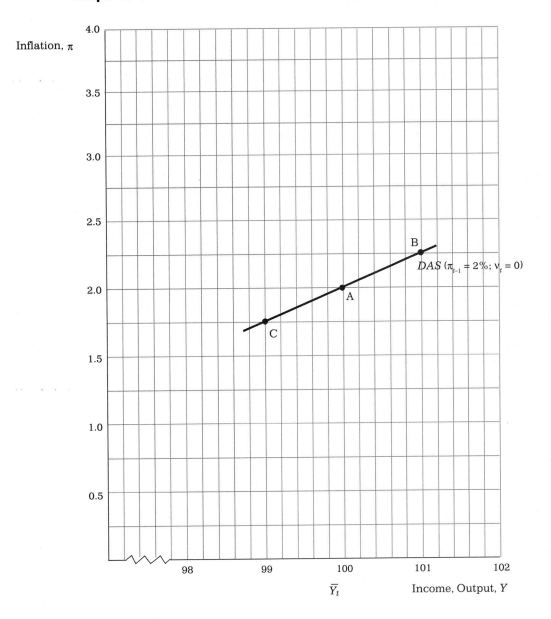

5. **Short-run Equilibrium and Aggregate Supply Shocks** *In this exercise, we introduce the short-run DAS-DAD equilibrium and examine the short-run and long-run effects of temporary supply shocks.*

   a. In Exercise 4, we examined the long-run *DAS-DAD* equilibrium conditions. In the short run, the model reaches an equilibrium when the *DAS* curve intersects the *DAD* curve. This occurs when the two endogenous variables, inflation and output, have adjusted so that both the *DAS* and the *DAD* equations are satisfied:

   $$Y_t = \overline{Y}_t - [\alpha\theta_\pi/(1 + \alpha\theta_Y)](\pi_t - \pi_t^*) + [1/(1 + \alpha\theta_Y)]\varepsilon_t \qquad \textbf{(DAD)}$$

   $$\pi_t = \pi_{t-1} + \varphi(Y_t - \overline{Y}_t) + \upsilon_t. \qquad \textbf{(DAS)}$$

   The long-run equilibrium conditions derived in Exercise 4 do not necessarily hold in short-run equilibrium. Thus, when the *DAD* and *DAS* equations are satisfied, the inflation rate does not have to be equal to what it was in the preceding period, nor must it equal the inflation target. Similarly, output does not have to equal its _____. The economy, however, will adjust over time and converge to its long-run equilibrium, at which all of these three conditions do hold. The mechanism by which this occurs is contained in the *DAS* equation and the DAS curve, which will shift upward or downward whenever π_{t-1} changes until long-run equilibrium is attained.

   b. Suppose, for example, that inflation has been rising so that $\pi_{t-1} > \pi_{t-2}$. When this happens, the lagged inflation term π_{t-1} in this period's *DAS* equation will be greater than the lagged inflation term π_{t-2} in last period's *DAS* equation. As we saw in Exercise 3, an increase in the preceding period's inflation rate will shift the entire *DAS* curve <u>upward (to the left)/downward (to the right)</u>. The *DAS* curve will keep shifting until inflation no longer changes from one period to the next, that is, until inflation is <u>greater than/equal to/less than</u> inflation in the preceding period. From the *DAS* equation, we can see that, in the absence of any supply shocks, this will occur when output is equal to the

   _____.

   c. Now, consider what happens when the economy is hit by a supply shock that lasts for one period. This could result from an oil price shock or an increase in union power that pushes up wages and prices. For simplicity, let us assume we begin in Period $t - 1$ in long-run equilibrium so that $Y_{t-1} =$ _____ and $\pi_{t-1} = \pi_{t-2} = \pi_{t-1}^*$. Let us also assume that the natural level of output and the inflation target do not change over time so that $\overline{Y}_{t-2} = \overline{Y}_{t-1} = \overline{Y}_t = \overline{Y}_{all}$ and $\pi_{t-2}^* = \pi_{t-1}^* = \pi_t^*$. Thus, we start at Point A in Graph 14-4. Note that Point A is located at the intersection of the DAD_{t-1} curve and the DAS_{t-1} curve.

Graph 14-4

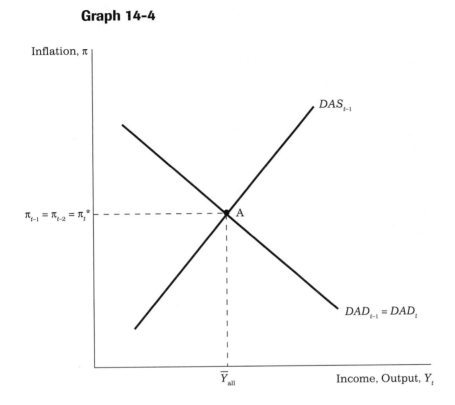

d. Recall that a supply shock represents an increase in v_t. Suppose that v_t rises from zero to 1 percent in Period t. According to the *DAS* equation and Exercise 3, the *DAS* curve will shift <u>upward (to the left)/downward (to the right)</u>. Draw the new *DAS* curve in Graph 14-4 and label it DAS_t. Since the *DAD* curve will not shift, we move to the intersection of the DAS_t curve and the $DAD_{t-1} = DAD_t$ curve. Locate this point in Graph 14-4, label it Point B, and label the inflation rate at Point B π_t. From Point A to Point B, output <u>increases/remains the</u> <u>same/decreases</u> while inflation <u>increases/remains the same/decreases</u>.

e. In Period $t + 1$, two important things happen. On the one hand, the temporary supply shock disappears, so the value of v_{t+1} returns to

_____. If nothing else occurred, the *DAS* curve would shift all the way back down to its original position at DAS_{t-1}. However, something else *has* happened. In Period t, the supply shock led to an increase in inflation. Thus, in Period $t + 1$, the inflation rate from the preceding period (π_t) is higher than π_{t-1}. And π_{t-1} was the inflation rate that partially determined inflation in Period t. If this is all that happened, the *DAS* curve would shift up because of the increase in the preceding period's inflation rate. If the system is stable, the combination of these two events will still shift the *DAS* curve down in Period $t + 1$, but not all the way to DAS_{t-1}. Consequently, draw a *DAS* curve on graph 14-4 in between DAS_{t-1} and DAS_t and label it DAS_{t+1}. Find the new short-run equilibrium in Period $t + 1$, label it Point C, and label the inflation rate at Point C π_{t+1}. From Point B to Point C output <u>increases/remains the same/decreases</u> while inflation <u>increases/remains the same/decreases</u>.

f. In Period $t + 2$ the supply shock remains equal to zero, but inflation continues to fall because inflation in the preceding period π_{t+1} is less than it was in period t. Thus, inflation expectations will rise/fall, and the *DAS* curve will continue to shift downward (to the right) until it reaches long-run equilibrium at the natural level of output. Consequently, relabel the initial *DAS* curve $DAS_{t-1} = DAS_{\text{Final}}$.

g. Thus, a supply shock that temporarily increases v_t will lead to temporarily higher/lower output and temporarily higher/lower inflation. In the long run, however, the economy returns to its long-run equilibrium.

6. **The Dynamic Response to Aggregate Supply Shocks and Impulse Response Functions** *In this exercise, we introduce simple impulse response functions to track the dynamic response to aggregate supply shocks.*

a. In Exercise 5, we used *DAS-DAD* graphs to illustrate the response to a temporary aggregate supply shock. In this exercise, we place values on the parameters in the *DAS* and *DAD* equations to illustrate how one can calculate the paths of both output and inflation after a supply shock.

b. Recall our basic *DAD* and *DAS* equations:

$$Y_t = \overline{Y}_t - [\alpha\theta_\pi/(1 + \alpha\theta_Y)](\pi_t - \pi_t^*) + [1/(1 + \alpha\theta_Y)]\varepsilon_t \qquad \textbf{(DAD)}$$

$$\pi_t = \pi_{t-1} + \varphi(Y_t - \overline{Y}_t) + v_t. \qquad \textbf{(DAS)}$$

In order to calculate numerical values of output and inflation, we use the numerical values of the relevant parameters suggested in the textbook, which are: $\overline{Y}_t = 100$; $\pi_t^* = 2.0$; $\alpha = 1.0$; $\varphi = 0.25$; $\theta_\pi = 0.5$; and $\theta_Y = 0.5$. Substituting these values into the *DAD* and *DAS* equations yields:

$$Y_t = \underline{\hspace{1.5cm}} - \underline{\hspace{1.5cm}}(\pi_t - \underline{\hspace{1cm}}) + \underline{\hspace{1.5cm}} \varepsilon_t \qquad \textbf{(14-11)}$$

$$\pi_t = \pi_{t-1} + \underline{\hspace{1.5cm}}(Y_t - \underline{\hspace{1cm}}) + v_t. \qquad \textbf{(14-12)}$$

c. Assume that we begin in period $t - 2$ at long-run equilibrium. Thus, output is equal to its natural level and inflation is and has been equal to its target rate. As in Exercise 5, we make two additional assumptions. First, the natural level of output does not change over time so that $\overline{Y}_{t-2} = \overline{Y}_{t-1} = \overline{Y}_t = \overline{Y}_{t+1} = \overline{Y}_{\text{all}} = \underline{\hspace{1.5cm}}$. Second, the inflation target π_t^* remains constant over time so that $\pi_{t-2}^* = \pi_{t-1}^* = \pi_t^* = \underline{\hspace{1.5cm}}$ (percent). These results are shown in the first row of Table 14-4:

Table 14-4

(1) Period	(2) Supply Shock υ	(3) Demand Shock ε	(4) Inflation in Preceding Period	(5) Output Y	(6) Inflation π
$t-2$	0	0	2	100.	2
$t-1$	0	0	_____	100	_____
t	1	0	_____	_____	_____
$t+1$	0	0	_____	_____	_____
$t+2$	0	0	_____	_____	_____
$t+3$	0	0	_____	_____	_____

d. We now use Equations 14-11 and 14-12 to complete the second row of Table 14-4. In period $t-1$, inflation in the preceding period (i.e., in period $t-2$) is given in the first row of Column 6. This number is _____ (percent). Enter this number in Column 4 of period $t-1$. If we are still in long-run equilibrium in period $t-1$, output will still be equal to its natural level of 100, which is entered in Column 5. Finally, if there are no supply shocks in period $t-1$, we can use Equation 14-12 to calculate inflation in period $t-1$ as $\pi_{t-1} = \pi_{t-2} +$ _____ $(Y_{t-1} -$ _____$) + 0 =$ _____ $+ 0.25($ _____ $-$ _____$) + 0 =$ _____. Enter this number in the second row of Column 6. Since this also becomes the preceding period's inflation rate for period t, enter it again in the third row of Column 4.

e. In period t, suppose a temporary supply shock increases υ_t from zero to 1 as shown in Column 2. The economy will no longer be in long-run equilibrium. Instead, it will move to a new intersection of the *DAS* and *DAD* curves at Point B in Graph 14-4 of Exercise 5. In order to calculate the values of output and inflation at Point B (in period t), we substitute the expression on the right-hand side of Equation 14-12 for π_t in Equation 14-11 to obtain:

$$Y_t = 100 - (1/3)[\pi_{t-1} + 0.25(Y_t - 100) + \upsilon_t - 2] + (2/3)\varepsilon_t. \qquad \textbf{(14-13)}$$

We have one more step to derive the equation we can use to calculate the value of Y_t in all periods once we know the values π_{t-1} and the two shocks. We need to solve Equation 14-13 for Y_t by multiplying through the right-hand side, collecting terms, and solving for Y_t. You should try this yourself, but the result is:

$$Y_t = 100.6154 - (4/13)\pi_{t-1} - (4/13)\upsilon_t + (8/13)\varepsilon_t. \qquad \textbf{(14-14)}$$

Inserting the values in Columns 2, 3, and 4 of Row 3 into Equation 14-14 gives $Y_t = 100.6154 - (4/13)$_____ $- (4/13)$_____ $+ (8/13)$_____ $=$ _____. Enter this number in Column 5 of Table 14-4.

f. Finally, we can calculate inflation in period t by substituting the values of π_{t-1}, v_t, and Y_t into Equation 14-12, which yields $\pi_t =$ _____ + 0.25(_____ − 100) + _____ = _____. Enter this number in Column 6. We now have the values for output and inflation in period t, which are the values at Point B in Graph 14-4.

g. Equations 14-14 and 14-12 can now be used to calculate the values of output and inflation in all future periods. In period $t + 1$, the supply shock disappears and the value of v_t returns to 0, as shown in Column 2 of Table 14-4. The value of ε_t remains equal to 0. The value of inflation in the preceding period is the rate of inflation in period t, which we calculated to be _____. Enter this number in Column 4. Then, use Equation 14-14 to calculate $Y_{t+1} =$ 100.6154 − (4/13) _____ − (4/13)_____ + (8/13)_____ = _____ and enter this number in Column 5. Finally, use Equation 14-12 to calculate $\pi_{t+1} = \pi_t +$ 0.25(Y_{t+1} − 100) + v_{t+1} = _____ − _____ + _____ = _____ and enter this number in Column 6. The numbers in Columns 5 and 6 are the values of output and inflation at Point C in Graph 14-4.

h. In Period $t + 2$, the values of both shocks are again 0, and inflation in the preceding period (i.e., π_{t+1}) is equal to _____. Enter this number in Column 4 and use Equations 14-14 and 14-12 to calculate Y_{t+2} and π_{t+2} as follows: $Y_{t+2} =$ 100.6154 − (4/13)_____ − (4/13)_____ + (8/13)_____ = _____, and $\pi_{t+2} = \pi_{t+1} +$ 0.25(Y_{t+2} − 100) + v_{t+2} = _____ − _____ + _____ = _____. Enter these values in Columns 5 and 6. If you feel courageous, try to complete the last row of Table 14-4 by yourself to verify that $Y_{t+3} =$ 99.758 and $\pi_{t+3} =$ 2.726.

i. We shall now use the numbers in Table 14-4 to derive what economists call *impulse response functions*, which are graphs of the time paths of variables after a shock. The impulse response functions for v and Y are illustrated in the top two panels of Graph 14-5. The values for periods $t - 2$ and $t - 1$ are those before the shock, when the value of $v = 0$ and the value of $Y = 100$. In period t, the value of v_t = _____ and the value of Y_t rises/falls to _____. In period $t + 1$, the value of v_{t+1} returns to _____ and the value of Y_{t+1} rises/falls to _____. In period $t + 2$, $v_{t+2} =$ _____ and $Y_{t+2} =$ _____. As we noted in Exercise 5, in the period in which a supply shock occurs that increases v for one period, output rises/falls. In future periods, output starts to rise/fall until we return to the long-run equilibrium.

Graph 14-5

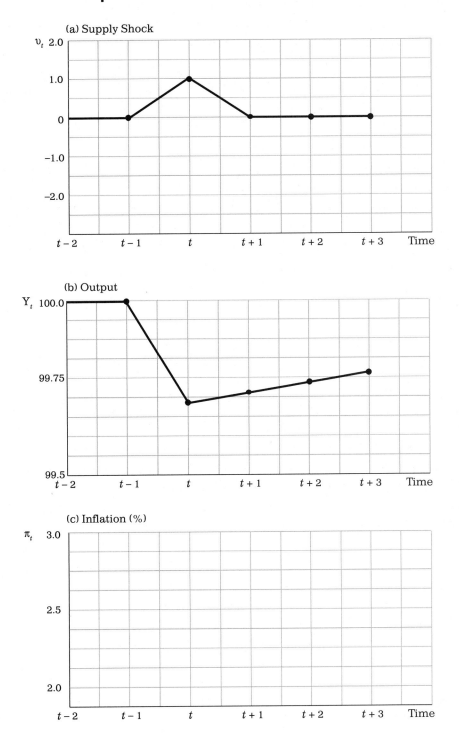

(a) Supply Shock

(b) Output

(c) Inflation (%)

j. Use the data in Table 14-4 to draw the impulse response function for inflation in the bottom section of Graph 14-5. As we noted in Exercise 5, in the period in which a supply shock occurs that increases v_t for one period, inflation rises/falls. In future periods, inflation starts to rise/fall until we return to the long-run equilibrium. As your text illustrates, we could also use the monetary policy rule to derive impulse response functions for the nominal and real interest rates.

7. **Aggregate Demand Shocks** *In this exercise, we analyze an aggregate demand shock that lasts for two periods.*

a. Recall that the random variable ε_t in the *DAD* equation represents an aggregate demand shock. An aggregate demand shock might be caused by an increase in government purchases, a sudden change in the stock market that affects household wealth, and thereby consumption, or a change in consumer or business optimism. The text analyzes a shock that lasts for five periods, but in this exercise, we analyze one that lasts for two. Starting with our basic *DAD* and *DAS* equations,

$$Y_t = \overline{Y}_t - [\alpha\theta_\pi/(1 + \alpha\theta_Y)](\pi_t - \pi_t^*) + [1/(1 + \alpha\theta_Y)]\varepsilon_t \qquad \textbf{(DAD)}$$

$$\pi_t = \pi_{t-1} + \varphi(Y_t - \overline{Y}_t) + v_t \qquad \textbf{(DAS)}$$

we again assume that we have been in long-run equilibrium at Point A in Graph 14-6 for several periods $t - 1$, $t - 2$, etc. We also assume that both the natural level of output and the inflation target remain constant over time. Starting at Point A, suppose there is a demand shock in period t that increases the value of ε to 1.0 for two periods. According to the *DAD* equation, an increase in ε_t will increase/decrease the value of Y_t in the period in which it occurs. Consequently, the *DAD* curve will shift to the right/left. Draw the new *DAD* curve in Graph 14-6 and label it DAD_t.

Graph 14-6

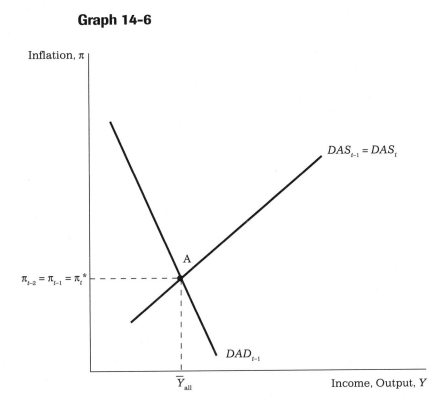

b. Because ε_t is not explicitly included in the *DAS* curve, it will not shift in period t. Hence, $DAS_t = DAS_{t-1}$ and the economy moves to the intersection of the DAD_t curve and the DAS_t curve. Locate this point in Graph 14-6 and label it Point B. From Point A to Point B, output has <u>increased/decreased</u> and inflation has <u>increased/decreased</u>.

c. Since the demand shock lasts for two periods, the value of ε_t will remain equal to _____ in period $t + 1$. Consequently, the *DAD* curve will not shift again, so add the label $DAD_t = DAD_{t+1}$ to your DAD_t curve in Graph 14-6. Because inflation has increased from period $t - 1$ to period t, expected inflation in period $t + 1$ will <u>rise/fall</u>, which will shift the *DAS* curve <u>upward (to the left)/downward (to the right)</u>. Draw a new *DAS* curve and label it DAS_{t+1}. Locate the new equilibrium at the intersection of the DAS_{t+1} and DAD_{t+1} curves and label it Point C. From Point B to Point C, output has <u>increased/decreased</u> and inflation has <u>increased/decreased</u>. These changes occur partially because the central bank has responded to the changes in output and inflation in period t by <u>increasing/decreasing</u> the real interest rate in period $t + 1$.

d. In period $t + 2$, the demand shock disappears and the value of ε_{t+2} falls back to zero. This will shift the *DAD* curve permanently back to DAD_{t-1}, so modify your label of this curve to $DAD_{t-1} = DAD_{t+2}$. Because inflation has increased from period t to period $t + 1$, expected inflation in period $t + 2$ will <u>rise/fall</u>, which will shift the *DAS* curve upward (to the left)/downward (to the right). Draw the new *DAS* curve, label it DAS_{t+2}, locate the new equilibrium and label it Point D. From Point C to Point D, output will definitely increase/decrease because both the *DAS* and *DAD* curves have shifted left. Inflation may continue to rise temporarily, depending on the parameter values in the model, but it will soon begin to fall. When it starts to fall, the *DAS* curve will shift upward (to the left)/downward (to the right) until the economy returns to long-run equilibrium at Point A. At Point A, inflation will again equal the _____, and output will return to the _____.

e. As in Exercise 6, we could construct the impulse response functions using the numbers suggested in the textbook, and this is left as one of the problems that follow the Exercise section of this *Study Guide*.

8. **A Change in Monetary Policy** *In this exercise, we analyze the effects of a reduction in the target for the inflation rate.*

a. In earlier exercises, the central bank used a monetary policy rule to change the real interest rate in response to deviations of inflation from its target and deviations of output from its natural level. The central bank may also change its target for inflation. Suppose we again start in long-run equilibrium in period $t - 1$ at Point A in Graph 14-7. Inflation has been constant for several periods and is equal to the central bank's initial target π_1^*.

Graph 14-7

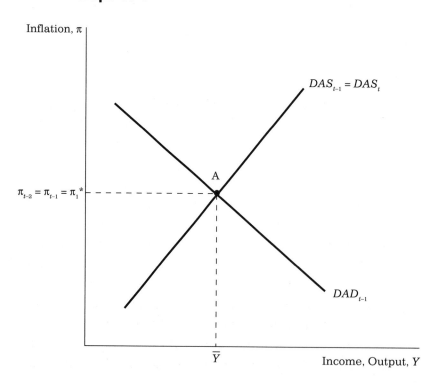

Now, suppose the central bank reduces its target for the inflation rate π_t^* to π_2^* in period t. Since π_t^* does not appear in the DAS equation, the DAS curve will not immediately be affected, so $DAS_t = DAS_{t-1}$. In the DAD equation, however, π_t^* does appear as an exogenous variable. As we discussed in Exercise 1, a reduction in π_t^* will shift the DAD curve downward (to the left)/upward (to the right). Draw the new DAD curve and label it DAD_t. Then, locate the short-run equilibrium in period t and label it Point B. From Point A to Point B, output increases/decreases and inflation increases/decreases.

b. After the initial decline in the inflation target, the DAD curve will not shift again. Therefore, relabel the DAD_t curve $DAD_t = DAD_{t+1...}$. When inflation starts to fall from Point A to Point B, however, inflation expectations will fall, and the DAS curve will start to shift upward (to the left/downward (to the right). Draw the new DAS curve and label it DAS_{t+1}. Locate the new short-run equilibrium and label it Point C. From Point B to Point C, output increases/decreases and inflation increases/decreases.

c. In period $t + 2$ and thereafter, the DAS curve will continue to shift upward (to the left/downward (to the right) until a new long-run equilibrium has been reached at the natural level of output. Draw the final DAS curve in Graph 14-7 and label it DAS_{Final}. Locate the final equilibrium and label it Point Z. At Point Z, inflation will be greater than/equal to/less than the new, lower inflation target π_2^*.

d. Throughout these exercises, we have assumed that people have adaptive expectations. If, however, people have rational expectations, they optimally use all available information in making their predictions. In this case, if the central bank's announcement of a lower inflation target is credible, the DAS curve will shift down more quickly/slowly, and the economy may move immediately to the new long-run equilibrium.

9. **The Tradeoff Between Output Variability and Inflation Variability** *In this exercise, we illustrate how the monetary policy rule can affect the variability of output and inflation.*

a. The slope of the DAD curve determines whether a supply shock has a big or small impact on output and inflation. Graph 14-8 has one DAS curve and two DAD curves. One DAD curve is flat, and the other is steep. Point A is the initial equilibrium because it is the intersection of the DAS curve and both DAD curves. Now, suppose there is a supply shock, such as an oil price increase. This will shift the DAS curve upward. Draw the new DAS curve in Graph 14-8 and label it DAS_{t+1} ($\upsilon_{t+1} > 0$). Locate the two new equilibria, one for each DAD curve. Label the equilibrium along the flat DAD curve Point B, and label the equilibrium along the steep DAD curve Point C. Your graph indicates that a supply shock that shifts the DAS curve upward (to the left) will reduce output by more when the DAD curve is flat/steep, while inflation rises by more when the DAD curve is flat/steep.

Graph 14-8

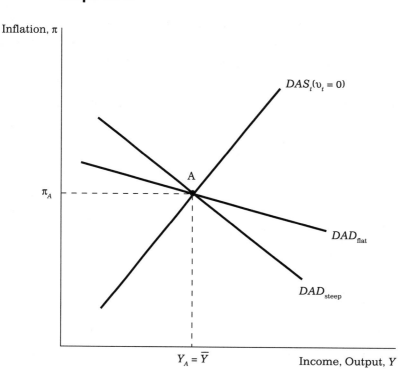

b. The central bank can influence the slope of the *DAD* curve through its monetary policy rule. Remember the equation for the monetary policy rule:

$$i_t = \pi_t + \rho + \theta_\pi(\pi_t - \pi_t^*) + \theta_Y(Y_t - \overline{Y}_t) \tag{14-4}$$

where the parameter θ_π represents the responsiveness of the central bank to inflation and the parameter θ_Y represents the responsiveness of the central bank to output. Both parameters are assumed to be greater than zero. If we then take the *DAD* equation,

$$Y_t = \overline{Y}_t - [\alpha\theta_\pi/(1 + \alpha\theta_Y)](\pi_t - \pi_t^*) + [1/(1 + \alpha\theta_Y)]\varepsilon_t, \tag{DAD}$$

after some manipulation and re-arranging, we can write the *DAD* equation in terms of inflation:

$$\pi_t = \pi_t^* - [(1 + \alpha\theta_Y)/\alpha\theta_\pi](Y_t - \overline{Y}_t) + (1/\alpha\theta_\pi)\varepsilon_t. \tag{14-15}$$

If there is no demand shock (i.e., $\varepsilon_t = 0$) and output is equal to its natural level, Equation 14-15 indicates that inflation will be <u>greater than/equal to/less than</u> its target. Furthermore, for every unit that output rises above its natural level, inflation falls by _____. Since the brackets in Equation 14-15 are preceded by a minus sign, the slope of the *DAD* curve is

_____. If the term in brackets in Equation 14-15 is large, the *DAD* curve will be steep. If the term in brackets is small, the *DAD* curve will be flat.

c. If the central bank responds strongly to inflation, θ_π will be large/small. Since θ_π appears in the denominator of the term in brackets in Equation 14-15, the entire term in brackets will then be large/small, and the *DAD* curve will be flat/steep. As a result, when the central bank responds strongly to inflation, a supply shock will result in a large/small increase in inflation and a large/small decrease in output. This occurs because a central bank that responds strongly to inflation will respond to a supply shock by increasing the real interest rate a lot/a little. As a result, the variability in inflation will be relatively high/low, and the variability in output will be relatively high/low.

d. Conversely, if the central bank responds strongly to output, θ_Y will be large/small. Since θ_Y appears in the numerator of the term in brackets in Equation 14-15, the entire term in brackets will then be large/small, and the *DAD* curve will be flat/steep. As a result, when the central bank responds strongly to output, a supply shock will result in a large/small increase in inflation and a large/small decrease in output. This occurs because a central bank that responds strongly to output will respond to a supply shock by increasing the real interest rate a lot/a little. As a result, the variability in inflation will be relatively high/low, and the variability in output will be relatively high/low.

Problems

Answer the following problems on a separate sheet of paper.

1. a. What determines the size of α, which appears in the equation representing the demand for goods and services?

    b. How does the size of α affect the flatness or steepness of the *DAD* curve? Briefly explain.

    c. Use the appropriate graph to illustrate and then describe how the value of α (and hence the steepness or flatness of the *DAD* curve) will affect the economy's short- and long-run responses to a reduction in the central bank's target for the inflation rate.

2   According to the Taylor rule, what are the recommended values for the nominal and real federal funds rates if:

    a. inflation is 4 percent and the GDP gap is 2 percent (i.e., GDP is 2 percent below its natural level)?

    b. inflation is 1 percent and unemployment is at its natural rate?

3. In this question, apply the Taylor rule.

   a. According to Okun's law, the GDP gap is twice the difference between the actual unemployment rate and the natural rate of unemployment. If the natural rate of unemployment is 5.4 percent, and the actual unemployment rate is 8.9 percent, calculate the GDP gap.

   b. Assume that the inflation rate is 0 percent. According to the Taylor rule, what were the recommended nominal and real interest rates that the central bank should set?

   c. The nominal interest rate cannot fall below zero. What might the central bank do to try to achieve the optimal real interest rate you calculated in Part a? (These data represent the actual situation in the U.S. in April 2009.)

4. Suppose inflation expectations for period $t + 1$ depended on both current inflation and last period's inflation such that $E_t\pi_{t+1} = \frac{1}{2}\pi_t + \frac{1}{2}\pi_{t-1}$. How would this affect the speed with which inflation expectations would change in response to a sudden change in the inflation rate resulting from a supply shock? Consequently, how would it affect the speed with which the economy returned to its long-run equilibrium following a temporary supply shock?

5. Use the *DAD* and *DAS* equations:

$$Y_t = \overline{Y}_t - [\alpha\theta_\pi/(1 + \alpha\theta_Y)](\pi_t - \pi_t^*) + [1/(1 + \alpha\theta_Y)]\varepsilon_t \qquad \textbf{(DAD)}$$

$$\pi_t = \pi_{t-1} + \varphi(Y_t - \overline{Y}_t) + \upsilon_t \qquad \textbf{(DAS)}$$

along with the values of the parameters, inflation target, and natural level of output given in the textbook (i.e., $\overline{Y}_t = \overline{Y}_{all} = 100$; $\pi_t^* = 2.0$; $\alpha = 1.0$; $\varphi = 0.25$; $\theta_\pi = 0.5$; and $\theta_Y = 0.5$) to derive the equations we used in Exercise 6 to solve for the endogenous variables in each period:

$$Y_t = 100.6154 - (4/13)\pi_{t-1} - (4/13)\upsilon_t + (8/13)\varepsilon_t, \text{ and} \qquad \textbf{(14-14)}$$

$$\pi_t = \pi_{t-1} + 0.25(Y_t - 100) + \upsilon_t. \qquad \textbf{(14-12)}$$

6. Suppose the economy has been in long-run equilibrium and experiences a demand shock that lasts for two periods starting in period t, as in Exercise 7. Use the values of the parameters, inflation target, and natural level of output given in the textbook (i.e., $\overline{Y}_t = \overline{Y}_{all} = 100$; $\pi_t^* = 2.0$; $\alpha = 1.0$; $\varphi = 0.25$; $\theta_\pi = 0.5$; and $\theta_Y = 0.5$) and Equations 14-14 and 14-12 from Problem 5 to complete Table 14-5. Then, draw the impulse response functions for periods $t - 2$ through $t + 3$ for the demand shock, output, and inflation.

Table 14-5

(1) Period	(2) Supply Shock υ_t	(3) Demand Shock ε_t	(4) Inflation in Preceding Period	(5) Output Y_t	(6) Inflation π_t
$t-2$	0	0	2	100_	2
$t-1$	0	0	2	100	2
t	0	1	2	_____	_____
$t+1$	0	1	_____	_____	_____
$t+2$	0	0	_____	_____	_____
$t+3$	0	0	_____	_____	_____

7.
C

a. Use the *DAD* equation

$$Y_t = \overline{Y}_t - [\alpha\theta_\pi/(1 + \alpha\theta_Y)](\pi_t - \pi_t^*) + [1/(1 + \alpha\theta_Y)]\varepsilon_t, \qquad \textbf{(DAD)}$$

to derive the inverted *DAD* equation introduced in Exercise 9:

$$\pi_t = \pi_t^* - [(1 + \alpha\theta_Y)/\alpha\theta_\pi](Y_t - \overline{Y}_t) + (1/\alpha\theta_\pi)\varepsilon_t. \qquad \textbf{(14-15)}$$

b. The slope of the *DAD* curve is $d\pi_t/dY_t$. Use Equation 14-15 to calculate this slope.

c. Recall that θ_π and θ_Y measure the central bank's responses to inflation and output, respectively. Use calculus to determine whether an increase in θ_π increases or decreases the slope of the *DAD* curve. Consequently, will an increase in the central bank's responsiveness to inflation make the *DAD* curve flatter or steeper? (Be careful about the minus sign.)

d. Use calculus to determine whether an increase in θ_Y increases or decreases the slope of the *DAD* curve. Consequently, will an increase in the central bank's responsiveness to output make the *DAD* curve flatter or steeper?

e. Confirm the answer to Problem 1 mathematically by using calculus to prove that an increase in α makes the *DAD* curve flatter.

8. Use the appropriate graph to illustrate how the steepness or flatness of the *DAD* curve will affect the economy's response to an adverse demand shock, defined as $\upsilon_t < 0$, in the period in which it occurs. (Hint: A demand shock will shift the *DAD* curve by the same *horizontal amount* regardless of its slope.)

chapter 15

Stabilization Policy

Fill-in Questions

Use the key terms below to fill in the blanks in the following statements. Each term may be used more than once.

automatic stabilizers
index of leading indicators
inflation targeting
inside lag
Lucas critique

monetarists
outside lag
political business cycle
time inconsistency

1. The _____ is the time between a shock to the economy and the policy action responding to that shock.

2. The _____ is the time between a policy action and its ultimate influence on the economy.

3. Fiscal policy has a relatively long _____; monetary policy has a relatively long _____.

4. _____ stimulate or depress the economy when necessary without any deliberate policy changes.

5. The _____ is composed of 10 data series that signal future changes in real output. Economists use this measure to forecast future economic conditions.

6. The _____ argues that traditional methods of policy evaluation did not adequately take into account the impact of policy on expectations.

7. The manipulation of the economy by politicians in an attempt to gain reelection is called the _____.

8. The phenomenon of _____ implies that policymakers can sometimes better achieve their own goals by having their discretion taken away from them.

9. _____ advocate that the Bank of Canada keep the money supply growing at a steady rate as a method of preventing most large fluctuations in real output.

10. _____ may be viewed as fiscal policy without any inside lag.

11. Since the Bank of Canada has adopted a policy of _____, it announces a target for the rate of inflation and then adjusts the money supply accordingly whenever the actual inflation rate deviated from its target.

Multiple-Choice Questions

1. The outside lag is the time between a:
   a. shock to the economy and the policy action responding to that shock.
   b. policy action and its influence on the economy.
   c. shock to the economy and the realization that some policy action needs to be taken.
   d. decision to implement a policy and the enactment of that policy.

2. The following statement is TRUE:
   a. monetary policy has an especially long outside lag.
   b. fiscal policy has an especially long inside lag.
   c. automatic stabilizers eliminate part of the inside lag in the conduct of fiscal policy.
   d. all of the above.

3. Arguments against the use of active stabilization policy include all of the following EXCEPT the:
   a. existence of long inside and outside lags.
   b. limited ability of economic forecasters to predict future economic conditions accurately.
   c. responsiveness of labour force participation rates to changes in national output.
   d. historical view that ill-advised policy choices were the cause of the Great Depression.

4. The system of employment insurance can be used to illustrate:
   a. the time inconsistency of policy.
   b. the way that the economy is automatically stabilized in the event of a shock.
   c. the Lucas critique.
   d. long inside lags in policy implementation.

5. Countries with more independent central banks tend to have:
   a. lower unemployment rates.
   b. lower inflation rates.
   c. higher rates of economic growth.
   d. all of the above.

6. Suppose that the index of leading indicators falls. Economic forecasters will expect all of the following to occur EXCEPT:

   a. the unemployment rate will increase.
   b. real output will decrease.
   c. inflation will increase.
   d. tax revenues will decrease.

7. According to the Lucas critique:

   a. traditional methods of policy evaluation do not adequately account for the impact of policy changes on expectations.
   b. traditional estimates of the sacrifice ratio are unreliable.
   c. economists cannot be completely confident when they make assessments about the effects of alternative economic policies.
   d. all of the above.

8. Comparing the time period before World War I with the period after World War II, Christina Romer found that:

   a. real GDP and unemployment have been much more stable in the later period.
   b. real GDP and unemployment have been much less stable in the later period.
   c. real GDP and unemployment have been slightly more stable in the later period.
   d. the levels of real GDP and unemployment have been approximately equal in the two periods.

9. I: The Bank of Canada's policy of limiting price volatility means that demand shocks affect real output less than they otherwise would. II: The Bank of Canada's policy of limiting price volatility means that supply shocks affect real output less than they otherwise would.

   a. I is true; II is not.
   b. II is true; I is not.
   c. Both I and II are true.
   d. Neither I nor II is true.

10. All of the following are examples of a policy conducted by rule EXCEPT:

    a. the Bank of Canada automatically increases the money supply every year by 3 percent.
    b. the federal government is required, by a constitutional amendment, to balance the budget every year.
    c. the Bank of Canada adopts the following monetary policy for the indefinite future: % Change in $M = 3\% + 2 \times$ (Actual Unemployment Rate $- 6.5\%$).
    d. after a decline in private spending, federal parliament debates and then decides to stimulate aggregate demand by reducing taxes.

11. The following statement is FALSE:

    a. a policy that is active cannot be conducted by rule.

    b. the problem of time inconsistency is especially relevant to policy conducted by discretion.

    c. the conflicting interests of politicians reduce the desirability of policy conducted by discretion compared with policy conducted by rule.

    d. monetary policy currently is conducted by discretion.

12. If the Bank of Canada conducts monetary policy by setting a targeted unemployment rate of 6.5 percent, then the:

    a. unemployment rate will never fall above or below 6.5 percent.

    b. natural rate of unemployment will converge to the Bank of Canada's target.

    c. Bank of Canada will increase the growth rate of the money supply whenever unemployment exceeds this targeted rate.

    d. Bank of Canada will adjust its target whenever unemployment deviates from this rate.

13. Which of the following policies might lead to suboptimal results in the long run because of time inconsistencies?

    a. negotiation with terrorists who have taken hostages after a policy of nonnegotiation has been announced

    b. the enactment of a temporary "tax amnesty" for tax evaders

    c. the use of discretionary monetary policy rather than monetary rules

    d. all of the above

14. The best argument against the monetarists' view that a steady growth in the money supply would prevent most large fluctuations in output and unemployment is that:

    a. steady growth in the money supply would prevent fluctuations in output only if the aggregate price level is constant.

    b. steady growth in the money supply need not stabilize aggregate demand because the velocity of money is not always stable.

    c. large fluctuations in the money supply do not occur because there is a limited amount of money available in the economy.

    d. fluctuations in output and unemployment are best treated by fiscal policy because the federal government has a more direct control over the economy through its use of the tax system.

Exercises

1. **Active versus Passive Macroeconomic Policies** *In this exercise, we review the arguments for active and passive policy responses to fluctuations in real output.*

    a. Suppose that the economy is initially at Point A on Graph 15-1.

    Graph 15-1

    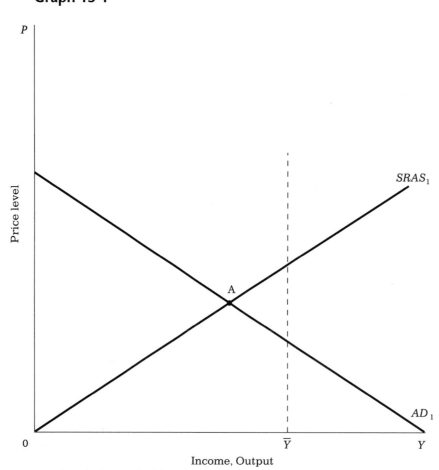

    Clearly, at Point A, real output Y is greater than/equal to/less than the natural rate of output $\overline{Y}$. Consequently, the actual price level P must be greater than/ equal to/less than the expected price level EP.

    b. In future years, therefore, EP will rise/fall/remain the same. If macroeconomic policies remain unchanged, the change in EP will shift the short-run aggregate supply curve upward/downward until eventually actual output is greater than/ equal to/less than the natural rate of output. Draw the final short-run aggregate supply curve on Graph 15-1 and label it $SRAS_F$. Label the final equilibrium Point F. Comparing Points A and F, one can conclude that if no policy response is taken, real output will eventually rise/fall/remain the same, and the price level will rise/fall/remain the same.

c. The initial equilibrium from Graph 15-1 is redrawn on Graph 15-2.

Graph 15-2

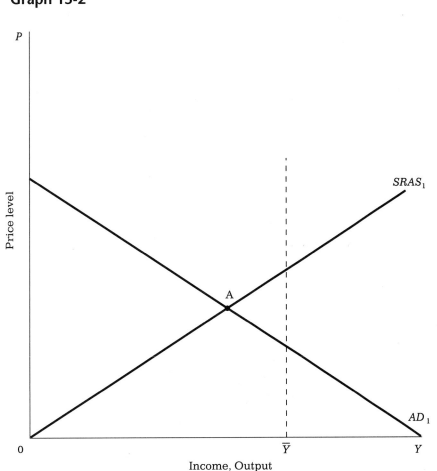

If policymakers wanted to increase output to the natural rate quickly, they could increase/decrease the money supply, increase/decrease government purchases, or increase/decrease taxes. These policies would shift the aggregate demand curve to the left/right. Draw the new aggregate demand curve on Graph 15-2, label it AD_2, and label the new equilibrium Point B. Comparing Points A and B, one can conclude that if an active policy response is taken, real output will rise/fall/remain the same, and the price level will rise/fall/remain the same.

d. In Parts a and b, the economy eventually reaches the natural rate of output. If an active policy response is taken, however, the eventual price level is greater than/ equal to/less than the eventual price level if no policy response is taken.

The case for an active policy response to fluctuations in output relies partially on the belief that the transition back to the natural rate will be longer/shorter if expansionary monetary and fiscal policies are pursued than if no new policies are pursued. It also relies on the belief that policymakers will be able and willing to implement the appropriate policies.

e. In Chapter 13 of the textbook, there is a discussion of some of the issues that determine the speed with which the economy approaches the natural rate of output when policy is passive. Instead of assuming that expected inflation is equal to last year's actual rate of inflation, suppose that inflationary expectations are rational. Then real output will return to its natural rate more/less rapidly. If wages and prices are flexible rather than sticky, real output will return to its natural rate more/less rapidly. If the duration of wage and price contracts is relatively long rather than short, real output will return to its natural rate more/less rapidly.

f. In Chapter 15 of the textbook, there is a discussion of several problems that commonly arise when active policy measures are taken to stabilize output. One limitation of active policy concerns the fact that fiscal policy has a relatively long inside/outside lag, whereas monetary policy has a relatively long inside/outside lag. Another limitation is that the track record of economic forecasters has not been especially good. Finally, policymakers occasionally seem to be unwilling or unable to implement the appropriate macroeconomic policies because of political considerations.

2. **The Lucas Critique** *In this exercise, we use a simple Phillips curve example to illustrate the Lucas critique.*

a. Suppose that the following equation represents the Phillips curve for an imaginary economy:

$$u = u^n - \beta\,(\pi - E\pi) = 6 - 0.2(\pi - E\pi). \tag{15-1}$$

According to Equation 15-1, the natural rate of unemployment is _____ percent. Furthermore, whenever the actual inflation rate exceeds the expected rate of inflation by 1 percentage point, the unemployment rate is _____ percentage points above/below the natural rate of unemployment.

b. During the nineteenth century, suppose that the actual rate of inflation was +5 percent half the time and –5 percent the remaining half. In the absence of any prior information, the average or expected rate of inflation for any year would be

$$E\pi = 0.5 \times 5\% + 0.5 \times (-5\%) = \underline{\hspace{1cm}}\%.$$

During those years in which the actual rate of inflation turned out to be +5 percent, the Phillips curve equation indicates that the actual unemployment rate was 6 – 0.2(_____ – _____) = _____ percent. On the other hand, during those years in which the actual rate of inflation was –5 percent, the actual rate of unemployment was 6 – 0.2 (_____ – _____) = _____ percent. Since each of the two rates occurred half of the time, the average unemployment rate during the entire century was _____ percent.

c. After a century of this pattern, advisers recommended policies designed to keep the inflation rate equal to +5 percent in every year. It was the advisers' hope that people's expectations of inflation would remain equal to the last century's expected inflation rate of _____ percent, so that the unemployment rate would be 6 − 0.2(_____ − _____) = _____ percent in every year.

d. Alas, after several years of these new policies and persistent 5 percent inflation, people soon increased their forecast of inflation to 5 percent. As a result, unemployment thereafter equaled 6 − 0.2(_____ − _____) = _____ percent in every year, which was <u>more than/less than/equal to</u> the average during the preceding century.

e. This example illustrates the Lucas critique, whereby an evaluation of a change in economic policy must take into account the impact of the policy change on people's expectations of the future. Several economists believe that the imaginary economy in this exercise resembles the experience of the Canadian economy during the past two centuries. Finally, the more quickly people changed their expectations in response to the more inflationary policies, the more <u>quickly/slowly</u> unemployment returned to its natural rate.

3. **Rules versus Discretion** *In this exercise, we present and evaluate several rules for the conduct of monetary and fiscal policy.*

a. As stated in Exercise 1, many observers are wary about the ability and/or willingness of policymakers to implement the appropriate macroeconomic policies. Some economists believe that monetary and/or fiscal policy should be governed by a set of rules or formulas. One example is the constant-growth-rate rule, advocated by many monetarists, in which the Bank of Canada would increase the money supply by a fixed percentage each year. Suppose, for example, that the goal of monetary policy is to fuel noninflationary long-run economic growth. Recall the quantity equation presented in Chapter 7 of the textbook.

$$MV = PY \qquad\qquad (15\text{-}2)$$

The percentage change version of the quantity equation is

% Change in M + % Change in V = % Change in P + % Change in Y.

The long-run rate of growth of output is about 3 percent per year. If velocity were constant, growth that kept the price level stable would require that % Change in M = % Change in P + % Change in Y − % Change in V or

_____ + _____ − _____ = _____%.

b. One frequently mentioned problem with the constant-growth-rate rule is that large fluctuations in velocity would lead to large fluctuations in aggregate demand. As a result, some economists advocate a money-growth rule that sets a target for nominal income PY. Suppose that the target growth rate for nominal income is 3 percent per year. If velocity were constant, this target growth rate would require a _____ percent annual increase in the money supply M. Suppose, however, that nominal income increases by 7 percent in one year. If the money supply continued to grow by _____ percent, then velocity must have increased/decreased by _____ percent. Following a nominal-income targeting rule, the Bank of Canada would then reduce the growth rate of the money supply to dampen aggregate demand. If, on the other hand, nominal income increased by 1 percent in one year and the money supply continued to grow at its initial rate, then velocity must have increased/decreased by _____ percent. The Bank of Canada would then increase the growth rate of the money supply to spur aggregate demand. In this way, the Bank of Canada would have the ability and the authority to offset fluctuations in the velocity of money.

c. A third group of economists believes that price stability should be the sole goal of monetary policy. Consequently, they advocate a money-growth rule that is based on a target price level. If the actual price level were to exceed the target, money growth would increase/decrease. If the actual price level were less than the target, money growth would increase/decrease.

Problems

Answer the following problems on a separate sheet of paper.

1. Suppose you do not know the exact natural rate of unemployment, but you are confident that it is between 4.5 and 6 percent. Given the evidence cited in the textbook concerning the accuracy of economic forecasts and policy time lags, what might you reasonably conclude about the appropriate changes in monetary and fiscal policies if:

   a. the actual unemployment rate is 6.1 percent? Explain.

   b. the actual unemployment rate is 10.1 percent? Explain.

2. Explain why you agree or disagree with the following statement: The acceptance of rational expectations *totally* discredits the notion that policy activism should be pursued if output lies below its natural rate.

3. As the textbook notes, countries with more independent central banks tend to have lower average inflation rates. Nevertheless, the average unemployment rates among countries are unrelated to the degree of central bank independence. How would one explain this finding using the Phillips curve?

4. **a.** According to what measure has real GDP become much less variable (volatile) in the post–World War II period relative to its variability in the 40-year period prior to World War II?

   b. According to what measure has the volatility of real GDP been roughly the same in these two periods?

   c. Why is this issue important for the debate concerning the desirability of pursuing macroeconomic stabilization policies when the economy is in a boom or a recession?

5. Suppose a central banker was concerned *only* about price stability, resulting in the
   A loss function $L(\pi) = \pi^2$.
   C

   a. Use calculus to derive the optimal level of inflation for this central banker. (The answer should not be surprising.)

   b. What will be the resulting rate of unemployment in the long run? Explain.

6. **a.** Many economists advocate a reduction in the capital gains tax in order to stimu-
   ▣ late saving and investment. Briefly explain these economists' reasoning.

   b. Other economists believe that a capital gains tax reduction on past acquisitions would reduce tax revenues without stimulating additional saving and investment. Briefly explain their reasoning.

   c. Instead, this second group of economists suggests that saving and investment could be stimulated more by focusing all of the tax reduction on new acquisitions. This action would allow the tax rates on additional saving and investment to be reduced even more. Explain how the problem of time inconsistency might be used to dispute their assertion.

7. Suppose current consumption depends on current disposable income and expected future disposable income. In forming their expectations of future disposable income, households must also forecast future taxes.

   a. During his election campaign, Barack Obama promised to reduce taxes for 95% of Americans. If people believed these promises, how would his election in November 2008 affect consumption in 2008? Explain your answer.

   b. After the election, it took many months for Congress to pass some of the proposed tax cuts. Once they were finally passed, what effect would their passage have on consumption? Explain your answer.

   c. How do your answers to Parts a and b illustrate the Lucas critique?

8. Canada's target range for the inflation rate has been 1%–3%. Some argue that it should be zero. But zero inflation prevents the central bank from pushing interest rates below zero—something bank officials may want to do in a severe recession. Why does zero inflation have this effect?

Questions to Think About

1. **a.** Are inflationary expectations rational?

    b. What empirical tests would prove or disprove the hypothesis that expectations are rational?

2. As the textbook illustrates, different economists believe in different models of the economy. In what sense, then, can everyone have a rational expectation of the effects of various policies on real output?

3. If policymakers decided to conduct monetary and fiscal policy by rules, should they be allowed to change the rules? If so, under what circumstances?

4. If monetary and fiscal policies are governed by rules, but policymakers are allowed to change these rules, how can one apply the problem of time inconsistency to the debate about whether policy should be conducted by rules or by discretion?

5. How might policymakers make a commitment to a policy rule? Might the policymakers' reputation be a form of commitment?

6. If you believe that democracy is the best form of government, how could you justify greater central bank independence from a political perspective?

chapter **16**

Government Debt
and Budget Deficits

Fill-in Questions

Use the key terms below to fill in the blanks in the following statements. Each term may be used more than once.

cyclically adjusted budget deficit   interest rate
government debt   Ricardian equivalence
growth rate   traditional view of government debt

1. When the conventionally measured government budget deficit is positive, there is an increase in the nominal value of the _____.

2. The _____ measures what the budget deficit would be if the economy were operating at its natural rate of output and employment.

3. According to the _____, a tax cut that is unaccompanied by current or expected future reductions in government spending stimulates current consumption.

4. According to the _____ hypothesis, a tax cut that is unaccompanied by current or expected future reductions in government spending has no effect on current consumption.

5. If the primary deficit is zero, the level of the government debt-to-GDP ratio must increase if the _____ exceeds the _____.

6. If the overall deficit is zero, the government debt-to-GDP ratio must decrease if the _____ exceeds zero.

Multiple-Choice Questions

1. The ratio of federal government debt to GDP:
   a. has never been higher than it was in 1995.
   b. peaked during the Great Depression of the 1930s.
   c. has never been lower than it has been during the past 15 years.
   d. is much smaller today than it was at the end of World War II.

2. If no changes are made to our public health care systems, projected demographic changes will:

   a. worsen our budgetary problems in the next 30 years.

   b. alleviate our budgetary problems in the next 30 years.

   c. have little effect on our budgetary problems in the next 30 years.

3. Ignoring interest payments on the debt, the government budget deficit is equal to:

   a. $G - T$.

   b. $T - G$.

   c. $G + T$.

   d. $-G$.

4. The stock of government debt is equal to:

   a. the current government budget deficit.

   b. the total debt of all individuals in the nation.

   c. the sum of all past budget deficits.

   d. government expenditures minus the tax revenues.

5. During periods of inflation, the official measure of the budget deficit:

   a. overstates the change in the government's real indebtedness.

   b. understates the change in the government's real indebtedness.

   c. equals the change in the government's real indebtedness.

   d. should equal the expected rate of inflation.

6. Economists argue that the official measure of the budget deficit is an incomplete measure of the change in the government's overall indebtedness because it:

   a. measures the change in the nominal debt rather than the real debt.

   b. does not consider any changes in the value of government assets.

   c. excludes the accrual of future pension benefits that must be paid to government employees.

   d. all of the above.

7. During recessions the:

   a. actual budget deficit will be smaller than the cyclically adjusted budget deficit.

   b. actual budget deficit will be greater than the cyclically adjusted budget deficit.

   c. actual budget deficit will be equal to the cyclically adjusted budget deficit.

   d. cyclically adjusted budget deficit will always be positive.

8. According to the traditional view of government debt, a tax cut will lead to all of the following in the short run EXCEPT a(n):

   a. increase in consumption.

   b. increase in private saving.

   c. increase in investment.

   d. decrease in public saving.

9. According to the traditional view of government debt, a tax cut will lead to all of the following in the long run EXCEPT a:

    a. decrease in public saving.
    b. decrease in national saving.
    c. decrease in net exports.
    d. depreciation of the foreign exchange rate.

10. According to the Ricardian view of government debt, consumers will treat a current tax cut as an increase in:

    a. their wealth.
    b. the sum of their current and expected future income.
    c. their current disposable income accompanied by a future tax increase.
    d. public saving.

11. According to the Ricardian view of government debt, consumers will respond to a current tax cut by:

    a. increasing their current consumption.
    b. increasing their private saving by the amount of the tax cut.
    c. increasing their future consumption.
    d. decreasing their private saving by the amount of the tax cut.

12. According to the Ricardian view of government debt, a current tax cut will:

    a. decrease public saving.
    b. increase private saving.
    c. have no effect on national saving.
    d. all of the above.

13. According to the Ricardian view of government debt, the relevant decision-making unit is the:

    a. infinitely lived family.
    b. finitely lived family.
    c. finitely lived individual.
    d. infinitely lived world community.

14. During the early 1980s, taxes were cut substantially in the United States, and national saving in that country fell. This evidence by itself would seem to support:

    a. the traditional view of government debt.
    b. the Ricardian view of government debt.
    c. neither view of government debt.
    d. the view that government debt is neutral.

15. The events of the early 1980s, when taxes were cut and national saving fell in the United States, are consistent with the Ricardian view of government debt if:

    a. people suddenly became less optimistic about future economic growth.
    b. people expected future reductions in government spending.
    c. people expected that the tax cuts were temporary.
    d. the tax cuts were unexpected.

16. High budget deficits may:

    a. encourage excessively expansionary monetary policy.

    b. increase the risk of government default on its debt.

    c. reduce a nation's political influence throughout the world.

    d. all of the above.

17. If higher deficits raise fears of default on a country's national debt:

    a. domestic interest rates will rise.

    b. the foreign exchange rate will depreciate.

    c. capital flight may occur.

    d. all of the above.

18. Indexed government bonds:

    a. have higher interest rates than nonindexed bonds.

    b. reduce the government's incentive to produce surprise inflation.

    c. were introduced in Canada in 1999.

    d. all of the above.

19. Adherence to a balanced-budget rule by the federal government results in:

    a. an inability to use monetary policy to stimulate the economy when it slips into a recession.

    b. persistent inflation.

    c. an inability to lower tax rates to stimulate the economy when it slips into a recession.

    d. all of the above.

20. If the government always balances its overall budget, the debt-to-GDP ratio:

    a. cannot increase indefinitely.

    b. must increase indefinitely if the interest rate exceeds the growth rate.

    c. must increase indefinitely if the nominal GDP growth rate is negative.

    d. must increase indefinitely if the real interest rate is negative.

Exercises

1. **Adjusting the Budget Deficit for Inflation** *In this exercise, we illustrate how inflation can lead to an overestimate of the correctly measured budget deficit and how the inclusion of real, rather than nominal, interest payments in government expenses overcomes this problem.*

   Consider Table 16-1 on next page.

Table 16-1

(1)	(2) Country A	(3) Country B
Initial debt (in billions of dollars)	$2,000	$2,000
Nominal government outlays (made near the end of the year), excluding interest payments (in billions of dollars)	$200	$200
Price level at the beginning of the year	1.0	1.0
Annual inflation rate	0	0.10
Nominal interest rate	0.03	0.13
Nominal taxes (in billions of dollars)	$260	$260

Countries A and B are identical, except that Country B has 10 percent more inflation and, therefore (assuming that real interest rates are 3 percent in both economies), a 10 percent higher nominal interest rate than Country A.

a. Using these data, we see that government (nominal) interest payments during the year in Country A = 0.03 × $2,000 = $_____ billion. In Country B, however, government (nominal) interest payments during the year = _____ × $2,000 = $_____ billion.

b. The official government deficit in each country is equal to nominal government outlays, *including* nominal interest payments minus nominal taxes. In Country A, this amount equals $200 + (0.03 × $2,000) − $260 = $_____ billion. In Country B, however, the official government budget deficit equals $_____ + (_____ × $2,000) − $_____ = $_____ billion.

c. The nominal value of outstanding government debt at the end of the fiscal year is equal to the initial value of debt plus any additional nominal budget deficits during the year. Consequently, the nominal value of outstanding government debt at the end of the fiscal year in Country A equals $2,000 + $_____ = $_____ billion, whereas in Country B it equals $_____ + $_____ = $_____ billion.

d. Given the initial price level of 1.0 in both countries and the different inflation rates in Table 16-1, the price level at the end of the fiscal year is _____ in Country A and _____ in Country B. The real value of outstanding government debt at the end of the fiscal year in Country A is equal to the nominal debt at the end of the year divided by the aggregate price level at the end of the year, or $_____ / _____ = $_____ billion. The real value of outstanding government debt at the end of the fiscal year in Country B is equal to $_____ / _____ = $_____ billion. The real value of government debt at the end of the year in Country A is greater than/less than/equal to the real value of government debt at the end of the year in Country B. If deficits truly measured changes in the real value of outstanding government debt, the budget deficits in both countries would equal $_____$ billion. Thus, during periods of high inflation, as in Country B, official deficit measures tend to understate/ overstate the true value of the deficit.

e. Suppose that one counts only *ex post* real interest payments in the deficit. The *ex post* real interest rate is _____ (or _____ percent) in Country A and _____ in Country B. Consequently, real interest payments are $_____ billion in Country A and $_____ billion in Country B. The adjusted budget deficit would then equal nominal government outlays excluding interest payments plus real interest payments minus nominal taxes. This adjusted budget deficit would equal $_____ + $_____ – $_____ = $_____ billion in both countries. Thus, one way to eliminate the distortionary effects of inflation on the deficit is to include in the budget only real interest payments on the government debt.

2. The Traditional View of Government Debt *In this exercise, we review the short- and long-run effects of tax cuts according to the traditional view of government debt.*

a. In a closed economy in the short run, a tax cut will shift the *IS/LM* curve to the left/right. This shift will increase/decrease real income, increase/decrease consumption, and increase/decrease the real interest rate. As a result, investment will rise/fall and the tax cut partially crowds out government purchases/investment.

b. In an open economy, the short-run effects of the tax cut will depend upon whether the foreign exchange rate is fixed or floating. If the country is a small open economy, the real interest rate will increase/decrease/remain constant. If the foreign exchange rate is floating, a tax cut will lead to a(n) appreciation/ depreciation of the domestic currency and national income will increase/ decrease/remain constant. Disposable income and consumption, however, will increase/decrease/remain constant, and the tax cut will completely crowd out investment/government purchases/net exports. If the foreign exchange rate is fixed, the tax cut will increase/decrease/have no effect on real income and increase/decrease/have no effect on consumption. To maintain the fixed exchange rate, the central bank will have to increase/decrease the money supply.

c. In the long run, output will be at its natural rate. According to the traditional view of government debt, if the steady-state capital stock is unaffected, then in a closed economy the tax cut will increase/decrease/have no effect on national saving in the long run and increase/decrease/have no effect on consumption.

d. If the steady-state capital stock is affected and the economy starts from a
CH position below the Golden Rule level of capital, the tax cut will increase/
decrease/have no effect on the saving rate. Consequently, the steady-state level
of the capital stock will increase/decrease/remain constant, and the steady-
state levels of output and consumption will rise/fall/remain constant.

3. The Ricardian View of Government Debt *In this exercise, we present the Ricardian
view that tax cuts will increase saving and have no effect on current consumption.*

a. According to the Ricardian view of government debt, a tax cut does not stimulate consumption because it does not affect the current and expected future
income of current citizens and their descendants. Let us begin by analyzing a
simple two-period model. Suppose that the government cuts taxes by $1,000 in
Period 1. If this tax cut represents an increase in current and expected future
income, consumers will respond by increasing/decreasing/not changing
consumption.

b. Now suppose that the government finances the tax cut by issuing a bond
for $1,000 plus interest of 10 percent. When the government pays back its
loan in Period 2, it will pay $1,000 + 0.10($1,000) = $_____.
To pay this amount, it will have to increase taxes in Period 2 by
$_____. If in Period 1 you had saved all of the money you
received from the initial tax cut and put it into the bank at an interest rate of
10 percent, you would have $1,000 + 0.10($1,000) = $_____
in Period 2. Consequently, after you pay the tax increase in Period 2, you will be
better off/worse off/equally well off compared with your situation before the
initial tax cut in Period 1. As a result, the early tax cut and the later tax increase
will increase/decrease/have no effect on the sum of your current and expected
future income, and consumption in Period 1 will increase/decrease/remain
constant.

c. Ricardians expand this simple model to include many periods in the distant
future. Any tax reduction in the current period unaccompanied by current or
future reductions in government spending will eventually lead to a tax increase
in the future that is equal to the amount of money that will accumulate if current
citizens save all of the current tax reduction. (Alternatively, the "present value"
of the future tax increase is equal to the initial tax cut.) Consequently, if the
indefinite future is considered, an early tax cut and a later tax increase will
increase/decrease/have no effect on the sum of current and expected future
income, and consumption in Period 1 will increase/decrease/remain constant.

4. **Fiscal Policy Rules** *Chapters 14 and 15 examined several policy rules for monetary policy. In this exercise we present and evaluate several rules for the conduct of fiscal policy.*

   a. The most well-known rule for fiscal policy is one that requires the federal budget to be balanced in each year, that is, $G - tY = 0$ where t is the tax rate. This balanced-budget rule would obviously reduce the ability of policymakers to use fiscal policy to offset fluctuations in real output. It might even exacerbate these fluctuations. If, for example, the economy slipped into a recession, tY would <u>increase/remain constant/decrease</u>. To keep the budget balanced, policymakers might then have to <u>increase/decrease</u> G or <u>increase/decrease</u> the tax rate t. Either change would shift the aggregate demand curve to the <u>left/right</u> and thereby magnify the reduction in output.

   b. As the textbook states, policymakers should avoid large changes in tax rates in order to minimize the distortion of incentives caused by the tax system. Relatively constant tax rates, however, would lead to government <u>surpluses/ deficits</u> during recessions and <u>surpluses/deficit</u> during economic booms. Finally, budget deficits may be the appropriate way to shift a portion of the burden of a current government expenditure to future generations if they, too, benefit from the expenditure.

   c. To avoid the first problem mentioned in Part a, the reduction in the ability of policymakers to use fiscal policy to offset fluctuations in real output, some economists have advocated a rule that balances the "cyclically adjusted budget deficit," which is the budget deficit that would occur if $Y = \overline{Y}$. (See Problem 4 in Chapter 16 of the textbook.) This amount is roughly equal to $G - t\overline{Y}$. Consequently, if the economy slipped into a recession, tax rates <u>would/ would not</u> have to be increased because the cyclically adjusted budget deficit <u>would/would not</u> increase.

Problems

Answer the following problems on a separate sheet of paper.

1. Individual contributions to the Canada and Quebec public pension plans are made by the federal government levying payroll taxes. How does an increase in this payroll tax, unaccompanied by any changes in CPP/QPP benefits or changes in government spending, affect current consumption in a closed economy, according to the traditional and Ricardian views of government debt? Explain.

2. Suppose the government cuts taxes by $100 billion. According to Ricardian equivalence, indicate what will happen to each of the following and briefly explain your answer.

   a. current consumption

   b. current private saving

c. current national saving

3. Suppose that the assumptions behind the Ricardian view of government debt are true, and you are planning to emigrate to another country with your family next year. How would you respond to a tax reduction in this year? If the Ricardian view of government debt is true, how would the economy as a whole respond?

4. ◘ How does an expected future reduction in government purchases affect current consumption and current private saving, according to the traditional and Ricardian views of government debt? Explain.

5. ◘ Consider Table 16-2.

Table 16-2

(1)	(2) Country A	(3) Country B
Initial debt (in billions of dollars)	$2,000	$2,000
Nominal government outlays (made near the end of the year), excluding interest payments (in billions of dollars)	$200	$200
Price level at the beginning of the year	1.0	1.0
Annual inflation rate	0	−0.05
Nominal interest rate	0.07	0.02
Nominal taxes (in billions of dollars)	$340	$340

Countries A and B are identical, except that Country B has 5 percent less inflation and, therefore (assuming that the real interest rate is 7 percent in both economies), a 5 percent lower nominal interest rate than Country A.

a. What is the nominal value of government interest payments in each economy?

b. What are the official government deficits in each economy?

c. Calculate the nominal value of outstanding government debt at the end of the fiscal year in each economy.

d. Show that the real value of outstanding government debt at the end of the fiscal year is the same in both economies, so that the difference in official deficits does not reflect any real difference in the governments' net debt positions.

e. Show that, if one counts only *ex post* real interest payments in the deficit, then Country A's and Country B's deficits are equal.

f. During deflationary periods, do official deficit measures tend to understate or overstate the true value of the deficit? Explain.

6. Suppose that you are the president of a country facing budget deficits. You ask your economic advisers to solve the following dilemma: you would like to reassure the "financial markets" that you are serious about proposing a long-run plan that will eventually reduce the federal budget deficit further, but you are concerned that any contractionary fiscal policy might push the economy into a recession. One adviser suggests that you pass a law *now* that will raise taxes, *starting four years from now*. Assume throughout this problem that everyone believes that taxes will indeed rise four years from now.

a. Why would the simple Keynesian consumption function predict that this strategy would work?

   b. Your adviser's view is that the tax law will affect the economy now even if taxes do not increase for another four years. Explain her reasoning and the theory (or theories) she uses.

   c. Another group of economists argues that the tax increase will have no effect on real GDP, regardless of when it takes effect. Why?

   d. Even if the theory cited by economists in Part c is correct, other economists argue that the tax increase will still affect consumption when it takes effect if people have liquidity constraints. Explain their reasoning.

7. During the Mexican crisis of 1994–1995, the United States government guaranteed up to $50 billion of Mexican government debt. This guarantee helped to calm the crisis, and the Mexican government did not default. Explain what the effect of a United States guarantee for another country's debt (for example, Brazil) would be on the United States budget deficit.

8. Many people associate high budget deficits with high real interest rates and rising prices. Taxes are primarily linked to income. Throughout this problem assume that $T = tY$, where t is the net tax rate.

   a. Use *IS-LM* and *AS-AD* graphs to illustrate and explain whether this association (that is, high budget deficits with high real interest rates and rising prices) is true in the short run if the deficits are primarily due to expansionary fiscal policies (like increases in government purchases).

   b. Use *IS-LM* and *AS-AD* graphs to illustrate and explain whether this association is true in the short run if there is a sudden decline in consumer or business confidence.

9. At the end of January 2009, China owned about $740 billion in U.S. Treasury bonds. Along with a comparable amount of bonds issued by U.S.–government-sponsored enterprises, like Fannie Mae and Freddie Mac, and other assets, China owned an estimated $1.5–$2.5 trillion in dollar-denominated assets. In April, 2009, China's Premier Wen Jiabao expressed concern that President Obama's fiscal stimulus package and the Federal Reserve's expansionary monetary policies might adversely affect the value of China's dollar-denominated assets in two ways: They might lead to inflation and they might lead to a reduction in the foreign exchange rate of the dollar. Use the traditional view of government debt and the appropriate graphs to determine whether his concerns were justified in:

   a. the short run and

   b. the long run.

   (*Hint:* Somewhere in your answer, consider the possible effects of an increase in the risk premium on dollar-denominated assets.)

Data Questions

Instead of asking you to look up actual data, these questions ask you to generate hypothetical data, and then to compare what you find to the actual historical outcome. The purpose of the exercise is to let you form your own opinion about a controversy regarding the history of our federal government's debt.

By the end of the 1970s, the federal debt-to-GDP ratio was 27% (in the notation of the text, $b = 0.27$). The program spending ratio did not exceed the tax-to-GDP ratio by much: $(g-t)$ averaged about 0.007 during the 1975–1979 period. Fourteen years later, by 1993, the debt ratio had risen to 73 percent—an increase of 46 percentage points. The controversy has concerned how much of this increase should we "blame on" each of two causes: systematic overspending by the government versus world developments and contractionary Canadian monetary policy—both of which caused lower real growth rates and higher real interest rates during this 14-year period. These developments meant that the government lost revenue at the very time that it had higher employment-insurance obligations. Thus, even though $(g-t)$ rose over the 14-year period, many have argued that a significant part of that increase should not be interpreted as "overspending" by the government. According to this view, the $(g-t)$ *had* to rise because of the developments that were beyond the control of fiscal policy.

As a base for comparison, let us assume that those external events did not happen. Also, let us assume that there was no independent increase in $(g-t)$ either. Finally, let's assume that the gap between the interest rate and the growth rate was only 2.6 percentage points—1.5 percentage points below the gap that actually occurred over the 1980–1993 period. By making these assumptions, we can have some idea about what the debt buildup would have looked like if *neither* of the alleged causes was in effect.

1. Use a spreadsheet to conduct this simulation. As explained in the text, the relationship involved is:

$$(\text{next year's } b) = (g-t) + (r-n)(\text{this year's } b).$$

Start off with this year's b equal to 0.27; and assume that $(r-n)$ and $(g-t)$ remain constant at 0.026 and 0.007, respectively. What values does b reach after 14 years?

2. Now let us add the "bad news" events that were beyond the control of the government. Let's assume that these events (the downturn in productivity growth and the contractionary monetary policy) had two effects: they widened the $(r-n)$ gap by 1.5 percentage points and forced the government to double its $(g-t)$ gap. To simulate this second scenario, use the same equation and the same starting value for b (0.27). But this time, set $(r-n)$ and $(g-t)$ to 0.041 and 0.014, respectively. What value does b reach after 14 periods this time?

3. If you have done the simulations correctly, you should find that the second scenario reproduces the actual history of the debt ratio—an increase of 46 percentage points in that 14-year period. In the first scenario, with absolutely no increase in the primary deficit, the increase in the debt ratio is just half that amount. If these simulations are representative, the conclusion appears to be that the government "couldn't help" *any* of the increase in debt! Half was caused by the "bad luck" of having to endure contractionary monetary policy and the slowdown in world growth, and the other half was caused by the unfortunate fact that interest rates exceeded growth rates. By working through the simulations, you have learned that this popular interpretation of the episode is misleading. With r exceeding n, it is in the very nature of the government accounting identity that the debt ratio had to explode—even with no increase in $(g-t)$ or any "bad luck." In this environment, even a constant primary deficit has to be interpreted as "overspending."

Questions to Think About

1. Would your own spending change in response to a tax cut that was not linked to current or future changes in government spending? Explain.

2. Why does the government have to pay off its debt at some point in the future? Can debt continue to grow at any rate indefinitely? Examine two cases, one in which the real interest rate on government debt exceeds the economy's long-run rate of growth of real output, and a second in which the economy's long-run growth rate exceeds the real interest rate.

3. Under what circumstances do you think indexed bonds would be especially attractive?

chapter 17

Consumption

Fill-in Questions

Use the key terms below to fill in the blanks in the following statements. Each term may be used more than once.

average propensity to consume	marginal propensity to consume
behavioural economics	marginal rate of substitution
borrowing constraint	normal good
budget constraint	permanent income
discounting	permanent-income hypothesis
income effect	precautionary saving
indifference curve	random walk
intertemporal budget constraint	substitution effect
life-cycle hypothesis	transitory income

1. The amount that an individual consumes out of an additional dollar of (disposable) income is called the _____.

2. According to the Keynesian consumption function, as income rises an individual's _____ falls. In household studies, however, the _____ tends to rise with income. This phenomenon can be explained by both the _____ and the _____.

3. All consumers face a(n) _____, which is a limit on how much they can spend.

4. When consumers are deciding how much to consume today versus how much to save for future consumption, they face a(n) _____.

5. Since saving earns interest, one should compare future income with current income by _____, which reduces the value of $10,000 of income received in the future below the value of $10,000 of current income.

6. In Irving Fisher's model of consumption, a(n) _____ shows the combinations of first-period consumption and second-period consumption that make the consumer equally happy.

7. The slope of the indifference curve equals the _____, which represents the amount of second-period consumption the consumer requires to be compensated for a one-unit reduction in first-period consumption.

8. If a consumer wants to consume more of a good when his or her income rises, that good is said to be a(n) _____.

9. When the real interest rate changes, the change in consumption can be divided into two components. The change in consumption resulting from the movement to a higher indifference curve is called the _____. The change in consumption arising from the change in the relative price of consumption between different periods is called the _____.

10. When the interest rate rises, the _____ tends to make consumers choose more consumption in all periods, and the _____ tends to make consumers choose less consumption in the current period and more consumption in future periods.

11. A consumer who wishes to consume more than her current income may be unable to borrow against her future income if she faces a(n) _____.

12. The _____ suggests that people save their income in order to smooth their consumption over their entire adult lifetime. In reality, the elderly do not dissave to the extent predicted by this model, possibly because of _____, which is additional saving that arises from uncertainty.

13. The _____ distinguishes between two types of income that affect consumption. _____ is the part of income that people expect to persist in the future. The part of income that people do not expect to persist is called _____.

14. The combination of the permanent-income hypothesis and rational expectations implies that consumption follows a(n) _____. A(n) _____ is the term that economists use to describe the path of a variable whose changes are unpredictable.

15. _____ is a new subfield of economics that infuses psychology into economics and often finds that human behaviour is far from rational.

Multiple-Choice Questions

1. According to the Keynesian theory of consumption, when individuals experience an increase in their income their:
   a. consumption will rise by the total amount of the increase in income.
   b. consumption will rise by less than the increase in income.
   c. average propensity to consume will increase.
   d. marginal propensity to consume will increase.

2. According to the Keynesian theory of consumption, the primary determinant of consumption is the:
   a. interest rate.
   b. wealth of the consumer.
   c. consumer's ability to borrow.
   d. consumer's income.

3. According to Fisher's model of consumption, all of the following statements about the intertemporal budget constraint are true EXCEPT:
   a. if current consumption rises, the resources available for future consumption will fall.
   b. consumption in Period 1 must be less than or equal to consumption in Period 2.
   c. in the first period, saving is equal to first-period income minus consumption.
   d. consumers take into account both current income and expected future income when making consumption choices.

4. In the Fisher model, if the real interest rate is positive:
   a. second-period consumption costs less in terms of first-period income than the same amount of first-period consumption.
   b. second-period income is worth more than an equal amount of first-period income.
   c. consumers will be unwilling to borrow money, so their consumption in Period 1 will be less than their income in Period 1.
   d. all of the above.

5. All of the following statements about indifference curves are true EXCEPT:
   a. if first-period consumption is decreased, second-period consumption must be increased in order for the consumer to remain equally satisfied.
   b. the slope is equal to the marginal rate of substitution.
   c. the greater the decrease in first-period consumption, the less second-period consumption must increase to keep the consumer's utility constant.
   d. the consumer prefers to be on a higher indifference curve than a lower one.

6. According to the Fisher model, the optimal level of consumption for a consumer occurs when the marginal rate of substitution:
   a. equals one.
   b. equals zero.
   c. equals the slope of the budget line.
   d. is maximized.

7. An increase in the real interest rate leading to an increase in consumption in all periods because of a movement to a higher indifference curve is an example of:
   a. the substitution effect.
   b. the income effect.
   c. the life-cycle hypothesis.
   d. the permanent-income hypothesis.

8. Which of the following may NOT occur when the real interest rate increases?

    a. The income effect works to increase consumption in both Periods 1 and 2 for consumers who initially save part of their income in Period 1.

    b. Consumption rises in all periods.

    c. A consumer who saves part of her income in Period 1 will move to a higher indifference curve.

    d. The substitution effect works to increase second-period consumption and reduce first-period consumption.

9. If a consumer wishes to consume more than his current income in Period 1:

    a. he will be unable to consume anything in Period 2.

    b. the real interest rate must be greater than one.

    c. the decision to consume more must satisfy both his budget constraint and his borrowing constraint.

    d. none of the above.

10. If a consumer faces a borrowing constraint:

    a. she will be unable to consume anything in the second period.

    b. she may or may not be less satisified than if she was able to borrow.

    c. consumption in the first period must be less than consumption in the second period.

    d. all of the above.

11. The life-cycle consumption function takes into account all of the following EXCEPT the:

    a. amount of wealth.

    b. government budget deficit.

    c. expected number of working years.

    d. expected number of years of retirement.

12. According to the life-cycle hypothesis, a consumer who expects to work 40 more years before retiring and who expects to live a total of 50 more years will have the following consumption function:

    a. $C = 0.2W + 0.6Y$.

    c. $C = 0.04W + 0.8Y$.

    b. $C = 0.2W + 0.8Y$.

    d. $C = 0.02W + 0.8Y$.

13. Under the life-cycle hypothesis, the consumption function, $C = 0.025W + 0.5Y$, implies that:

    a. the individual expects to live 40 more years.

    b. half of the person's expected remaining life will be spent in retirement.

    c. for every additional dollar of wealth, consumption increases by 2.5 cents.

    d. all of the above.

14. An example of precautionary saving is when:

    a. a newly married couple saves to buy a house in 10 years.

    b. high interest rates cause a business professional to reduce investment.

    c. an individual automatically deposits a fraction of his weekly income in a Christmas Club to save for the coming holiday.

    d. an individual increases her saving in preparation for retirement because she fears that poor health may lead to added expenses.

15. According to the permanent-income hypothesis:

    a. the average propensity to consume is the ratio of transitory income to current income.

    b. consumption depends equally on permanent and transitory income.

    c. people use saving to smooth consumption in response to transitory changes in income.

    d. none of the above.

16. A change in permanent income occurs when a(n):

    a. Florida resort owner enjoys unusually good business during a particularly harsh winter.

    b. individual wins $10,000 in a lottery.

    c. injured worker receives workers' compensation benefits for six months.

    d. tenured university professor receives a $10,000 increase per year in her salary.

17. Which of the following statements is TRUE?

    a. Studies indicate that households with high incomes tend to have low average propensities to consume.

    b. Over long periods of time, the average propensity to consume is fairly constant.

    c. The life-cycle and permanent-income hypotheses can explain most of the empirical facts about the average propensity to consume.

    d. all of the above.

18. According to the permanent-income hypothesis, an artist whose income fluctuates from year to year will:

    a. have a higher average propensity to consume in years of lower income.

    b. have a higher average propensity to consume in years of high income.

    c. have a constant average propensity to consume every year.

    d. never save any of her income.

19. According to the permanent-income hypothesis, which of the following is likely to happen if Parliament enacts a temporary tax cut?

    a. Consumers will view the year as a temporarily good one and will increase their saving by almost the full amount of the tax cut.

    b. Consumers will increase their consumption by the full amount of the tax cut.

    c. The tax cut will have a large effect on aggregate demand.

    d. Both b and c are true.

20. When a consumer borrows money to allow for greater consumption, he is:

   a. increasing his total income.

   b. escaping his intertemporal budget constraint.

   c. borrowing against his future income.

   d. able to increase his consumption in all periods.

21. Many economists believe that Americans should save a greater fraction of their incomes because:

   a. people would be better prepared for retirement.

   b. greater national saving and investment would increase the nation's productive capacity in the long run.

   c. less domestic investment would need to be financed by further increases in U.S. foreign debt.

   d. all of the above.

22. Behavioural economics suggests that all of the following measures would induce people to save more EXCEPT:

   a. forcing all workers to participate in a retirement savings plan at their place of employment.

   b. automatically enrolling workers in a retirement savings account at their place of employment, but giving them the opportunity to opt out.

   c. allowing people to borrow more on their credit cards.

   d. having people commit in advance to saving a portion of their future salary increases.

Exercises

1. **The Keynesian Consumption Function** *In this exercise, we use a Keynesian consumption function to illustrate the algebraic and graphical differences between the marginal and average propensities to consume.*

   a. Consider the simple consumption function

$$C = 125 + 0.75(Y - T), \tag{17-1}$$

where T = taxes and $Y - T$ = disposable income. If $T = 0$, we may write

$$C = 125 + 0.75Y, \tag{17-2}$$

where Y is both national income and disposable income. Graph this equation on Graph 17-1 and label the curve C.

Graph 17-1

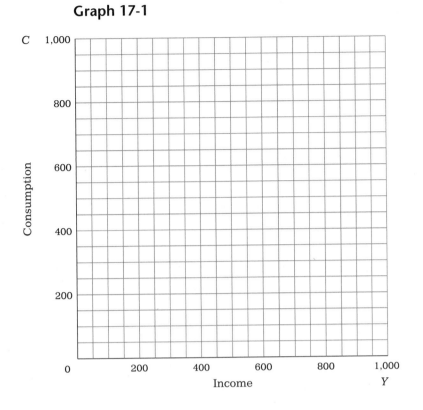

b. The marginal propensity to consume (*MPC*) is defined as:

The value of the *MPC* in this model is _____. This fraction is also equal to the slope of the consumption function in Graph 17-1. As *Y* increases in this model, the value of the *MPC* increases/decreases/remains constant. Furthermore, Keynes postulated that the *MPC* would always be greater than _____ but less than _____.

c. The average propensity to consume (*APC*) is defined as the ratio of consumption to disposable income, which, when $T = 0$ as in this model, is equal to Y. Thus, in this model, $APC = C/Y$. Substituting Equation 17-2 into the numerator of the *APC* and simplifying yields

$APC = $ _____ $ + $ _____ $\times (1/Y)$.

When $Y = 250$, $APC = $ _____ $ + $ _____ $\times (1/250) = $ _____ .

When $Y = 500$, $APC = $ _____ $ + $ _____ $\times (1/500) = $ _____ .

When $Y = 1{,}000$, $APC = $ _____ $ + $ _____ $\times (1/1{,}000) = $ _____ .

This example illustrates that as Y increases, the value of the *APC* <u>increases/ decreases/remains constant</u>.

d. The value of the *APC* can also be illustrated on Graph 17-1. Suppose that $Y = 1{,}000$. According to Equation 17-2, when $Y = 1{,}000$, $C = $

_____. Locate this point on Graph 17-1, label it Point A, and draw a line between Point A and the origin. The slope of this line is equal to the rise over run, or _____ / _____ =

_____. This is equal to the *MPC/APC* when $Y = 1{,}000$. Consequently, the slope of the line connecting the origin to any point on the consumption function is equal to the *MPC/APC* at that level of income. Note that the slope of this line <u>increases/decreases/remains constant</u> as Y increases.

2. **The Short-Run and Long-Run Consumption Functions** *In this exercise, we review the cross-section and time-series evidence concerning the average propensity to consume and discuss the resulting short-run and long-run consumption functions.*

a. Data collected from various households at any one point in time, called *cross-sectional data*, confirm the basic implications of the Keynesian consumption function. In these studies, the *MPC* is greater than _____ and less than _____. Furthermore, people with higher incomes tend to save a greater percentage of their income, which is another way of saying that the *APC* <u>increases/decreases/remains constant</u> as Y increases. Aggregate (economywide) data over short time periods also confirm these implications.

b. Aggregate data collected over long periods of time, called *time-series data*, however, seem to contradict some of the implications of the Keynesian consumption function. Greater amounts of inputs and improved technology lead to rising income over time. As income rises, the Keynesian consumption function predicts that the APC will increase/decrease/remain constant. Economists who have studied the data, however, find that the APC tends to increase/decrease/remain constant over long periods of time despite substantial increases in Y.

c. These contradictory findings have led economists to conclude that the aggregate short-run consumption function is different from the aggregate long-run consumption function. The short-run consumption function is very similar to the Keynesian consumption function: the MPC lies between _____ and _____, and the APC increases/decreases/remains constant as Y increases. Draw an arbitrary line on Graph 17-2 that satisfies these properties and label it SRCF (short-run consumption function). As stated in Part b, in the long run, the APC tends to increase/decrease/remain constant as Y increases. Draw an arbitrary line on Graph 17-2 that satisfies these properties and label it LRCF (long-run consumption function). (You may find it useful to review Part d of Exercise 1.) Note that any positively sloped straight line with a y intercept of _____ will satisfy the properties of the LRCF.

3. **Present and Future Value** *In this exercise, we present the concepts of present and future value.*

a. Suppose you have $100 and the bank interest rate is 5 percent. If you put this $100 in the bank, at the end of one year you would have $100 + 0.05 ($100) = $_____. Note that we can express this algebraically as:

$$FV_1 = PV + i(PV)(1 + i) \qquad \text{(17-3)}$$

where FV_1 is the future value at the end of year 1, PV represents the present (initial) value, and i represents the annual interest rate.

Graph 17-2

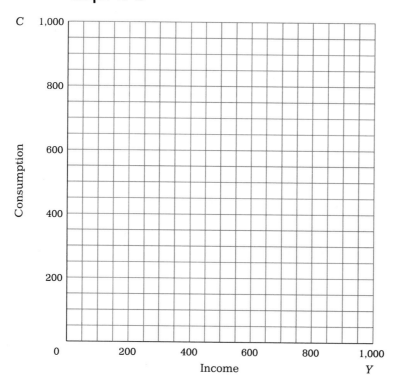

b. Conversely, if you knew you could get $\$FV_1$ at the end of one year and the interest rate is i, you could calculate the "present value" of this option by solving Equation 17-3 for PV:

$$PV = FV_1/(1 + i) \qquad \text{(17-4)}$$

As you might expect, the present value of receiving $105 at the end of one year with an interest rate of 5 percent is therefore $\$$_____/(1 + 0.05) = $\$$_____.

c. If you keep your original $100 in the bank, you would earn interest in the second year on the full amount of money you had at the end of the first year. Consequently, at the end of two years, you would have $105 + 0.05($105) = $\$$_____. Note that this can be written as 1[$100(1 + i)] + i[$100(1 + i)] or (1 + i)$100(1 + i), which is also equal to $100(1 + i)^2$. Thus, we can write:

$$FV_2 = PV(1 + i)^2 \qquad \text{(17-5)}$$

d. Conversely, if you knew you could get $\$FV_2$ at the end of two years and the annual interest rate is i, you could calculate the "present value" of this option by solving Equation 17-5 for PV:

$$PV = FV_2/(1 + i)^2 \qquad \text{(17-6)}$$

As you might expect, the present value of receiving $110.25 at the end of two years with an interest rate of 5 percent is therefore $_____$/ $(1 + 0.05) = \$_____$.

e. Using the results from Parts a–d, you may surmise that the formula for determining the amount you would have if you left your money in the bank for T years at annual interest rate i is _____. Conversely, if you know the future value in year T, FV_T, and the interest rate i, the formula for determining the present value is _____.

4. **The Intertemporal Budget Constraint** *In this exercise, we use a simple two-period model to derive the intertemporal budget constraint.*

a. Suppose that a typical consumer named Jennifer lives for two consumption periods. Her real income in each of Periods 1 and 2, Y_1 and Y_2, equals 12. Designate consumption during Periods 1 and 2 as C_1 and C_2, respectively. The portion of Jennifer's income in Period 1 that she does not consume in Period 1 is her saving S. Obviously,

$$S = Y_1 - C_1 = \underline{\hspace{3cm}} - C_1. \qquad \text{(17-7)}$$

Assume that any saving from Period 1 earns interest at a real interest rate of 50 percent, or 0.50. Since Jennifer knows she will die at the end of Period 2, she does not save in the second period. Consequently, her consumption in Period 2, C_2, is equal to her income in Period 2, $(Y_2 = 12)$, plus any saving from Period 1 plus accumulated interest:

$$C_2 = Y_2 + S + rS = Y_2 + (Y_1 - C_1) + r(Y_1 - C_1) = \qquad \text{(17-8)}$$

$$\underline{\hspace{2cm}} + (\underline{\hspace{2cm}} - C_1) + \underline{\hspace{2cm}} (\underline{\hspace{2cm}} - C_1), \text{ or}$$

$$C_2 = \underline{\hspace{4cm}} - \underline{\hspace{4cm}} C_1.$$

Graph this equation on Graph 17-3 and label it *IBTC* (intertemporal budget constraint).

Graph 17-3

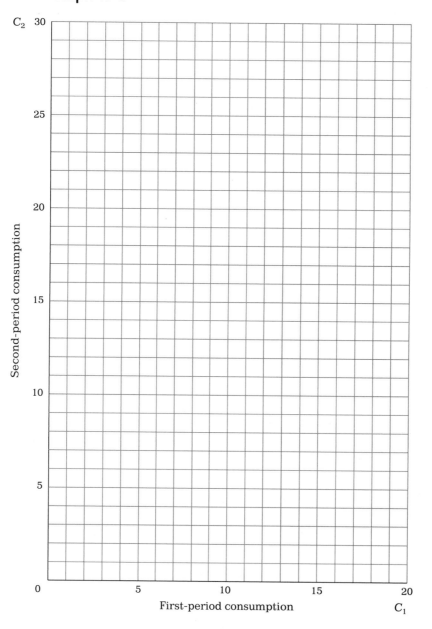

b. The line you drew on Graph 17-3 is called the *intertemporal budget constraint.* Given Jennifer's income and the real interest rate, the intertemporal budget constraint depicts the combinations of C_1 and C_2 that are available to her. The slope of this line is equal to $-(1 + r) = -(1 +$ _____$) = -$ _____. This number indicates that each unit of consumption in Period 1 can be transformed into _____ units of consumption in Period 2 because any saving earns interest at the rate of _____ percent.

c. Although Jennifer can consume at any point along her intertemporal budget constraint, three points are worth noting. Locate the point on Graph 17-3 at which Jennifer consumes all of her current income in each of the two periods and label it Point A. At Point A, $C_1 = Y_1 = $ _____. Consequently, during Period 1, saving $S = $ _____, and $C_2 = Y_2 = $ _____. Now locate the point on Graph 17-3 at which Jennifer saves all of her income in Period 1 in order to maximize C_2 and label it Point B. At Point B, $C_1 = $ _____. Consequently, during Period 1, $S = $ _____ and $C_2 = Y_2 + S + rS = $ _____ + _____ + _____ × _____ = _____. Graph 17-3 can also be used to illustrate the situation in which Jennifer borrows at the same real interest rate to finance a level of consumption during Period 1 that exceeds her income in Period 1. Locate the point on Graph 17-3 at which Jennifer maximizes C_1 by borrowing against all of her income in Period 2 and label it Point C. At Point C, $C_2 = $ _____ and $C_1 = Y_1 + [Y_2/(1 + r)] = $ _____ + [_____ / _____] = _____.

5. **The Consumer's Optimal Levels of Consumption** *In this exercise, we derive a set of indifference curves from a specific utility function and illustrate the optimal consumption pattern given the intertemporal budget constraint in Exercise 3.*

a. Suppose that Jennifer, the same consumer from Exercise 3, lives for two periods and derives pleasure from her consumption in each of them. Assume, furthermore, that the amount of her total satisfaction is given by this utility function:

$$U = C_1 \times C_2 = C_1 C_2. \tag{17-9}$$

Given this utility function, complete Table 17-1. Round off your answers to one decimal place.

Table 17-1

(1)	(2)	(3)	(4)	(5)	(6)	(7)	(8)
C_1	8.0	9.0	_____	_____	12.0	14.0	16.0
C_2	18.0	16.0	14.4	13.09	_____	_____	_____
$U = C_1 C_2$	_____	_____	144.0	144.00	144.0	144.0	144.0

b. Plot the numbers from Columns 2–8 on Graph 17-4, connect them (try to make the curve smooth), and label this curve $IC_{U=144}$.

Inasmuch as Jennifer's levels of utility at these seven combinations of C_1 and C_2 all equal _____, Jennifer is indifferent among them. Hence, $IC_{U=144}$ is called the indifference curve for a level of utility equal to 144.

c. Now complete Table 17-2, which lists all the combinations of C_1 and C_2 for which Jennifer's level of utility would equal 150.

Graph 17-4

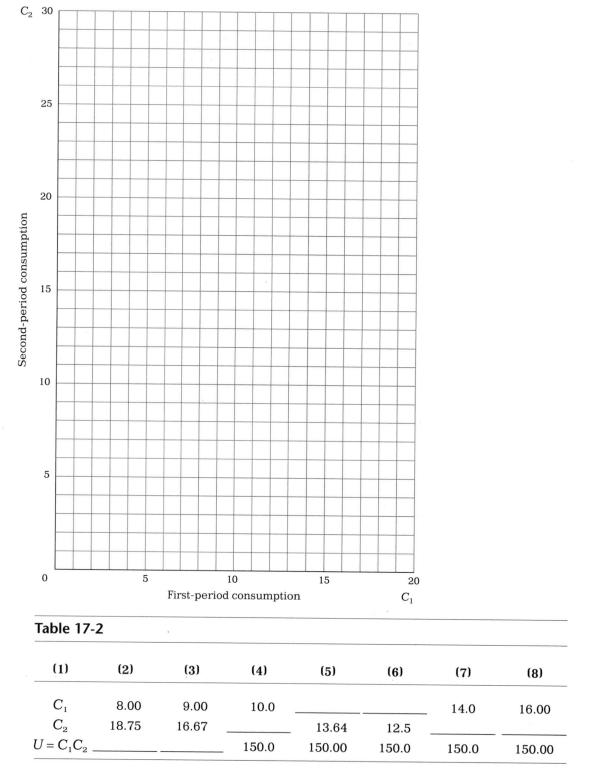

Table 17-2

	(1)	(2)	(3)	(4)	(5)	(6)	(7)	(8)
C_1		8.00	9.00	10.0	_____	_____	14.0	16.00
C_2		18.75	16.67	_____	13.64	12.5	_____	_____
$U = C_1C_2$		_____	_____	150.0	150.00	150.0	150.0	150.00

Plot the numbers from Table 17-2 on Graph 17-4, connect them (again, try to make the curve smooth), and label this curve $IC_{U=150}$.

d. Finally, complete Table 17-3, which lists the combinations of C_1 and C_2 for which Jennifer's level of utility would equal 162.

Table 17-3

(1)	(2)	(3)	(4)	(5)	(6)	(7)	(8)
C_1	8.00	9.0	10.0	_____	_____	14.0	16.0
C_2	20.25	18.0	_____	14.73	13.5	_____	_____
$U = C_1 C_2$	_____	_____	162.0	162.00	162.0	162.0	162.0

Plot the numbers on Graph 17-4, connect them (again, try to make the curve smooth), and label this curve $IC_{U=162}$.

e. Along each indifference curve, the level of utility is held constant. As the level of utility increases, the entire indifference curve shifts to the <u>left (downward)/ right (upward)</u> because, in order to achieve the higher level of utility, consumption in one or both periods must <u>increase/decrease</u>. The slope of the indifference curve at any point shows how much second-period consumption Jennifer requires to be compensated for a one-unit reduction in first-period consumption and remain equally satisfied. This slope is called the _____ between first-period consumption and second-period consumption.

f. Suppose that Jennifer faces the same intertemporal budget constraint that she did in Exercise 3 (that is, $C_2 = 30 - 1.5C_1$). Graph this equation on Graph 17-4 and label it *ITBC*.

g. If Jennifer follows Polonius's advice to Laertes ("neither a borrower nor a lender be") and decides to consume all of her current income in each period, then $C_1 = Y_1 =$ _____ and $C_2 = Y_2 =$ _____. Locate this point on Graph 17-4 and label it Point A. Because Point A lies on the indifference curve labeled _____, Jennifer's level of utility at Point A equals _____.

h. Note, however, that Jennifer can move to a higher indifference curve and a higher level of utility by saving some of her income in Period 1 and increasing her consumption in Period 2. Indeed, she can move up to the indifference curve labeled _____ on Graph 17-4 and achieve a level of utility equal to _____ by reducing C_1 to 10 and thereby saving _____ in Period 1. If this amount of saving is put in a bank and earns interest of 50 percent, it will grow to _____ by Period 2, at which time Jennifer can add it to her income in Period 2 to obtain C_2 $= Y_2 + (1 + r)S =$ _____ + _____ = _____. Locate this point on Graph 17-4 and label it Point D. At Point D, $U = C_1 C_2 =$ _____ × _____ = _____. Also note that at Point D, Jennifer's indifference curve is just tangent to her intertemporal budget constraint line, which means that the slopes of these two curves are equal. Thus, at her optimal levels of consumption, Jennifer's marginal rate of substitution is equal to $1 + r$. All indifference curves corresponding to a still higher level of utility, such as $IC_{U=162}$, lie to the left (below)/right (above) of Jennifer's intertemporal budget constraint line and are consequently unattainable.

6. **The Effects of Changes in Income and the Real Interest Rate on the Consumer's Optimal Levels of Consumption** *In this exercise, we graphically illustrate the effects of increases in income and the real interest rate on the consumer's optimal levels of consumption and discuss the income and substitution effects.*

    a. Graph 17-5 illustrates Jennifer's initial optimal levels of consumption at Point D from Exercise 4 and the indifference curves corresponding to utility levels of 150 and 162, respectively. The real interest rate equals 50 percent. The curve labeled $ITBC_1$ represents Jennifer's initial intertemporal budget constraint. Suppose that Jennifer's income in Period 1 rises to 12.78, while Y_2 remains equal to 12. Consequently, Jennifer's intertemporal budget constraint would change to the following:

    $$C_2 = Y_2 + S + rS = Y_2 + (Y_1 - C_1) + r(Y_1 - C_1)$$

    $$= 12 + (12.78 - C_1) + 0.50(12.78 - C_1), \text{ or}$$

    $C_2 = $ _____ $-$ _____ $C_1.$

    Graph this new intertemporal budget constraint on Graph 17-5 and label it $ITBC_2$.

Graph 17-5

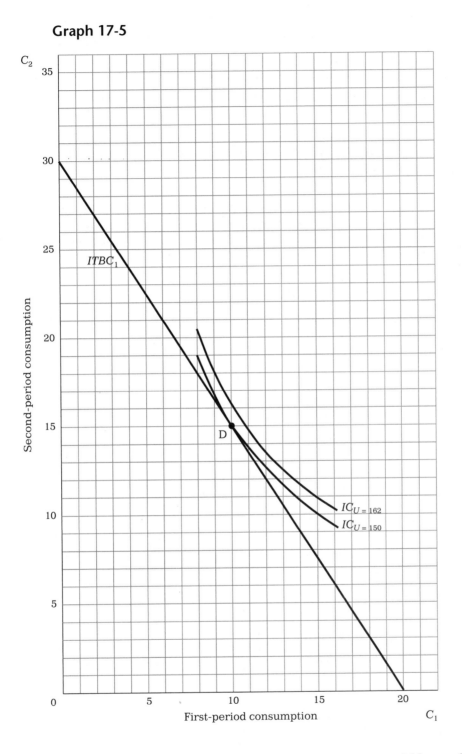

This shift of the intertemporal budget constraint curve could have also occurred from an increase in income in Period 2 or from increases in income in both periods. The slope of $ITBC_2$ is <u>greater than/less than/equal to</u> the slope of $ITBC_1$.

b. As a result of her increase in income, Jennifer is now able to move to a higher indifference curve. Indeed, the new optimum occurs at the tangency of $ITBC_2$

with $IC_{U=162}$, indicating that Jennifer is able to increase her level of utility to
_____. Locate this point on Graph 17-5 and label it Point
E. At Point E, $C_1 = 10.39$. Since $U = C_1 C_2$ and $U =$ _____, C_2
$= U/C_1 =$ _____. We can see that consumption during
each period has increased/decreased. The changes in consumption between
Points D and E are the result of the income effect, which measures the change in
consumption resulting from the movement to a higher indifference curve, holding the slope of the intertemporal budget constraint (whose absolute value is
equal to 1 plus the real interest rate) constant.

c. Finally, suppose that Jennifer's income in each period returns to its former level
of 12 and that the real interest rate rises to 100 percent, or 1.0. Jennifer's
intertemporal budget constraint becomes

$$C_2 = Y_2 + S + rS = Y_2 + (Y_1 - C_1) + r(Y_1 - C_1), \text{ or}$$

$$C_2 = \underline{\hspace{1cm}} + (\underline{\hspace{1cm}} - C_1) + 1.0\underline{\hspace{1cm}} - C_1), \text{ or}$$

$$C_2 = \underline{\hspace{3cm}} - \underline{\hspace{3cm}} C_1.$$

Graph Jennifer's new intertemporal budget constraint on Graph 17-5 and label
it $ITBC_3$. Once again, Jennifer is able to move to a higher indifference curve.
Indeed, the new optimal levels of consumption occur at the tangency of $ITBC_3$
with $IC_{U=162}$, which is where the new intertemporal budget constraint just
touches $IC_{U=162}$ and has the same slope. Thus, Jennifer is again able to
increase her level of utility to _____. Plot this point
on Graph 16-5 and label it Point F. At Point F, $C_1 = 9$. Since $U = C_1 C_2$ and $U =$
_____, $C_2 = U/C_1 =$ _____.

d. The changes in consumption between Points D and F resulting from the increase
in the real interest rate can be decomposed into two different effects. The first
reflects the change in consumption resulting from Jennifer's ability to move to a
higher indifference curve while holding the real interest rate constant. This
effect is called the income/substitution effect, and it is represented by a hypothetical movement from Point D to Point E (since Point E lies on the new indifference curve but would be the equilibrium only if the slope of the intertemporal
budget constraint had remained unchanged, as in Part b). The change in consumption from Point E to Point F reflects the second effect, called the
income/substitution effect. This represents the change in consumption arising
from the change in the relative price of consumption in the two periods. As the
interest rate increases from 50 percent to 100 percent, Jennifer must now give

up less first-period consumption to obtain an extra unit of second-period consumption. Comparing Points E and F, Jennifer responds to this change in the relative price of consumption in the two periods by increasing/decreasing C_1 and increasing/decreasing C_2.

e. In Part d, the income effect increases/decreases C_1 and increases/decreases C_2, while the substitution effect increases/decreases C_1 and increases/decreases C_2. The combination of these two effects will always increase/decrease C_2. Depending on the specific circumstance, however, C_1 can either increase or decrease. In this example, C_1 obviously increases/decreases.

7. **The Life-Cycle Hypothesis** *In this exercise, we develop a simple life-cycle model of consumption and derive some of its implications.*

a. The life-cycle hypothesis is based on the assumption that people try to smooth their consumption over their (adult) lifetimes. Assume that a typical adult named Tanya expects to live for another T years. She intends to work for R years, earning an annual real income equal to Y, and then retire for $(T - R)$ years. If Tanya wishes to smooth her annual consumption C over her remaining lifetime, she will plan to spend her lifetime earnings $(R \times Y)$ over her remaining T years in equal amounts so that

$$C \times T = R \times Y, \qquad\qquad \textbf{(17-10)}$$

or $C = Y \times ($_____ / _____$)$. This equation implies that Tanya will consume a fraction of her income during her working years and save the remaining portion to fund her consumption during her retirement. (Although the real interest rate is implicitly assumed to equal zero here, a positive real interest rate could easily be incorporated into the model.)

b. Suppose that Tanya begins working at age 20, intends to retire at age 65 after working for 45 years, and expects to live until age 80. Thus, $T = 80 - 20 =$ _____, $R = 65 - 20 =$ _____, and $T - R =$ _____. If $Y = \$40,000$, then Tanya's annual consumption will be $C = \$$_____ $\times ($_____ / _____$) =$ \$_____. During each of her working years, Tanya will consume \$_____, or _____ / _____ of her income, and will save \$_____, or _____ / _____ of her income. During her working years, therefore, Tanya's consumption function will be $C =$ _____ Y. An extra dollar of annual income would raise consumption by _____ cents.

c. Draw a rectangle on Graph 17-6 whose height is equal to $Y = \$$_____ and whose width is equal to $R =$ _____ years. The area of this rectangle represents Tanya's total lifetime earnings and is equal to \$_____. Now draw a second rectangle whose height is equal to C and whose width is equal to T. The area of this second rectangle, representing Tanya's total lifetime consumption, is equal to \$_____. Now shade in the area of a third rectangle, labeled saving, which represents Tanya's total saving during her working years, and a fourth rectangle, labeled dissaving, which represents her total consumption during retirement. The size of the shaded rectangle representing Tanya's total saving is <u>greater than/less than/equal to</u> the size of the shaded rectangle representing her total consumption during retirement.

Graph 17-6

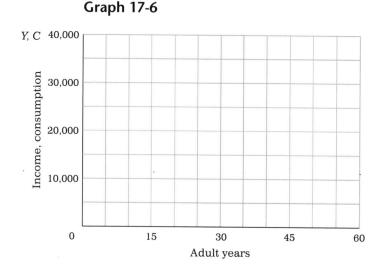

d. Now suppose that Tanya begins her adult life with an initial wealth equal to W. Consequently, the total amount that she will now have available to spend during her lifetime will equal $RY + W$. If Tanya still wishes to consume equal amounts in every year,

$$C \times T = (R \times Y) + W, \tag{17-11}$$

or $C = [(\underline{\hspace{1.5cm}} / \underline{\hspace{1.5cm}}) \times Y] + W/ \underline{\hspace{1.5cm}}$. Substituting from Part c the values for $T = \underline{\hspace{1.5cm}}$ and $R = \underline{\hspace{1.5cm}}$, we obtain Tanya's new consumption function, $C = \underline{\hspace{1.5cm}} Y + \underline{\hspace{1.5cm}} W$. An extra dollar of wealth raises consumption by $\underline{\hspace{1.5cm}}$ cents. Draw this consumption function on Graph 17-7 and label it C. The y intercept of this line is $\underline{\hspace{1.5cm}} W$, and the slope of the line equals $\underline{\hspace{1.5cm}}$.

Graph 17-7

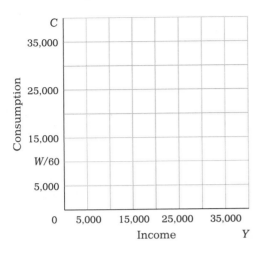

e. As Chapter 17 of the textbook states, the life-cycle model can explain the cross-sectional evidence concerning the average propensity to consume. Dividing the consumption function in Part d by Y yields $APC = C/Y =$ _____ + _____ × (W/Y). Suppose that $W = \$120,000$ and $Y = \$40,000$. Then $APC =$ _____ + _____(_____ / _____) = _____. As Chapter 17 of the textbook explains, in the short run, wealth does not vary with income from person to person or from year to year. Consequently, if Y rises to $\$80,000$ and W remains equal to $\$120,000$, $APC =$ _____ + _____(_____ / _____) = _____. Obviously, as income rises, APC rises/falls. Conversely, if Y falls to $\$20,000$ and W remains equal to $\$120,000$, $APC =$ _____.

f. The life-cycle model can also explain the time-series evidence concerning the relative constancy of the economy's APC in the long run. Over long periods of time, wealth and income grow together. If $W = 3Y$ in the long run, then, in this model, $APC =$ _____.

8. **The Permanent-Income Hypothesis** *In this exercise, we present the permanent-income model of consumption and discuss its implications.*

a. According to the permanent-income hypothesis, current income Y is the sum of permanent income Y^P plus transitory income Y^T, or $Y = Y^P + Y^T$. Permanent income is a measure of expected or average income. Transitory income is the random difference between current income Y and permanent income Y^P that occurs because of unexpected and temporary increases or decreases in income. On average, however, transitory income equals zero. Consumption is a function of permanent income. For example, assume the following:

$$C = aY^P = 0.75Y^P. \qquad \text{(17-12)}$$

Equation 17-12 suggests that people consume _____ percent of their permanent income; the remainder is saved, presumably for retirement.

b. Let us examine the consumption patterns of three people: a university professor having a typical year; an artist who is experiencing an especially good year, having just sold several paintings; and another artist who is having a dry spell, having sold only two paintings during the year. Assume that the average or permanent income of each of these three people equals $40,000 and that $C = 0.75Y^P$. Now complete Table 17-4.

Table 17-4

(1)	(2) Y^P	(3) $C = 0.75Y^P$	(4) Y	(5) $APC = C/Y$	(6) Y^T
University professor	$40,000	_____	$40,000	_____	_____
Artist in a good year	$40,000	_____	$50,000	_____	_____
Artist in a bad year	$40,000	_____	$30,000	_____	_____

c. The data in Table 17-4 indicate that changes in transitory income will increase/decrease/not change consumption. Consequently, if a person's actual current income temporarily rises above her permanent income, then her consumption will increase/decrease/not change. This situation will increase/decrease/not change her *APC*. Conversely, if a person's actual current income temporarily falls below her permanent income, her consumption will increase/decrease/not change but her *APC* will increase/decrease/not change.

d. As stated previously, cross-sectional household data indicate that the average propensity to consume tends to increase/decrease/remain constant as income increases. If, at any one time, people who have high incomes are generally having temporarily good years and those who have low incomes are generally having temporarily bad years, data in Table 17-4 indicate that the *APC* will increase/decrease/remain constant as current income *Y* increases.

e. This theory can also be used to explain short-term variations in the average propensity to consume. If the economy slips into a recession and the majority of the population is having a bad year, the *APC* will increase/decrease/remain constant. If, on the other hand, the economy is in a temporary boom and the majority of the population is having a good year, the *APC* will increase/decrease/remain constant.

f. Alternatively, if the government enacts a temporary tax cut, everyone will experience a temporarily good year, but the *APC* will increase/decrease/remain constant and most of the tax cut will be consumed/saved. If, on the other hand, the government enacts a permanent tax cut, everyone will experience an increase in permanent/transitory income, and most of the tax cut will be consumed/saved.

g. Over time, the good and bad years will cancel out. In the long run, as the economy grows, permanent income also grows. Thus, if the economywide permanent income Y^P equals actual income Y in the long run, the APC will increase/decrease/remain constant, just as the time-series evidence indicates.

Problems

Answer the following problems on a separate sheet of paper.

1. Consider the Keynesian consumption function $C = 100 + 0.8(Y - T)$.

    a. If $T = 0$, calculate the value of the marginal propensity to consume (MPC) and the formula for the average propensity to consume (APC).

    b. Choose two values of Y and compute the directional changes in the MPC and APC when Y increases.

2. Suppose someone offers you a piece of paper (a bond) that will pay you a (coupon) payment of $100 at the end of *each* of the next three years. You will also get an additional $1,000 at the end of the third year.

    a. Calculate the present value of this bond if the prevailing interest rate is 5 percent per year.

    b. Calculate the present value of this bond if the prevailing interest rate rises to 15 percent per year.

    c. Consequently, what do you conclude about the relationship between the present value of a bond and the prevailing interest rate?

3. a. Suppose that income in each of two periods is equal to 100 and the interest rate is 10 percent per year. Draw a graph of the intertemporal budget constraint and calculate its slope.

    b. On the same graph, draw a hypothetical indifference curve that is tangent to this intertemporal budget constraint at a point at which saving in the first period is positive, and label it IC_1. Label the initial equilibrium Point A.

    c. Suppose that the interest rate rises to 25 percent. Draw the new budget line on your graph. Draw a new indifference curve that is tangent to this budget line and label it IC_2. Label the new equilibrium Point B.

    d. On the same graph, illustrate both the income and substitution effects of this increase in the interest rate.

    e. From your answer to Part d, under what circumstances might an increase in the interest rate lead to an *increase* in C_1 and hence a *reduction* in saving?

4. Suppose that Bart has the following utility function: $U = (C_1 C_2)^{1/2}$, where C_1 and C_2 are Bart's levels of consumption in Periods 1 and 2, respectively. Suppose that his income is $120 in Period 1 and $100 in Period 2, and the real interest rate is 25 percent.

    a. Calculate Bart's optimal levels of consumption in Periods 1 and 2 and his saving in Period 1. (You may wish to use a Lagrange multiplier to solve this problem, but it isn't necessary.)

b. Suppose that the real interest rate increases to 50 percent. Calculate Bart's new optimal levels of consumption in Periods 1 and 2 and his saving in Period 1.

5. Consider the Keynesian consumption function, $C = a + b(Y - T)$, where a and b are
C constants.

   a. Let $T = 0$ and calculate the value of the marginal propensity to consume and the formula for the average propensity to consume.

   b. Differentiate your answers to Part a with respect to income Y to calculate the directional changes in the *MPC* and *APC* when Y increases.

6. What does the life-cycle model of consumption predict about the relative saving
○ rates between:

   a. a country with a rapidly increasing population and a country with a steady population, all other things being equal? Explain.

   b. a country where real GDP per capita is growing rapidly and a country with a stagnant economy, all other things being equal? Explain.

7. People who support an active role for macroeconomic policymakers occasionally argue that policy activism is necessary to buffer the economy from extreme fluctuations in private spending. What do the life-cycle and permanent-income models of consumption imply about this argument, especially as it relates to consumption, which is by far the largest component of private spending? Explain.

8. Suppose that Yan expects to live for 25 more years and work for 10 of those years.

   a. Derive Yan's consumption function in terms of her annual income Y and initial wealth W according to the life-cycle model.

   b. Suppose that Yan expects her income to be $50,000 per year until she retires. In addition, she has accumulated $250,000 in wealth. Calculate her annual level of consumption.

9. Many economists advocate a reduction in tax rates on interest and dividends to stimulate saving and investment. What does the Fisher model of consumption imply about the effects of such a tax reduction on saving?

10. In 1981, the U.S. Congress passed President Ronald Reagan's proposed tax cuts.
CH This legislation called for a permanent reduction in tax *rates* by 5 percent in 1981,
another 10 percent in 1982, and an additional 10 percent in 1983. If people had ratio-
○ nal expectations, fully expected all of the tax cuts to occur (which they did), and incorporated these expectations into their estimates of their permanent incomes, in what years would the permanent-income hypothesis predict that the greatest *change* in consumption would occur? Explain.

Data Questions

Locate the necessary economic data and apply them to answer the following data questions. For advice on how to access the data, see the Preface, and the Economic Data on the Web section on page xi.

1. **a.** Graph annual data (1960–2000) for the personal saving rate (Statistics Canada series 498187) and the GDP-deflator inflation rate (Statistics Canada series 1997756) on the same graph.

b. Try to account for the fact that both these time series move together through the 1970s and 1980s. (*Hint:* With sustained inflation, much of one's nominal interest earnings represent an inflation premium, and *all* of this part must be saved just to keep *real* asset holdings constant. Thus, measured saving overstates actual saving during inflationary times, and the recent "drop" in the savings rate is an overstatement.)

Questions to Think About

1. **a.** Which aspects of your family's consumption behaviour are described by each of the four models of consumption presented in Chapter 17 of the textbook? Which aspects are not described by these theories?

    b. Which of the four models is the most appropriate for describing your family's consumption behaviour? Explain.

2. Does the life-cycle model of consumption accurately explain the consumption behaviour of your grandparents? Why or why not?

3. If you won $10,000,000 in the lottery, how and when would you spend it? Which of the four models of consumption presented in Chapter 17 of the textbook would be consistent with your behaviour?

4. In the recession of 2009, the Canadian government introduced a temporary tax break on home renovation expenditures, while the U.S. government introduced a temporary "cash for clunkers" program for those who traded in their old car for a new one. Explain whether these initiatives would be supported by those who believe in the permanent-income hypothesis concerning household consumption expenditure.

chapter 18

Investment

Fill-in Questions

Use the key terms below to fill in the blanks in the following statements. Each term may be used more than once.

accelerator model
business fixed investment
corporate profits tax
depreciation
efficient markets hypothesis
financing constraints
inventories as a factor of production
inventory investment
investment tax credit
neoclassical model of investment

net investment
production smoothing
real cost of capital
residential construction
stock market
stock-out avoidance
subprime
Tobin's q
work in process

1. Economists distinguish among three types of investment spending: _____ includes the new housing that people buy to live in and that landlords buy to rent out; _____ includes the equipment and structures that businesses buy to use in production; and _____ includes materials, supplies, and finished goods that businesses put aside in storage.

2. The _____ examines the benefit and cost to firms of owning capital goods by showing how investment is related to the marginal product of capital, the interest rate, and the tax rules affecting firms.

3. As capital ages, it undergoes wear and tear, which decreases its value. This process is called _____.

4. The cost of buying and renting out a unit of capital, measured in units of the economy's output, is called the _____.

5. The change in the capital stock is called _____. Recall from Chapter 2 of the textbook that it is equal to gross investment minus _____.

6. According to the _____, firms find it profitable to add to their capital stock if the marginal product of capital exceeds the _____.

7. The _____ is a tax on corporate profits.

8. Many economists believe that the _____ may discourage investment because it does not define profit as the rental price of capital minus the cost of capital.

9. A(n) _____ reduces a firm's taxes by a certain amount for each dollar that the firm spends on capital goods. It works as a subsidy on investment.

10. According to one theory of investment, firms base their investment decisions on the ratio of the market value of installed capital divided by the replacement cost of installed capital. This ratio is known as _____.

11. According to Tobin's q-theory of investment, net investment will be positive whenever managers can raise their firm's market value by buying more capital. More precisely, if the _____ value of capital exceeds its replacement cost, _____ will exceed 1.0, and net investment will be positive.

12. According to the _____, the price of a company's stock is the fully rational valuation of that company's value, given current information about the company's business prospects.

13. When firms are limited in the amount that they can raise in financial markets, they are said to face _____.

14. Firms have several motives for holding inventories. One motive, called _____, exists when it is cheaper for a firm to produce goods at a steady rate when that firm experiences temporary booms and busts in sales. Firms can also view _____ when inventories increase output by improving efficiency. A third motive, called _____, exists when firms hold inventories to avoid running out of goods when sales are unexpectedly high. A final motive exists because many goods take time to produce, so they are counted as part of a firm's inventory when they are only partly completed. These inventories are called _____.

15. According to the _____, investment depends on the change in the firm's level of output. When output is increasing, investment will be greater than when output is decreasing.

16. In 2008 and 2009, many banks in the United States became practically insolvent. This resulted in a credit crunch, which may be viewed as a period of increasing _____ on business.

17. One of the causes of the recession of 2008–2009 was the rising default rate on mortgages in the United States made to households with questionable credit histories, called _____ borrowers.

Multiple-Choice Questions

1. According to the neoclassical model of investment:
   a. investment falls as the real interest rate rises.
   b. investment falls as the real interest rate falls.
   c. an increase in the marginal product of capital causes the investment function to shift to the left.
   d. both a and c are true.

2. In equilibrium, the real rental price of capital is equal to:
   a. 1.0.
   b. the marginal product of capital.
   c. the price of output.
   d. all of the above.

3. In a Cobb-Douglas production function, the equilibrium rental price of capital increases as:
   a. the stock of capital used by the firm falls.
   b. the amount of labour employed by the firm rises.
   c. technology improves.
   d. all of the above.

4. The cost of capital is determined by all of the following EXCEPT the:
   a. rate of depreciation.
   b. corporate profit rate.
   c. interest rate.
   d. price of capital and its rate of change.

5. Assume that the price of capital goods rises at the same rate as the price of other goods. If the price of capital is $1,500 per unit, the real interest rate is 4 percent, and the depreciation rate is 6 percent, then the cost of capital equals:
   a. $30.   b. $300.   c. $150.   d. $100.

6. If the price of capital goods rises at the same rate as the price of other goods, the real cost of capital may be written as:
   a. $(P_K/P)(r + \delta)$.   b. $(P_K/P)(r - \delta)$.   c. $(P/P_K)(i + \delta)$.   d. $(P/P_K)(r - \delta)$.

7. Firms find it profitable to add to their capital stock if the:
   a. real cost of capital exceeds the marginal product of capital.
   b. marginal product of capital exceeds the real cost of capital.
   c. marginal product of capital exceeds the real interest rate.
   d. rental price of capital exceeds the marginal product of capital.

8. Expansionary monetary policy spurs investment in the short run via:

   a. a decrease in inflation.

   b. a decrease in the cost of capital.

   c. an increase in the rental price of capital.

   d. all of the above.

9. An event that decreases the marginal product of capital will:

   a. shift the investment function to the left.

   b. shift the investment function to the right.

   c. raise the real cost of capital.

   d. raise the rate of depreciation.

10. The corporate profits tax discourages investment because it:

    a. defines profit as the rental price of capital minus the cost of capital.

    b. taxes profits at an exorbitant rate of 60 percent.

    c. does not appropriately take inflation into account in calculating depreciation and profit.

    d. all of the above.

11. All of the following statements about the investment tax credit are true EXCEPT:

    a. it stimulates investment.

    b. it continues to be one of the most influential tax provisions in Canada.

    c. it reduces the after-tax cost of capital.

    d. it operates as an indirect subsidy for investment.

12. All of the following statements about the q-theory of investment are true EXCEPT:

    a. Tobin's q is equal to the market value of installed capital divided by the replacement cost of installed capital.

    b. if Tobin's q is greater than 1.0, firms will allow their capital to wear out without replacing it.

    c. it assumes that stock prices play an influential role in investment decisions.

    d. it implies that investment depends on the current and expected future profits from installed capital.

13. A policy that allows firms to deduct the cost of depreciation earlier in the life of an investment project will:

    a. reduce the after-tax cost of capital.

    b. make investment more profitable.

    c. increase the amount of investment.

    d. do all of the above.

14. According to the efficient markets hypothesis, an increase in today's stock price may reflect all of the following EXCEPT:

    a. a new invention by the company.

    b. a merger with another company that was announced last year.

    c. an announcement of a future merger with another company.

    d. a new earnings report.

15. Financing constraints that limit the amount of money firms can raise in financial markets:

    a. tend to reduce the length of recessions.

    b. induce firms to invest on the basis of their current cash flow rather than their expected profitability.

    c. make investment less sensitive to current economic conditions.

    d. do all of the above.

16. Residential investment depends on:

    a. the relative price of housing P_H/P.

    b. the real interest rate.

    c. the size of the adult population.

    d. all of the above.

17. Some firms hold inventories in order to avoid changing production frequently in response to fluctuations in sales. This motive is called:

    a. holding inventories as a factor of production.

    b. production smoothing.

    c. stock-out avoidance.

    d. holding inventories as work in process.

18. According to the accelerator model of investment, investment:

    a. is high when the real interest rate is low.

    b. remains fairly constant at all times.

    c. is high when output grows rapidly.

    d. is high when corporate profits are high.

Exercises

1. **The Demand for Capital** *In this exercise, we use a numerical example to illustrate how the demand for capital is related to the real rental price of capital.* Note: *Students may wish to review Exercises 1–3 in Chapter 3 of this Study Guide.*

    a. The owners of Acme Car Wash must decide how many units of capital to rent. They have the data shown in Columns 1 and 2 of Table 18-1 to help them in making a decision. (All data are for a given number of workers.)

Table 18-1

(1) Units of Capital	(2) Number of Cars Washed per Hour	(3) Marginal Product of Capital
0	0	
		_____
1	20	
		_____
2	35	
		_____
3	45	
		_____
4	50	

Recall that the marginal product of capital MPK is the extra output produced when one unit of capital is added. Thus, the MPK for the first unit of capital is equal to $20 - 0 =$ _____. Use this information to complete Column 3 in Table 18-1. Then use the data from Columns 1 and 3 to plot and draw the MPK curve on Graph 18-1, and label it MPK.

Graph 18-1

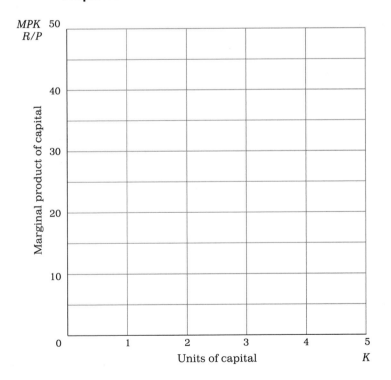

b. To maximize profits, firms rent capital until *MPK* is equal to the real rental price of capital, where the latter is defined as the rental rate of capital *R* divided by the price of the firm's output *P*, or *R/P*. Thus, in equilibrium, *R/P* = *MPK*. Using the data from Table 18-1, if *R/P* = 15, Acme will want to rent _____ units of capital because this is the point at which *R/P* = *MPK*. Remember that this will occur if *R* = $15 and *P* = $1 or if *R* = $30 and *P* = $2. (*Note:* Review the exercises in Chapter 3 if this is not clear.) If *R/P* = 5, Acme will want to rent _____ units of capital because this is now the point at which *R/P* = *MPK*. Thus, the demand curve for capital is the same as the *MPK* curve. Consequently, add *R/P* as an additional label for the vertical axis on Graph 18-1, and add Capital demand as an additional label for the *MPK* curve. Obviously, as the real rental price of capital falls, firms will want to rent <u>more/fewer</u> units of capital.

c. You can construct an aggregate *MPK* and an aggregate capital demand curve for the entire economy in a similar way. One such curve is depicted on Graph 18-2. On this graph, *P* represents the aggregate price level, which can also be viewed as the price of output for a representative firm.

Graph 18-2

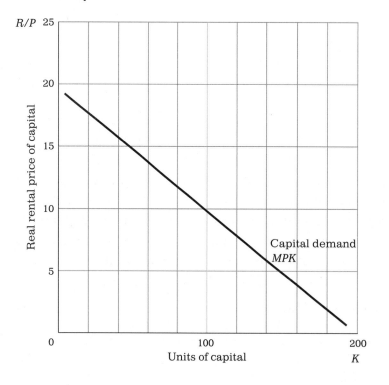

In the short run, the total amount of capital in the economy is fixed at $\overline{K}$. Suppose that $\overline{K}$ = 100. Draw a vertical capital supply curve at $\overline{K}$ = 100 on Graph 18-2, and label it Capital supply. In this case, the equilibrium real rental price of capital *R/P* will equal _____ in the short run because at this price the supply of capital equals the demand for capital.

d. Several factors can affect the equilibrium real rental price of capital R/P. Chapter 18 of the textbook illustrates some of these factors using the Cobb-Douglas production function, but one can also present them intuitively. If the capital stock were to increase suddenly, the capital supply curve would shift to the left/right and the equilibrium real rental price of capital would rise/fall. If capital and labour both became more productive, the marginal product of each unit of capital would be higher/lower, thereby shifting the capital demand curve to the left/right and increasing/decreasing the equilibrium real rental price of capital. If more workers were employed, each unit of capital would probably become more productive, thereby increasing the *MPK* at each level of capital, shifting the capital demand curve to the left/right, and increasing/decreasing the equilibrium real rental price of capital.

2. The Cost of Capital *In this exercise, we derive the cost of capital.*

a. Following the simplification introduced in Chapter 18 of the textbook, assume that the firms in Exercise 1 rent capital from other firms that own it. The nominal rent received by these other firms per unit of capital is R; the real rent is R/P, where P is the aggregate price level. As Chapter 18 of the textbook illustrates, the nominal cost of one unit of capital per period to the firm that owns it is

$$\text{(Nominal) Cost of Capital} = iP_K - \Delta P_K + \delta P_K, \qquad \textbf{(18-1)}$$

where i equals the nominal interest rate, P_K equals the purchase price of a unit of capital, ΔP_K equals the change in the price of (new) capital, and δ equals the rate of physical or technological depreciation. The first term on the right-hand side of Equation 18-1, iP_K, represents the foregone interest revenue the firm could have earned had it put its money in the bank or purchased bonds instead of purchasing capital. The second term, ΔP_K, represents the amount by which capital prices increase, and the third term, δP_K, reflects the amount by which the capital is reduced by depreciation. The minus sign before ΔP_K indicates that the cost of capital to firms that own it falls when capital prices increase, because the capital can then be sold to other firms that own capital for a higher price. Factoring P_K from the right-hand side of Equation 18-1 by P_K yields

$$\text{(Nominal) Cost of Capital} = P_K[i - \Delta P_K/P_K + \delta], \qquad \textbf{(18-2)}$$

where $\Delta P_K/P_K$ equals the rate at which capital prices are changing.

Now complete Table 18-2.

Table 18-2

(1) Price of Capital P_K	(2) Nominal Interest Rate i	(3) Rate of Growth of Capital Prices	(4) Rate of Depreciation δ	(5) Cost of Capital
$100	0.05	0.05	0.10	_____
$100	0.10	0.05	0.10	_____
$100	0.10	0.08	0.10	_____
$100	0.10	0.08	0.20	_____
$200	0.10	0.08	0.20	_____
$100	_____	0.08	0.20	$15

b. Equation 18-2 and the data in Table 18-2 indicate that an increase in the nominal interest rate will increase/decrease the cost of capital, and an increase in the rate of growth of capital prices will increase/decrease the cost of capital. Finally, an increase in the rate of depreciation will increase/decrease the cost of capital because the capital now wears out more quickly/slowly, thereby lasting for a longer/shorter period of time.

c. If capital prices are rising at the same rate as the aggregate price level, then $\Delta P_K / P_K = \pi$, and Equation 18-2 becomes

$$\text{(Nominal) Cost of Capital} = P_K[i - \pi + \delta] = P_K[r + \delta], \qquad \textbf{(18-3)}$$

where r is the real interest rate. Given this assumption, the real interest rate in the first row of Table 18-2 is _____ percent, and the real interest rate in the second row of Table 18-2 is _____ percent.

d. Finally, recall that the nominal rental cost of capital R for the firms that rent capital must be divided by the price level to obtain the real rental cost of capital R/P. Similarly, the real cost of capital to the firms that own the capital is $(P_K/P)(r + \delta)$. An increase in the real interest rate will increase/decrease the real cost of capital, and an increase in the rate of depreciation will increase/decrease the real cost of capital.

3. **The Determinants of Investment** *In this exercise, we combine the results from Exercises 1 and 2 to illustrate the determinants of investment.*

a. In Exercise 1, it was shown that firms rent additional units of capital until the marginal product of capital *MPK* is greater than/less than/equal to the real rental cost of capital R/P. In Exercise 2, it was also shown that if capital prices rise at the same rate as the aggregate price level, the real cost of capital to the firms that own it is $(P_K/P)[\underline{\qquad} + \underline{\qquad}]$. Consequently, the real profit rate from owning one unit of capital and renting it is

$$\text{Profit Rate} = MPK - (P_K/P) \times (\underline{\qquad} + \underline{\qquad}). \qquad \textbf{(18-4)}$$

If the profit rate is positive, firms that own capital will add to/subtract from their capital stock, resulting in positive/negative net investment. If the profit rate is negative, firms that own capital will add to/subtract from their capital stock, leading to positive/negative net investment. Total, or gross, business fixed investment is equal to net investment plus replacement investment, where the latter is equal to δK. Consequently, total investment may be positive even if net investment is negative.

b. In competitive long-run equilibrium, *MPK* is greater than/less than/equal to the real cost of capital $(P_K/P)(r + \delta)$, and the profit rate is positive/zero/negative. Starting from equilibrium, a reduction in the real interest rate r (resulting from either a(n) increase/decrease in the nominal interest rate or a(n) increase/decrease in the rate of inflation) will increase/decrease the real cost of capital and hence increase/decrease the profit rate from owning capital. As a result, firms that own capital will add to/subtract from their capital stock, resulting in a(n) increase/decrease in investment. Thus, as r falls, investment rises/falls. This result is similar to/different from that obtained in earlier textbook chapters. As capital is added and lent out, firms move along the aggregate *MPK* curve, and the marginal product of capital will rise/fall until it equals the new real cost of capital.

c. Starting from equilibrium again, a technological innovation that increases the marginal product of capital will increase/decrease/have no immediate effect on the real cost of capital, but it will increase/decrease the profit rate from owning capital. As a result, firms that own capital will add to/subtract from their capital stock, resulting in a(n) increase/decrease in investment. As capital is added/subtracted and lent out, firms move along the aggregate *MPK* curve, and the marginal product of capital will rise/fall until it equals the real cost of capital.

d. As Chapter 18 of the textbook indicates, various tax measures encourage or discourage the accumulation of capital by firms. Most economists believe that a reduction in the corporate tax on accounting profits will increase/decrease investment. The investment tax credit reduces a firm's taxes by a certain amount for each dollar the firm spends on investment goods. An increase in the investment tax credit would <u>increase/decrease</u> the real after-tax cost of capital and thereby <u>increase/decrease</u> investment. The <u>same/opposite</u> effect occurs following a fiscal policy that makes depreciation allowances less generous.

4. **Residential Investment** *In this exercise, we discuss the supply and demand for housing and residential investment.*

    a. Graph 18-3 depicts an initial equilibrium in the housing market at Point A. Housing demand, labeled D_1, is negatively related to the relative price of housing P_H/P. Housing supply, labeled S_1, is fixed in the short run. If the residential construction industry is perfectly competitive, economic profits will be <u>positive/negative/zero</u>.

Graph 18-3

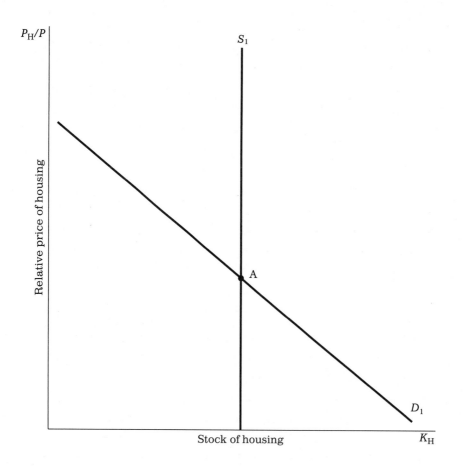

b. An economic boom that increases households' income will shift the housing demand curve to the left/right. Draw the new demand curve on Graph 18-3, label it D_2, and label the new short-run equilibrium Point B. Obviously, the relative price of housing will increase/decrease. This trend will induce the residential construction industry to increase/decrease the production of new houses, which will increase/decrease residential investment. This change in residential investment will eventually shift the housing supply curve on Graph 18-3 to the left/right. As it shifts, the relative price of housing will rise even more/fall from Point B.

c. Starting again at Point A, an increase in mortgage interest rates will shift the housing demand curve to the left/right. Draw the new demand curve on Graph 18-3, label it D_3, and label the new short-run equilibrium Point C. Obviously, the relative price of housing will increase/decrease, and residential investment will increase/decrease.

5. The Accelerator Model *In this exercise, we present a numerical example of the accelerator model to illustrate how changes in output can affect investment.*

a. The accelerator model has been used to analyze several types of investment, especially inventory investment. In this model, investment I is a function of the change in output ΔY from one period to another:

$$I = \beta(\Delta Y) = \beta(Y - Y_{-1}). \qquad \textbf{(18-5)}$$

When output Y rises, firms want to hold more inventories, so they invest in them. When Y falls, firms want to hold fewer inventories, so they run them down, and inventory investment is negative. If $\beta = 0.2$, complete Table 17-3.

Table 18-3

(1) Period	(2) Output Y	(3) Change in Y	(4) % Change in Y	(5) $I = 0.2(\Delta Y)$ $= 0.2(Y - Y_{-1})$	(6) % Change in I
0	1,000				
		100	_____		
1	1,100			20	
		_____	_____		_____
2	1,200			_____	
		_____	_____		_____
3	1,300			_____	
		_____	_____		_____
4	1,350			_____	
		_____	_____		_____
5	1,350			_____	

b. Compare the percentage changes in output Y in each period from Period 2 through Period 5 with the comparable percentage changes in investment I. One of the major implications of the accelerator model is that relatively small changes in the growth rate of output Y lead to <u>even smaller/much larger</u> changes in the growth of investment I. Consequently, investment I is likely to be <u>stable/volatile</u>.

Problems

Answer the following problems on a separate sheet of paper.

1. In Chapters 10 and 11 of the textbook, it was assumed that investment I depends on the real interest rate r but is independent of changes in real output Y. Now suppose that I also increases as Y rises and decreases as Y falls.

   a. Draw an investment curve that illustrates this relationship between I and Y.

   b. Explain why I might be an increasing function of Y.

   c. If I increases as Y rises and decreases as Y falls, what would happen to the:

       i. slope of the planned expenditure curve? Explain.

       ii. government-purchases multiplier? Explain using the round-by-round story.

       iii. slopes of the IS and LM curves?

       iv. slopes of the AD and $SRAS$ curves?

2. **a.** Consider a harvester that costs $10,000. If harvester prices are rising at 3 percent per year, the interest rate is 6 percent, and harvesters depreciate by 20 percent per year, calculate the cost of capital on this investment.

   b. Now consider a computer that costs $10,000. Once again, assume that the interest rate is 6 percent and computers depreciate by 20 percent per year. Computer prices, however, *fall* by 15 percent per year. Calculate the cost of capital on this investment.

3. Suppose that there were large increases in the prices of certain basic commodities, such as oil and food. Consequently, the prices of capital goods increase by less than the overall rate of inflation. Would the use of the real interest rate in the cost-of-capital equation over- or underestimate the true cost of capital? Explain.

4. **C** Consider the following Cobb-Douglas production function:

$$Y = 12(K^{1/3}L^{2/3}). \text{ Assume that labour } L = 64.$$

   a. Derive the equation for the marginal product of capital MPK.

   b. Find the specific values for MPK when capital $K = 1, 8, 27$, and 64. Plot these values of MPK on a graph and draw the resulting capital demand curve.

   c. Now suppose that L rises to 125, and repeat Parts a and b.

5. Suppose that there is a reduction in personal income taxes. Use the *IS-LM* model and the relevant sections in Chapter 18 of the textbook to illustrate what happens to investment according to the:

   a. neoclassical (cost-of-capital) model of investment.

   b. accelerator model of investment.

6. In its first public stock market trade in August 2004, the price of one share of Google stock sold for $95. In February 2006, one share was selling for $475. What may have cause the stock price to quintuple according to each of the following theories: the efficient markets hypothesis and Keynes's "beauty contest" hypothesis about stock prices?

7. Mortgage interest payments are tax deductible in the United States. Many economists have argued for the elimination of this provision. What would the effects of an elimination on the tax deductibility on mortgage interest payments be on the demand for housing, the relative price of housing, investment in housing, and the profits of residential construction firms in the short run?

8. a. Define what is meant by an investment tax credit of 8 percent.

   b. Consider a closed economy in which the government enacts an investment tax credit of 8 percent. If the aggregate price level is held constant, what happens to the *IS* and/or *LM* curves in the short run? Briefly explain.

   c. Now consider an open economy. If the price level is still held constant and government enacts an 8 percent investment tax credit for domestic firms only, explain what happens to each of the following in the short run:

      i. the *IS* and/or *LM* curves.
      ii. domestic net foreign investment.
      iii. the domestic trade surplus and the domestic real exchange rate.

   d. In these models, does the investment tax credit have a greater short-run effect on output in a closed economy or in an open economy? Where does it have the greater effect on investment? Explain your answers intuitively.

Data Questions

Locate the necessary economic data and apply them to answer the following data questions. For advice on how to access the data, see the Preface, and the Economic Data on the Web section on page xi.

1. a. Complete Table 18-4 (in billions of 2002 dollars), which presents data about various forms of real private gross investment.

   To get this data, follow the procedure outlined in the Preface. Through your university library's e-resources on the Internet, go to *Canadian Economic Observer Historical Supplement* (under Statistics Canada). Then, under the National Accounts section, go to the table entitled Gross Domestic Product, by income and *expenditure* in chained 2002 dollars.

Table 18-4

(1) Year	(2) Real Nonresidential Construction Investment	(3) Real Investment in Machinery and Equipment	(4) Real Residential Construction Investment	(5) Real Change in Business Inventories
1995	_____	_____	_____	_____
2000	_____	_____	_____	_____
2005	_____	_____	_____	_____

b. Calculate the percentage change in each category of investment between its highest and lowest values (defined as the absolute change divided by the average of the two values). What do you conclude about the relative volatility of the different components of investment?

Questions to Think About

1. Why do you think banks use the nominal interest rate in determining the creditworthiness of their potential customers?

2. Studies of the Swedish "investment funds" indicate that investment tended to rise during periods of recession above what it would have been without these temporary investment subsidies. Critics argue, however, that investment may merely get crowded into recessions in anticipation of the subsidies—that is, critics suggest that firms may wait until recessions to invest in order to receive the investment subsidy. How might one control for this potential effect in an academic study?

3. Discuss the efficient markets hypothesis with your parents or grandparents. Ask them how, if at all, it has influenced their investment behaviour.

c h a p t e r **19**

Money Supply and
Money Demand

Fill-in Questions

Use the key terms below to fill in the blanks in the following statements. Each term may be used more than once.

100-percent-reserve banking
balance sheet
bank capital
Bank Rate
Baumol-Tobin model
capital requirement
currency-deposit ratio
deposit switching
dominated asset
financial intermediation
fractional-reserve banking
high-powered money

inflation rate
leverage
monetary base
money multiplier
near money
open-market operation
portfolio theories
reserve-deposit ratio
reserve requirements
reserves
transactions theories

1. A bank's _____ is a statement of its assets and liabilities.

2. The deposits that banks receive but do not lend out are called
   _____. Under a(n) _____ system,
   banks hold all deposits as reserves and are, therefore, unable to create money by
   making loans.

3. Under a(n) _____ system, banks keep a fraction of their
   deposits in reserve.

4. The _____ represent(s) the fraction of deposits banks keep
   in reserve. The _____ reflects the preferences of the public
   about how to apportion their money holding between currency and deposits.

5. Institutions that act as go-betweens for those individuals who wish to save some of
   their income for future consumption and those individuals who wish to borrow
   engage in _____.

6. The _____ is the sum of currency and bank reserves. It can be easily controlled by the Bank of Canada, and it is sometimes called _____.

7. The money supply is equal to the monetary base multiplied by the _____, where the latter is equal to (one plus the _____) divided by (the _____ plus the _____).

8. The Bank of Canada uses two tools to control the money supply. The tool most often used is a(n) _____, by which the Bank of Canada purchases and sells government bonds. The Bank of Canada may also alter the _____ by _____. The Bank of Canada changes the _____, which is the interest rate it charges banks that wish to borrow reserves from the Bank of Canada, as a summary indicator of these initiatives.

9. Money demand theories that emphasize the role of money as a store of value are called _____. Some economists question the usefulness of these theories for studying money demand because money is a(n) _____, that is, there are other financial assets that are equally safe and offer a higher return.

10. _____ of money demand emphasize the role of money as a medium of exchange. The _____ of cash management is perhaps the most prominent model of this type.

11. In the _____, people compare the opportunity costs of holding currency with the benefits resulting from making fewer trips to the bank.

12. Nonmonetary assets that have acquired some of the liquidity of money are called _____.

13. Bank of Canada policy involves trying to keep the _____ between 1 and 3 percent.

14. The financial resources bank owners use to start a bank are called the equity of the bank's owners, or _____.

15. The process by which banks use borrowed money to create and acquire assets that greatly exceed the amount of bank capital is called _____.

16. In order to ensure that banks have enough capital to pay off their depositors if their assets lose some of their value, bank regulators establish a _____.

Multiple-Choice Questions

1. The money supply as defined by $M1$ is roughly equal to currency held by the:

   a. public.
   b. public plus demand and chequing deposits at chartered banks.
   c. public plus chartered bank reserves.
   d. public plus chartered bank loans.

2. In a 100-percent-reserve banking system, if a bank receives $500 in new deposits:

   a. the bank's assets will increase by $500.
   b. the bank's liabilities will increase by $500.
   c. the bank's loans will remain unchanged.
   d. all of the above.

3. The monetary base is equal to:

   a. currency held by the public plus bank reserves.
   b. currency held by the public plus bank deposits.
   c. $M1$.
   d. total bank deposits.

4. In a 100-percent-reserve banking system, the money multiplier equals:

   a. 0.
   b. 1.
   c. 10.
   d. 100.

5. In a fractional-reserve banking system, if the reserve-deposit ratio is 30 percent and the currency-deposit ratio is 40 percent, then the money multiplier equals:

   a. 1.
   b. 0.5.
   c. 1.5.
   d. 2.

6. If the monetary base is $60 billion and the money multiplier is 3, then the money supply equals:

   a. $20 billion.
   b. $60 billion.
   c. $63 billion.
   d. $180 billion.

7. If the monetary base doubles and both the currency-deposit and reserve-deposit ratios remain constant, the money supply will:

   a. fall by half.
   b. remain constant.
   c. double.
   d. increase by a factor of $2 \times [(1 + cr)/(cr + rr)]$.

8. An increase in the currency-deposit ratio leads to a(n):

   a. increase in the money supply.
   b. decrease in the money supply.
   c. increase in the money multiplier.
   d. increase in the reserve-deposit ratio.

9. An open-market operation occurs when:

   a. there is an emergency appendectomy at the farmers' market.

   b. the Bank of Canada buys government bonds from the public.

   c. the Bank of Canada sells government bonds to the public.

   d. both b and c.

10. Switching a government deposit from the Bank of Canada to a chartered bank: (I) increases the money supply; (II) increases the national debt.

    a. I is true; II is not.

    b. II is true; I is not.

    c. Both I and II are true.

    d. Neither I nor II is true.

11. The Bank Rate is the:

    a. top classification assigned to borrowers by international debt-rating agencies.

    b. interest rate charged by banks on loans to their best customers.

    c. interest rate charged by the Bank of Canada to banks that borrow reserves from the Bank of Canada.

    d. difference between the interest rate on Treasury bills and the prime rate of interest.

12. If the Bank of Canada wishes to increase the money supply, it may:

    a. perform an open-market purchase.

    b. switch deposits to chartered banks.

    c. lower the Bank Rate.

    d. all of the above.

13. A decrease in the reserve-deposit ratio will increase the money supply by:

    a. increasing the monetary base.

    b. increasing the money multiplier.

    c. decreasing the currency-deposit ratio.

    d. decreasing the Bank Rate.

14. Between 1929 and 1933, during the Great Depression, the U.S. money supply fell for all of the following reasons EXCEPT the:

    a. reserve-deposit ratio increased.

    b. currency-deposit ratio increased.

    c. monetary base decreased.

    d. money multiplier decreased.

15. According to portfolio theories of money demand, all of the following affect money demand EXCEPT the:

    a. expected real return on bonds.

    b. usefulness of money in making transactions.

    c. expected rate of inflation.

    d. expected real return on stocks.

16. According to transactions theories of money demand, the demand for money is primarily a result of the:

    a. risk involved in buying stocks and bonds.
    b. unpredictability of the inflation rate.
    c. desire of individuals to engage in illegal activities such as the drug trade.
    d. convenience of money in making purchases.

17. The Baumol-Tobin model of money demand considers all of the following factors EXCEPT:

    a. the return on stocks.
    b. expenditures.
    c. the interest rate.
    d. the cost of going to and from the bank.

18. According to the Baumol-Tobin model, average money holding will rise if:

    a. the fixed cost of going to and from the bank falls.
    b. the inflation rate rises.
    c. the interest rate falls.
    d. expenditures fall.

19. Each of the following will result in a decrease in the fixed cost of going to the bank (denoted by F in the Baumol-Tobin model of money demand) EXCEPT:

    a. a decrease in banking fees.
    b. a decrease in real wages.
    c. the spread of automatic teller machines.
    d. a reduction in downtown traffic.

20. Empirical studies indicate that the actual elasticities of money demand with respect to income and the interest rate are:

    a. equal to those predicted by the Baumol-Tobin model.
    b. larger than they would be if the Baumol-Tobin model were completely correct.
    c. different from what they would be if the Baumol-Tobin model were completely correct. The estimated interest elasticity is larger (in absolute value) and the estimated income elasticity is smaller.
    d. different from what they would be if the Baumol-Tobin model were completely correct. The estimated interest elasticity is smaller (in absolute value) and the estimated income elasticity is larger.

21. A bank's capital, or owner's equity, is calculated as:

    a. reserves minus deposits.
    b. assets minus liabilities.
    c. reserves and loans minus deposits.
    d. assets minus deposits.

22. A bank's leverage ratio is the ratio of its:

    a. assets to liabilities.
    b. deposits to reserves.
    c. assets to bank capital.
    d. assets to debt.

23. A bank's capital requirement is calculated as the minimum acceptable ratio of its:

a. assets to liabilities.

b. reserves to deposits.

c. bank capital to assets.

d. assets to debt.

Exercises

1. Fractional-Reserve Banking *In this exercise, we illustrate how money is created by an open-market purchase in a fractional-reserve banking system.*

a. Imagine an economy with three banks, each of which has the following initial balance sheet:

Initial Balance Sheet of
First, Second, and Third National Banks

Assets		Liabilities	
Reserves	$250 million	Deposits	$1,000 million
Loans	$750 million		

If there is no currency held outside the three banks, the total initial money supply will equal total deposits, or 3 × $_____ million = $_____ million. The reserve-deposit ratio in this economy is _____ percent.

b. Suppose that the central bank makes an open-market purchase of $10 million by buying $10 million in government bonds from Tara, a typical citizen. It pays Tara with a $10 million cheque, which Tara takes to her bank, the First National Bank. When the bank presents the cheque to the central bank, the central bank credits the First National Bank with an additional $10 million in reserves, and Tara's deposits at the First National Bank officially increase by the amount of the cheque, or $_____ million. At that point, the bank's balance sheet will be:

First National Bank

Assets		Liabilities	
Reserves	$_____ million	Deposits	$_____ million
Loans	$_____ million		

The balance sheets of the two remaining banks have not yet changed.

c. If the First National Bank wishes to maintain its initial reserve-deposit ratio of
_____ percent, it must keep _____
percent of the additional $_____ million in reserves, and
it can lend out the remaining $_____ million. Suppose it
lends all this money to Fred, who is not a depositor at the bank. When it makes
the loan, its reserves fall and its loans rise by the same amount, and its deposits
do not change. Thus, the First National Bank's balance sheet becomes:

First National Bank

Assets			Liabilities		
Reserves	$_____ million		Deposits	$_____ million	
Loans	$_____ million				

d. Now suppose that Fred takes his $_____ million loan and
either deposits it in the Second National Bank or buys a baseball team, and the
seller of the team deposits the proceeds in the Second National Bank. In either
case, both the reserves and deposits of the Second National Bank will rise by
$_____ million above their initial levels in Part a, and its
balance sheet will be:

Second National Bank

Assets			Liabilities		
Reserves	$_____ million		Deposits	$_____ million	
Loans	$_____ million				

e. If the Second National Bank wishes to maintain its initial reserve-deposit ratio of
_____ percent, it must keep _____
percent of the additional $_____ million in deposits (and
reserves) obtained from Fred, and it can lend out the remaining
$_____ million. Suppose it lends this amount to Eileen,
who is not a depositor at the bank. Consequently, its reserves fall and its loans
rise by the same amount, and the Second National Bank's balance sheet
becomes:

Second National Bank

Assets			Liabilities		
Reserves	$_____ million		Deposits	$_____ million	
Loans	$_____ million				

f. Eileen takes her $_____ million loan and either deposits it in the Third National Bank or donates it to her university, and the university deposits it in the Third National Bank. In either case, both the reserves and deposits of the Third National Bank will rise by $_____ million above their initial levels in Part a, and its balance sheet will be:

Third National Bank

Assets		Liabilities	
Reserves	$_____ million	Deposits	$_____ million
Loans	$_____ million		

g. The money supply has now grown by more than the $10 million open-market purchase that the central bank made in Part b. From Parts c, e, and f, total deposits in the three banks now equal $_____ million, compared with the initial level of $3 \times$ $_____ million = $_____ million. Thus, the money supply has increased by $_____ million.

h. The process is not yet over. The Third National Bank will now increase its loans, and deposits at one of the three banks will rise even more when the borrower deposits the proceeds of his or her loan in the bank. According to the textbook, the total increase in deposits is equal to the initial infusion of reserves, or $10 million, multiplied by $1/rr$, where rr is the reserve-deposit ratio expressed as a decimal. (In this exercise, we implicitly assume that the currency-deposit ratio equals zero.) In this exercise, $rr =$ _____; thus, deposits (and the money supply) will eventually increase by $_____ million.

i. Note that reserves in all three banks increased by a total of $_____ million above its initial level. Thus, when $cr = 0$, an open-market purchase of $10 million will increase bank reserves by <u>more than/exactly/less than</u> $10 million, while it eventually increases the money supply by <u>more than/exactly/less than</u> $10 million.

2. **The Money Multiplier** In this exercise, we review the determinants of the money multiplier.

According to the model of the money supply presented in Chapter 19 of the textbook, the money supply can be written as

$$M = [(cr + 1)/(cr + rr)] \times B, \qquad \text{(19-1)}$$

where M equals the money supply, B is the monetary base, and the term in brackets is called the money multiplier.

a. The money supply consists of currency plus reserves/deposits/loans. The monetary base consists of currency plus reserves/deposits/loans, and it is sometimes called high-powered money. The reserve-deposit ratio is equal to rr, and cr is the currency-deposit ratio.

b. Complete Table 19-1.

Table 19-1

(1) Currency-Deposit Ratio cr	(2) Reserve-Deposit Ratio rr	(3) Money Multiplier $[(cr + 1)/(cr + rr)]$
0.2	0.2	_____
0.2	0.4	_____
0.6	0.4	_____
0.2	1.0	_____
0.6	1.0	_____
0	0.2	_____

c. From Table 19-1, note that an increase in the reserve-deposit ratio rr will increase/decrease the money multiplier, and an increase in the currency-deposit ratio cr will increase/decrease the money multiplier in a fractional-reserve banking system. If $rr = 1.0$, all deposits are held as reserves, there are no loans, and we have a 100-percent-reserve banking system. In this case, the money multiplier is equal to _____, and the money supply is greater than/less than/equal to the monetary base. Finally, if cr equals 0, the formula for the money multiplier becomes _____. In this case, the entire money supply would be in the form of currency/deposits.

3. The Monetary Transmission Mechanism *In this exercise, you work through the brief self-directed learning sequence that is available at the Bank of Canada's website.*

Go to *http://www.bankofcanada.ca* and then click on "Monetary Policy," and then on "How monetary policy works," and "Decision-making process." Proceed at your own pace through the several screens that appear in the first of these two links.

4. Bank Capital, Leverage, and Capital Requirements *In this exercise, we develop a more realistic bank balance sheet to illustrate the relationships among bank capital, leverage, and capital requirements.*

In Exercise 1, we considered a simple balance sheet in which a bank's assets consisted solely of its reserves and loans, and its only liabilities were its deposits. Furthermore, we made the simplifying assumption that assets always equal liabilities. In order to understand the bank crisis of 2008–2009, we present the following, more realistic initial bank balance sheet for Bank A:

Initial Balance Sheet for Bank A

Assets		Liabilities and Owner's Equity	
Reserves	$50	Deposits	$300
Loans	$250	Debt	$180
Securities	$200	Capital (Owner's Equity)	$20

As described in Chapter 19, a bank obtains resources from its owners, who provide capital, and also by taking deposits and issuing debt. Some of these resources are held as bank reserves. The remaining amounts are used either to make loans or to buy financial securities, such as government and corporate bonds. Total assets on the left-hand side of the balance sheet must equal the sum on the right-hand side of the balance sheet, which is equal to total liabilities (deposits plus debt) plus bank capital. Bank capital is also called owner's equity. If the bank's assets grow faster than its liabilities, the value of the bank's capital (or equity) will also grow. If the bank's assets grow less rapidly than its liabilities, the value of the bank's capital (or equity) will fall.

a. In the initial balance sheet, Bank A's total assets equal $_____. Its total liabilities, consisting of its deposits and debt, equal $_____. The value of its capital (or equity) is calculated as Assets minus Liabilities, which equals $_____.

b. A bank's capital ratio is calculated as the total value of its capital divided by its assets. Bank A's capital ratio is $_____/$_____ = _____ percent. Bank regulators require banks to maintain a minimum capital ratio to ensure that the bank can pay its depositors.

c. Clearly, Bank A's assets greatly exceed the value of its capital. The bank has used leverage to purchase assets by borrowing from its depositors and its creditors. A bank's leverage ratio is calculated by dividing its total assets by the value of its capital. Bank A's leverage ratio is equal to $_____/$_____ = _____.

d. Now suppose that some of Bank A's securities were bonds whose value was linked to risky (subprime) mortgages. When some homeowners could not pay their monthly mortgage payment, the value of these bonds fell. Suppose the value of Bank A's securities fell by $10 to $190. In this case Bank A's balance sheet would become:

Second Balance Sheet for Bank A

Assets		Liabilities and Owner's Equity	
Reserves	$50	Deposits	$300
Loans	$250	Debit	$180
Securities	$190	Capital (Owner's Equity)	_____

Note that the value of Bank A's other assets and liabilities remains the same. Since the total value of its assets, including its securities, falls to $_____, while its total liabilites remain equal to $_____, the value of its capital, or owner's equity, calculated as Assets minus Liabilities, will now equal $_____. (Put this number in the appropriate spot in the balance sheet.) Because of its high leverage ratio, the _____ percent reduction in the value of its securities led to a _____ percent reduction in the value of its capital. This is exactly what happened to many U.S. banks in 2008–2009.

e. Furthermore, now suppose that some of Bank A's car loans could not be repaid because the car owners lost their jobs during the recession. If the value of Bank A's loans also fell by $10, its balance sheet would be:

Third Balance Sheet for Bank A

Assets		Liabilities and Owner's Equity	
Reserves	$50	Deposits	$300
Loans	$240	Debit	$180
Securities	$190	Capital (Owner's Equity)	_____

The value of Bank A's assets have now fallen to $_____, while its total liablities remain equal to $_____. Thus, the value of its capital, or owner's equity, calculated as Assets minus Liabilities, now equals $_____. (Put this number in the balance sheet.) Consequently, Bank A is now insolvent.

f. In order to ensure that banks can pay their depositors, bank regulators require banks to maintain a minimum ratio of bank capital to assets, called capital requirements. Suppose Bank A's capital requirement was 4 percent. In the initial balance sheet, Bank A's actual ratio of capital to assets was $_____/$_____ = _____ percent, so its capital requirements were/were not met. In the second balance sheet, Bank A's actual rate of capital to assets was $_____/$_____ = _____ percent, so its capital requirements were/were not met. As in Part e, Bank A could acquire new bank capital by issuing stock to private investors or the government.

Problems

Answer the following problems on a separate sheet of paper.

1. In the simple fractional-reserve model of the banking system, how much would the money supply rise if someone received an additional $1,000 in currency and the reserve-deposit ratio were 0.10? Explain.

2. Calculate the money multiplier for the following values of the currency-deposit ratio *cr* and the reserve-deposit ratio *rr*:

   a. $cr = 0.5$; $rr = 0.25$.

   b. $rr = 1.0$; cr = any fraction. Explain this result.

3. **a.** Differentiate the formula for the money multiplier with respect to *rr*, and determine whether an increase in the reserve-deposit ratio will increase or decrease the money supply.

   b. Differentiate the formula for the money multiplier with respect to *cr*, and determine whether an increase in the currency-deposit ratio will increase or decrease the money supply.

4. According to the Baumol-Tobin model of cash management, the combined opportunity and transactions cost of holding currency is $C = FN + iY/2N$.

   a. Differentiate *C* with respect to *N*.

   b. Find the first-order condition for the optimal value of *N*, that is, N^*.

   c. Check the second-order condition to confirm that total costs are minimized at the N^* you calculated in Part b.

5. Suppose that the nominal interest rate *i* was 10 percent per year, the cost of each round-trip to and from the bank *F* was $25, and total annual expenditure *Y* was $72,000.

   a. Calculate the optimal number of withdrawals N^* according to the Baumol-Tobin model of cash management.

   b. How often would an optimizing individual go to the bank, and how much would she withdraw from the bank each trip?

   c. Calculate the average money holding.

6. Use the formula for the optimal value of *N* in the Baumol-Tobin model of cash management to show that at the optimal *N* (that is, N^*), the opportunity cost of holding money $iY/2N$ is equal to the cost of foregone trips to the bank *FN*.

7. Recall from Chapter 4 of the textbook that the elasticity of money demand with respect to the interest rate is $|(dM/di)| \times (i/M)$, and the income elasticity of money demand is $(dM/dY) \times (Y/M)$. Show that both the interest and income elasticity of money demand equal 1/2 in the Baumol-Tobin model of the transactions demand for money.

8. Re-examine State Bank's initial balance sheet in Exercise 4. If the value of its securities fell by $30 to $170, what would happen to the value of its bank capital?

9. Although most bank assets have explicit market prices, some do not. In 2009, many economists believed banks were over-valuing the assets on their balance sheets in order to maintain their capital requirements. Explain how more realistic valuations would affect the banks' actual capital ratios.

10. What is the mathematical relationship between a bank's capital ratio and the percentage by which the value of its assets could fall before the bank became insolvent?

Data Question

Locate the necessary economic data and apply them to answer the following data question. For advice on how to access the data, see the Preface, and the Economic Data on the Web section on page xi.

1. Between August 2008 and March 2009, the U.S. central bank was very worried about a recession and a possible collapse of the banking and financial system. As a result, the Fed doubled the monetary base. But during this same period, the excess reserves of the banking system skyrocketed—going up by a staggering 364 times! Find out what the Fed did to raise the monetary base so quickly. Why do you think that banks chose to hold such large amounts of excess reserves?

Questions to Think About

1. The Bank Rate is frequently below the interest rate banks receive on new loans. During these periods, why don't banks increase their profits by borrowing an infinite amount (or extremely large finite amounts) from the Bank of Canada and increasing the money supply infinitely?

2. To estimate the cost of traveling to and from the bank, the textbook multiplied the wage rate by the travel time. This method is commonly used by economists to estimate the opportunity cost of time. What is the reasoning behind this method? Under what conditions is it valid? When might it be invalid?

Answers

Chapter 1

Fill-in Questions

1. Macroeconomics; Microeconomics
2. Real GDP; recession; depression
3. unemployment
4. inflation
5. models
6. exogenous; endogenous
7. price flexibility; price stickiness
8. market-clearing

Multiple-Choice Questions

1. b   2. d   3. b   4. d   5. c

Exercises

1. **a.** 20 percent   **b.** 325 percent   **c.** −20 percent
2. **a.** $Y = 3.5$; $Y = 4.0$; $Y = 4.5$
   b. Graph 1-1

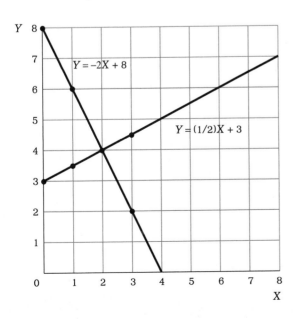

c. Slope = 1/2, or 0.5. Every time the value of X increases by 1 unit, the value of Y increases by 1/2.

d. Y intercept = 3. When $X = 0$, $Y = 3$.

e. $Y = 6$; $Y = 4$; $Y = 2$

f. See Graph 1-1.

g. Slope = -2; Y intercept = 8

h. $X = 2$ and $Y = 4$

i. By definition, the point of intersection must lie on both lines. This means that the values of X and Y at this point must satisfy both equations, that is, $Y = (1/2)X + 3$, and $Y = -2X + 8$. Consequently, at the intersection $(1/2)X + 3 = -2X + 8$.

3. a. 8; 9; 5

b. 1/8; 1/3; 1/1,000

c. $5^5 = 3{,}125 = 25 \times 125$; $6^2 = 36 = 216 \times 1/6$; $4^1 = 4 = 2 \times 2$

Problems

1. a. In a controlled experiment, researchers observe changes in two or more samples in which the only conditions that are different in the two samples are the variables whose effects are being tested. All other variables are held constant.

b. In experiments that are not controlled, it is often difficult to attribute any differences in the results from the two (or more) samples to the differences in the variables that were purposefully changed because other influencing variables may have also changed.

c. It is extremely difficult to hold constant all of the macroeconomic variables we would ideally like to hold constant. Even if it could be done, it would be very expensive and often politically impossible.

2. a. Graph for Problem 2a.

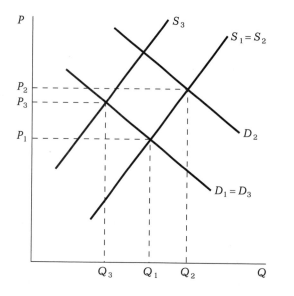

b. The demand curve for coal shifts to the right to D_2, and the supply curve does not shift. The equilibrium price of coal rises, and the equilibrium quantity of coal also rises.

c. The supply curve of coal shifts to the left to S_3, and the demand curve does not shift. The equilibrium price of coal rises and the equilibrium quantity of coal falls.

Chapter 2

Fill-in Questions

1. Nominal gross domestic product; Real gross domestic product
2. unemployment rate; labour force
3. value added
4. Okun's law
5. consumer price index; Laspeyres
6. GDP deflator; nominal gross domestic product; real gross domestic product; Paasche
7. stock; flow
8. Depreciation
9. labour-force participation rate
10. personal disposable income
11. imputed value
12. recession; unemployment rate
13. Nominal gross national product; Nominal gross domestic product
14. national income, accounting identity, consumption investment, government purchase, and net exports

Multiple-Choice Questions

1. c 2. b 3. c 4. c 5. c 6. c 7. a 8. d 9. b 10. b

11. a 12. c 13. c 14. a 15. a 16. d 17. c 18. d 19. b 20. d

21. a

Exercises

1. **a.** intermediate; intermediate; final; final
   b. $3,000 million
   c.

	Value-Added per Unit	Number of Units	Company Value-Added
Intel	$200	1 million	$200 million
Samsung	$300	1 million	$300 million
IBM	$700	1 million	$700 million
Sleeman's	$9.00	200 million	$1,800 million
Total			$3,000 million

2. **a.** Nominal GDP in 2000 = $15 billion; nominal GDP in 2010 = $40 billion
   b. $15 billion
   c. $48 billion
   d. 220 percent
   e. Real GDP in 2000 using 2010 as base year = $21 billion; real GDP in 2010 using 2010 as base year = $40 billion.
   f. 73.1 percent
   g. In 2000, computers were expensive relative to automobiles. Consequently, when 2000 is used as the base year, the dramatic increase in the quantity of computers produced between 2000 and 2010 is multiplied by a big price ($6,000), resulting in a large increase in real GDP. In 2010, however, computers were cheap relative to automobiles. Consequently, when 2010 is used as the base year, the large change in the quantity of computers produced in the period is multiplied by a relatively low price ($2,000), resulting in a much smaller increase in real GDP.

3. **a.** 140
   b. 83.3
   c. $40 billion; 0.833; $48 billion
   d. CPI: 40%; GDP deflator: −16.7%
   e. In 2000, computers comprised a small portion of the consumer market basket. Therefore, in a Laspeyres index like the CPI, the dramatic reduction in the price of computers will be outweighed by the increase in the price of automobiles. For a Paasche index like the GDP deflator, however, the weight given to computers is much greater because they comprise a much larger portion of the GDP in 2010 than in 2000. Consequently, in this index the reduction in computer prices will outweigh the increase in automobile prices.

4. **a. and b.**

Table 2-3

(1) Period	(2) Nominal GDP (PY)	(3) % Change in PY	(4) P	(5) % Change in P	(6) Y	(7) % Change in Y
1	100		1.00		100	
		5		2		3
2			1.02		103	

   c. 2; 3; 5
   d. 1.02; 103; 105.06; 105.06; 5.06
   e. 2
   f. minus; 3

5. **a.** **Table 2-4**

(1) Event	(2) Included in Canadian GNP	(3) Included in Canadian GDP
1. Blue Rodeo perform a rock concert in Vancouver	Yes	Yes
2. Blue Rodeo perform a rock concert in London (UK)	Yes	No
3. The Rolling Stones perform a concert in Vancouver	No	Yes
4. The Rolling Stones perform a concert in London (UK)	No	No
5. Toyota earns profits from its car factory in Ontario	No	Yes
6. Ford earns profits from its car factory in England	Yes	No

6. **a.** Graph 2-1

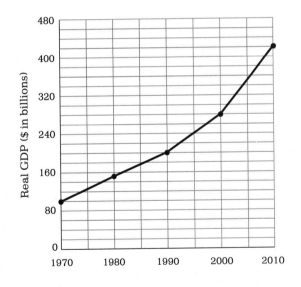

b. Graph 2-2

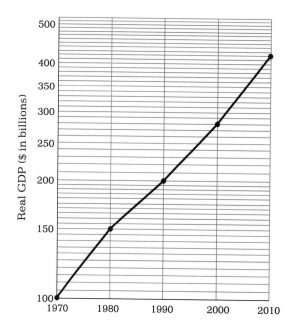

Problems

1. $560.8 billion

2. Prices are a better measure than weight of the (marginal) value that consumers place on various goods and services.

3. Education may be viewed as an investment because part of its value lies in its ability to increase a student's future production, just like a new piece of equipment. Economists sometimes refer to education as an investment in human capital.

4. There are at least two reasons why the ratios in GNP per capita may overstate the true differences in standards of living between the United States, on the one hand, and Bangladesh, Ethiopia, and Burundi, on the other. First, many researchers think that nonmarketed household production, which is usually not included in the official GDP statistics, may be larger relative to measured GDP in these three countries than in the United States. Second, the official GNP per capita measures generally use the market exchange rates to convert different currencies. These exchange rates are usually determined by the flows of tradable goods, services, and assets among countries. If the relative prices of non-tradable and tradable goods and services are not the same in all countries, this conversion will not accurately reflect differences in standards of living. Very few people, however, would deny that the standard of living in the United States is many times that in Bangladesh, Ethiopia, and Burundi.

5. **a.**   Yes. It represents consumption.
   b.   No. The purchase of a used computer from a friend does not increase GDP.
   c.   No. Although many people think of stock purchases as investment, this is not true in the national accounting sense.
   d.   Yes. It represents investment.
   e.   Yes. It represents investment.
   f.   No. Your grandmother's pension cheque is a transfer payment.
   g.   Yes. It represents a government purchase of a good.
6. Investment rises by $300,000, consumption rises by $12,000.
7. **a.**   Canadian GNP falls.
   b.   Canadian GDP remains unchanged.
8. **a.** $220,000
   b. $250,000
   c.   88

Chapter 3

Fill-in Questions

1.   Factors of production
2.   Factor prices
3.   marginal product of labour; marginal product of capital
4.   production function
5.   constant returns to scale
6.   competition; marginal product of labour; real rental price of capital
7.   real wage
8.   Accounting profit
9.   Euler's theorem; economic profit
10. Cobb-Douglas production function
11. diminishing marginal productivity
12. consumption function; marginal propensity to consume; disposable income
13. nominal interest rate; real interest rate
14. national saving
15. private saving
16. public saving; crowding out
17. loanable funds, loanable funds, loanable funds
18. Financial intermediaries

Multiple-Choice Questions

1. c	2. d	3. b	4. c	5. a	6. a	7. a
8. b	9. b	10. a	11. c	12. d	13. d	14. a
15. c	16. d	17. c	18. b	19. b	20. c	21. c

Exercises

1. **a.** Graph 3-1

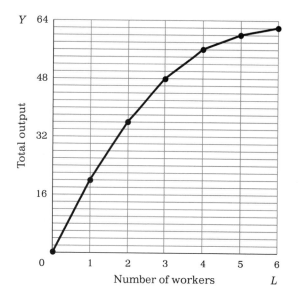

The positive slope indicates that as the number of workers employed increases, total output increases. The decreasing slope indicates that as more workers are hired, each additional worker adds less to total output.

b. Table 3-1

(1) No. of Workers (L)	(2) No. of Loaves Baked per Hour	(3) Marginal Product of Labour (MPL)	(4) Price per Loaf	(5) Price per Loaf × MPL	(6) Nominal Wage Rate (W)	(7) Real Wage Rate (W/P)
0	0				$8	8
		20	$1	$20		
1	20				$8	8
		16	$1	$16		
2	36				$8	8
		12	$1	$12		
3	48				$8	8
		8	$1	$8		
4	56				$8	8
		4	$1	$4		
5	60				$8	8
		2	$1	$2		
6	62				$8	8

c. Graph 3-2

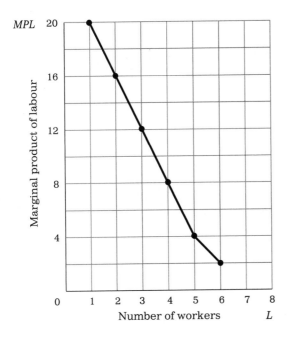

d. See Table 3-1 in Part b.

e. See Table 3-1 in Part b. The company hires four bakers.

f. Graph 3-3

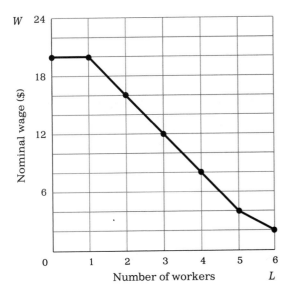

2. **a.** See Table 3-1 in the answer to Exercise 1.

b. Table 3-2

(1) No. of Workers (L)	(2) No. of Loaves Baked per Hour	(3) Marginal Product of Labour (MPL)	(4) Price per Loaf	(5) Price per Loaf × MPL	(6) Nominal Wage Rate (W)	(7) Real Wage Rate (W/P)
0	0				$16	8
		20	$2	$40		
1	20				$16	8
		16	$2	$32		
2	36				$16	8
		12	$2	$24		
3	48				$16	8
		8	$2	$16		
4	56				$16	8
		4	$2	$8		
5	60				$16	8
		2	$2	$4		
6	62				$16	8

c. Four

d. $32; right

Graph 3-4

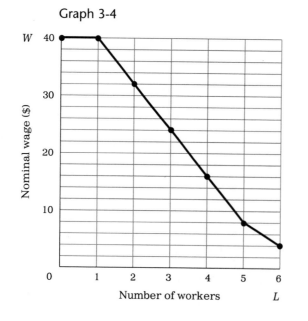

e. **Table 3-3**

(1) Nominal Wage (W)	(2) Price of Bread (P)	(3) Real Wage (W/P)	(4) Number of Bakers Hired
$20	$1	20	1
$40	$2	20	1
$16	$1	16	2
$32	$2	16	2
$12	$1	12	3
$24	$2	12	3
$ 8	$1	8	4
$16	$2	8	4
$ 4	$1	4	5
$ 8	$2	4	5

Graph 3-5

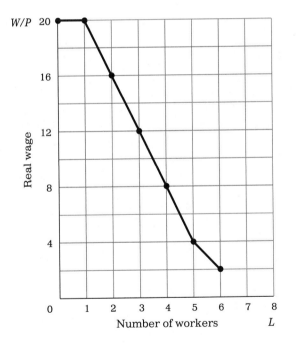

3. **a.** $Y = 50$

    b. Constant returns to scale refers to a production function in which an x percentage change in all inputs leads to the same x percentage change in output.

Table 3-4

K	L	$Y = K^{1/2}L^{1/2}$
100	25	50
200	50	100
2,500	625	1,250

doubled; increased 25-fold

   c. $MPL = 1$; equilibrium real wage $= 1$

   d. $MPK = 0.25$; equilibrium real rental price of capital $= 0.25$

   e. Step 1: 50

   Step 2: 1; 25

   Step 3: 1/2

   Step 4: 0.25; 25

   Step 5: 1/2

   Step 7: When $K = 100$ and $L = 625$, $Y = 250$, $MPL = W/P = 0.2$, $MPK = R/P = 1.25$, factor payments to labour $= 0.2(625) = 125$, factor payments to capital $= 1.25(100) = 125$, labour's share $=$ capital's share $= 1/2$.

   f. $25 + 25 = 50$

4. **a. Table 3-5**

(1) Disposable Income $(Y - T)$	(2) Consumption (C)
$ 0	125
100	200
200	275
500	500
800	725
1,000	875

b. Graph 3-6

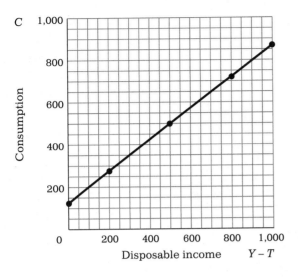

c. 125

d. 0.75; The slope is equal to the marginal propensity to consume here because it measures the change in consumption resulting from a $1 increase in disposable income.

5. a. 100; 50; –50

b. Table 3-6

(1) Net Taxes (T)	(2) Government Purchases (G)	(3) Budget Surplus	(4) Budget Deficit
200	100	100	–100
200	200	0	0
100	200	–100	100
–100	100	–200	200

6. **a.**   950

    b.   100; 100; r = 10

    c.   Graph 3-7

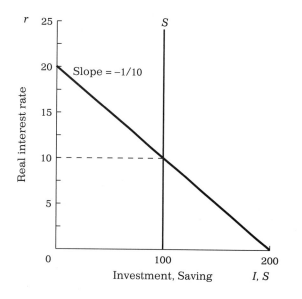

    d.   public saving = –50; private saving = 150; national saving = 100

7. **a.**   fall; 50; 50; left; 50

    Graph 3-8

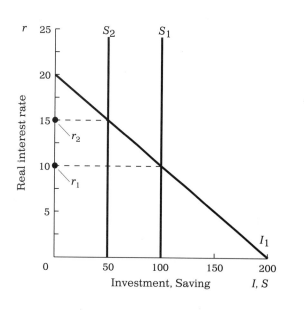

    b.   fall; 50; 50; movement along; rise; $r = 15$

    c.   decrease; increase; decrease

    d.   increase; 965; decrease; 85; left; 15; fall; 15; 85; movement along; rise

e. right

Graph 3-9

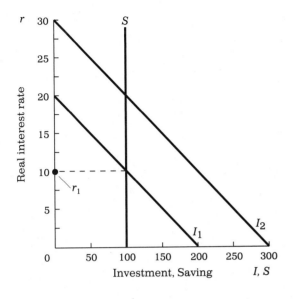

remain constant; not shift; rise; 100

f. positive; right; increase

Graph 3-10

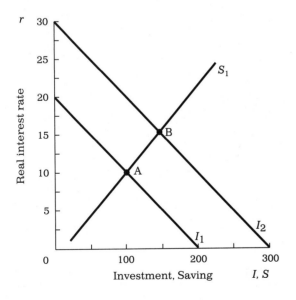

8. **a.** decrease; left

Graph 3-11

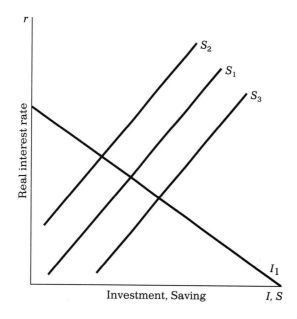

rise; fall; negative

b. increase; right; see Graph 3-11; fall; rise; negative

c. right; increase; left; decrease; positive

d. negative; positive

Problems

1. Graphs for Problem 1

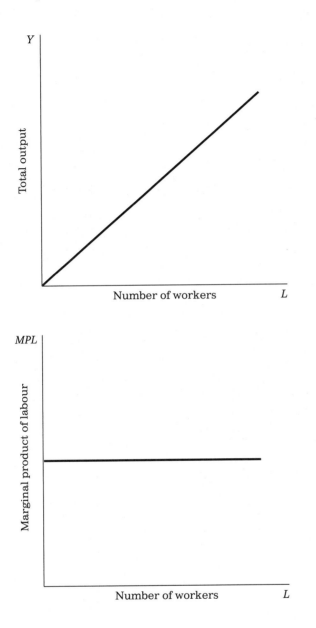

2. **a.** The profit-maximizing rule sets the real wage equal to the marginal prod-
    uct of labour. The average products of labour in British Columbia and Nova
    Scotia could be very different even if the marginal products of labour were
    equal.

    b. Once again, the average products of labour in British Columbia and Nova
    Scotia could be very different even if the marginal products of labour were
    equal. If all orchards are maximizing profits, then the *MPL* is the same in all
    orchards. Thus, the movement of a worker from Nova Scotia to British
    Columbia would reduce output in Nova Scotia by the same amount that
    output increased in British Columbia, resulting in no change in total apple
    production.

3. **a.** $Y = 960$; $Y = 1,920$; $Y = 2,880$. When all of the inputs were doubled, output doubled. When all of the inputs were tripled, output tripled. Consequently, these results illustrate the property of constant returns to scale.

   b. $MPL = 40K^{1/3}L^{-1/3} = 40(K/L)^{1/3}$

   c. $MPL = 80$; $W/P = 80$

   d. $MPK = 20K^{-2/3}L^{2/3} = 20(L/K)^{2/3}$

   e. $MPK = 5$; $R/P = 5$

   f. total real labour payments = 640;
   total real payments to capital = 320;
   labour's share = 640/960 = 2/3;
   capital's share = 320/960 = 1/3.

   g. Since $W/P = MPL$ and $R/P = MPK$, $(W/P)L = (MPL)L$ and $(R/P)K = (MPK)K$.
   $(MPL)L = 40(K/L)^{1/3}L = 40(K^{1/3}L^{2/3}) = (2/3)Y$.
   $(MPK)K = 20(L/K)^{2/3}K = 20(K^{1/3}L^{2/3}) = (1/3)Y$.

   h. $(W/P)L + (R/P)K = (MPL)L + (MPK)K = 40(K/L)^{1/3}L + 20(L/K)^{2/3}K =$
   $40(K^{1/3}L^{2/3}) + 20(K^{1/3}L^{2/3}) = 60K^{1/3}L^{2/3} = Y$.

4. **a.** The deficit would fall.

   b. Disposable income would fall by the full amount of the tax increase. Since consumption would fall by only a fraction (MPC) of this amount, private saving would also decrease. Public saving would increase by the amount of the tax increase plus the reduction in government spending. Consequently, national saving would increase.

   c. S would shift right to S_2. I would not shift. Consequently, the real interest rate would fall and investment would rise.
   Graph for Problem 4c

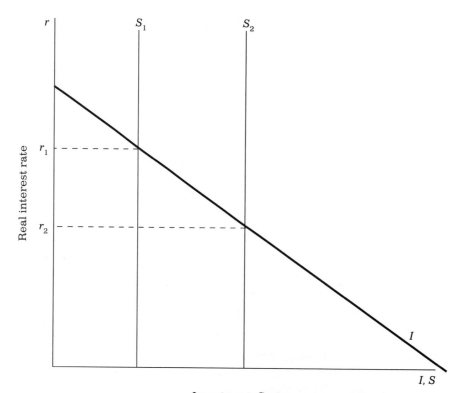

Investment, Saving

5. **a.** If both taxes and government purchases were reduced by equal amounts, the government budget surplus $T - G$, and hence public saving, would remain unchanged (at a negative value). The reduction in net taxes, however, would increase the amount of disposable income, $Y - T$, at the full employment level of GDP, Y, by the full amount of the tax cut. Consequently, the level of consumption would increase at Y by $MPC \times (\Delta T)$, since consumption rises with disposable income. Since $MPC < 1$, some of the additional disposable income will go toward increasing private saving. (Alternatively, note that $S_{PR} = (Y - T) - C$. Disposable income at Y rises by the full amount of the tax decrease while consumption rises by only a fraction of the increase.) Thus, the level of private saving would increase at Y, along with the level of national saving S. This shifts the S curve to the right below. As a result, the equilibrium level of the real interest rate would fall and investment would rise.

   b. Graph for Problem 5b

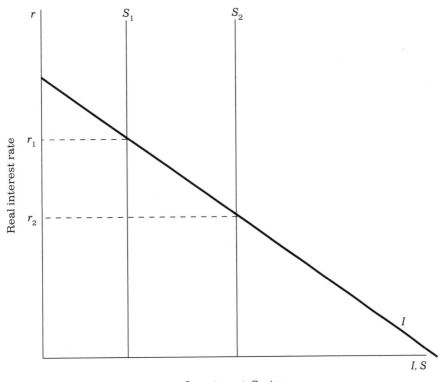

Investment, Saving

c. The increases in consumption and private saving at $\overline{Y}$ following an equal reduction in taxes and government purchases depend on the value of the marginal propensity to consume. The increase in disposable income at $\overline{Y}$ will equal the full amount of the tax reduction regardless of the value of *MPC*. If the *MPC* is large, that is, close to 1.0, the increase in consumption will be large, and the increases in private and national saving will be small. Consequently, the saving curve will shift only slightly to the right, the decline in the real interest rate will be small, and investment will rise by only a small amount. If, on the other hand, the *MPC* is small, the increase in consumption will be smaller and the increase in private saving will be larger. This will result in a large increase in national saving, a big shift to the right in the saving curve, a large decline in the real interest rate, and a big increase in investment.

6. The savings schedule shifts to the right, as in the diagram in the answer for Problem 5b, leading to higher investment.

7. The savings schedule shifts to the left, exactly opposite to what is shown in the diagram in the answer for Problem 5b, leading to an increase in the real interest rate.

Chapter 4

Fill-in Questions

1. inflation
2. hyperinflation
3. Money; store of value; unit of account; medium of exchange (last three terms in any order)
4. double coincidence of wants
5. fiat money
6. commodity money; gold standard
7. money supply; central bank; Bank of Canada
8. monetary policy; Bank of Canada or central bank; open-market operations
9. *M*1; currency; *M*2
10. quantity equation; transactions velocity of money; quantity theory
11. income velocity of money
12. real money balances
13. money demand function
14. seigniorage
15. nominal interest rate; Fisher equation; real interest rate; nominal interest rate; Fisher effect
16. *ex ante* real interest rate; *ex post* real interest rate
17. shoe-leather cost; menu cost; disincentive for saving
18. real variables; nominal variables
19. classical dichotomy; real variables; real variables; monetary neutrality

Multiple-Choice Questions

1. d	2. c	3. d	4. b	5. d	6. a	7. b
8. c	9. d	10. b	11. d	12. c	13. a	14. c
15. d	16. b	17. b	18. d	19. d	20. c	21. a

Exercises

1. a. 1.8

b. % change in M + % change in V = 4 + 1 = 5

% change in P + % change in Y = 3 + 2 = 5

2. a. 0; 3; 3

b. and c.

Table 4-2

(1)	(2)	(3) % Change in M	(4)	(5) % Change in V	(6)	(7) % Change in P	(8)	(9) % Change in Y
Period	M		V		P		Y	
1	100		2.0		1.0		200	
		3		0		0.0		3.0
2	103		2.0		1.0		206	
		−5.8		0		−8.8		3.0
3	97		2.0		0.912		212.2	
		10.3		0		7.3		3.0
4	107		2.0		0.978		218.5	

d. Period 2: $P = MV/Y = 103(2)/206 = 1.0$

Period 3: $P = 97(2)/212.2 = 0.91$

Period 4: $P = 107(2)/218.5 = 0.98$

3. a. **Table 4-3**

(1) Real Interest Rate (%)	(2) Nominal Interest Rate (%)	(3) Inflation Rate (%)
6	10	4
2	10	8
−2	10	12
4	7	3
−2	12	14
3	8	5
−2	7	9

$r + \pi$

b. 3

Table 4-4

(1) % Change in P	(2) % Change in M	(3) Inflation Rate (%)	(4) Real Interest Rate (%)	(5) Nominal Interest Rate (%)
0	3	0	3	3
1	4	1	3	4
2	5	2	3	5
−1	2	−1	3	2
5	8	5	3	8

4. a. π; $E\pi$

b.

Table 4-5

(1) Nominal Interest Rate (%)	(2) Expected Inflation (%)	(3) *Ex Ante* Real Interest Rate (%)	(4) Actual Inflation (%)	(5) *Ex Post* Real Interest Rate (%)
8	3	5	3	5
8	3	5	5	3
8	3	5	1	7
2	−1	3	1	1

c. **(i)** equal to **(ii)** lower than; lower than; borrowers; lenders **(iii)** higher than; higher than; lenders; borrowers

5. a. 21,000; 12,000; 9,000; 3; 3

b. 21,000; 18,000; 3,000; 1; 1

6. a.

Table 4-6

(1) Nominal Interest Rate i	(2) $i^{-0.1}$	(3) Real Output Y	(4) Real Money Demand $(M/P)^d$
0.12 (= 12%)	1.236	100	123.6
0.08	1.287	100	128.7
0.05	1.349	100	134.9
0.03	1.420	100	142.0
0.01	1.585	100	158.5

increases

b. Graph 4-1

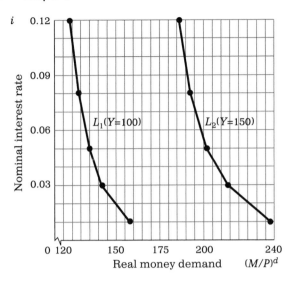

c. Table 4-7

(1) Nominal Interest Rate i	(2) $i^{-0.1}$	(3) Real Output Y	(4) Real Money Demand $(M/P)^d$
0.12 (= 12%)	1.236	150	185.4
0.08	1.287	150	193.1
0.05	1.349	150	202.4
0.03	1.420	150	213.0
0.01	1.585	150	237.8

   d. right

   e. left

7. a. 142

   b. 142

   c. 8; 128.7

   d. 1.103; an increase

8. a. **(i)** 6   **(ii)** 9; 2

   b. 6; 4; 4; 4; 0

   c. increases; stays constant; 9; 6; 6; 7; −1

   d. decrease

   e. 1,800; 1,500; 300; 20; 100; 200; 13.33

   f. 1,625.1; 1,486.4; loss; 138.7; 8.53; 100; 1,403.8; 221.3; 13.6

Problems

1. a. store of value, medium of exchange, and unit of account

   b. store of value and medium of exchange

   c. store of value

2. **a.** 6

   b. 12

   c. $n(n-1)$, where n equals the number of goods

3. Noninflationary growth in $M = 2\%$ per year

4. 3,178 australs

5. 4

6 **a.** As prices rise, the real value of the dollars people hold in their wallets falls. When the government prints new money for its use, it makes the old money in the hands of the public less valuable.

   b. It is a tax in that, solely as a result of inflation, people have to give up some real resources to maintain the same level of real money balances. It is not a tax in that people don't explicitly "pay" the government.

   c. Holders of money pay for the inflation tax.

7. **a.** $\ln(M) + \ln(V) = \ln(P) + \ln(Y)$.

   b. $dM/M + dV/V = dP/P + dY/Y$. Hence, for small percentage changes, % Change in M + % Change in V = % Change in P + % Change in Y.

   c. If V is constant, % Change in $V = 0$, and for small changes, % Change in P = % Change in M − % Change in Y. Since % Change in Y in the long run is determined by population growth, technology, and other exogenous factors, changes in the money supply lead to equal percentage changes in the price level, that is, to inflation.

8. **a.** $[d(M/P)/dY][Y/(M/P)] = 1$

   b. $[d(M/P)/di][i/(M/P)] = -0.1$

9. **a.** $3

   b. 2.0

   c. $1/1.0 = $1; $3/2.0 = $1.50

   d. ($1.50 − $1)/$1 = 50\%

Chapter 5

Fill-in Questions

1. net exports

2. Net capital outflow

3. net foreign investment; net exports; trade balance

4. small open economy

5. world interest rate

6. nominal exchange rate

7. real exchange rate; nominal exchange rate

8. purchasing-power parity

9. trade surplus; trade deficit; balanced trade

Multiple Choice Questions

1. c	**2.** a	**3.** b	**4.** d	**5.** d	**6.** c	**7.** c
8. d	**9.** d	**10.** b	**11.** a	**12.** c	**13.** b	**14.** b
15. c	**16.** c	**17.** d	**18.** c	**19.** c	**20.** b

Exercises

1. a. Table 5-1

(1)	(2)	(3)	(4)
	Purchases of Goods and Services Produced in Canada ($ in billions)	Purchases of Goods and Services Produced Elsewhere ($ in billions)	Total Purchases ($ in billions)
Group			
Canadian households	$C^d = \$310$	$C^f = \$40$	$C = \$350$
Canadian businesses	$I^d = \$\ 60$	$I^f = \$20$	$I = \$\ 80$
Canadian governments	$G^d = \$\ 90$	$G^f = \$10$	$G = \$100$
Total	$\$460$	$\$70$	$\$530$

b. 460

c. imports; 70

d. 530

e. 70; $C = 350$; $I = 80$; $G = 100$; Exports = 90; Imports = 70; $Y = 550$

f. 20

g. $C^d = 310$; $I^d = 60$; $G^d = 90$; Exports = 90; $Y = 550$

2. a. surplus; positive; positive; lend; positive; greater

b. negative; negative; borrowing

c. Table 5-2

				($ in billions)					
(1)	(2)	(3)	(4)	(5)	(6)	(7)	(8)	(9)	(10)
Case	Y	C	I	G	NX	T	Private Saving	Public Saving	National Saving
1.	5,000	3,000	700	1,000	300	900	1,100	−100	1,000
2.	5,000	3,200	900	1,000	−100	900	900	−100	800
3.	5,000	3,200	900	900	0	1,000	800	100	900

d. 300; 300; −100; −100; 0; 0

e. −100; 100

3. a. 950; 100; 150; 0; 0

b. 1,100; 150; −50; 100; 0; 0

c. Graph 5-1

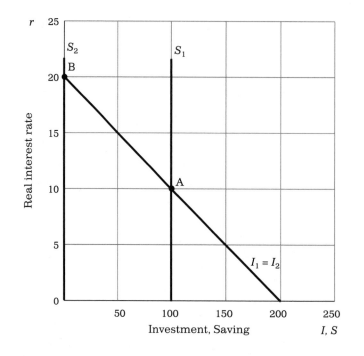

d. left; 100; not shift
e. 0; 0; 20
f. 100; −100; −100; fall; 100
g. increase; decrease; does not change; does not change; down; deficit
h. right; not shift

Graph 5-2

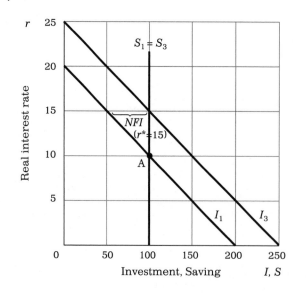

−50; −50
i. increase; decrease; 50; not change; 50; 50

4. **a.** **Table 5-3**

(1) U.S. Nominal Foreign Exchange Rate (euros per dollar)	(2) Price of IBM Computer in the U.S.	(3) Price of IBM Computer in Germany	(4) Price of Siemens Computer in Germany	(5) Price of Siemens Computer in the U.S.
1.0	$10,000	10,000 euros	15,000 euros	$15,000
1.5	$10,000	15,000 euros	15,000 euros	$10,000
2.0	$10,000	20,000 euros	15,000 euros	$7,500

b. increases; decrease

c. remains constant; decreases; increase

d. exports; imports; decrease

e. decrease

5. **a.** **Table 5-4**

(1) U.S. Nominal Foreign Exchange Rate (euros per dollar)	(2) Price of IBM Computer in the U.S.	(3) Price of IBM Computer in Germany	(4) Price of Siemens Computer in Germany	(5) Price of Siemens Computer in the U.S.
1.5	$10,000	15,000 euros	15,000 euros	$10,000
1.5	$12,000	18,000 euros	15,000 euros	$10,000

b. equal to; greater than; decrease

c. **Table 5-5**

(1) U.S. Nominal Foreign Exchange Rate (euros per dollar)	(2) Price of IBM Computer in the U.S.	(3) Price of IBM Computer in Germany	(4) Price of Siemens Computer in Germany	(5) Price of Siemens Computer in the U.S.
1.50	$10,000	15,000 euros	15,000 euros	$10,000
1.25	$12,000	15,000 euros	15,000 euros	$12,000

20; 20; remain equal to; not change

d. 0.67; 1.0; 1.0; 1.2; 1.33

e. decrease; increase; decrease; increases; increases; decreases

6. **a.** decreases

 b. Graph 5-3

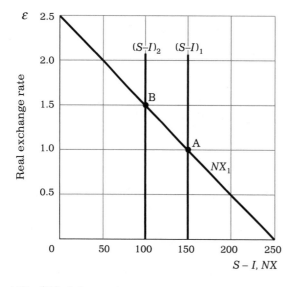

 c. 150; 150; 1.0

 d. decrease; 50; remains the same; decrease; 50; 100; left; 50; decrease; borrowing; decrease; 50; 100; 1.5; increase

 e. Graph 5-4

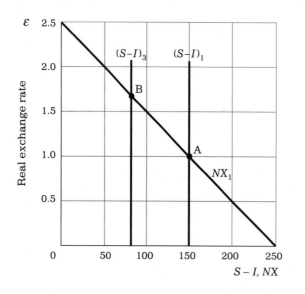

 increase; decrease; increase; decrease; left; decrease; decrease; rise

7. **a.** % Change in $\varepsilon + \pi^* - \pi$; decrease; depreciate; increase; appreciates

 b. 20; 100; 5

 c. 40; 100; fall; 2.5

 d. 200; increase; 10

e. **Table 5-7**

(1) Long-Run Nominal Foreign Exchange Rate (zlotys per dollar)	(2) Canadian Price Level	(3) Polish Price Level	(4) Long-Run Real Foreign Exchange Rate
5.0	20	100	1.0
2.5	40	100	1.0
10.0	20	200	1.0

1.0; horizontal

f.   1.0; 0; $\pi^* - \pi$; all

Problems

1. a.   U.S. investment would be low relative to our trading partners because relatively low U.S. saving would lead to a relatively high U.S. real interest rate, which would dampen U.S. investment.

   b.   Net capital outflow has been negative; the United States has had a trade deficit.

2. a.   Under purchasing-power parity, the nominal exchange rate between any two countries can take on any value.

   b.   It implies that the real exchange rate between any two countries will always equal 1.0.

   c.   Purchasing-power parity implies that almost all goods are freely and easily tradeable among countries. Consequently, if the real exchange rate deviates from 1.0, all consumers will prefer to buy all commodities from one country and none from the other. This, of course, cannot occur. If the real exchange rate cannot deviate from 1.0, the answer to Part a follows directly from the definition of the real exchange rate $\varepsilon = eP/P^*$.

3. a.   According to purchasing-power parity, the long-run real foreign exchange rate will eventually approach 1.0 and stay there. In the long run, according to the classical dichotomy, it is unaffected by nominal variables, such as the growth of the money supply.

   b.   According to the Quantity Theory, velocity is constant in the long run and the long-run rate of inflation is equal to the growth of the money supply minus the long-run growth rate of real output (real GDP). Thus, a reduction in the growth rate of the money supply would reduce the rate of inflation in Canada below that prevailing abroad. The real foreign exchange rate can be written as:

$$\varepsilon = e(P/P^*).$$

   The percentage change in the *nominal* foreign exchange rate can be written as:

$$\%\Delta e = \%\Delta\varepsilon + \%\Delta P^* - \%\Delta P.$$

According to purchasing-power parity, in the long run $\%\Delta\varepsilon = 0$. Thus, if foreign inflation exceeds domestic inflation, the nominal Canadian foreign exchange rate will increase.

4. **a.** According to the quantity equation, $MV = PY$.

Taking percentage changes of both sides yields

% Change in M + % Change in V = % Change in P + % Change in Y.

If the money supply grows at 3 percent per year, velocity remains constant, and real GDP grows at 3 percent per year in the long run, then

3% = % Change in P + 3%, or

$\pi = 0\%$.

If money supply growth rises to 10 percent per year, $\pi = 10\% - 3\% = 7\%$, that is, it rises by 7 percent (points) per year.

b. According to the classical dichotomy, real variables, like the real interest rate, are not affected by nominal variables, like the money supply, in the long run. Instead, the real interest rate is typically determined by investment and saving. Consequently, the real interest rate would remain unchanged.

c. Recall $i = r + \pi$. Because r remains constant in the long run and inflation rises by 7 percentage points, the nominal interest rate will also rise by 7 percentage points.

d. Following the classical dichotomy, the real exchange rate will remain unchanged in the long run. This is also true if purchasing-power parity prevails.

e. Because $\varepsilon = e\,(P/P^*)$,

% Change in ε = 0 = % Change in e + % Change in P – % Change in P^*, or

% Change in e = % Change in P^* – % Change in P.

If foreign inflation is unaffected and Canadian inflation rises by 7 percentage points per year, the Canadian nominal exchange rate will fall by 7 percentage points per year.

f. Because investment is a function of the real interest rate, which is unchanged, investment will also be unchanged.

g. In the long run, real GDP is a function solely of technology and the amount of factor inputs, such as labour and capital. Because these are unchanged, real GDP will not be affected by the increase in money growth in the long run.

5. **a.** $\varepsilon = e\,(P/P^*) = 6.83\ \text{yuan}/\$1 \times (\$4.09/\text{Big Mac})/(12.50\ \text{yuan}/\text{Big Mac}) = 2.23$.

b. **i.** According to purchasing-power parity, the real exchange rate will eventually be 1.0. At any other real exchange rate, trade would theoretically go in only one direction.

ii. Recall $\varepsilon = e\,(P/P^*)$. Thus if $\varepsilon = 1.0$,

1.0 = e ($4.09/Big Mac)/(12.5 yuan/Big Mac)

e = 12.5 yuan/$4.09 = 3.06 yuan per dollar

6. a. In Germany net capital outflow would decrease, the German trade surplus would decrease, and the German foreign exchange rate would increase.

b. As German government spending increases, German saving would decrease, thereby decreasing net capital outflow and the German trade surplus even more, and increasing the German foreign exchange rate further.

7. a. In the long run, the tax increase will decrease disposable income by ΔT. Consumption will fall by $MPC (\Delta T)$. Private saving will fall by $(1 - MPC) \Delta T$. Public saving $T - G$ will rise by the increase in taxes plus the reduction in government spending. Thus, national saving will rise by the reduction in government spending plus MPC times the increase in taxes.

b. Graph for Problem 7b.

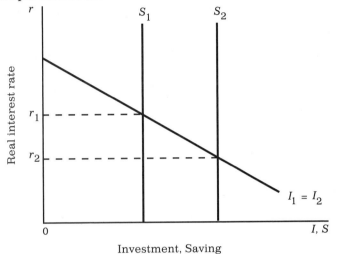

The increase in T and reduction in G would both shift the national saving curve to the right, from S_1 to S_2. In a closed economy $I = S$. Because the investment curve would not shift, the real interest rate would fall and the level of investment would rise.

c. Graph for Problem 7c.

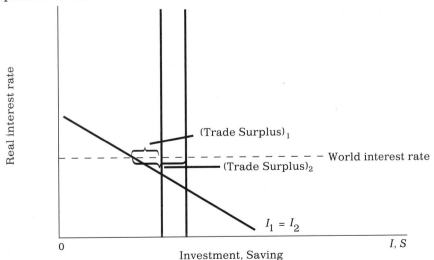

d. See graph for Part b.

In a small open economy, the real interest rate is unaffected by saving and investment decisions within the country. Although national saving will still increase, leading to the same shift in S to S_2, as in Part b, the real interest rate and the level of investment will remain constant. Consequently, $S - I$ will rise (or $I - S$ will fall) and the trade surplus will rise.

e. In the following graph, the $S - I$ curve shifts to the right following an increase in S. Consequently, the real exchange rate would fall, thereby increasing the quantity of net exports.

Graph for Problem 7e.

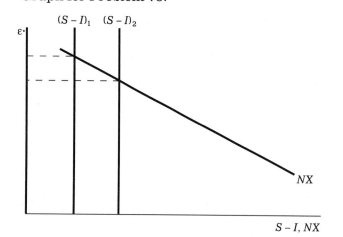

f. The longer-run effects of deficit reduction involve a shift back to the left of the $(S - I)$ line in the previous graph—as explained in the discussion of Figure 5-17 on page 169 of the text.

8. In a closed economy, saving and investment are equal. Consequently, investment will be low in a country with low saving and high in a country with high saving. In a small open economy, the levels of saving and investment are theoretically independent because a country can borrow unlimited amounts from abroad to finance any gaps between investment and saving at the world real interest rate.

9. Assume that the tax policy stimulates domestic investment. Initially, as a result, $(S-I)$ falls. Equilibrium requires that net exports fall as well, and this requires a rise in the real exchange rate. But this is not the end of the story. Consider the foreign debt accumulation equation:

$$\Delta Z = rZ - NX.$$

With no change in the world interest rate, and no change (yet) in accumulated debt, Z, the fall in NX forces ΔZ to become positive. This means that the level of foreign debt begins to rise. In the new full equilibrium, the product rZ is, therefore, higher. Since $rZ = NX$ in the new steady state, NX will be higher as well. So NX will be higher in the new full equilibrium (than it was before the government policy was initiated). Overall, then, the real exchange rate first rises, then falls to below its initial starting value.

10. a. The U.S. tax cuts and increased defense spending decreased world saving and, thereby, increased the world real interest rate.

   i. as r^* increases, investment in Europe and Japan falls.

   ii. Since national saving in Europe and Japan remains constant, as investment falls, $S - I$ increases, and European and Japanese net capital outflow rises.

   iii. Recall that $S - I - NX$. As European and Japanese net capital outflow increases, their trade surpluses NX increase (or their trade deficits decrease).

   iv. For their trade surpluses to increase, the real exchange rates in Europe and Japan must decrease.

11. Recall $\varepsilon = e\,(P/P^*)$

   Thus, % change in ε = % changed in e + % change in P – % change in P^*.
   Since both Germany and France use the euro, % change in e = 0. Thus,
   % change in ε = % change in P – % change in P^*.
   The French real exchange rate relative to Germany has risen because French inflation (that is, % change in P) has exceeded German inflation (% change in P^*)

12. a. and b. The increased demand for Chilean wine will shift its NX curve to the right. Since neither S, I, nor $(S - I)$ has changed, this would merely result in an increase in Chile's real exchange rate and no change in Chile's trade surplus.

Graph for Problem 13a and b

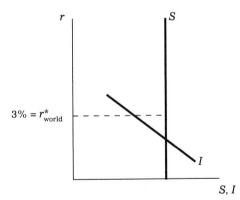

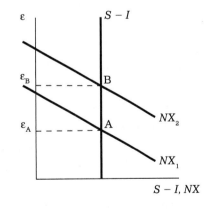

c. To keep Chile's real exchange rate unchanged the government could increase national saving by increasing taxes. The real interest rate would remain unchanged at the world real interest rate and Chilean investment would not change. Consequently, net capital outflow = $S - I$ would increase along with the trade surplus.

Graph for Problem 13c

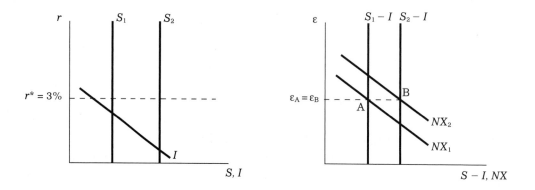

13. a. Since purchasing-power parity (PPP) holds at every moment in the past, present, and future, the real exchange rate will always equal 1.0, and will not change.

b. If the expected real interest rates are equal, the difference in nominal interest rates must reflect differences in expected future inflation rates of $3.5 - 2 = 1.5$ percentage points. Thus, U.S. inflation was expected to exceed Swiss inflation by 1.5 percentage points per year.

c. Recall $\varepsilon = e\,(P/P^*)$.

Thus, % change in ε = % change in e + % change in P − % change in P^* and % change in e = % change in ε + % change in P^* − % change in P.

If PPP holds and the real exchange rate always equals 1.0, % change in $\varepsilon = 0\%$. From Part b we know % change in P^* − % change in $P = -1.5\%$.

Thus, the U.S. nominal exchange rate was expected to fall by 1.5 percent per year.

Chapter 6

Fill-in Questions

1. labour force
2. steady state; unemployment rate; natural rate of unemployment
3. frictional unemployment; sectoral shift; frictional unemployment; employment insurance
4. Wage rigidity; structural unemployment
5. insiders; outsiders
6. Efficiency wage; wage rigidity
7. discouraged workers

Multiple-Choice Questions

1. b   2. a   3. d   4. c   5. b   6. d   7. b

8. d   9. d   10. d   11. d   12. c   13. b

Exercises

1. a. **(i)** 46   **(ii)** 46   **(iii)** 46; 46; 200; 46; 46; 2,300   **(iv)** Because the flows into and out of unemployment are equal, and the unemployment rate is constant from one period to the next.

   b. 8 percent

   c. $s/(s + f) = 0.02/(0.02 + 0.23) = 0.08 = 8$ percent

2. a. **(i)** 40   **(ii)** 69   **(iii)** 229; 2,271   **(iv)** 9.16

   b. **(i)** 46   **(ii)** 68   **(iii)** 229; 46; 68; 251; 2,271; 46; 68; 2,249   **(iv)** 10.04

   c. 13.0%

3. a. Male $u = 2.5\%$; Total $u = 5\%$.

   b. Women had a looser attachment to the labour force, moving in and out more frequently. Women also worked at lower-paying jobs, with higher job turnover and higher unemployment rates. Women may have also suffered from sex discrimination.

   c. Female $u = 10\%$; Male $u = 2.5\%$; Total $u = 5.5\%$.

   d. The unemployment rates for both sexes remained constant.

   e. The total unemployment rate increased.

   f. This occurs when the relative size of the groups (and, hence, their relative weights in the total labour force) change.

   g. cannot

   h. decrease

Problems

1. a. By allowing unemployed people to search longer before accepting a job and by cushioning the loss of income from unemployment, employment insurance reduces the probability of finding a job. Because employees and firms know that people who are laid off will receive employment-insurance benefits, firms' reluctance to lay off workers may be reduced, thereby increasing the probability of being separated from a job.

   b. i. By giving income to those who have recently experienced a sharp decline in their income and by easing the emotional pain of unemployment.

      ii. By allowing unemployed workers to wait until they find a job that fully utilizes their skills.

2. a. If the demand for low-wage workers is inelastic, total wage income accruing to low-wage workers will increase following an increase in the minimum wage; if demand is elastic, it will fall.

   b. Policymakers are more likely to support higher minimum wages if demand for low-wage workers is very inelastic because the reduction in employment would be small, and the increase in income accruing to low-wage workers would be large.

    c.   Teenagers are less likely to be the primary wage earners in the family, and they "pay" for some kinds of on-the-job training by accepting low wages now for high wages after they are trained.

    d. **i.** If employers respond to the subminimum wages by firing adults and hiring teenagers, adult employment could fall.

        ii. If adults and teenagers are complements, a reduction in the price of teenage labour via the subminimum wage for teenagers would increase the demand for adult workers. If adults and teenagers are substitutes, a reduction in the price of teenage labour would decrease the demand for adult workers.

4. **a.** $du/df = -s/(s + f)^2 < 0$. As f increases, u decreases.

    b. $du/ds = f/(s + f)^2 > 0$. As s increases, u increases. As a greater percentage of those employed lose their jobs, the unemployment rate increases.

5. As we shall see in later chapters, the natural rate of unemployment is the rate toward which we should aim when using macroeconomic stabilization policies. It is also the rate toward which the economy is heading in the long run.

6. Case I: When both employment earnings and EI receipts are taxed, the key equations are $w(1 - a)(1 - t) = b$ and $b = (1 - u)w(1 - t) + cw(1 - t)$. These equations lead to $u = a/(1 - c)$. Case II: when just EI receipts are taxed, the key equations are $w(1 - a) = b$ and $b = (1 - u)w + cw(1 - t)$. These equations lead to $u = a/(1 - c(1 - t))$. This unemployment rate must be smaller, since both c and t are positive fractions. Using the suggested parameters values, shifting from Case I to Case II lowers the natural unemployment rate from 6% to 5.5%.

7. Unions may increase the natural rate of unemployment if nonunion employers raise their wages to prevent their workers from joining a union.

Chapter 7

Fill-in Questions

1.   Solow growth model
2.   steady state
3.   level effect
4.   growth effect
5.   Golden Rule level of accumulation

Multiple-Choice Questions

1. a	2. d	3. c	4. b	5. b	6. d	7. c
8. a	9. a	10. b	11. a	12. b	13. d	14. a
15. c	16. b	17. c	18. b	19. a	20. b	21. c
22. d	23. b					

Exercises

1. **a.** doubles

   b. –1/2; 1/2; 1/2

   c. **Table 7-1**

(1) Capital per Worker k	(2) Output per Worker $y = k^{1/2}$	(3) Consumption per Worker c	(4) Investment per Worker i	(5) Depreciation per Worker δk	(6) Change in Capital per Worker Δk
0	0	0	0	0	0
4	2.0	1.6	0.4	0.2	0.2
12	3.464	2.771	0.693	0.6	0.093
16	4.0	3.2	0.8	0.8	0.0
20	4.472	3.578	0.894	1.0	–0.106
36	6.0	4.8	1.2	1.8	–0.6

   d. Graph 7-1

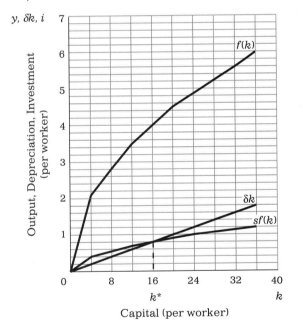

   Capital (per worker)

   marginal product of capital

   e. 20; 0.8; 80; see Table 7-1

   f. sy; 0.2; see Table 7-1 and Graph 7-1

   g. 20; 0.05; see Table 7-1 and Graph 7-1

   h. 0.05; $0.2(k)^{1/2}$; $0.05k$; see Table 7-1

   i. 0; 16; 4; 3.2; 0.8; less than; falls; greater than; rises

   j. 16

   k. upward; greater than; rise; rise; increase; higher; remain constant; have no effect on; lower; have no effect on

2. a.

Table 7-2

(1) Year	(2) Capital per Worker k	(3) Output per Worker y	(4) Consumption per Worker c	(5) Investment per Worker i	(6) Depreciation per Worker δk	(7) Change in k Δk
1	25	5	4	1.0	1.25	−0.25
2	24.75	4.975	3.980	0.995	1.238	−0.243
3	24.507	4.950	3.960	0.990	1.225	−0.235
•						
•						
•						
30	20.063	4.479	3.583	0.896	1.003	−0.107
31	19.956	4.467	3.574	0.893	0.998	−0.105
•						
•						
•						
100	16.6657	4.081	3.265	0.816	0.833	−0.017
101	16.640	4.079	3.263	0.816	0.832	−0.016
•						
•						
•						
∞	16.000	4.0	3.2	0.8	0.8	0.0

    b.   25; 0.25; 24.75

    c. and **d.** see Table 7-2

    e.   0

    f.   16

3. **a.**   increases; 1/2

    b.   0.05

Table 7-3

(1) Capital per Worker k^*	(2) Output per Worker $f(k^*) = k^{*1/2}$	(3) Depreciation per Worker δk^*	(4) Consumption per Worker $c^* = f(k^*) - \delta k^*$	(5) Saving per Worker $sf(k^*)$
0	0	0	0	0
4	2.0	0.2	1.8	1.0
16	4.0	0.8	3.2	2.0
36	6.0	1.8	4.2	3.0
64	8.0	3.2	4.8	4.0
100	10.0	5.0	5.0	5.0
121	11.0	6.05	4.95	5.5
144	12.0	7.2	4.8	6.0

c. Graph 7-2

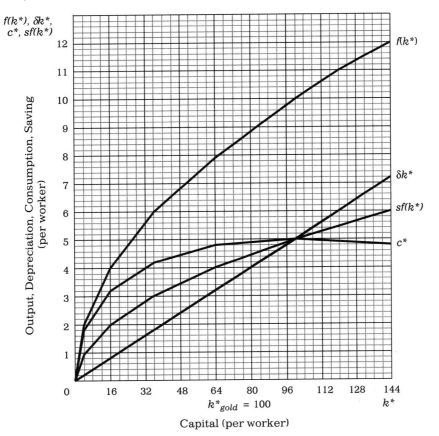

100; 100

d. 5; 10; 0.5; increase

e. higher; higher; greater; less

f. 0.05; greater; increases; less; decreases; greater; 0.05; 0.05

g. 0.05; 100; 100; 10; 101; 10.0499; 0.0499

h. 0.5; equal to

i. up; high; down; low

4. a. 0.5; 100; 10; 5

b. 16; 4; 4; 3.2; increase

c. 3.2; 5

d. 2; fall

e. decrease; 0.8; 2; 0.8; 2; 0.8; 17.2; 4.15; 4.15; 2.075

f. fall; increase; rise

g. increase; greater; fall

h. 400; 20; 20; 0; 10; higher; lower; increase; fall

i. rise; fall; higher

5. a. 2; −2; 2; 2

b. **Table 7-4**

(1) Capital per Worker k	(2) Output per Worker $f(k) = k^{1/2}$	(3) Investment per Worker $sf(k)$	(4) Break-even Investment per Worker $(\delta + n)k$	(5) Change in Capital per Worker $sf(k) - (\delta + n)k$
0	0	0	0	0
4	2.0	0.4	0.28	0.12
8	2.828	0.566	0.56	0.006
16	4.0	0.8	1.12	−0.32
36	6.0	1.2	2.52	−1.32

c.   Graph 7-3

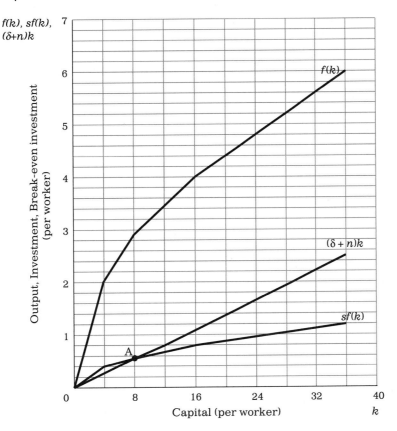

d.   0; $(\delta + n)k$; 8.16

e.   shift up; not shift; decrease; lower; lower

f.   0.07; δ; n; increases; decreases; decrease

Problems

1. $k = 256$; $y = 40$; $c = 34.88$; saving per worker $= i = 5.12$; $\delta k = 5.12$.

2. **a.** $sf(k) = (\delta + n)k$

    b.   consumption per worker

    c. $MPK = \delta + n$

3. **a.**   An increase in the saving rate would shift the $sf(k)$ curve up and increase the steady-state level of capital per worker.

Graph for Problem 3a

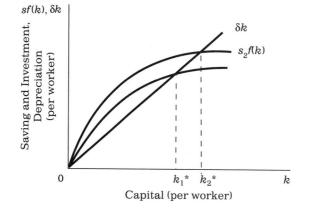

b. Since k^* rises, the steady-state level of output per worker will also rise.

c. In the new steady state, the amount of capital per worker will remain constant, so the amount of output per worker will also remain constant.

d. The Golden Rule level of capital per worker is independent of the saving rate (although only one saving rate will move the economy to the Golden Rule level), so it will not change.

e. In the initial steady state, the rate of growth of output per worker is zero. Since the level of output per worker is higher in the final steady state, the rate of growth of output per worker will increase during the transition to the final steady state.

4. a. Graph for Problem 4a

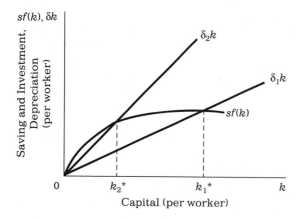

The steady-state level of capital per worker falls.

b. The Golden Rule level of capital per worker falls because as δ rises, *MPK* must also rise, and this requires a reduction in k^*_{gold}. Alternatively, at the old Golden Rule level, too much output must now be devoted to replacing the existing capital stock.

5. a. If the saving rate fell, the *sf(k)* curve would shift down. By itself, this reduction in *s* would lower the steady-state level of capital per worker k^*. In addi-

tion, however, the reduction in the rate of depreciation δ will reduce the slope of the δk line. By itself, this reduction in δ would increase k^*. When the two changes occur simultaneously, however, the net effect on k^* is ambiguous. It could fall, rise, or stay the same. In the following diagram, k^* could fall to k_2^* or rise to k_3^*.

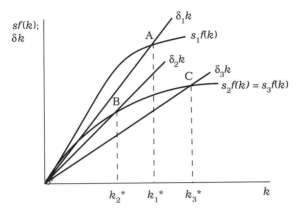

Graph for Problem 5a

b. At the initial Golden Rule level of capital accumulation k^*_{gold1} the marginal product of capital, which is the slope of the production function $f(k)$, is equal to the rate of depreciation δ. When δ falls, therefore, the *MPK* at the new k^*_{gold} must also be lower. Given the shape of the $f(k)$ curve, this must occur to the right of the initial equilibrium, and k^*_{gold} must rise. (Note that the shape of $f(k)$ is unaffected when the saving rate falls.)

Graph for Problem 5b

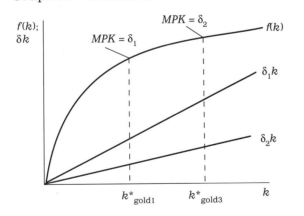

6. In Chapter 3, $MPK = dY/dK$. In Chapter 7, $y = Y/L = f(k)$, where $k = K/L$. Thus, $Y = Lf(k)$. Using the chain rule, $dY/dK = Ldf(k)/dK = Lf'(k)(L/L^2) = f'(k)$.

7. a. When $d(c)/dk = 0$, $f'(k) = δ = 0.02$. This occurs when $2.5(k)^{-3/4} = 0.02$, or when $k^*_{gold} = 625$.

b. $y = 50$; $δk = i = 12.5$; $s = 0.25$; $c = 37.5$

8. $dk = d(K/L) = (LdK − KdL)/L^2 = dK/L − (dL/L)(K/L)$. Since $dK/L = i − δk$ and $dL/L = n$, $dk = i − δk − nk$.

9. **a.** The saving rate must rise.

   b. In the short run, consumption per worker will fall; in the long run, it will rise.

   c. tax incentives to save, increases in the interest rate, or a tax on consumption

10. On the path to the new steady state, the rate of growth of k will rise, the rate of growth of output per worker will rise, and the rate of growth of total output may rise or fall. At the new steady state, the rates of growth of k and output per worker will be the same as they were initially, and the rate of growth of total output will be lower.

11. **a.** Total output is a function of the amounts of capital and labour. If the capital stock is unaffected and the number of workers falls by half, total output will also fall (but by less than half).

   b. Output per worker is a function of the amount of capital per worker k. Since the capital stock is unaffected and the number of workers falls by half, k will double, thereby increasing the amount of output per worker.

   c. Graph for Problem 11c

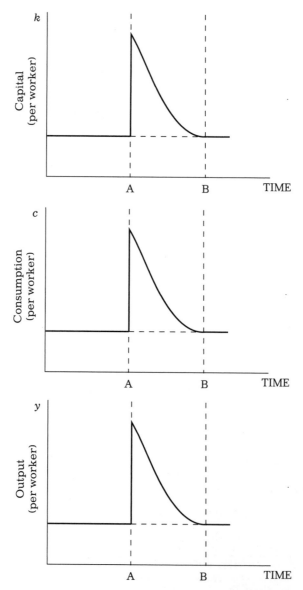

Chapter 8

Fill-in Questions

1. labour-augmenting technological progress; efficiency of labour
2. efficiency of labour
3. effective workers; efficiency of labour
4. labour-augmenting technological progress
5. Human capital
6. labour-augmenting technological progress; human capital
7. technological externality
8. endogenous growth theory

Multiple-Choice Questions

1.	a	2.	c	3.	a	4.	b	5.	a	6.	c	7.	d	8.	d
9.	d	10.	a	11.	a	12.	d	13.	b	14.	b	15.	a	16.	a
17.	d	18.	c	19.	d	20.	c								

Exercises

1. **a.** n; g
   b. 0; 1; −1; 1; 1
   c. Table 8-1

Table 8-1

(1) Capital per Effective Worker k	(2) Output per Effective Worker $f(k) = k^{1/2}$	(3) Investment per Effective Worker $sf(k)$	(4) Break-even Investment per Effective Worker $(\delta + n + g)k$	(5) Change in Capital per Effective Worker $sf(k) - (\delta + n + g)k$
0	0	0	0	0
4	2.0	0.4	0.32	0.08
6	2.45	0.49	0.48	0.01
8	2.83	0.57	0.64	−0.07
16	4.0	0.8	1.28	−0.48
36	6.0	1.2	2.88	−1.68

d. Graph 8-1

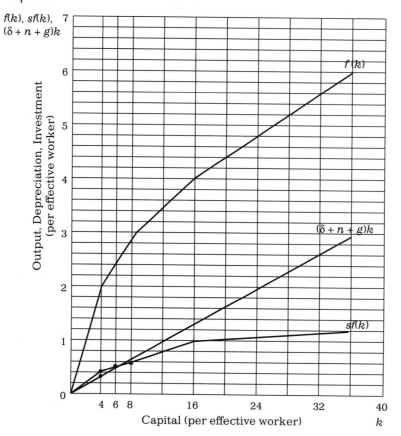

e. 0; $(\delta + n + g)k$; 6.25

f. g; technological change

g. n; g

2. **a.** $\delta + n + g$; δ; n; g

b. n; g

c. decreases; increase; increasing

d. decreasing; decreasing

3. **a.** Y/K

b. % Change in K; $\Delta Y/Y$; $\Delta K/K$

c. sY/K; δ

d. A

e. sA; δ

4.   **a.**   0.9; 4; 0.9; 8; 2; 7.59

   b.   0.1; 0.1, 10

   c.   14.4; 28.8; 8; 15.18

   d.   doubled

   e.   double

   f.   double; constant

   g.   10; increase; increase

5.   **a.**   0.3; 0.7

   b.   % Change in $Y - 0.3 \times$ (% Change in $K) - 0.7 \times$ (% Change in L)

   c.   3.6; 1.2; 1.2; 1.2

Problems

1.   **a.** $y = f(k) = 10k^{1/4}$

   b. $k^* = 16$; $y = 20$; $c = 17.44$; saving per effective worker $= i = 2.56$; $\delta k^* = 1.6$

   c.   They all grow at $g = 2$ percent per year.

   d.   They all grow at $n + g = 6$ per year.

2. a. Graph for Problem 2a

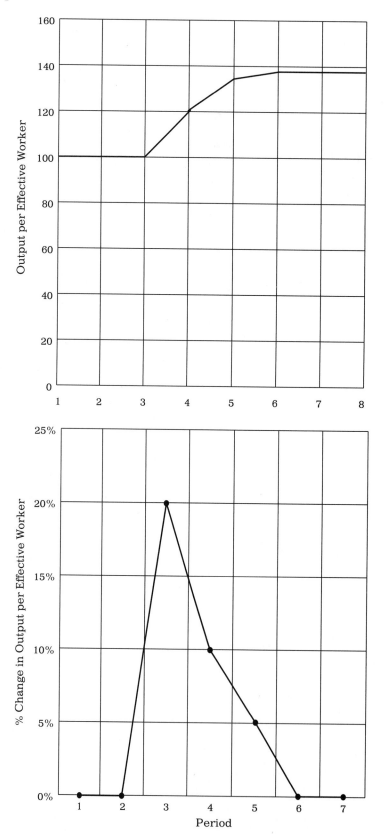

3. a. $sf(k) = (\delta + n + g)k$ In the steady state the amount of saving per effective worker equals the amount of capital per effective worker times the sum of the rates of depreciation, population growth and technological progress.

   b.   consumption per effective worker in the steady state.

   c. $MPK = \delta + n + g$

4. a. $y = f(k) = 10k^{1/4}$

   b. $k^*_{gold} = 39.0625$; $s = 0.25$

   c. $y = 25$; saving per effective worker $= i = 6.25$; $c = 18.75$

5. a. $y = f(k) = 10k^{1/4}$

   b. $MPK = f'(k) = 2.5\,(k)^{-3/4}$

   c. $f'(k^*_{gold}) = (\delta + n + g)(k^*_{gold})$; $k^*_{gold} = 39.0625$

6. a. $dk = [(EL)dK - k(EdL + LdE)]/E^2L^2$

   $\qquad = dK/EL - (K/EL)(dL/L) - (K/EL)(dE/E)$

   Since $dK/EL = i - \delta k$, $dL/L = n$, and $dE/E = g$,

   $dk = i - \delta k - nk - gk$

7. a.   An increase in the saving rate will shift the $sf(k)$ curve up and increase the steady-state capital stock per effective worker.

   Graph for Problem 7a

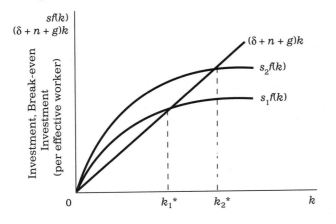

b. Graphs for Problem 7b

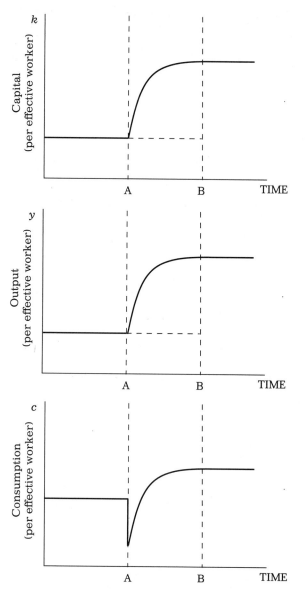

8. a. k^* will fall.

b. The growth rates of k and y will become negative.

c. They all equal zero.

d. All the growth rates rise from the old rate of technological progress to the new rate of technological progress.

9. a. $MPK - \delta = .10 - .04 = .06$; $n + g = .04 + .03 = .07$

Since $MPK - \delta < n + g$, the level of k is greater than the Golden Rule level.

b. $MPK - \delta = .09 - .05 = .04$; $n = g = .04$

Since $MPK - \delta = n + g$, the level of k is equal to the Golden Rule level.

10. a. 3 percent

b. 3.3 percent

11. In Chapter 3, $MPK = dY/dK$. In Chapter 8, $y = Y/EL = f(k)$, where $k = K/EL$. Thus, $Y = ELf(k)$. Using the chain rule, $dY/dK = ELdf(k)/dK = ELf'(k)(1/EL) = f'(k)$.

Chapter 9

Fill-in Questions

1. sticky wages and prices
2. aggregate demand
3. aggregate supply; aggregate demand

4. Stagflation
5. stabilization policy
6. supply shock; demand shock

Multiple-Choice Questions

1. c   **2.** d   **3.** c   **4.** b   **5.** a   **6.** d   **7.** b

8. b   **9.** a   **10.** c   **11.** c

Exercises

1. a. Table 9-1

(1)	(2)	(3)	(4)	(5)
M	V	PY	P	Y
1,000	2.0	2,000	2.0	1,000
1,000	2.0	2,000	1.5	1,333
1,000	2.0	2,000	1.0	2,000
1,000	2.0	2,000	0.8	2,500
1,000	2.0	2,000	0.5	4,000

b. Graph 9-1

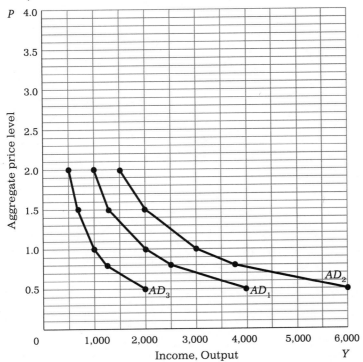

    c.   rises

    d.   1,500; 2,000; 3,000; 3,750; 6,000

    f.   the same; increase; right

    g.   500; 667; 1,000; 1,250; 2,000

    i.   the same; decrease; left

2. **a.** and **b.** 2,000

    Graph 9-2

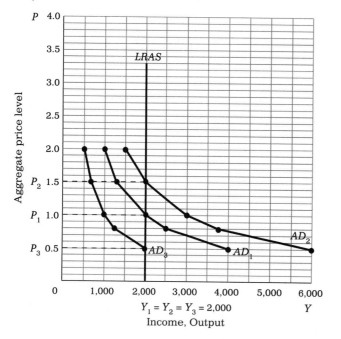

    c.   right

    d.   vertical; increase; not change; increase; 1.5

    e.   left

    f.   decrease; decrease; not change

3. **a.** 2,000

Graph 9-3

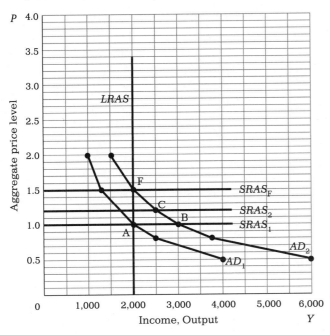

b. sticky

d. right

e. increase; not change; 3,000; 1.0

f. exceeds; increase; 2,500; 1.2

g. exceeds; increase; shift upward; 2,000; 1.5

h. decrease; not change; decrease; less than; downward; 2,000; decreased

i. output; the price level

4. **a.** upward

Graph 9-4

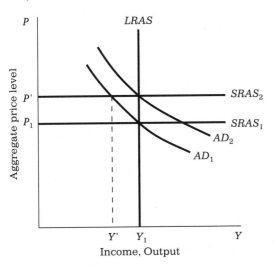

b. decrease; increase; stagflation
c. increase; right
d. higher; higher
e. decrease; lower; higher

Problems

1. a. The reduction in the money supply would shift the aggregate demand curve to the left (from AD_1 to AD_2) in the short run. Output would decrease, while the aggregate price level would remain constant as the economy moved from point A to point B.
        Graph for Problem 1a

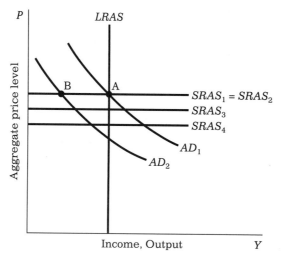

b. If there were no further reductions in the money supply, the aggregate demand curve would not shift any further. Over time, however, the short-run aggregate supply curve would shift down (to $SRAS_3$, $SRAS_4$, etc.). Output would rise toward its natural rate and the price level would fall.

c. The long-run aggregate supply curve is vertical. Hence, the contractionary monetary policy would have no effect on output in the long run. It would, however, reduce the long-run price level.

2. $MdV + VdM = PdY + YdP$. Along a stationary aggregate demand curve, $dV = dM = 0$, so $YdP = -PdY$, or $dP/dY = -P/Y < 0$.

3. Those economists who believe that sticky wages and prices make the movement to the natural rate a long drawn-out process generally believe that stabilization policies have an important role to play so that the economy need not languish for long periods of time below full employment. Those economists who believe that prices and wages are sufficiently flexible to move the economy to its natural rate rapidly are less enthusiastic about the use of stabilization policy for several reasons: the policy effects and their timing are often unpredictable, policymakers may not act in the best interest of the economy, and the public's expectations of policy changes may mitigate their efficacy.

5. **a.** If velocity is stable, the Bank of Canada can easily ascertain the shape and position of the aggregate demand curve. Once the Bank of Canada located the position of the new short-run aggregate supply curve, it could implement the appropriate policy change to shift the aggregate demand curve and keep output stable.

    b. If velocity is unstable and unpredictable, it will be difficult for the Bank of Canada to ascertain the exact shape and position of the aggregate demand curve. Consequently, it would be difficult to determine the required change in the money supply even if the new short-run aggregate supply curve can be located precisely.

Chapter 10

Fill-in Questions
1. Actual expenditure; Planned expenditure
2. Keynesian cross
3. Keynesian cross; multiplier
4. *IS* curve
5. *LM* curve
6. *IS* curve; *LM* curve
7. liquidity preference theory

Multiple-Choice Questions

1. a	2. b	3. d	4. a	5. d	6. d	7. c
8. c	9. d	10. c	11. b	12. c	13. b	14. d
15. a	16. d	17. b	18. d			

Exercises
1. **a.** the amount by which consumption increases when disposable income increases by $1; 0.75; 125; 0.75

    b. 50; 0.75

Graph 10-1

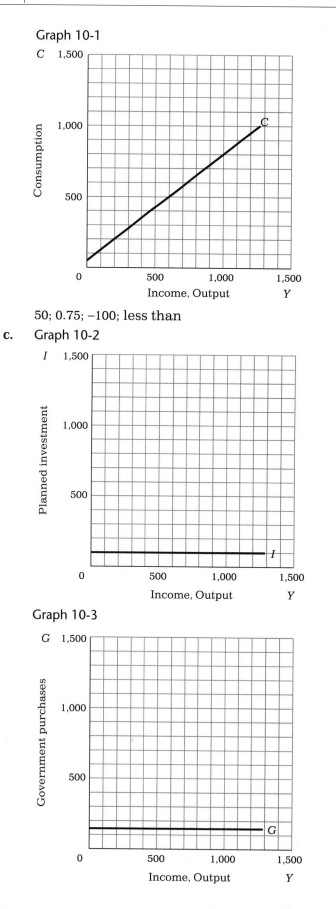

50; 0.75; −100; less than

c.   Graph 10-2

Graph 10-3

d.   Graph 10-4

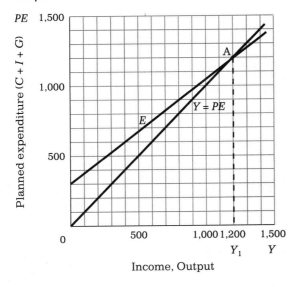

e.   50; 100; 150; 300; 0.75; 0; 0; 0.75

f.   300; 0.75

g.   1.0; 1,200

h.   1,500; 1,500; 100; lay off; decrease; fall; 1,200; 0

i.   1,050; 1,050; –50; hire more; increase; rise; 1,200; 0

2. **a.**   150; 151; 1

    b.   1

Graph 10-5

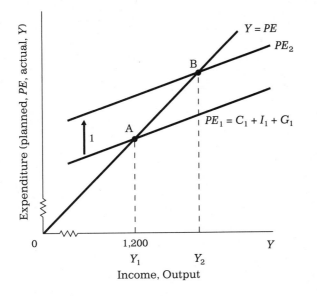

Graph 10-6

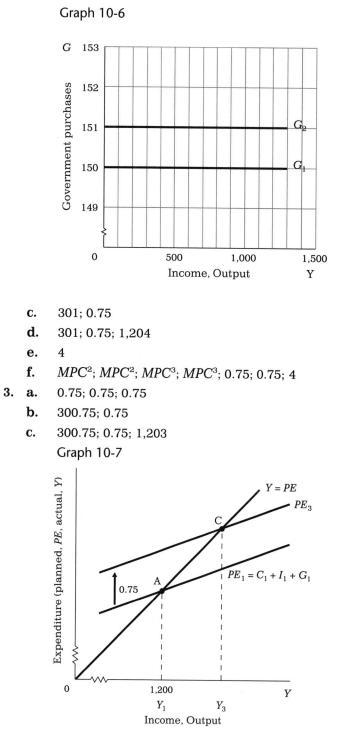

c. 301; 0.75

d. 301; 0.75; 1,204

e. 4

f. MPC^2; MPC^2; MPC^3; MPC^3; 0.75; 0.75; 4

3. a. 0.75; 0.75; 0.75

b. 300.75; 0.75

c. 300.75; 0.75; 1,203

Graph 10-7

d. 3

e. MPC^2, MPC^2; MPC^3; MPC^3; 0.75; 0.75; 0.75; 3

f. $MPC/(1 - MPC)$

g. upward; 1; downward; 0.75; upward; 0.25; rise, larger; 4; 3; decrease; 3; increase; 1

4. a. 10

Table 10-3

(1) Interest Rate (%)	(2) Planned Investment	(3) Equilibrium Level of Income
0	200	1,600
5	150	1,400
10	100	1,200
15	50	1,000
20	0	800

Graph10-9

b. 400; 0.75; 10

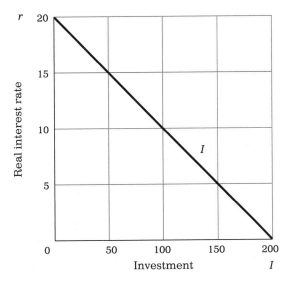

c. 400; 0.75; 10; 1,600; 40
d. 100; 1,200
e. 50; 50

Graph 10-10

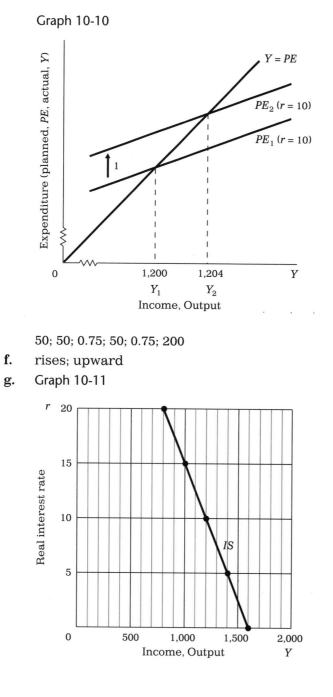

50; 50; 0.75; 50; 0.75; 200

f.   rises; upward

g.   Graph 10-11

5. a. 100; 1,200; 0.75; 4; 1,204

b. Graph 10-12

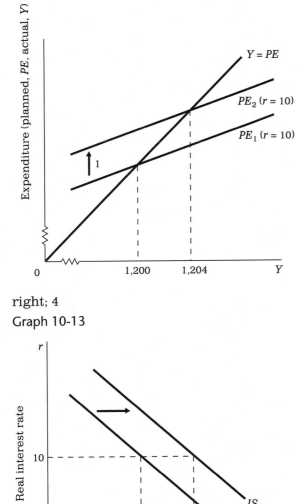

c. right; 4

Graph 10-13

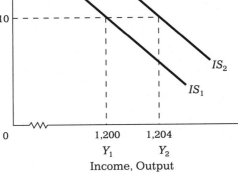

d. right; left; government-purchases multiplier

e. smaller; larger; larger; larger; larger

f. 1; 0.75; 0.75; 3; 1,203

Graph 10-14

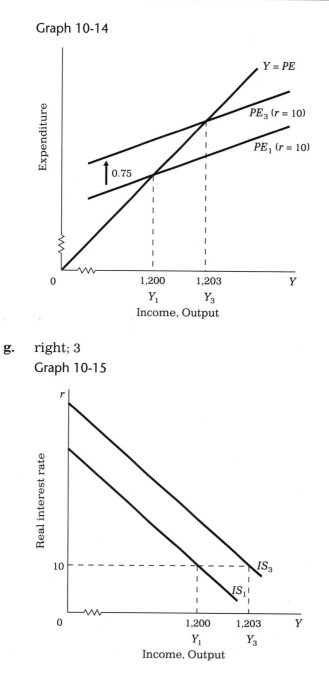

g. right; 3

Graph 10-15

h. right; left; tax multiplier
i. larger; smaller; larger; larger; larger; larger; flatter

6. **a.** Graph 10-16

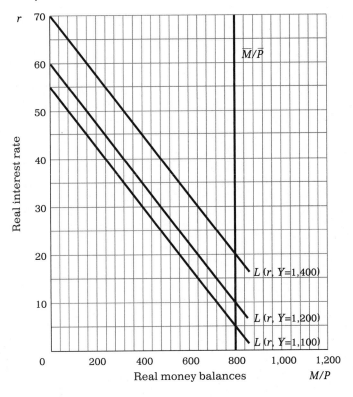

b. 0; 480; 720; 800; 880

c. 5

d. 0; 160; 560; 800; 880; right; rises; 10

e. 0; 320; 720; 960; 1,120; right; rises; 20

f. 800; 5; 10; 20

Graph 10-17

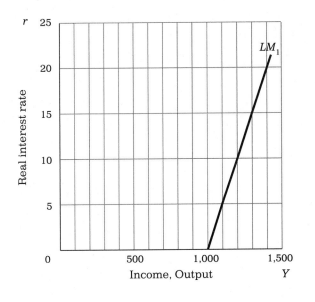

g. increase; rise

h. 800; 800; −50; 0.05; −50; 0.05

7. a. −50; 0.05

Graph 10-18

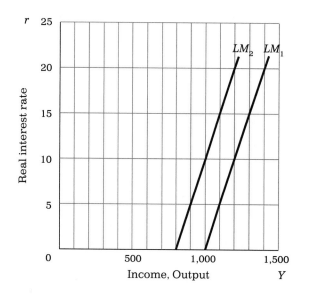

b. −40; 0.05; equal to; greater than; left (upward)

c. increase; decrease; left (upward); right (downward)

8. a. 40; −0.025

Graph 10-19

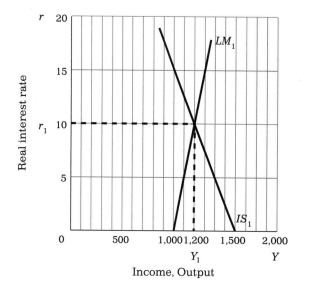

b. −50; 0.05

c. 1,200; 10

Problems

1. **a.** 0.8

   b. Graph for Problem 1b

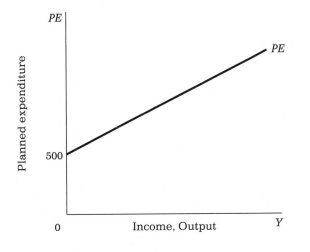

   slope = 0.8; *y* intercept = 500

   c. 2,500

   d. 100

2. **a.** 2,500

   b. i. The planned expenditure curve shifts upward by 10.

   ii. The equilibrium level of income increases by 50.

   iii. The level of consumption rises by 40.

   iv. The government budget deficit will rise by 10.

   c. i. The planned expenditure curve shifts downward by 8.

   ii. The equilibrium level of income decreases by 40.

   iii. The level of consumption decreases by 40.

   iv. The government budget deficit decreases by 10.

   d. i. The planned expenditure curve shifts upward by 2.

   ii. The equilibrium level of income increases by 10.

   iii. The level of consumption remains constant.

   iv. The government budget deficit remains unchanged.

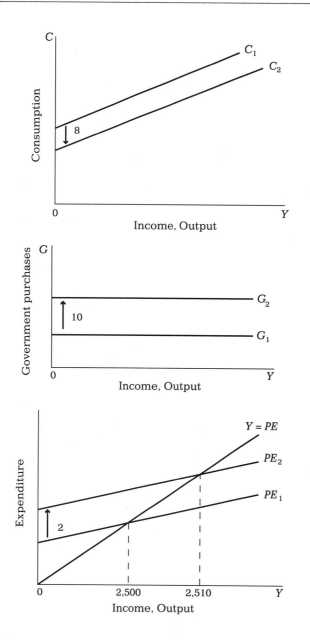

3. **a.** 0.6

   b. 100

   c. 1,500

   d. 2.5

   e. 50/2.5 = 20

5. **a.** $Y = 1{,}250 - 10r$

   b. $Y = 980 + 8r$

c. $r = 125 - (1/10)Y$ (*IS* curve equation)

$r = -122.5 + (1/8)Y$ (*LM* curve equation)

Graphs for Problem 5c

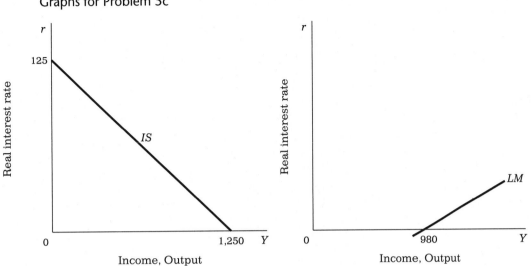

slope of *IS* curve $= -1/10$; slope of *LM* curve $= 1/8$

d. $r = 15$ (percent); $Y = 1,100$; $I = 40$; $C = 710$

e. -150

7. The money demand curve would shift to the right and the *LM* curve would shift to the left.

8. a. The *IS* curve becomes flatter.

b. The *IS* curve becomes flatter.

Chapter 11

Fill-in Questions

1. Pigou effect

2. debt-deflation theory

3. liquidity trap

Multiple Choice Questions

1. b	2. a	3. d	4. c	5. d	6. d	7. d
8. a	9. c	10. b	11. d	12. a	13. a	14. d
15. c	16. b	17. c	18. d	19. d	20. b	21. d
22. c	23. a					

Exercises

1. **a.**   1,200; 10
    b.   upward; 100; right; 400

    Graph 11-1

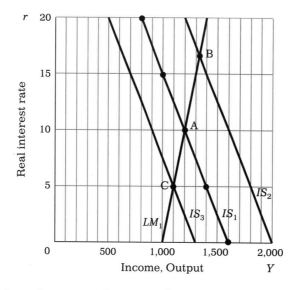

    c.   rises; increase; decrease; less
    d.   downward; 75; left; 300
    e.   falls; decrease; increase; less
    f.   downward (to the right); fall; rise; lower; increases; increases

    Graph 11-2

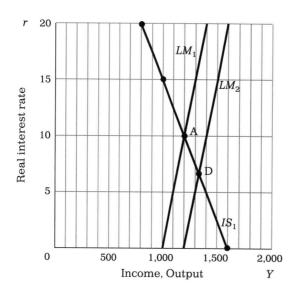

    upward (to the left); rise; fall
    g.   *IS*; right; rise; rise; *IS*; left; fall; fall; right; *LM*; upward (to the left); fall; rise
2. **a.**   downward (to the right)

Graph 11-3 and Graph 11-4

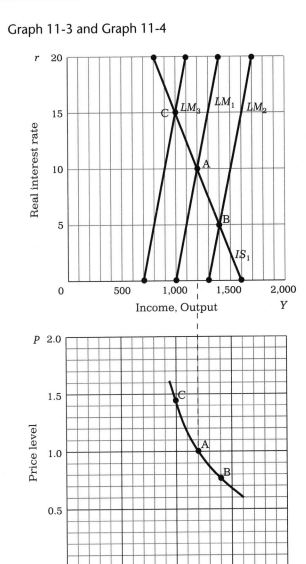

b. upward (to the left)

c. 1.0; 1,200

d. 0.77; 1,400

e. 1.43; 1,000

f. increase; *LM*; downward (to the right); decreases; increases; increases

3. a. 1.0; 1,000; 1,600; 1,300

Graph 11-5 and Graph 11-6

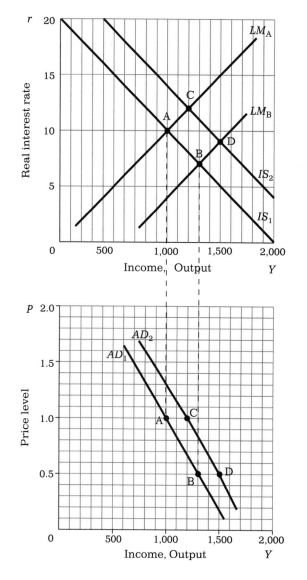

b. 4; right; 400

c. less

e. higher than; equal to; higher than; equal to

f. right; right; right; right

4. a. 1.0; 1,000

Graph 11-7

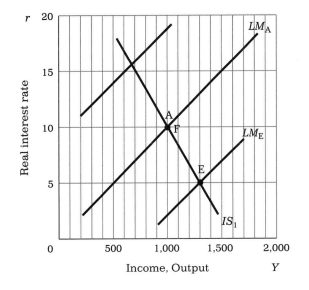

Graph 11-8

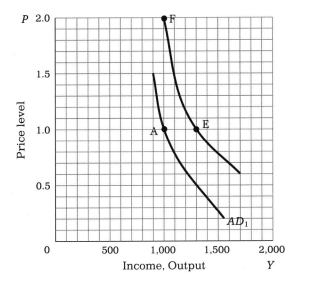

b. 1,600; downward (to the right)

c. higher than; equal to; right; left

d. 800; 1,000

5. **a.** Graph 11-9

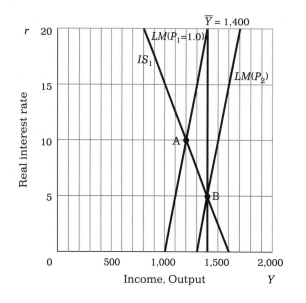

Graph 11-10

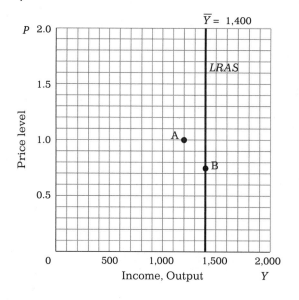

b. −50; 0.05

c. 1,200; 10

d. less; sticky; horizontal

e. flexible; fall; increase; downward (to the right)

f. 5; 1,040; 0.77

g. rise; *LM*; upward (to the left)

6. a. Graph 11-11

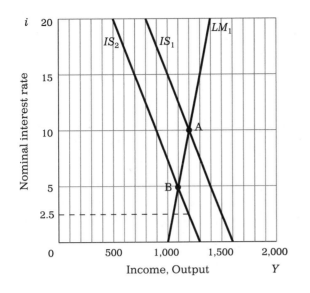

b. 1,200; 10; 10

c. 10; 17.5; higher; 10; 10; 10; –7.5; 2.5; 7.5; downward; 7.5

d. 1,100; 5

e. decrease; decrease; 10; 0; 10; 5; –7.5; 12.5; rises

Problems

1. a. $Y = 1,250 - 10r$

   b. $Y = 980 + 8r$

   c. $r = 125 - (1/10)Y$ (IS curve equation)

      $r = -122.5 + (1/8)Y$ (LM curve equation)

      Graphs for Problem 1c

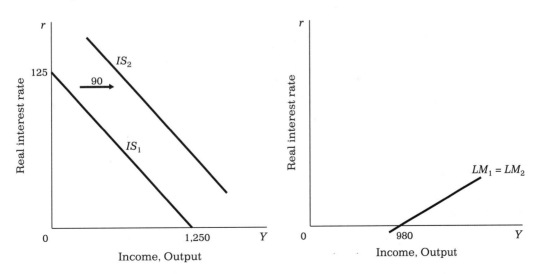

      slope of IS curve = –1/10; slope of LM curve = 1/8

   d. $r = 15$ (percent); $Y = 1,100$; $I = 40$; $C = 710$

   e. -150

   f.   The *LM* equation remains unchanged. The new *IS* equation is $Y = 1,340 - 10r$.

   g.   The shift in the *IS* curve is equal to 90. The *LM* curve does not shift.

   h. $Y = 1,140$; $r = 20$; $I = 20$; $C = 734$

   i.   54

   j.   Government purchases are higher in Part h. Since taxes and output are the same as Parts h and i, consumption is also the same. Since the interest rate is lower in Part i, investment is higher. Advocates of expansionary fiscal policy may argue that the United States is badly in need of public spending in areas like education, defense, and infrastructure. Advocates of expansionary monetary policy, on the other hand, would tout its effect on investment, which might spur economic growth as the capital stock grows.

2. **a.**   The *IS* curve would shift left to IS_2. Both Y and r would fall.

   Graph for Problem 2a

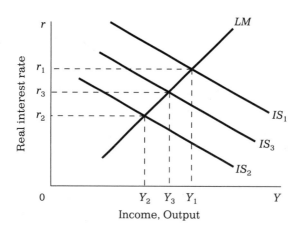

   b.   Since part of transfers are saved, the reduction in G would dominate. The *IS* curve would shift left (to IS_3) by a smaller amount than in Part a. Both Y and r would fall.

   c.   The reductions in Y and r would be smaller in Part b than in Part a.

   d.   If the money supply does not change, the results would be almost identical to those in Part a. The reductions in Y and r may not be as great if these countries spent some of their grants to increase their imports from Canada.

3. **a.** By reducing household wealth, the stock market crash would shift both the consumption and total planned expenditure curves downward.

b. Consequently, the *IS* curve would shift to the left, and both Y and r would fall. Graph for Problem 3b

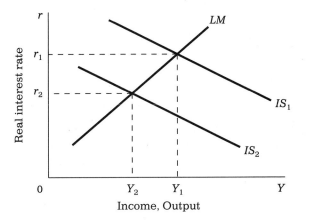

5. **a.** When the *MPC* is large, *ceteris paribus*, the slope of the planned expenditure curve will be large, and the multiplier will be large, resulting in a flatter *IS* curve in Country A. Intuitively, as r falls, investment rises and GDP increases via the direct effect on investment and multiplier effects on consumption. The latter will be larger when *MPC* is bigger, since people will then consume a greater fraction of the increase in disposable income in each successive round. The shape of the *LM* curve is unaffected by the *MPC*. Graph for Problem 5a

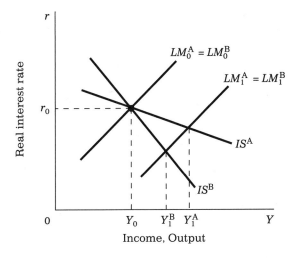

b. Monetary policy will be more effective in changing Y in Country A, where the *IS* curve is flatter.

6. a. The LM curve would remain stationary. The economy would move along a stationary LM curve in response to shifts in the IS curve. GDP would rise when private spending increases and would fall when private spending decreases.

Graph for Problem 6a

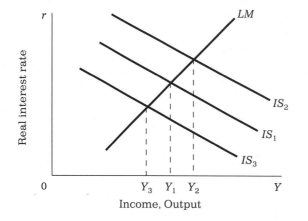

b. As Y increases in response to a shift in the IS curve to the right, the money demand curve would shift to the right. To keep the interest rate constant, the money supply would have to rise, shifting the LM curve downward (to the right).

Graphs for Problem 6b

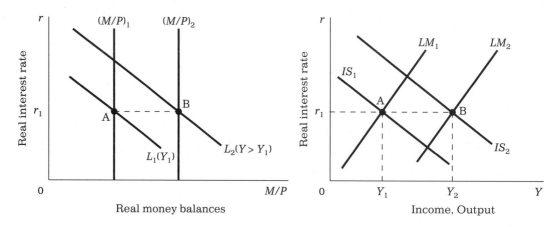

c. As Y decreases in response to a shift in the IS curve to the left, the money demand curve would shift to the left. To keep the interest rate constant, the money supply would have to fall, shifting the LM curve upward (to the left).

d. In Parts b and c, the central bank's policy exacerbates the fluctuations in Y following shifts in the IS curve. Consequently, a stable money supply would better stabilize the economy if the disturbances stem primarily from shifts in the IS curve.

7. a. An increase in government spending and a decrease in taxes both shift the
IS and *AD* curves to the right. The *SRAS* and *LM* curves do not shift in the
short run.

Graphs for Problem 7a

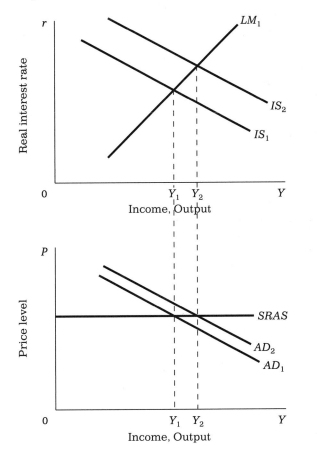

The equilibrium levels of *Y*, *r*, and *C* all rise. The equilibrium level of *I* falls,
and *G* and *P* do not change in the short run (given the horizontal *SRAS*
curve of Chapter 9).

b. The Bank of Canada increased the money supply at the same time as taxes fell and spending was increased. Consequently, both the *IS* and *LM* curves shifted to the right. This shifted the *AD* curve even farther to the right. Graphs for Problem 7b

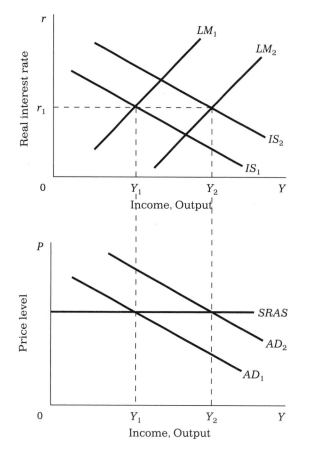

The levels of *Y* and *C* rise by more in Part b than in Part a. The remaining variables, *r*, *I*, *G*, and *P* remain constant.

8. The central bank should increase the money supply (which would shift the *LM* curve down, or to the right), and the government should simultaneously reduce *G* and/or increase *T* (which would shift the *IS* curve left). Real GDP could remain unchanged, but the reduction in the real interest rate would increase investment.

9. a. If consumption rises as the interest rate falls, the *IS* curve would be flatter because now both consumption and investment would increase when *r* falls. The *LM* curve is unaffected.

   b. A flat *IS* curve will enhance the short-run effectiveness of monetary policy.

   c. A flat *IS* curve will flatten the slope of the *AD* curve.

10. a. Graphs for Problem 10a

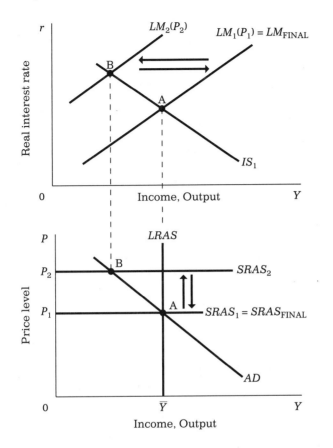

b. In the short run, the *SRAS* curve shifts upward. This increases *P* and thereby shifts the *LM* curve upward (to the left). Since output falls below its natural rate, the *SRAS* curve will shift downward in subsequent periods. As it does, *P* will fall and the *LM* curve will shift back downward (to the right) until it reaches its initial position, at which point *Y* and *P* will also reach their initial levels. (This assumes that the natural rate of output is unaffected.)

11. If expected inflation rises from 0 to 10 percent, the real interest rate would fall by 10 percentage points at each level of the nominal interest rate. Consequently, the *IS* curve would shift upward by 10 percentage points. The *LM* curve would not shift. The equilibrium levels of *i* and *Y* would rise, and the equilibrium level of *r* would fall.

Graph for Problem 11

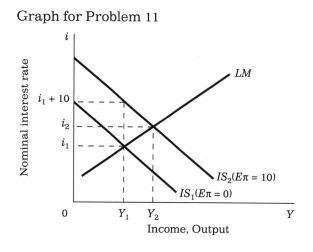

14. At the initial equilibrium the nominal interest rate is almost zero. If the announced monetary expansion increases expected inflation, the real interest rate would fall by the full amount of the increase in expected inflation at each level of the nominal interest rate. Consequently, the *IS* curve would shift upward by the increase in expected inflation. As the Japanese central bank increases the nominal money supply, the *LM* curve will also shift right. The equilibrium levels of *i* and *Y* would rise and the equilibrium level of *r* would fall.

Graph for Problem 14

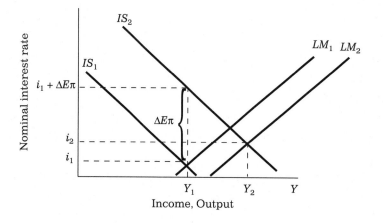

Chapter 12

Fill-in Questions

1. floating exchange rate
2. fixed exchange rate
3. fixed exchange rate; floating exchange rate
4. devaluation; revaluation
5. Mundell-Fleming model; devaluation; revaluation
6. fixed exchange rate
7. speculative attack; fixed exchange rate
8. currency board
9. Dollarization
10. impossible trinity; fixed exchange rate

Multiple-Choice Questions

1. c	2. d	3. c	4. c	5. a	6. b	7. a
8. b	9. d	10. c	11. b	12. d	13. d	14. a
15. b	16. c	17. d	18. c	19. b	20. d	21. b
22. d	23. d	24. b	25. b			

Exercises

1. **b.** 2; 50; 400; 0.75; 10

   c. 40; 0.025

   Graph 12-1

   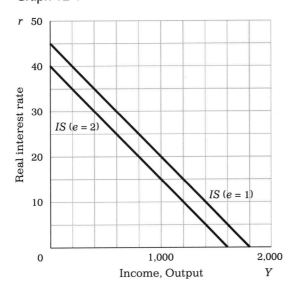

   d. depreciation; rise; 1; 100; 45; 0.025

   e. depreciation; increase; upward; right; 50; upward; 50; right; 50; 4; 200; appreciation; decrease; downward; left

2. **a.** 50; 1,200

Graph 12-2

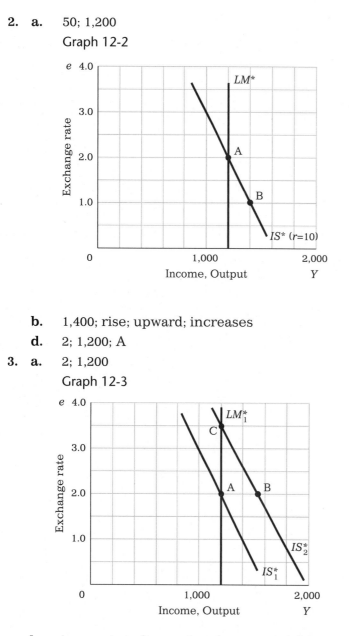

b. 1,400; rise; upward; increases

d. 2; 1,200; A

3. **a.** 2; 1,200

Graph 12-3

b. increasing; decreasing; increase; right

c. greater than; decreases; increase; rises; decrease; increase; rises above; increases

d. has no effect on; increases; fall; has no effect on; decreases

e. right (downward); rise; right

Graph 12-4

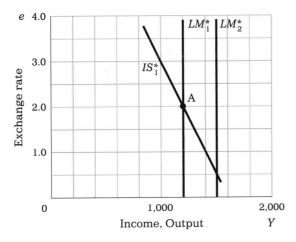

increases; decreases; rise

f. increase; the interest rate; out of; depreciate; increases

4. a. 2

Graph 12-5

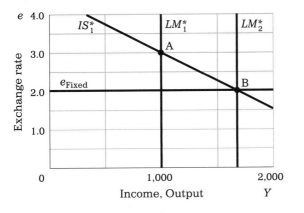

b. greater than; 3; 3; 3; 1.50

c. increases; right; increase; right

d. less than; 1; 1; 2

Graph 12-6

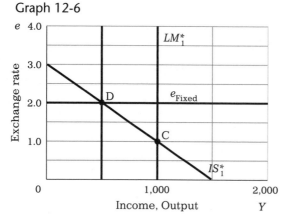

e. decreases; left; decrease; left

5. a. Graph 12-7

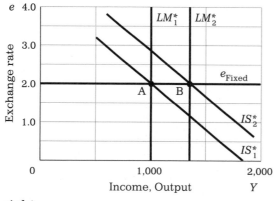

right

b. have no effect on; increase; increase; right; 2; increase; have no effect on

c. right

Graph 12-8

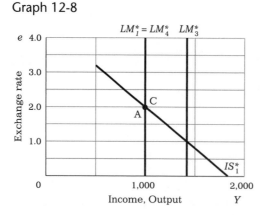

increase; decrease; falls below; selling; buying; decrease; left; 2; have no effect on; have no effect on; equal to; remain constant

d. buying; selling; increase; right; increase; left; decrease

6. a. higher

   b. rises; decrease; left

   c. decrease; right

   Graph 12-9

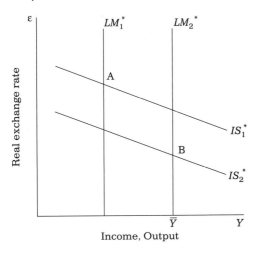

7. a. less than; remain constant

   b. downward; fall; rise

   Graph 12-10

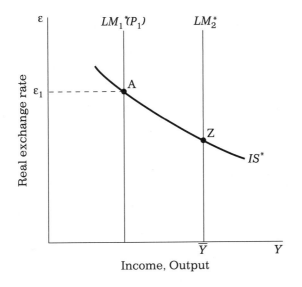

d. depreciation; increase

e. increases; LM*; left; decrease; LM*; left; LM*; left

Graph 12-11

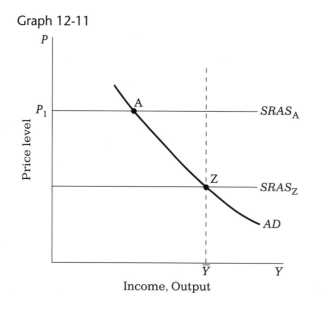

c.   increase; supply; LM^*; right; fall; rise; rises; rise; remains the same; remain the same

Problems

1. As the money supply begins to contract, the domestic interest rate will begin to rise above the world interest rate. Capital flows into the domestic economy as both foreigners and domestic investors wish to buy additional domestically issued bonds and assets. This will push the foreign exchange rate above the initial fixed exchange rate. Arbitragers will then sell foreign currency to (and buy domestic currenty from) the central bank. As a result, the domestic money supply will rise until the foreign exchange rate and the domestic interest rate fall back to their initial levels, at which point the money supply and real income will be equal to their initial levels.

2. The main advantage to leaving the EMS was that Britain regained control over the use of monetary policy for stabilization purposes. Specifically, Britain wanted to pursue policies to end a severe recession. The main disadvantage was increased uncertainty regarding future exchange-rate movements among European Economic Community (EEC) members, which might impede trade. Other critics believed that Britain's departure removed a mechanism that provided useful discipline to British monetary authorities.

3. a.   Participating countries would lose the limited ability they currently have to conduct independent monetary policies, but much of this has already been lost. Future monetary stabilization policies would have to be coordinated. The effects of fiscal policies would increase slightly.

    b.   Nonparticipating countries currently have considerable ability to conduct countercyclical monetary policies, but these policies would have to be coordinated in the future. Fiscal policies would become more powerful because under their current floating exchange rates, fiscal policy does not affect output.

4. During a recession, actual output is presumably less than the natural rate of output. Consequently, over time the domestic price level will fall. This will increase the real money supply and shift the *LM** curve to the right. As a result, the real exchange rate will fall, and the trade balance will rise along with national income.

5. The export restrictions will shift the *NX* curve to the left. Consequently, the *IS** curve will shift to the left.

   a. If the country has a flexible exchange rate, the *LM** curve is vertical. Consequently, the exchange rate will fall, but real GDP will remain unchanged.

   Graph for Problem 5a

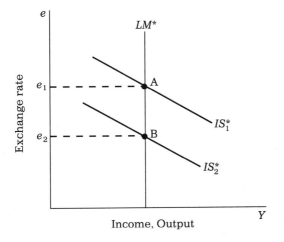

   b. If the country has a fixed exchange rate, the *LM** curve will also shift to the left to keep the exchange rate constant. Consequently, real GDP will fall.

   Graph for Problem 5b

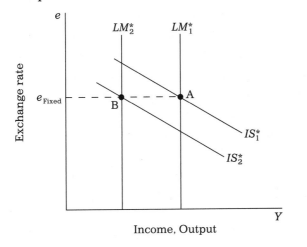

6. A crisis in confidence will raise a country's risk premium. Consequently, the domestic interest rate will rise. This will shift the *IS** curve to the left and the *LM** curve to the right. If, however, the country has a fixed exchange rate, it will be compelled to sell foreign currency and shift its *LM** curve to the left of its original position. This will reduce real GDP.

Graph for Problem 6

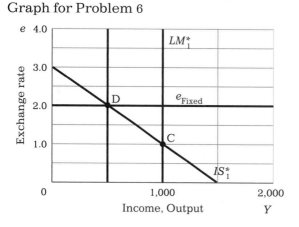

7. Renewed stability reduced these countries' risk premiums. Consequently, their domestic interest rates fell. This shifted the *IS** curve to the right and the *LM** curve to the left. Under a regime of flexible exchange rates, the countries' exchange rates would rise while real GDP would fall. (In reality, other developments may help these countries increase their real GDP as noted in the Appendix to Chapter 12 in the textbook.)

Graph for Problem 7

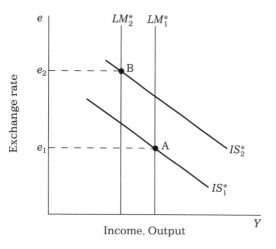

8. **a.** The shift in Argentina's net export curve would also shift its *IS** curve to the left. If Argentina kept the initial dollar-peso exchange rate of 1:1, it would have to buy up pesos, thereby shifting its *LM** curve to the left. Consequently,

its real GDP would fall. Since Argentina is being treated as a small open economy, its interest rate would remain at the world interest rate:

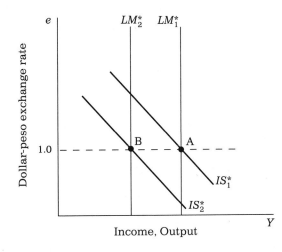

b. Once again, the shift in the net export curve would shift the *IS** curve to the left. If Argentina abandoned its fixed dollar-peso exchange rate, however, it would have fallen (i.e., the peso would have depreciated) to point B and there would have been no effect on real GDP:

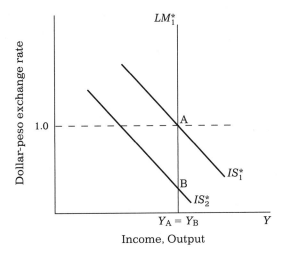

9. In favour of this strategy, you should note that international differences in saving and investment make it necessary for there to be adjustments in real exchange rates. Sticky wages and prices make it appealing to allow this flexibility to occur via changes in the nominal exchange rate, so a flexible system is appealing. But too much flexibility allows disruptive variations in the exchange rate that have nothing to do with long-term fundamentals, so the short-term smoothing strategy is a good compromise.

To argue against this policy, you should note that the reasoning in the previous paragraph ignores the Lucas critique. The smoothing policy makes it rational for market participants to forecast a significant degree of period-to-period persistence in the exchange rate. When today's exchange rate depends heavily on yesterday's exchange rate, shocks that might otherwise have only mattered for a short time have impact for a prolonged time. Thus, by affecting expectations, the smoothing strategy raises the variance of the exchange rate. You might, therefore, argue that—without an effective option to smooth—the government might be better advised to fix the exchange rate. Also, you might also point out that the traditional argument in favour of flexible exchange rates assumes that the country is an optimal currency area. This may not be the case.

10. Let the short-run aggregate supply function be $P^d = \Phi Y$. Use this relationship to eliminate P^d in the standard open-economy IS equation. The result is the equation of the IS^* locus, and you can use the equation to rationalize that this locus is negatively sloped, and that it shifts left with a rise in r^*, as usual. Now consider substituting the P^d equation into the definition of the price index, $P = \lambda P^d + (1-\lambda)(P^f/e)$. With P^f given from outside, and with P fixed by the monetary authority, this is the second equation in the two endogenous variables (e and Y) that you need to draw the usual diagram. This equation implies a positively sloped relationship in e-Y space, so it takes the place of the LM^* curve that was appropriate when the money supply was the exogenous variable of monetary policy. In this case, however, the LM function is not involved in the diagram. Its role is simply to indicate the value of the money supply that is needed for the central bank to fix P. The important difference in this case is that this analogue of the LM^* locus does not shift with changes in r^*. Thus, an increase in r^* moves IS^* to the left, so that it crosses the nonshifting positively sloped replacement for LM^* at a point to the left. Thus, a recession *must* occur.

Chapter 13

Fill-in Questions

1. sticky-price model
2. imperfect-information model
3. sticky-price, imperfect-information
4. Phillips curve
5. NAIRU
6. Phillips curve; demand-pull inflation
7. cost-push inflation
8. adaptive expectations
9. rational expectations
10. sacrifice ratio; rational expectations; adaptive expectations
11. natural-rate hypothesis
12. Hysteresis

Multiple-Choice Questions

1. d	2. c	3. c	4. a	5. b	6. b	7. a
8. b	9. a	10. d	11. d	12. a	13. a	14. c
15. d	16. a	17. a	18. b			

Exercises

1. **a.** equal to; greater than

   b. Graph 13-1

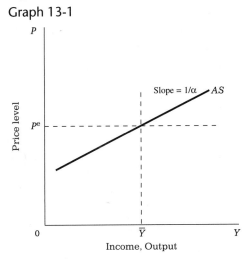

   slope $= 1/\alpha$

   c. upward (to the left); downward (to the right); increase

2. **b.** rise; raise; increase; increase

   c. 0; equal to; greater than; decreases; increase; decreases; decreases; flatter; horizontal; 1; all

3. **b.** $1; 1; 1; 100

   Graph 13-2

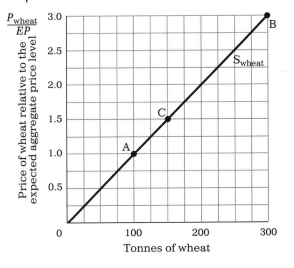

   c. $3; 1; 3; rise; 300

   d. $1; 1; 1; 100

e. 200; 200; 100; 2; 2; 1.5; 150

Graph 13-3

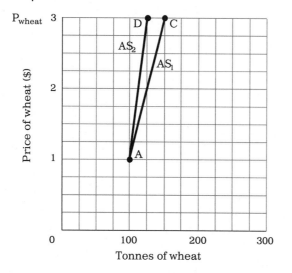

f. 1; greater; less

g. 200; 200; 140; 2.4; 2.4; 1.25; 125; steeper; steep; 1; 100; vertical

4. a. increase; *LM*; downward (to the right); increases; rises above; flexible; equal to

b. equal to; 1

c. increase; decrease; increase; 1; 1,400; 1.4

d. greater than; increase

e. 1.4; 1.4; upward; 1.4

Graph 13-4

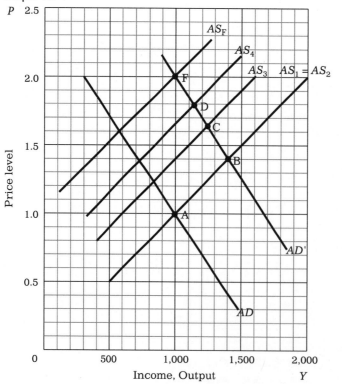

   f.   approximately 1,220; approximately 1.65; fallen; risen

   g.   greater than; increase; 1.65; 1.65; upward; 1.65

   h.   greater than; increase; upward; greater than; 1,000; 2; 2

   i.   no change; an increase

   j.   more; more

5. **a.**   positive; less

   b.   10; 0.4;

   Graph 13-5

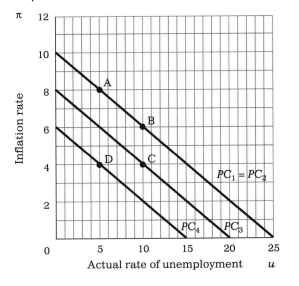

   equal to

   c.   decreasing; increasing; decreasing; 8; right

   d.   10; 6

   e.   less than; fall; downward

   f.   6; 6; 6; 8; 0.4

   g.   10; 4

   h.   less than; fall; downward; 4; 4; 4; 6; 0.4

   i.   5; 4; equal to; stay the same; remain stationary

   j.   4; 5; 5; 10; 4; 4; 2.5; 5; sacrifice

   k.   more; more; lower

l.   5; 8; 15; 4; 4; 4; 6; 0.4

Graph 13-6

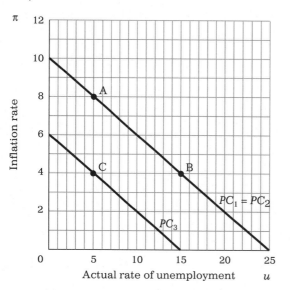

5; 4; equal to; 10; 4; equal to

m.   shift upward

6. b.

Table 13-1

(1) Time Period	(2) Inflation	(3) Excess Unemployment $(u-u^n)$
1	0%	0%
2	0%	0%
3	3%	−3%
4	6%	−3%
5	6%	0%
6	3%	+6%
7	0%	+6%
8	0%	0%

c.   In the first two periods, both inflation and excess unemployment are zero. In periods 3 and 4, inflation averages 4.5%, while unemployment has fallen by an average amount of 3 percentage points. This inverse relationship illustrates the short-run tradeoff.

d. Over the longer time span including periods 2 through 7, inflation averages 1%, while unemployment averages one percentage point *above* its initial value. Compared to time periods 1 and 2 there is not a tradeoff. Average unemployment and inflation are both higher after the temporary bout of inflationary monetary policy.

e. While both inflation and excess unemployment have returned to zero by period 8, the nonlinearily in the short-run Phillips curve means that the transition between steady states involves a net positive amount of *both* inflation and unemployment. The more nonlinear is the short-run tradeoff, the less desirable it is to have to undergo temporary bouts of inflation.

Problems

1. As the fraction of firms that have flexible prices becomes greater, the short-run aggregate supply curve becomes steeper because prices will adjust more quickly whenever real GDP deviates from its natural level. Monetary and fiscal policy changes affect real GDP by shifting the aggregate demand curve. If the aggregate supply curve is steep, shifts in the aggregate demand curve will have smaller short-run effects on output and bigger effects on the price level. Thus, as the fraction of firms with flexible prices becomes greater, the power of monetary and fiscal policy to change real GDP becomes weaker.

2. Graph for Problem 2

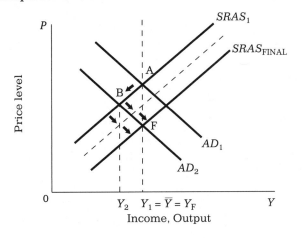

a. If expectations were rational, people would probably lower their expectations of future price levels more rapidly. Consequently, the *SRAS* curve would move toward its final position at Point F more rapidly.

b. If a greater fraction of firms have flexible prices, the short-run aggregate supply curve would be steeper than that depicted in the Graph for Problem 2. As a result, the price level would fall by more in the short run following a decrease in aggregate demand. Consequently, the expected price level would also fall more rapidly, and the economy would move toward its final position at Point F more quickly.

3. If real GDP falls (or unemployment rises) along with an increase in inflation, this probably represents a supply shock or an upward shift of the Phillips curve. Since the economy began at the natural rate of output, there is no reason for expected inflation or the expected price level to rise suddenly. Consequently, we could characterize the inflation as cost-push. If real GDP rises (or unemployment falls) along with the increase in inflation, this probably results from a shift in aggregate demand or a movement along a Phillips curve. Consequently, we could characterize the inflation as demand-pull.

4. $d[(1-s)a/s]/ds = -a/s^2 < 0$. When the fraction of firms with sticky prices s rises, the slope falls and the short-run aggregate supply curve flattens.

5. **a.** The natural rate of unemployment is 0.04, or 4 percent.

   b. Graph for Problem 6b

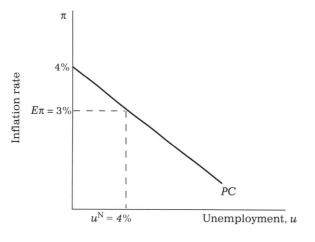

   c. 8

6. Your answer will depend on the most recent unemployment and inflation data and whether the economy is experiencing a supply shock. Most economists believe that the natural rate of unemployment lies between 4.5 and 6 percent. If the most recent unemployment rate is below this range and there are no supply shocks, the actual inflation rate would exceed the expected inflation rate. Consequently, expected inflation would increase over time, thereby shifting the Phillips curve up, and unemployment would move toward its natural rate. If the most recent unemployment rate is above this range and there are no supply shocks, the reverse would be true.

8. According to the hysteresis theory, the natural rate of unemployment may rise during a recession, leading to a reduction in the natural rate of output. This would shift the long-run aggregate supply curve to the left.

CHAPTER 14

Fill-in Questions

1. natural rate of interest
2. random variable
3. Taylor rule
4. predetermined variable

5. impulse response function
6. Taylor Principle
7. Taylor Principle

Multiple-Choice Questions

1. d   2. d   3. c   4. d   5. a   6. c   7. d   8. d   9. c   10. d

11. d   12. a   13. d   14. a   15. b   16. d   17. c   18. a   19. c   20. a

21. d   22. d   23. c   24. d   25. a   26. a   27. c   28. d   29. b   30. b

31. b   32. a   33. b   34. b   35. d   36. b

Exercises

1. **a.** fall; more
   b. $t + 1$; t
   c. 2
   d. t
   e. π_t; increasing; decrease; increasing; decrease; decrease; ρ
   f. falls; decreases; decreases
   g. $\overline{Y}_t - [\alpha\theta_\pi/(1 + \alpha\theta_Y)](\pi_t - \pi_t^*) + [1/(1 + \alpha\theta_Y)]\varepsilon_t$

h.   falls; equal to

Graph 14-1

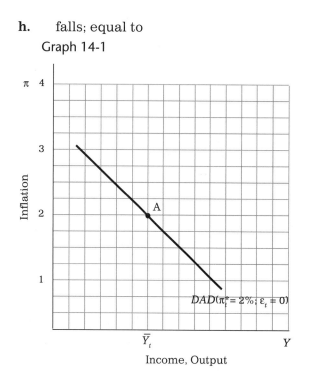

i.   rise; upward (to the right); increase; upward (to the right); equal to

2.   **a.**   2; 2

b.   0; 2; 2; 0; 4; rises

c.   1; rises; decreases

d. and **e.**

Table 14-1

(1)	(2)	(3)	(4)	(5)	(6)
		Natural		Nominal	Real
	Actual	Level	GDP	Federal	Federal
Inflation	GDP	of GDP	gap	Funds Rate	Funds Rate
(%)	$ billions	$ billions	(%)	(%)	(%)
2	100	100	0	4	2
3	100	100	0	5.5	2.5
2	94	100	6	1	−1
2	106	100	−6	7	5
4	96	100	4	5	1

minus

f.   1.5; rose; 0.5

3.   **a.** $t - 1$; t

b.   falls below

c.   negative

d.   2; 2.25; 1.75; 3; 3.25

e. 2; 1; 2.25; 1; 1.75

Graph 14-2

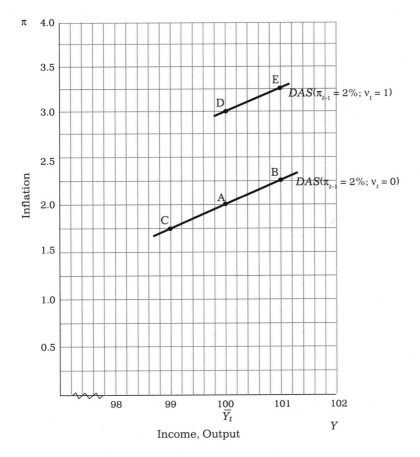

f. 0.25; φ; rise; bigger; steeper

g. 3; 3.25; upward; 1

h. 3; 3.25; 3; 3.25; upward; 1; downward (to the right)

Graph 14-3

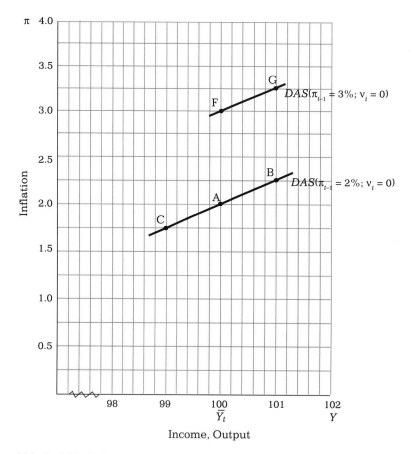

Income, Output

   i. 100; 3; 110; 0; 3

4. **b.** $\overline{Y}_t$

   c. ρ

   d. π_t^*; target rate of inflation; π_t^*; target

   e. π_t^*; target rate of inflation

5. **a.** natural level

   b. upward (to the left); equal to; the natural level of output

   c. $\overline{Y}_{t-1}$

Graph 14-4

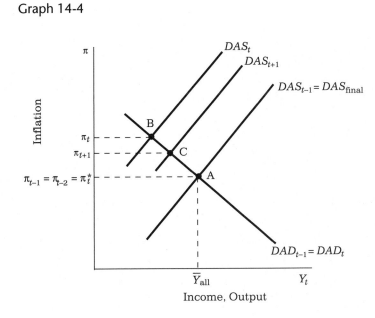

d. upward (to the left); decreases; increases

e. 0; increases; decreases

f. fall

g. lower; higher

6. b. 100; 1/3; 2; 2/3; 0.25; 100

c. 100; 2

d. 2; 0.25; 100; 2; 100; 100; 2

e.

Table 14-4

(1)	(2)	(3)	(4)	(5)	(6)
	Supply Shock	Demand Shock	Inflation in Preceding Period	Output	Inflation
Period	ν	ε		Y	π
$t-2$	0	0	2	100	2
$t-1$	0	0	2	100	2
t	1	0	2	99.692	2.923
$t+1$	0	0	2.923	99.716	2.852
$t+2$	0	0	2.852	99.738	2.787
$t+3$	0	0	2.787	99.758	2.762

2; 1; 0; 99.692

f. 2; 99.692; 1; 2.923

g. 2.923; 2.923; 0; 0; 99.716; 2.923; 0.071; 0; 2.852

h. 2.852; 2.852; 0; 0; 99.738; 2.852; 0.0655; 0; 2.787

i. 1; falls; 99.692; 0; rises; 99.716; 0; 99.738; falls; rise

j. rises; fall

Graph 14-5

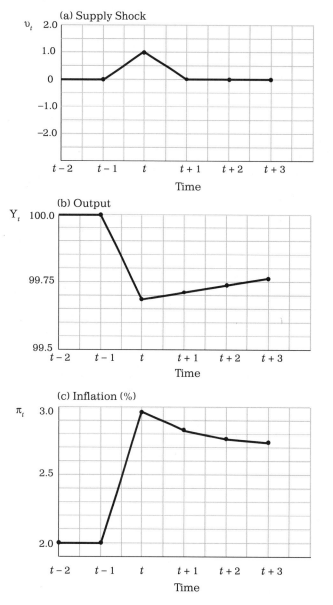

7. **a.** increase; right
    b. increased; increased
    c. 1; rise; upward (to the left); decreased; increased; increasing
    d. rise; upward (to the left); decrease; downward (to the right); target rate of inflation; natural level of output

Graph 14-6

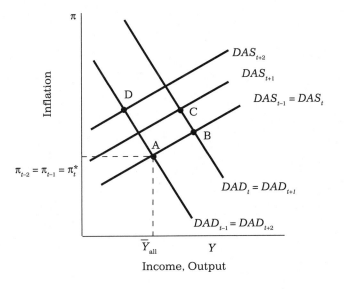

8. **a.** Graph 14-7

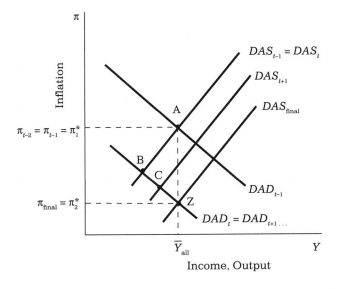

downward (to the left); decreases; decreases
b. downward (to the right); increases; decreases
c. downward (to the right); equal to
d. quickly

9. **a.** Graph 14-8

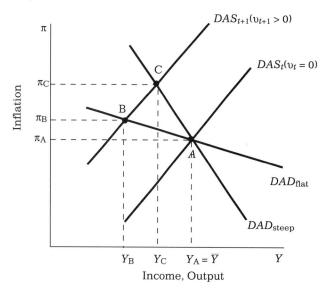

flat; steep

b. equal to: $[(1 + \alpha\theta_Y)/\alpha\theta_\pi]$; $- [(1 + \alpha\theta_Y)/\alpha\theta_\pi]$ (or negative)

c. large; small; flat; small; large; a lot; low; high

d. large; large; steep; large; small; a little; high; low

Problems

1. **a.** The size of α is determined primarily by the sensitivity of investment and consumption to changes in the real interest rate. If investment and consumption are very sensitive to changes in r, α will be large.

b. If α is large, an increase in r (in response to an increase in inflation) will lead to a big reduction in the demand for goods and services. Thus, the DAD curve will be flatter.

c. Graph for Problem 1c

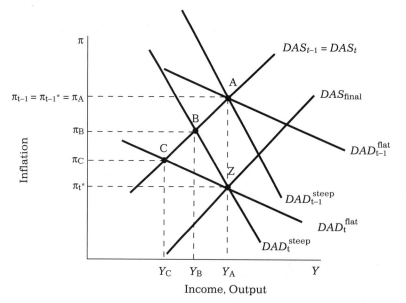

When the central bank reduces its target for the inflation rate, the *DAD* curve will shift down vertically by the change in the target. If the *DAD* curve is flat (and α is large), the short-run decline in output will be bigger (from Y_A to Y_C), as will the immediate decline in inflation (from π_A to π_C) than if the *DAD* curve is steep (and α is small). In the long run, there will be no differences in the responses since inflation will fall to the new target and output will be at its natural level at Point Z.

2. **a.** The recommended nominal federal funds rate = 6 percent, and the recommended real federal funds rate = 2 percent.

    b. The recommended nominal federal funds rate = 1.5 percent, and the recommended real federal funds rate = 0.5 percent.

3. **a.** 7 percent

    b. Both the recommended nominal and real interest rate = –2.5 percent.

    c. The central bank could increase the money supply to generate inflation and increase inflation expectations so that they both exceed 2.5 percent. At that point, a low nominal interest rate would result in a negative real interest rate.

4. Inflation expectations would change more slowly and the economy would return more slowly to its long-run equilibrium following a temporary supply shock.

5. **a.** $\pi_t = \pi_{t-1} + (1/4)(Y_t - 100) + v_t$

    Substituting for π_t in $Y_t = 100 - (1/3)(\pi_t - 2) + (2/3)\varepsilon_t$ yields

    $Y_t = 100 - (1/3)[\pi_{t-1} + (1/4)(Y_t - 100) + v_t - 2] + (2/3)\varepsilon_t$

    $(13/12)Y_t = 109 - (1/3)\pi_{t-1} - (1/3)\,v_t + (2/3)\varepsilon_t$

    $Y_t = 100.6154 - (4/13)\pi_{t-1} - (4/13)\,v_t + (8/13)\varepsilon_t$

6. **a.**

Table 14-5

(1)	(2)	(3)	(4)	(5)	(6)
	Supply Shock	Demand Shock	Inflation in Preceding	Output	Inflation
Period	v_t	ε_t	Period	Y_t	π_t
$t-2$	0	0	2	100	2
$t-1$	0	0	2	100	2
t	0	1	2	100.6154	2.1539
$t+1$	0	1	2.1539	100.5681	2.2959
$t+2$	0	0	2.2959	99.9090	2.2731
$t+3$	0	0	2.2731	99.9160	2.2521

Graphs for Problem 6

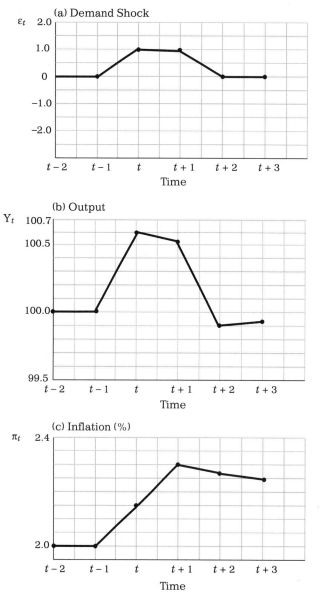

(a) Demand Shock

(b) Output

(c) Inflation (%)

7. **a.** Let $a = [\alpha\theta_\pi/(1 + \alpha\theta_Y)]$ and $b = [1/(1 + \alpha\theta_Y)]$

Then $Y_t = \overline{Y}_t - a\pi_t + a\pi_t^* + b\varepsilon_t$, and $\pi_t = \pi_t^* - (1/a)(Y_t - \overline{Y}_t) + (b/a)\varepsilon_t$. Substituting for a and b yields $\pi_t = \pi_t^* - [(1 + \alpha\theta_Y)/\alpha\theta_\pi](Y_t - \overline{Y}_t) + (1/\alpha\theta_\pi)\varepsilon_t$

b. Slope of $DAD = d\pi_t/dY_t = -[(1 + \alpha\theta_Y)/\alpha\theta_\pi]$

c. $d(\text{slope})/d\theta_\pi = -[-\alpha(1 + \alpha\theta_Y)/(\alpha\theta_\pi)^2] = (1 + \alpha\theta_Y)/\alpha\theta_\pi^2$

Since α, θ_Y, and θ_π^2 are always positive, the derivative will be positive. Thus, the value of the slope will get bigger (less negative), and the DAD curve will become flatter.

d. $d(\text{slope})/d\theta_Y = -1/\theta_\pi$, which is always negative. Thus, the value of the slope will get smaller (more negative), and the DAD curve will become steeper.

e. $d(\text{slope})/d\alpha = 1/(\alpha^2\theta_\pi)$, which is always positive. Thus, the slope will get bigger (less negative), and the DAD curve will become flatter.

8. As shown in the following graph, a steep *DAD* curve will lead to a bigger reduction in both inflation and output. A flat *DAD* curve will lead to smaller reductions in both inflation and output.

Graph for Problem 8

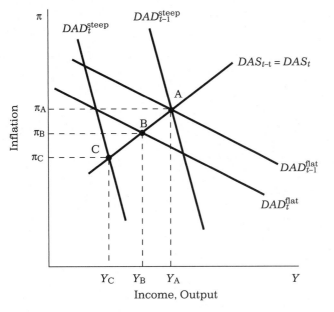

Chapter 15

Fill-in Questions

1. inside lag
2. outside lag
3. inside lag; outside lag
4. Automatic stabilizers
5. index of leading indicators
6. Lucas critique
7. political business cycle
8. time inconsistency
9. Monetarists
10. Automatic stabilizers
11. inflation targeting

Multiple-Choice Questions

1. b   2. d   3. c   4. b   5. b   6. c   7. d
8. c   9. a   10. d   11. a   12. c   13. d   14. b

Exercises

1. **a.** less than; less than
    b. fall; downward; equal to
    Graph 15-1

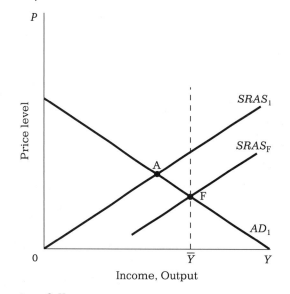

rise; fall
    c. increase; increase; decrease; right
    Graph 15-2

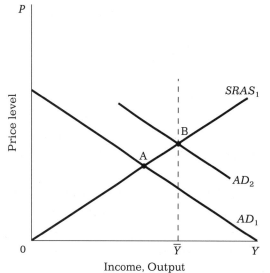

rise; rise
    d. greater than; shorter
    e. more; more; less
    f. inside; outside

2. **a.** 6; 0.2; below
   b. 0; 5; 0; 5; −5; 0; 7; 6
   c. 0; 5; 0; 5
   d. 5; 5; 6; equal to
   e. quickly
3. **a.** 0; 3; 0; 3
   b. 3; 3; increased; 4; decreased; 2
   c. decrease; increase

Problems

1. **a.** If the unemployment rate were 6.1 percent (which is close to the assumed estimate of the natural rate), it is probably better not to change either fiscal or monetary policy. The economy will soon correct itself, and the considerable lags in policy mean that they might take effect after the economy reaches the natural rate of unemployment, which will cause further fluctuations in output and unemployment.

   b. If the unemployment rate were 10.1 percent, it is probably better to pursue expansionary monetary and/or fiscal policy. In the absence of any policy changes, the unemployment rate would eventually return to its natural rate, but it might take a long time. Although economic forecasts are unreliable and policy lags exist, it is probable that the economy will still be far from its natural rate when the policies do take effect.

2. The acceptance of rational expectations may reduce the need for policy activism because it tends to shorten the amount of time it takes for the economy to return to the natural rate of output. If wages and/or prices are sticky, however, the economy will not immediately move back to the natural rate of output, and policy activism may be desirable.

3. According to the Phillips curve, in the long run the economy will be at its natural rate regardless of the rate of inflation. Therefore, while more independent central banks may choose to lower inflation rates, the rates will have no effect on the long-run level of unemployment.

4. **a.** According to the best measures of GDP available in each time period.
   b. According to the measure of GDP that is available for both time periods.
   c. It is generally acknowledged that macroeconomic stabilization measures have become more widely used since World War II. If the economy has also become more stable, this would support the continued use of these policies. If the economy has not become more stable, the effectiveness of these policies would be questionable.

5. **a.** Optimal $\pi = 0$.
   b. In the long run, unemployment will be at its natural rate since $\pi = \pi^e$.

7. **a.** After the election, people expected future tax cuts, resulting in higher expected future disposable income. As a result, consumption would immediately rise.

b. By the time the tax cut was eventually passed by Congress, households had already incorporated the tax cuts into their expected future disposable incomes. Consequently, their consumption would not increase any further.

c. According to the Lucas critique, traditional methods of policy evaluation do not adequately take into account the impact of policy on expectations. A traditional model that investigated the effects of the tax cut by looking only at its effects after the tax cut was enacted would erroneously conclude that the tax cut had no effect on consumption.

8. Recall that the real interest rate is equal to the nominal interest rate minus the inflation rate, that is, $r = i - \pi$. Central banks cannot reduce the nominal interest rate below zero. Consequently, the real interest rate can fall below zero only if inflation is positive.

Chapter 16

Fill-in Questions

1. government debt
2. cyclically adjusted budget deficit
3. traditional view of government debt
4. Ricardian equivalence
5. interest rate; growth rate
6. growth rate

Multiple-Choice Questions

1. d	2. a	3. a	4. c	5. a	6. d	7. b
8. c	9. d	10. c	11. b	12. d	13. a	14. a
15. b	16. d	17. d	18. b	19. c	**20.** c	

Exercises

1. **a.** 60; 0.13; 260
   b. 0; 200; 0.13; 260; 200
   c. 0; 2,000; 2,000; 200; 2,200
   d. 1; 1.1; 2,000; 1; 2,000; 2,200; 1.1; 2,000; equal to; 0; overstate
   e. 0.03; 3; 0.03; 60; 60; 200; 60; 260; 0

2. **a.** *IS*; right; increase; increase; increase; fall; investment
   b. remain constant; appreciation, remain constant; increase; net exports; increase; increase; increase
   c. decrease; increase
   d. decrease; decrease; fall

3. **a.** increasing
   b. 1,100; 1,100; 1,100; equally well off; have no effect; remain constant
   c. have no effect on; remain constant

4. **a.** decrease; decrease; increase; left

    b. deficits; surpluses

    c. would not; would not

Problems

1. According to the traditional view, households' current and expected future disposable incomes would fall and current consumption would fall. According to the Ricardian view, the current tax increase would be offset by an expected future reduction in taxes, resulting in no change in consumption.

2. **a.** Current consumption would remain unchanged because people would expect future taxes to rise.

    b. Current private saving would rise by $100 billion because current disposable income rises by $100 billion and consumption remains unchanged.

    c. Current national saving remains unchanged. Private saving rises by $100 billion, but public saving falls by the $100 billion tax cut.

3. For the prospective emigrant, a tax reduction in the current year represents an increase in income because the expected future tax increase will not have to be paid by either the emigrant or her descendants. Thus, the current consumption of the prospective emigrant will increase. In the whole economy, however, a tax reduction represents no change in the sum of current and expected future income, and current aggregate consumption is unaffected.

6. **a.** According to the simple Keynesian consumption function, current consumption is a function of current disposable income. Therefore, consumption will begin to be affected by the tax cut only when it takes effect, four years from now. Yet the plan still provides for an eventual reduction in the deficit.

    b. According to the forward-looking view of consumption (which will be called the permanent-income hypothesis or the life-cycle hypothesis in the next chapter), current consumption depends on the sum of current and expected future income. Since the future tax increase will decrease future income, it will also decrease *current* consumption, along with the eventual budget deficit.

    c. According to the theory of Ricardian equivalence, the future tax increase will affect the official deficit when it takes effect, but it will not affect consumption. According to the government budget constraint, people will merely expect a tax decrease sometime in the future (after four years), and they will dissave in order to maintain their levels of consumption.

    d. If people have liquidity constraints, the future tax increase will still reduce consumption when it takes effect even if Ricardian equivalence is valid. The tax increase will reduce disposable income when it becomes effective. Although people may wish to dissave and maintain consumption, they may not be able to do so if they do not have the resources (liquidity) and cannot borrow.

7. If Brazil does not default on its debt, the U.S. guarantee will probably have no effect on the U.S. budget deficit. One might, however, argue that the U.S. guarantee increases the riskiness of U.S. government debt. As a result, both U.S. government borrowing costs and U.S. government budget deficits might both rise, but this is unlikely.

8. **a.** Increases in government purchases will shift both the *IS* and *AD* curves to the right in the short run. Although the increase in real GDP will also increase tax revenues, the budget deficit will increase along with r, Y, and P. Thus, higher deficits will be associated with higher prices and higher interest rates. (Although the increase in P will also shift the *LM* curve upward a bit, both Y and r will still rise.)

Graphs for Problem 8a

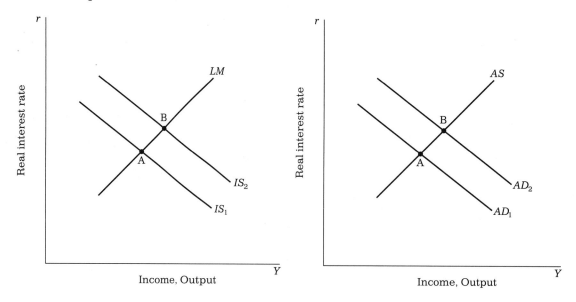

b. Declines in consumer or business confidence will shift the *IS* and *AD* curves to the left, reducing r, Y, and P. As Y falls, income tax revenues fall, and the budget deficit will increase. In this case higher deficits will be accompanied by *lower* prices and lower interest rates. (Although the decrease in P will also shift the *LM* curve downward a bit, both Y and r will still fall.)

Graphs for Problem 8b

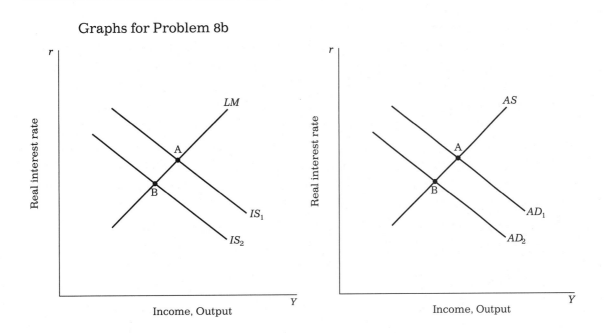

9. a. In the short run, President Obama's fiscal stimulus package would shift the
        IS and *AD* curves to the right. The expansionary monetary policy would shift
        the *LM* and *AD* curves to the right. The combined effect would be a shift of
        the *AD* curve to the right, which would increase real GDP and the price
        level in the short run. As the U.S. price level rises, the real value of the
        Chinese dollar-denominated assets would decline.

Graph for Problem 9a

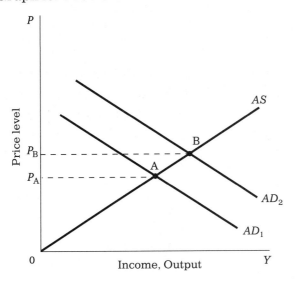

Since the United States is a large open economy, the rightward shift of the
IS and *LM* curves would have an ambiguous effect on the U.S. interest rate
in the short run and thus an ambiguous effect on the U.S. exchange rate.

If there was a substantial increase in the risk premium on dollar-denominated assets, the dollar would depreciate and the value of Chinese holdings of dollar-denominated assets would fall in terms of the Chinese currency, the renminbi.

b. In the long run, the expansionary monetary policy would increase the price level and thereby reduce the real value of the Chinese dollar-denominated assets. The expansionary fiscal policy would reduce national saving and, since the United States is a large open economy, it would increase the U.S. real interest rate. This would result in an appreciation of the dollar, contrary to the Chinese Premier's concern.

Graph for Problem 9b

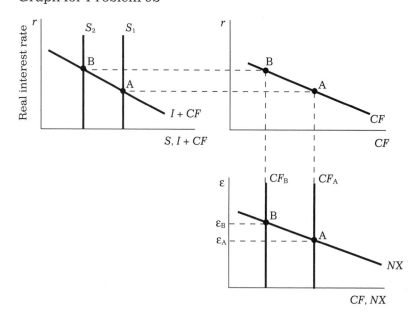

On the other hand, if the perceived risk premium of dollar-denominated assets rose, the dollar might depreciate and the value of Chinese holdings of dollar-denominated assets would fall in terms of the Chinese currency, the renminbi or yuan.

Chapter 17

Fill-in Questions

1. marginal propensity to consume
2. average propensity to consume; average propensity to consume; life-cycle hypothesis (or permanent-income hypothesis); permanent-income hypothesis (or life-cycle hypothesis)
3. budget constraint

4. intertemporal budget constraint
5. discounting
6. indifference curve
7. marginal rate of substitution
8. normal good
9. income effect; substitution effect
10. income effect; substitution effect
11. borrowing constraint
12. life-cycle hypothesis; precautionary saving
13. permanent-income hypothesis; Permanent income; transitory income
14. random walk; random walk
15. Behavioural economics

Multiple-Choice Questions

1. b	2. d	3. b	4. a	5. c	6. c	7. b
8. b	9. c	10. b	11. b	12. d	13. d	14. d
15. c	16. d	17. d	18. a	19. a	20. c	21. d
22. c						

Exercises

1. **a.** Graph 17-1

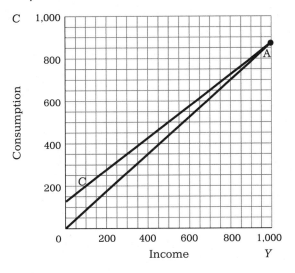

   b. the fraction of each additional dollar of disposable income that households spend on consumption; 0.75; remains constant; 0; 1
   c. 0.75; 125; 0.75; 125; 1.25; 0.75; 125; 1; 0.75; 125; 0.875; decreases
   d. 875; 875; 1,000; 0.875; *APC*; *APC*; decreases
2. **a.** 0; 1; decreases
   b. decrease; remain constant

c. 0; 1; decreases; remain constant; 0

Graph 17-2

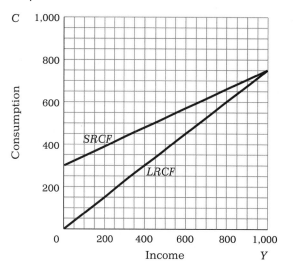

3. a. 105

b. 105; 100

c. 110.25

d. 110.25; 100

e. $FV_T = \$100 (1 + i)^T$; $PV = FV_T/(1 + i)^T$

4. a. 12; 12; 12; 0.50; 12; 30; 1.5

Graph 17-3

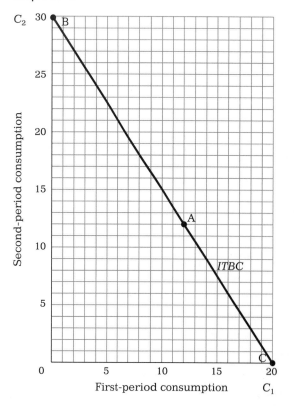

b. 0.50; 1.5; 1.5; 50

c. 12; 0; 12; 0; 12; 12; 12; 0.50; 12; 30; 0; 12; 12; 1.5; 20

5. a. **Table 17-1**

(1)	(2)	(3)	(4)	(5)	(6)	(7)	(8)
C_1	8.0	9.0	10.0	11.00	12.0	14.0	16.0
C_2	18.0	16.0	14.4	13.09	12.0	10.3	9.0
$U = C_1C_2$	144.0	144.0	144.0	144.00	144.0	144.0	144.0

b. Graph 17-4

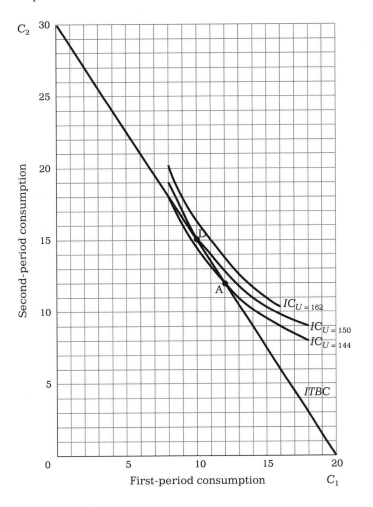

144

c. **Table 17-2**

(1)	(2)	(3)	(4)	(5)	(6)	(7)	(8)
C_1	8.00	9.00	10.0	11.00	12.0	14.0	16.00
C_2	18.75	16.67	15.0	13.64	12.5	10.7	9.38
$U = C_1 C_2$	150.00	150.00	150.0	150.00	150.0	150.0	150.00

d. **Table 17-3**

(1)	(2)	(3)	(4)	(5)	(6)	(7)	(8)
C_1	8.00	9.0	10.0	11.00	12.0	14.0	16.0
C_2	20.25	18.0	16.2	14.73	13.5	11.6	10.1
$U = C_1 C_2$	162.00	162.0	162.0	162.00	162.0	162.0	162.0

e. right (upward); increase; marginal rate of substitution

g. 12; 12; $IC_{U=144}$; 144

h. $IC_{U=150}$; 150; 2; 3; 12; 3; 15; 10; 15; 150; right (above)

6. a. 31.17; 1.5

Graph 17-5

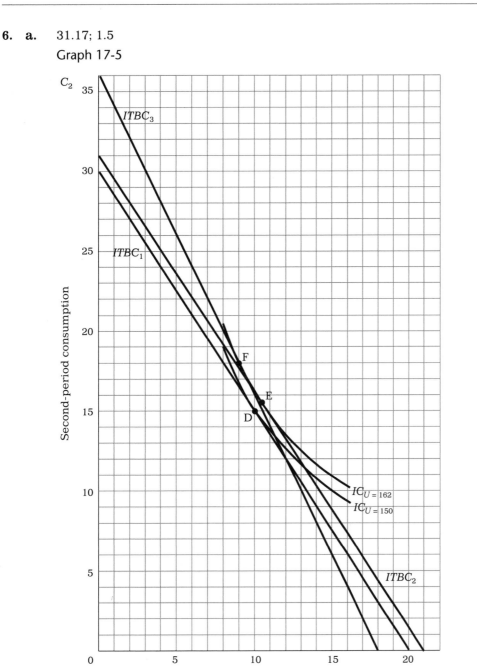

equal to

b. 162; 162; 15.59; increased

c. 12; 12; 12; 36; 2; 162; 162; 18

d. income; substitution; decreasing; increasing

e. increases; increases; decreases; increases; increase; decreases

7. **a.** R; T

b. 60; 45; 15; 40,000; 45; 60; 30,000; 30,000; 3; 4; 10,000; 1; 4; 0.75; 75

c. 40,000; 45; 1,800,000; 1,800,000; equal to

Graph 17-6

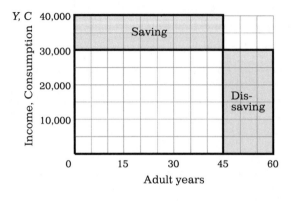

d. R; T; T; 60; 45; 0.75; 0.0167; 1.67

Graph 17-7

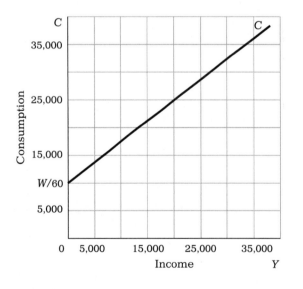

0.0167; 0.75

e. 0.75; 0.0167; 0.75; 0.0167; $120,000; $40,000; 0.80; 0.75; 0.0167; $120,000; $80,000; 0.775; falls; 0.85

f. 0.80

8. a. 75

b. **Table 17-4**

(1)	(2) Y^P	(3) $C = 0.75Y^P$	(4) Y	(5) $APC = C/Y$	(6) Y^T
University professor	$40,000	$30,000	$40,000	0.75	$0
Artist in a good year	$40,000	$30,000	$50,000	0.60	$10,000
Artist in a bad year	$40,000	$30,000	$30,000	1.00	−$10,000

c. not change; not change; decrease; not change; increase
d. decrease; decrease
e. increase; decrease
f. decrease; saved; permanent; consumed
g. remain constant

Problems

1. a. $MPC = 0.8$; $APC = (100/Y) + 0.8$
b. If $Y = 100$, $MPC = 0.8$ and $APC = 1.8$
If $Y = 200$, $MPC = 0.8$ and $APC = 1.3$
As Y rises, the MPC remains constant and the APC decreases.
2. $1136.16; $885.84; bond present values and prevailing interest rates move in opposite directions.
3. a. Graph for Problem 3a

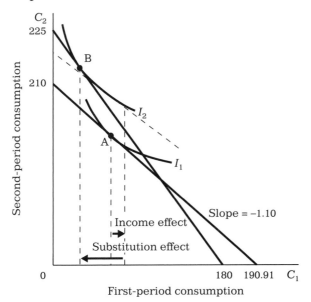

Note: We have assumed that the substitution effect is larger than the income effect.
e. if the income effect is bigger than the substitution effect
5. a. $MPC = b$; $APC = (a/Y) + b$

   b. $d(MPC)/dY = 0$; $d(APC)/dY = -a/Y^2 < 0$

7. The life-cycle and permanent-income models of consumption imply that consumption is relatively stable from one year to the next. Consumption is not as volatile as current income because people do not respond very much to temporary changes in income. Consequently, private spending will be relatively stable (since consumption is by far its largest component), and policy activism will usually be unnecessary.

8. **a.** $C = (1/25)W + (2/5)Y$

     b. $C = \$30,000$

9. A reduction in tax rates has two effects on current saving. The substitution effect reduces current consumption and increases current saving. The income effect, on the other hand, increases consumption in each period and, hence, reduces current saving. Consequently, the net effect of a reduction in tax rates on interest and dividends is ambiguous and depends on the relative sizes of the income and substitution effects.

Chapter 18

Fill-in Questions

1. Residential investment; business fixed investment; inventory investment
2. neoclassical model of investment
3. depreciation
4. real cost of capital
5. net investment; depreciation
6. neoclassical model of investment; real cost of capital
7. corporate profits tax
8. corporate profits tax
9. investment tax credit
10. Tobin's q
11. stock market; Tobin's q
12. efficient markets hypothesis
13. financing constraints
14. production smoothing; inventories as a factor of production; stock-out avoidance; work in process
15. accelerator model
16. financing constraints
17. subprime

Multiple-Choice Questions

1. a	2. b	3. d	4. b	5. c	6. a	7. b
8. b	9. a	10. c	11. b	12. b	13. d	14. b
15. b	16. d	17. b	18. c			

Exercises

1. **a.** 20; 15; 10; 5; 20

b. 2; 4; more

Graph 18-1

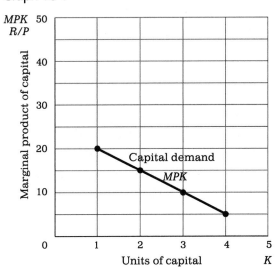

10

c. Graph 18-2

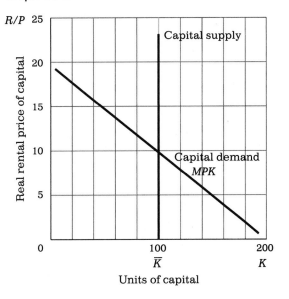

d. right; fall; higher; right; increasing; right; increasing

2. **a.** 0.03; $10; $15; $12; $22; $44

b. increase; decrease; increase; quickly; shorter

c. 0; 5

d. increase; increase

3. **a.** equal to; r; δ; r; δ; add to; positive; subtract from; negative

 b. equal to; zero; decrease; increase; decrease; increase; add to; increase; rises; similar to; fall

 c. have no immediate effect on; increase; add to; increase; added; fall

 d. increase; decrease; increase; opposite

4. **a.** zero

 b. right

 Graph 18-3

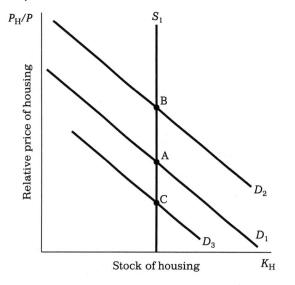

 increase; increase; increase; right; fall

 c. left; decrease; decrease

5. **a.** **Table 18-3**

(1) Period	(2) Output Y	(3) Change in Y	(4) % Change in Y	(5) $I = 0.2(\Delta Y)$ $= 0.2(Y - Y_{-1})$	(6) % Change in I
0	1,000				
		100	10.00		
1	1,100			20	
		100	9.09		0
2	1,200			20	
		100	8.33		0
3	1,300			20	
		50	3.85		−50
4	1,350			10	
		0	0.00		−100
5	1,350				0

 b. much larger; volatile

Problems

1. a.   Graph for Problem 1a

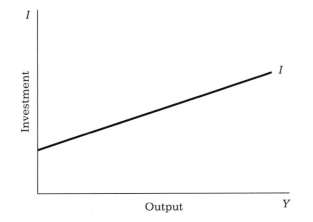

b.   Investment might rise as real output rises either because of an accelerator effect or because investment may be linked to sales or sales expectations that rise with Y.

c.   i.   The slope of the planned expenditure curve would become steeper. Now when Y increases, both consumption and investment will increase.

ii.   The government-purchases multiplier will increase. When government purchases increase by \$1, there will now be multiplier effects on both consumption and investment. Increases in government purchases will consequently lead to additional spending (and output) in each round.

iii.   The IS curve will become flatter; the slope of the LM curve is unaffected.

iv.   The AD curve will become flatter; the slope of the $SRAS$ curve is unaffected.

2. a.   \$2,300

b.   \$4,100

3.   The (nominal) cost of capital $= P_K[i - \Delta P_K/P_K + \delta]$, where the second term $\Delta P_K/P_K$ represents the rate at which capital prices are changing. If capital prices are rising at the same rate as the aggregate price level, $\Delta P_K/P_K = \pi$, and the cost of capital becomes $P_K[i - \pi + \delta] = P_K[r + \delta]$. If $\pi > \Delta P_K/P_K$, $(i - \pi) < (i - \Delta P_K/P_K)$ and the use of the real interest rate will underestimate the true cost of capital.

4. a. $MPK = 64(K)^{-2/3}$

b. 64; 16; 7.11; 4

Graph for Problem 4b

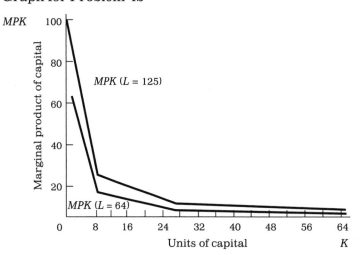

c. $MPK = 4(L/K)^{2/3} = 100(K)^{-2/3}$; $MPK = 100$; 25; 11.11; 6.25

5. The *IS* curve would shift to the right, increasing both the equilibrium levels of output and the interest rate.

    a. The increase in the interest rate would increase the cost of capital, reduce the profit rate from owning capital, and thereby decrease investment according to the neoclassical (cost-of-capital) theory of investment.

    b. The increase in *Y*, however, would increase investment (via an increase in inventories) according to the accelerator theory.

6. According to the efficient markets hypothesis, the price of one share of Google stock quintupled between August 2004 and February 2006 because of unexpected increase in the actual and expected future profitability of Google between those two dates. According to Keynes's "beauty contest" theory, the stock price quintupled because investors believed that Google would become increasingly attractive to stockholders, for reasons extending beyond reasonable expectations of future profitability.

7. The demand for housing would shift to the left, reducing the relative price of housing and investment in housing. The profits of home builders would fall in the short run.

Chapter 19

Fill-in Questions

1. balance sheet

2. reserves; 100-percent-reserve banking

3. fractional-reserve banking

4. reserve-deposit ratio; currency-deposit ratio

5. financial intermediation
6. monetary base; high-powered money
7. money multiplier; currency-deposit ratio; currency-deposit ratio; reserve-deposit ratio
8. open-market operation; monetary base; deposit switching; Bank Rate
9. portfolio theories; dominated asset
10. Transactions theories; Baumol-Tobin model
11. Baumol-Tobin model
12. near money
13. inflation rate
14. bank capital
15. leverage
16. capital requirement

Multiple-Choice Questions

1. b
2. d
3. a
4. b
5. d
6. d
7. c

8. b
9. d
10. a
11. c
12. d
13. b
14. c

15. b
16. d
17. a
18. c
19. c
20. d
21. b

22. c
23. c

Exercises

1. **a.** 1,000; 3,000; 25
   b. 10; Reserves = $260 million; Deposits = $1,010 million; Loans = $750 million
   c. 25; 25; 10; 7.5; Reserves = $252.5 million; Deposits = $1,010 million; Loans = $757.5 million
   d. 7.5; 7.5; Reserves = $257.5 million; Deposits = $1,007.5 million; Loans = $750 million
   e. 25; 25; 7.5; 5.625; Reserves = $251.875 million; Deposits = $1,007.5 million; Loans = $755.625 million
   f. 5.625; 5.625; Reserves = $255.625 million; Deposits = $1,005.625 million; Loans = $750 million
   g. 3,023.125; 1,000; 3,000; 23.125
   h. 0.25; 40
   i. 10; exactly; more than
2. **a.** deposits; reserves
   b. 3; 2; 1.6; 1; 1; 5
   c. decrease; decrease; 1.0; equal to; 1/*rr*; deposits
4. **a.** 500; 480; 20
   b. 20; 500; 4
   c. 500; 20; 25
   d. 490; 480; 10; 5; 50
   e. 480; 480; 0
   f. 20, 500; 4; were; 10; 490; 2.04; were not

Problems

1. $10,000; In this model, $cr = 0$. Thus, the money multiplier $= 1/rr = 10$.

2. **a.** $m = 2$

   b. $m = 1$; There is the case of a 100-percent-reserve banking system, in which there are no loans. Any increase in the monetary base leads to an equal increase in the money supply, either in the form of currency held by the public or deposits.

3. **a.** $dm/d(rr) = -(cr + 1)/(cr + rr)^2 < 0$

   b. $dm/d(cr) = (rr - 1)/(cr + rr)^2 < 0$, unless $rr = 1.0$

4. **a.** $dC/dN = F - iY/2N^2$

   b. At the optimum, $dC/dN = 0$. This implies that $N^* = \sqrt{iY/2F}$.

   c. $d^2C/dN^2 = iY/N^3 > 0$. This second-order condition confirms that the total cost of holding money reaches a local minimum at N^*.

5. **a.** $N^* = 12$

   b. monthly; $6,000

   c. $3,000

7. $|(dM/di)| \times (i/M) = (1/2)(YF/2i)^{-1/2}(YF/2i^2) \times i(YF/2i)^{-1/2} = (1/2)(2i/YF)(YF/2i) = 1/2$

   $(dM/dY) \times (Y/M) = (1/2)(YF/2i)^{-1/2}(F/2i) \times Y(YF/2i)^{-1/2} = (1/2)(2i/YF)(F/2i)Y = 1/2$

8. The value of Bank A's capital would fall to –$10.

9. The capital ratio is calculated as Capital/Assets. If the value of bank assets were reduced to reflect more realistic market valuations, both capital and assets would fall by the same dollar amount. Since Capital < Assets, the capital ratio would fall.

10. The two are equal to each other.